MODELS FOR WRITERS

SHORT ESSAYS FOR COMPOSITION

Fifth Edition

Karen Lynne Eberle
860 298· 8382

Karen Flint
8383 Pine St.
880 346 028

MODELS FOR WRITERS

SHORT ESSAYS FOR COMPOSITION
Fifth Edition

Ms. Karen L. Eberle
83 Maple Ave
Windsor CT 06095-2927

Editors

Alfred Rosa
Paul Eschholz
University of Vermont

ST. MARTIN'S PRESS   NEW YORK

Senior editor: Karen Allanson
Development editor: Clare Payton
Manager, publishing services: Emily Berleth
Editor, publishing services: Douglas Bell
Project management: Omega Publishing Services, Inc.
Production supervisor: Joe Ford
Cover art: Marjory Dressler

Library of Congress Catalog Card Number: 94-65175

Manufactured in the United States of America.
98765
fedcba

For information, write:
St. Martin's Press, Inc.
175 Fifth Avenue
New York, NY 10010

ISBN: 0-312-10120-1

Acknowledgments

It is a violation of the law to reproduce these selections by any means
whatsoever without the written permission of the copyright holder.

Page 25. "Give Us Jobs, Not Admiration" by Eric Bigler. From *Newsweek*.
Reprinted with the permission of the author.
Page 30. "Anxiety: Challenge by Another Name" by James Lincoln Collier. From
Reader's Digest, December 1986. Reprinted with the permission of the author
and *Reader's Digest*.
Page 37. "The Meanings of a Word" by Gloria Naylor. Copyright © 1986 by Gloria
Naylor. Reprinted with the permission of Sterling Lord Literistic, Inc.
Page 42. "Why 'Model Minority' Doesn't Fit" by Diane Yen-Mei Wong. From *USA
Weekend*, January 7–9, 1994, page 24. Reprinted with the permission of the
author.
Page 46. "Don't Let Stereotypes Warp Your Judgments" by Robert L. Heilbronner.
From *Think Magazine*, June 1961. Reprinted with the permission of the author.

Acknowledgments and copyrights are continued at the back of the book on
pages 450–453, which constitute an extension of the copyright page.

Preface

Models for Writers offers seventy-one short, lively essays that represent particularly appropriate models for use by beginning college writers. Most of our selections are comparable in length to the essays students will write themselves, and each clearly illustrates a basic rhetorical element, principle, or pattern. Just as important, the essays deal with subjects that we know from our own classroom experience will spark the interest of most college students. In making our selections, we have sought a level of readability that is neither so easy as to be condescending nor so difficult as to distract the reader's attention from the rhetorical issue under study. Most of the essays have been written in the last ten years. Drawn from a wide range of sources, they represent a variety of contemporary prose styles.

This fifth edition of *Models for Writers* has been revised based on our own recent experiences and on the many suggestions made by instructors who adopted and liked the first four editions.

The new essays, comprising almost half of this edition, were chosen with an eye toward critical thinking and writing as well as for their brevity, clarity, and suitability for student writers. We have included new pieces written by such popular writers as N. Scott Momaday, Audre Lorde, Barry Lopez, and Marianne Wiggins in an effort to ensure that this collection of essays reflects the wealth of cultural perspectives present in America today.

The introduction, which explains the purpose of the text and shows students how it can be used to improve their writing, includes three student essays—a personal narrative, an expository essay, and an argumentative essay. These three essays demonstrate the three major types of writing students will be doing throughout the term.

As in the fourth edition, the essays in *Models for Writers*, Fifth Edition, are grouped into eighteen chapters, each devoted to a particular element or pattern. Chapters 1–7 focus on the concepts of thesis, unity, organization, beginnings and endings, paragraphs, transitions, and effective sentences. Next, Chapters 8 and 9 illustrate some aspects of language: the effects of diction and tone and the uses of figurative language. Finally, Chapters 10–18 explore the various types of writing most often required of college students: illustration, narration, description, process analysis, definition, division and classification, comparison and contrast (including analogy), cause and effect, and argument. The arrangement of the chapters suggests a logical teaching sequence, moving from the elements of the essay to its language and to the different types of essays. An alternative teaching strategy might be to structure the course around Chapters 10–18, bringing in earlier chapters as necessary to illustrate various individual elements. Each chapter is self-contained, so that instructors may easily devise their own sequences, omitting or emphasizing certain chapters according to the needs of a particular group of students. Whatever sequence is followed, thematic comparisons among the selections will be facilitated by the alternate *Thematic Table of Contents* at the beginning of the book.

The chapters all follow a similar pattern. Each opens with an explanation of the element or principle to be considered, in many cases including paragraph-length examples. We then present three or four essays, each with its own brief introduction providing information about the author and directing the student's attention to specific rhetorical features.

Every essay is accompanied by the following apparatus:

Questions for Study and Discussion focus on the content, the author's purpose, and the rhetorical strategy used to achieve that purpose. Some questions allow brief answers, but most are designed to stimulate more searching analysis and to promote lively classroom discussion. In order to reinforce the lessons of other chapters and remind students that good writing is never one-dimensional, at least one question at the end of each series focuses on a writing concern other than the one highlighted in the chapter at hand.

Vocabulary sections draw from each reading several words that students will find worth adding to their vocabularies. These exercises ask them to define each word as it is used in the context of the selection and then to use the word in a new sentence of their own.

Suggested Writing Assignments provide two writing assignments for each essay. The first calls for an essay closely related to the content and style of the essay it follows, in effect encouraging the use of the reading selection as a direct model. The second writing assignment, while ranging a little further afield in subject, gives the student yet another opportunity to practice the particular rhetorical element or principle being illustrated.

A **Glossary of Useful Terms,** covering all rhetorical and literary terms, appears at the end of the text. Whenever possible in the apparatus, whether questions or writing assignments, we refer students to this helpful list and encourage them to connect the terms listed with concrete examples in the book.

In response to avid users of this book, we have kept the solid foundation of previous editions of *Models for Writers* while adding fresh readings and writing topics to stimulate today's student writers.

We are indebted to many people for their criticism and advice as we prepared this fifth edition of *Models for Writers*. We are especially grateful to:

Charlotte Alexander, College of Staten Island; John Alexander, St. John's University; Cheryl Allen-Pfitzner, Fullerton College; A. Patricia Bartinique, Essex County College; Barbara Bonander, College of Marin; Edna Burow, California State University, Northridge; Floyd Coleman, Grambling State; Sylvia H. Gamboa, College of Charleston; James Garmhausen, College of San Mateo; Lucie Greenberg, Washtenaw Community College; Judy Hathcock, Amarillo College; Winona Howe, La Sierra University; Mary Beth Inverso, Bentley College; Sandra Jerinsky, Rockland Community College; Phyllis Katz, University of Hartford; Charles K. Kenosian, Salem State College; David Lazzari, College of San Mateo; Pamela Mertsock, Rutgers University, Camden; Susan Reddington, Cabrillo College; Audrey J. Roth, Dade Community College, Miami; M. L. Shelden, Cochise College; Maryann Siebert, Rutgers University, Newark; David Stamper, Incarnate Word College; Bruce C. Swaffield, Roanoke College; Rebecca Warner, City University of New York, BMCC; Mary Beth Wilk, Des Moines Community College; Grady Wilson, Jersey City State College; Nancy Witherspoon, City University of New York, BMCC; and Linda Woodson, University of Texas at San Antonio.

It was our good fortune to have the editorial guidance of Edward Hutchinson and especially Clare Payton of St. Martin's Press as we worked on this new edition. Thanks to our colleagues Phoebe Bryan, Hal Cochran, Wright Danenbarger, Deborah D'Agati, Sue Dinitz, Nancy Disenhaus, Susan Frankson, Lynne Hefferon, Jim Juliano, Brian Kent, Edis Schneider, Dick Sweterlitsch, Melissa Tedrowe, Cherie Turpin, and Alex Vardamis, who have shared with us their experiences using *Models for Writers* in the class-room. Our greatest debt, as always, is to our students, for all that they have taught us.

Alfred Rosa
Paul Eschholz

Contents

II. The Language of the Essay   159

8. Diction and Tone   161

9. Figurative Language   186

III. Types of Essays   203

10. Illustration   205

Thematic Contents

Work

Language and Thought

Enduring Issues

Health and Medicine

MODELS FOR WRITERS
SHORT ESSAYS FOR COMPOSITION
Fifth Edition

INTRODUCTION

Models for Writers is designed to help you learn to write by providing you with a collection of model essays, essays that are examples of good writing. We know that one of the best ways to learn to write and to improve our writing is to read. By reading we can begin to see how other writers have communicated their experiences, ideas, thoughts, and feelings. We can study how they have used the various elements of the essay—words, sentences, paragraphs, organizational patterns, transitions, examples, evidence, and so forth—and thus learn how we might effectively do the same. When we see, for example, how a writer like James Lincoln Collier develops an essay from a strong thesis statement, we can better appreciate the importance of having a clear thesis statement in our writing. When we see the way Lisa Brown uses transitions to link key phrases and important ideas so that readers can recognize clearly how the parts of her essay are meant to fit together, we have a better idea of how to achieve such clarity in our own writing.

But we do not learn only by observing, by reading. We also learn by doing, by writing, and in the best of all situations we engage in these two activities in conjunction with one another. *Models for Writers* encourages you, therefore, to write your essays, to practice what you are learning, as you are actually reading and analyzing the model essays in the text.

The kind of composition that you will be asked to write for your college writing instructor is most often referred to as an essay—a relatively short piece of nonfiction in which a writer attempts to develop one or more closely related points or ideas. An effective essay has a clear purpose, often provides useful information, has an effect on the reader's thoughts and feelings, and is usually a pleasure to read.

All well-written essays also share a number of structural and stylistic features that are illustrated by the various essays in *Models for Writers*. One good way to learn what these features are and how you can incorporate them in your own writing is to look at each of them in isolation. For this reason we have divided *Models for Writers* first into three major sections and, within these sections, into eighteen chapters, each with its own particular focus and emphasis.

"The Elements of the Essay," the first section, includes chapters on the following subjects: thesis, unity, organization, beginnings and endings, paragraphs, transitions, and effective sentences. All these elements are essential to a well-written essay, but the concepts of thesis, unity, and organization underlie all the others and so come first in our sequence.

Briefly, "Thesis" shows how authors put forth or state the main ideas of their essays and how they use such statements to develop and control content; "Unity," how authors achieve a sense of wholeness in their essays; and "Organization," some important patterns that authors use to organize their thinking and writing. "Beginnings and Endings" offers advice and models of ways to begin and conclude essays, while "Paragraphs" concentrates on the importance of well-developed paragraphs and what is necessary to achieve them. "Transitions" concerns the various devices that writers use to move from one idea or section of an essay to the next. Finally, "Effective Sentences" focuses on techniques to make sentences powerful and create stylistic variety.

"The Language of the Essay," the second major section of the text, includes a chapter on diction and tone and one on figurative language. "Diction and Tone" shows how carefully writers choose words either to convey exact meanings or to be purposefully suggestive. In addition, this chapter shows how the words a writer uses can create a particular tone or relationship between the writer and the reader—one of irony, for example, or humor or great seriousness. "Figurative Language" concentrates on the usefulness of the special devices of language—such as simile, metaphor, and personification—that add richness and depth to one's writing.

The final section of *Models for Writers*, "Types of Essays," includes chapters on the various types of writing most often required of college writing students: "Illustration" (how to use examples to illustrate a point or idea); "Narration" (how to tell a story or give an account of an event); "Description" (how to present a verbal picture); "Process Analysis" (how to explain how something is done or happens); "Definition" (how to explain what something is); "Division and Classification" (how to divide a subject into its parts and place items into appropriate categories); "Comparison and Contrast" (how to demonstrate likenesses and differences); "Cause and Effect" (how to explain the causes of an event or the effects of an action); and, finally, "Argument" (how to use reason and logic to persuade someone to your way of thinking). These types of writing are referred to as *rhetorical modes*.

Studying the rhetorical modes and practicing using them is very important in any effort to broaden one's writing skills. In *Models for Writers* we look at each mode separately, one at a time; we believe this is the simplest and most effective way to introduce them. However, this does not mean that a well-written essay is necessarily one that chooses a single mode and sticks to it exclusively and rigidly. Confining oneself to comparison and contrast throughout an entire essay, for instance, might prove impractical and may yield a strained, unnatural piece of writing. In fact, it is often best to use a single mode to organize your essay, and then to use the other modes as your material dictates. When you read the student essays that follow, notice how, for example, Laura LaPierre's essay is basically organized as a narrative, but also includes a good deal of description and even some comparison and contrast. Jon Clancy's essay is an argumentative one that makes its point with strong illustrations, and vivid narrative examples. As you read the model essays included throughout this text, you will find that in the service of the dominant mode a good many of them utilize a combination of rhetorical modes.

Combining rhetorical modes probably is not something you want to think about or even plan when you first tackle a writing assignment. Rather, it should develop naturally as you organize, draft, and revise your materials. As long as your essay remains clear and logical, this combining process will only enhance the interest, impact, and persuasiveness of your writing.

All of the chapters are organized in the same way. Each opens with an explanation of the element or principle under consideration. These introductions are intended to be brief, clear, and memorable. Here you will also usually find one or more short examples of the feature or principle being studied. Following the introduction, we present three or four model essays, each with a brief introduction of its own providing information about the author and directing your attention to the highlighted rhetorical features. Every essay is followed by study materials in three parts: *Questions for Study and Discussion, Vocabulary,* and *Suggested Writing Assignments.*

Models for Writers, then, provides information, instruction, and practice in writing essays. By reading carefully and thoughtfully and by applying what you learn, you can begin to have more and more control over your own writing. Laura LaPierre, Courtney Smith, and Jon Clancy, three of our own writing students at the University of Vermont, found this to be true, and their work is a good example of what can be achieved from studying models.

Three Model Student Essays

After reading several personal narratives—Helen Keller's "The Most Important Day" and Dick Gregory's "Shame" in particular—Laura LaPierre decided to write one of her own. Only weeks prior to writing this essay Laura had received some very bad news. It was the experience of living with this news that she decided to write about. It was painful, and not everyone would feel comfortable with a similar task, but Laura welcomed the opportunity because she came to a better understanding of her own fears and feelings as she moved from one draft to the next. What follows is the final draft of Laura's essay.

Why Are You Here?
Laura LaPierre

BEGINNING SETS CONTEXT: when, where, to whom   Balancing between a crutch on one side and an I.V. pole with wheels on the other, I dragged my stiff leg along the smooth, sterile floor of the hospital hall. All around me nurses, orderlies, and doctors bustled about, dodging well-meaning

SELECTION OF DETAILS: harsh hospital environment   visitors laden with flowers and candy. The fluorescent lights glared down with a brightness so sharp that I squinted and thought that sunglasses

might be in order. Sticking close to the wall, I
rounded the corner and paused to rest for a moment.
I breathed in the hot, antiseptic-smelling air which I
had grown accustomed to and sighed angrily.

POINT OF VIEW: first person

Tears of hurt and frustration pricked at the
corner of my eyes as the now familiar pain seared
my leg. I tugged my bathrobe closer around my
shoulder and, hauling my I.V. pole with me, I
continued down the hall. One, two—second door on
the left, she had said. I opened the heavy metal
door, entered, and realized that I must be a little
early because no one else was there yet. After
glancing at my watch, I sat down and looked
around the room, noting with disgust the prevalence
of beige. Beige walls, beige ceiling, shiny beige
floor tiles. A small cot stood in one corner with a
beige bedspread, and in the opposite corner there
was a sink, mirror, and beige waste basket. The
only relief from the monotony was the circle of six
or seven chairs where I sat. They were a vivid rust
color and helped to brighten the dull room. The
shades were drawn and the lights were much
dimmer than they had been in the hall, and my eyes
gradually relaxed as I waited.

ORGANIZATION: chronological sequence of events

SELECTION OF DETAILS: dull, uninviting room (dominant impression)

ORGANIZATION: time reference

People began to drift in until five of the seats
were filled. A nurse was the head of the odd-
looking group. Three of us were attached by long
tubes to I.V. poles, and then there was a social
worker. The man to my left wore a slightly faded,
royal blue robe. He had a shock of unruly gray hair
above an angular face with deeply sunken cheeks.

His eyes were sunken, too, and glassy with pain. Yet he smiled and appeared untroubled by his I.V. pole.

Wearing a crisp white uniform and a pretty sweater, the nurse, a pleasant-looking woman in her late twenties, appeared friendly and sympathetic, though not to the point of being sappy. My impressions were confirmed as she began to speak.

Dialogue

"Okay. I guess we can begin. Welcome to our group, we meet every Monday at. . . ." She went on, but I wasn't paying attention anymore. I looked around the group and my eyes came to rest on the man sitting next to the nurse. In contrast to the other man's shriveled appearance, this man was robust. He was tall, with a protruding belly and a ruddy complexion. Unlike the other man, he seemed at war with his I.V. pole. He constantly fiddled with the tube and with the tape that held the needle in his arm. Eyes darting around the room, he nervously watched everyone.

Comparison and Contrast: points to differences between men

I heard the nurse continue, "So, let's all introduce ourselves and tell why we are here." We went around the circle clockwise, starting with the nurse, and when we got to the social worker, I looked up and surveyed her while she talked. Aside from contributing to the beige monotony with her pants, she was agreeable both in appearance and disposition.

Echo of Title

Selection of Details: reinforces earlier description of room

When it was my turn, I took a deep breath and with my voice quivering began, "My name is Laura an—"

Dialogue: shows instead of tells

"Hi, Laura!" interrupted the cheerful man on my left. I turned and smiled weakly at him.

Fighting back the tears, I continued, "And I have bone cancer."

ENDING: moment of truth

For an assignment following one of the readings in the chapter on unity, Courtney Smith was inspired by a television commercial to choose an unusual topic: cockroaches. In order to develop a thesis about these creatures, Courtney did some preliminary reading in the library, spoke to her biology professor who had some interesting exhibits to show her, and surveyed the roach control products available at her local supermarket. In sorting through the information she gathered, she was particularly surprised by the ability of cockroaches to survive under almost any circumstances. This ability seemed to her to provide a suitably narrow focus for a short, unified essay, so she began to analyze the various reasons for the insects' resiliency. By first making lists of the points she wanted to include in her essay, Courtney discovered that she could cluster the reasons into three groups. She was then able to formulate the following thesis: "Cockroaches are remarkably resilient creatures for three basic reasons." This thesis, in turn, helped Courtney to map her organization; she decided that her essay would have three major paragraphs to discuss each of the basic reasons cockroaches are so durable and that she would also need an introductory paragraph and a concluding paragraph. This five-paragraph pattern provided the basis for her first draft.

What follows is the final draft of Courtney's essay, which incorporates a number of changes she made based on a critical evaluation of her first draft.

Cockroaches

Courtney Smith

Have you ever tried to get rid of cockroaches? Those stupid little bugs refuse to go. You can chase them, starve them, spray them, and even try to squash them. But no matter what you do, they

BEGINNING: captures readers' attention

always come back. I have heard they are the only creatures that can survive a nuclear explosion. What do cockroaches have that enables them to be such **THESIS** extremely resilient insects? The answer is simple. Cockroaches have survived in even the most hostile environments because they possess several unique physical features, an amazing reproductive process, and an immune system that has frustrated even the best efforts of exterminators to get rid of them.

FIRST POINT: "physical features"

DESCRIPTION

Cockroaches are thin, torpedo-shaped insects. Their body shape allows them to squeeze into small cracks or holes in walls and ceilings or dart into drains, thus avoiding all dangers. Their outer shell is extremely hard, making them almost impossible to crush. Cockroaches have sticky pads on their claws that enable them to climb walls or crawl upside down on ceilings. They also have two little tails called "cerci" to alert them to danger. These cerci are covered with tiny hairs that, like antennae, are sensitive to things as small as a speck of dust or as seemingly innocent as a puff of air. Finally, if cockroaches can't find food, they can sustain themselves for up to a month without food, as long as

TOPIC SENTENCE: PARAGRAPH UNITY

they have water. Combined with their other physical features, this ability to go for long periods without food has made the cockroach almost invincible.

SECOND POINT: "reproductive process"

Cockroaches give credence to the old adage that there is safety in numbers. They reproduce at a truly amazing rate. About two months after mating, a new generation of cockroaches is born. One cockroach can produce about two dozen offspring each time it mates. To get some idea of their reproductive power, imagine that you start with three pairs of cockroaches that mate. Approximately three weeks after mating the females lay their eggs, which hatch some forty-five days later. If we assume two dozen eggs from each female, the first generation would number seventy-two offspring. These roaches would continue to multiply geometrically so that by year's end the colony's population would total more than 10,000 cockroaches. Stopping this process is almost impossible because, even if we were successful in annihilating the adult population, it is more than likely that a new generation would already be on the way.

ILLUSTRATION: **hypothetical example**

Finally, cockroaches have frustrated scientists with their ability to immunize themselves against drugs, poison, and bomb gases. The cockroaches then pass this new immunity on to the next generation quicker than a new poison can be made. Although scientists have studied the cockroach for a long time, they have not discovered the biological mechanism that enables them to develop immunity quickly. It is only natural, therefore, that many scientists have been at work on a "birth control" solution for cockroaches. By rendering at least some portion of the adult population sterile, scientists hope to gain a measure of control over the pesty creatures.

THIRD POINT: **"immune system"**

Today there are 3,500 different species of cockroaches. They have survived on this planet since the time of the dinosaurs some 350 million years ago. Whether or not scientists are successful

ENDING: **prediction for the future**

in their latest efforts to rid us of cockroaches is yet
to be determined. Odds are that they won't succeed.
Given the cockroach's amazing record of
survivability, it is not likely to turn up on the
world's list of endangered species.

Jon Clancy's paper grew out of his reading the essays in Chapter 18. His assignment was to write an argument and, like Laura and Courtney, he was free to choose his own topic. He knew from past experience that in order to write a good essay he would have to write on a topic he cared about. He also knew that he should allow himself a reasonable amount of time to find such a topic and gather his ideas. After studying Russian four years and French for six, Jon had begun to wonder why he wasn't learning the languages as quickly and as well as other people. Then, after meeting a Soviet couple and their eight-year-old daughter, he understood. The girl, after only a few months in the United States, spoke English with only a slight accent while her mother was not progressing nearly as quickly. Never before did he realize how the difference in age affected the attainment of fluency. This gave Jon the idea to write an essay on the need to teach languages at an early age rather than only at the secondary and post-secondary levels, something that would have helped him, as well as many others, he thought.

Jon began by brainstorming about the topic. He made lists of all the ideas, facts, issues, arguments, opposing arguments, and refutations that came to mind as a result of his own reflections on the topic, as well as ideas he had gathered from several educators he interviewed about the teaching of foreign languages. Once he was confident that he had amassed enough information to begin writing, he made a rough outline of an organizational pattern he felt would work well for him. Keeping this pattern in mind, Jon wrote a first draft of his essay, then went back and examined it carefully, assessing how it could be improved.

Jon was writing this particular essay in the second half of the semester, after he had read a number of essays and had learned the importance of such matters as good paragraphing, unity, and transitions. In rereading his first draft, he realized that his organizational pattern could be clearer if he did not mix the reasons why Americans need to learn foreign languages with his suggestion for how we should actually go about teaching and learning them. He also found places where phrases and even whole sentences could be added to make his meaning clearer. He repositioned some sentences, added some key transitions, and changed a number of words to create a more forceful effect.

The final draft of Jon's paper illustrates that he has learned how the parts of a well-written essay fit together, and how to make revisions that emulate some of the qualities of the model essays he has read and studied. The following is the final draft of Jon's essay.

Where Is Le Bathroom?

Jon Clancy

An American in Paris. To the French, this is a most hideous thought. Thousands of travellers from Boston to Boise head for the city of lights each year, and very few know enough French to ask for directions to the nearest metro stop, police station, or bathroom. Americans think that knowing the language of a foreign country is not necessary. The basic, arrogant assumption is, "Not to worry! The whole world knows English."

BEGINNING: a problem is announced

The typical traveller is in for a rude awakening when it is 3 a.m. on a remote European road and suddenly the engine overheats. The last gas station is 10 kilometers back, and there's not one English-speaking Austrian to be found. Quickly now! Refer to that dime store phrase book and attempt to say, "My car is broken." Too bad. What actually came out was, "My! Look at all the hedgehogs!" We Americans just do not have a strong knowledge of

ILLUSTRATION: hypothetical example

THESIS

languages, and something should be done to change this.

RHETORICAL QUESTION

ORGANIZATION: first argument

ORGANIZATION: second argument

ORGANIZATION: third argument

But why should we begin emphasizing foreign language study? Actually, the benefits are great. For example, the knowledge of a second language helps in learning others. Strong similarities exist within linguistic groups, such as the Romance and Slavic families. Of course it's not possible for Americans to know every language, but once someone understands the concepts of verb conjugation, noun cases, and noun gender, a foreign tongue will seem less intimidating.

We deal with many foreign speakers right here in the United States. For instance, those areas of the United States which are near French-speaking parts of Canada, such as New England, and those near Mexico, are often visited by our foreign neighbors. However, many Americans who often deal with them do not know the most basic French or Spanish phrases. People will argue that those travelling in the United States should know English. Fine. But when we travel to Quebec, what do we speak? That's right . . . "Garkon, I'd like un coca-cola, seel voos plate."

Also, most urban areas in the U.S., especially those in the southern states, are home to Mexican, Cuban, and other Latin American immigrants. These people have made Spanish our second language, yet most people do not bother to learn it at all. Wouldn't it be beneficial if these Hispanics and Americans who work and live with each other took the time to learn each other's native tongue, thus taking a big step in bettering the understanding between these two different but inevitably inseparable cultures? Latin Americans are making the more sincere effort in this case, and as usual, the arrogant, lazy Americans cannot be bothered broadening their horizons beyond "America's Funniest Home Videos" and "Wheel of Fortune."

Linguistically, politically, and economically, the world is growing closer each year. According to Senator Paul Simon of Illinois, "Cultural isolation is a luxury the United States can no longer afford" (qtd. in Seligmann 37). Places like China and the Soviet Union do not seem quite as far as they used to, and international business is on the rise. With the advent of international companies and a global economy, we need to enhance inter-nation communication. How can we expect to understand these new neighbors and business partners without knowing their language? Each culture has its own, distinct vocabulary which reflects its way of life. For example, the Russian word "blat," which is the highly developed system of favors between merchant and consumer, does not have a direct English translation, but it has significant economic, social, and political ramifications in the U.S.S.R. One surely cannot appreciate the importance and beauty of foreign cultures by reading such classics as Arabic at a Glance and Just Enough Serbo-Croat.

But exactly how should we go about making the United States more aware of the world and the

ORGANIZATION:
fourth
argument
QUOTATION:
supporting
opinion

EVIDENCE:
example used
as illustration

RHETORICAL
QUESTION

languages it speaks? Because a person's cognitive learning skills are at their peak at an early age, the first grade would be an excellent place to begin foreign language instruction. At birth, according to noted brain surgeon Wilder Penfield, there is a large area of the brain, known as the uncommitted cortex, which is not used. This part of the brain becomes a perfect tool for learning a second language in the early years—especially before the age of 12 (389).

Some would argue that the most efficient way of solving the language problem would be to work on the existing programs at the junior high and high school levels. However, these programs have been in effect for many years, and the results have been anything but promising. A high school student will study a language for two, three, or even four years and afterwards will not have attained fluency.

It should come as no surprise that students in the teenage years do not excel in the area of language study. On the other hand, younger children are still learning English in the first grade, so the teaching of a second tongue would not be a hindrance, but rather a complement. The children surely will not protest this addition, for if it is incorporated as part of their learning from day one they will always associate French, Spanish, or even Russian, with math and English, as part of the school day. Also, there is a good chance that children would consider learning a foreign language fun.

Children all over the world begin to study English as a second language at a very early age,

---

Margin annotations:

SOLUTION TO PROBLEM

EVIDENCE: paraphrase of scientific authority

ORGANIZATION: opposing argument

REFUTATION OF OPPOSING ARGUMENT

and despite its complexity, do amazingly well. For example, I just met the eight-year-old daughter of a Soviet family now living in the United States who participated in an intensive English instruction program. After only a few months, she learned the language so well that she was able to enter the fourth grade, speaking English with only a slight accent. On the other hand, her mother is taking much longer; she still has a strong accent and often stumbles over vocabulary. Young children have a clear advantage in learning languages.

EVIDENCE: personal experience

Young children have little difficulty switching between two languages. Many schools, such as those in Montreal and in Gates County, North Carolina, have instituted bilingual school days. The morning lessons are taught in French, and the afternoon lessons in English. The direct method, when a parent speaks to a child in a second language from day one, is the best way to create proficient speakers.

EVIDENCE: examples of effective programs

In order for Americans to better understand the world, we must be able to expand and grow with the world. The best way is through a second language. The present system of beginning instruction in junior high school does not create effective speakers and listeners. At this stage, the ability to learn a second language is severely diminished. However, starting in the primary years of a child's education, as has already been shown, will create a group of adept, bilingual people who will have no problems communicating and learning

ENDING: argument summarized

ENDING:
concluding
sentence
echoes title

from other cultures. Let's not raise another generation of ignorant Americans who can't communicate with their foreign neighbors and are forced to walk the streets of Europe in agony because they can't find le bathroom.

WORKS CITED

Penfield, Wilder. "Conditioning the Uncommitted Cortex for Language Learning." <u>Brain</u> 88.4 (1965): 387-398.

Seligmann, Jean. "Speaking in Tongues." <u>Newsweek</u> Fall/Winter Special Edition, 1990: 36-37.

I

THE
ELEMENTS
OF THE
ESSAY

1

THESIS

The *thesis* of an essay is its main idea, the point it is trying to make. The thesis is often expressed in a one- or two-sentence statement, although sometimes it is implied or suggested rather than stated directly. The thesis statement controls and directs the content of the essay: everything that the writer says must be logically related to the thesis statement.

Usually the thesis is presented early in an essay, sometimes in the first sentence. Here are some thesis statements that begin essays:

> One of the most potent elements in body language is eye behavior.
>
> Flora Davis

> Americans can be divided into three groups—smokers, non-smokers, and that expanding pack of us who have quit.
>
> Franklin E. Zimring

> Over the past ten to fifteen years it has become apparent that eating disorders have reached epidemic proportions among adolescents.
>
> Helen A. Guthrie

> Clutter is the disease of American writing. We are a society strangling in unnecessary words, circular construction, pompous frills, and meaningless jargon.
>
> William Zinsser

Each of these sentences does what a good thesis statement should do—it identifies the topic and makes an assertion about it.

Often writers prepare readers for a thesis statement with one or several sentences that establish a context. Notice, in the following example, how the author eases the reader into his thesis about television instead of presenting it abruptly in the first sentence:

> With the advent of television, for the first time in history, all aspects of animal and human life and death, of societal

and individual behavior have been condensed on the average to a 19 inch diagonal screen and a 30 minute time slot. Television, a unique medium, claiming to be neither a reality nor art, has become reality for many of us, particularly for our children who are growing up in front of it.

Jerzy Kosinski

On occasion a writer may even purposefully delay the presentation of a thesis until the middle or end of an essay. If the thesis is controversial or needs extended discussion and illustration, the writer might present it later to make it easier for the reader to understand and accept it. Appearing near or at the end of an essay, a thesis also gains prominence.

Some kinds of writing do not need thesis statements. These include descriptions, narratives, and personal writing such as letters and diaries. But any essay that seeks to explain or prove a point has a thesis that is usually set forth in a thesis statement.

THE MOST IMPORTANT DAY

Helen Keller

*Helen Keller (1880–1968) was afflicted by a disease
that left her blind and deaf at the age of eighteen
months. With the aid of her teacher, Anne Sullivan,
she was able to overcome her severe handicaps, to
graduate from Radcliffe College, and to lead a productive and challenging adult life. In the following
selection from her autobiography,* The Story of My
Life *(1902), Keller tells of the day she first met Anne
Sullivan, a day she regarded as the most important
in her life. Notice that Keller states her thesis in the
first paragraph and that it serves to focus and unify
the remaining paragraphs.*

The most important day I remember in all my life is the one
on which my teacher, Anne Mansfield Sullivan, came to me.
I am filled with wonder when I consider the immeasurable contrast between the two lives which it connects. It was the third of
March, 1887, three months before I was seven years old.

On the afternoon of that eventful day, I stood on the porch,
dumb, expectant. I guessed vaguely from my mother's signs and
from the hurrying to and fro in the house that something unusual
was about to happen, so I went to the door and waited on the
steps. The afternoon sun penetrated the mass of honeysuckle that
covered the porch and fell on my upturned face. My fingers
lingered almost unconsciously on the familiar leaves and blos-
soms which had just come forth to greet the sweet southern
spring. I did not know what the future held of marvel or surprise
for me. Anger and bitterness had preyed upon me continually for
weeks and a deep languor had succeeded this passionate struggle.

Have you ever been at sea in a dense fog, when it seemed as if
a tangible white darkness shut you in, and the great ship, tense
and anxious, groped her way toward the shore with plummet and
sounding-line, and you waited with beating heart for something
to happen? I was like that ship before my education began, only

I was without compass or sounding-line, and had no way of knowing how near the harbor was. "Light! give me light!" was the wordless cry of my soul, and the light of love shone on me in that very hour.

I felt approaching footsteps. I stretched out my hand as I sup- 4 posed to my mother. Someone took it, and I was caught up and held close in the arms of her who had come to reveal all things to me, and, more than all things else, to love me.

The morning after my teacher came she led me into her room 5 and gave me a doll. The little blind children at the Perkins Institution had sent it and Laura Bridgman had dressed it; but I did not know this until afterward. When I had played with it a little while, Miss Sullivan slowly spelled into my hand the word "d-o-l-l." I was at once interested in this finger play and tried to imitate it. When I finally succeeded in making the letters correctly I was flushed with childish pleasure and pride. Running downstairs to my mother I held up my hand and made the letters for doll. I did not know that I was spelling a word or even that words existed; I was simply making my fingers go in monkeylike imitation. In the days that followed I learned to spell in this uncomprehending way a great many words, among them *pin, hat, cup* and a few verbs like *sit, stand* and *walk*. But my teacher had been with me several weeks before I understood that everything has a name.

One day, while I was playing with my new doll, Miss Sullivan 6 put my big rag doll into my lap also, spelled "d-o-l-l" and tried to make me understand that "d-o-l-l" applied to both. Earlier in the day we had had a tussle over the words "m-u-g" and "w-a-t-e-r." Miss Sullivan had tried to impress it upon me that "m-u-g" is *mug* and that "w-a-t-e-r" is *water,* but I persisted in confounding the two. In despair she had dropped the subject for the time, only to renew it at the first opportunity. I became impatient at her repeated attempts and, seizing the new doll, I dashed it upon the floor. I was keenly delighted when I felt the fragments of the broken doll at my feet. Neither sorrow nor regret followed my passionate outburst. I had not loved the doll. In the still, dark world in which I lived there was no strong sentiment or tenderness. I felt my teacher sweep the fragments to one side of the hearth, and I had a sense of satisfaction that the cause of my discomfort was removed. She brought me my hat, and I knew I was going out into the warm sunshine. This thought, if a wordless sensation may be called a thought, made me hop and skip with pleasure.

We walked down the path to the well-house, attracted by the fragrance of the honeysuckle with which it was covered. Some one was drawing water and my teacher placed my hand under the spout. As the cool stream gushed over one hand she spelled into the other the word *water,* first slowly, then rapidly. I stood still, my whole attention fixed upon the motions of her fingers. Suddenly I felt a misty consciousness as of something forgotten—a thrill of returning thought; and somehow the mystery of language was revealed to me. I knew then that "w-a-t-e-r" meant the wonderful cool something that was flowing over my hand. The living word awakened my soul, gave it light, hope, joy, set it free! There were barriers still, it is true, but barriers that could in time be swept away.

I left the well-house eager to learn. Everything had a name, and each name gave birth to a new thought. As we returned to the house every object which I touched seemed to quiver with life. That was because I saw everything with the strange, new sight that had come to me. On entering the door I remembered the doll I had broken. I felt my way to the hearth and picked up the pieces. I tried vainly to put them together. Then my eyes filled with tears; for I realized what I had done, and for the first time I felt repentance and sorrow.

I learned a great many new words that day. I do not remember what they all were; but I do know that *mother, father, sister, teacher* were among them—words that were to make the world blossom for me, "like Aaron's rod, with flowers." It would have been difficult to find a happier child than I was as I lay in my crib at the close of that eventful day and lived over the joys it had brought me, and for the first time longed for a new day to come.

Questions for Study and Discussion

1. What is Helen Keller's thesis in this essay?
2. What is Helen Keller's purpose in this essay? (Glossary: *Purpose*)

3. What was Helen Keller's state of mind before Anne Sullivan arrived to help her? To what does she compare herself?

4. Why was the realization that everything has a name important to Helen Keller?

5. How was the "mystery of language" (7) revealed to Helen Keller? What were the consequences of this new understanding of the nature of language for her?

6. Helen Keller narrates the events of the day Anne Sullivan arrived (2–4), the morning after she arrived (5), and one day several weeks after her arrival (6–9). Describe what happens on each day, and explain how these separate incidents support her thesis.

Vocabulary

Refer to your dictionary to define the following words as they are used in this selection. Then use each word in a sentence of your own.

dumb (2)	plummet (3)
preyed (2)	tussle (6)
languor (2)	vainly (8)
passionate (2)	

Suggested Writing Assignments

1. Think about an important day in your own life. Using the thesis statement "The most important day of my life was _____," write an essay in which you show the significance of that day by recounting and explaining the events that took place.

2. For many people around the world, the life of Helen Keller stands as the symbol of what can be achieved by an individual despite seemingly insurmountable handicaps. Her achievements have also had a tremendous impact upon those who are not afflicted with handicaps, leading them to believe that they can accomplish more than they ever thought possible. Consider the role of handicapped people in our society, develop an appropriate thesis, and write an essay on the topic.

GIVE US JOBS, NOT ADMIRATION

Eric Bigler

Eric Bigler was born in Powhatan Point, Ohio, in 1958. Despite a diving accident while in high school that left him paralyzed from the chest down, Bigler went on to earn his bachelor's degree in social work and his master's degree in business and industrial counseling management at Wright State University. Bigler lives in Dayton, Ohio, and has been working for a software company since 1989. In his spare time, he actively trades commodities and stocks and is seriously considering changing careers to trade full-time. He also continues to write short stories and hopes someday to have his work published in outdoor magazines.

Tuesday I have another job interview. Like most I have had so far, it will probably end with the all-too-familiar words, "We'll let you know of our decision in a few days."

Many college graduates searching for their first career job might simply accept that response as, "Sorry, we're not interested in you," and blame the rejection on inexperience or bad chemistry. For myself and other disabled people, however, this response often seems to indicate something more worrisome: a reluctance to hire the handicapped even when they're qualified. I have been confined to a wheelchair since 1974, when a high-school diving accident left me paralyzed from the chest down. But that didn't prevent me from earning a bachelor's in social work in 1983, and I am now finishing up a master's degree in business and industrial management, specializing in employee relations and human-resource development.

Our government spends a great deal of money to help the handicapped, but it does not necessarily spend it all wisely. For example, in 1985 Ohio's Bureau of Vocational Rehabilitation (BVR) spent more than $4 million in tuition and other expenses so that disabled students could obtain a college education. BVR's philosophy is that the amount of money spent educating students will be repaid in disabled employees' taxes. The agency assists graduates by offering workshops on résumé writing and interviewing techniques, skills many already learned in college. BVR also maintains files of résumés that are matched with help-wanted notices from local companies and employs placement specialists to work directly with graduates during their job search.

Even with all this assistance, however, graduates still have 4 trouble getting hired. Such programs might do better if they concentrated on the perceptions of employers as well as the skills of applicants. More important, improving contacts with prospective employers might encourage them to actively recruit the disabled.

Often, projects that *do* show promise don't get the chance to 5 thrive. I was both a client and an informal consultant to one program, Careers for the Disabled in Dayton, which asked local executives to make a commitment to hire disabled applicants whenever possible. I found this strategy to be on target, since support for a project is more likely when it is ordered from the top. The program also offered free training seminars to corporations on how they can work effectively with the disabled candidate. In April of 1986—less than a year after it was started and after only three disabled people were placed—the program was discontinued because, according to the director, they had "no luck at getting [enough] corporations to join the program."

Corporations need to take a more independent and active part 6 in hiring qualified handicapped persons. Today's companies try to show a willingness to innovate, and hiring people like myself would enhance that image. Madison Avenue has finally recognized that the disabled are also consumers; more and more often, commercials include them. But advertisers could break down even more stereotypes. I would like to see one of those Hewlett-Packard commercials, for instance, show an employee racing down the sidewalk in his wheelchair, pulling alongside a pay phone and calling a colleague to ask "What if . . .?"

Corporate recruiters also need to be better prepared for meet- 7 ing with disabled applicants. They should be ready to answer queries about any barriers that their building's design may pose, and they should be forthright about asking their own questions. It's understandable that employers are afraid to mention matters that are highly personal and may prove embarassing—or, even worse, discriminatory. There's nothing wrong, however, with an employer reassuring him or herself about whether an applicant will be able to reach files, operate computers or even get into the bathroom. Until interviewers change their style, disabled applicants need to initiate discussion of disability-related issues.

Government has tried to improve hiring for the disabled through Affirmative Action programs. The Rehabilitation Act of 1973 says institutions or programs receiving substantial amounts of federal money can't discriminate on the basis of handicap. Yet I was saddened and surprised to discover how many companies spend much time and money writing great affirmative-action and equal-opportunity guidelines but little time following them. Then there are the cosmetic acts, such as the annual National Employ the Handicapped Week every October. If President Reagan (or anyone else) wants to help the disabled with proclamations, more media exposure is necessary. I found out about the last occasion in 1985 from a brief article on the back of a campus newspaper—a week after it had happened. 8

As if other problems were not enough, the disabled who search unsuccessfully for employment often face a loss of self-esteem and worth. In college, many disabled people I have talked to worked hard toward a degree so they would be prepared for jobs after graduation. Now they look back on their four or more years as wasted time. For these individuals, the days of earning good grades and accomplishing tough tasks fade away, leaving only frustrating memories. Today's job market is competitive enough without prejudice adding more "handicaps." 9

About that interview . . . five minutes into it, I could feel the atmosphere chill. The interviewer gave me general information instead of trying to find out if I was right for the job. I've been there before. Then the session closed with a handshake, and those same old words: "We'll let you know." They said I should be so proud of myself for doing what I am doing. That's what they always say. I'm tired of hearing how courageous I am. So are other disabled people. We need jobs, and we want to work like anyone else. 10

But still, I remain an optimist. I know someday soon a company will be smart enough to realize how much I have to offer them in both my head and my heart. 11

Maybe then I'll hear the words so many of us really want to hear: "You're hired." 12

Questions for Study and Discussion

1. What does Bigler feel is wrong with government programs aimed at helping the disabled? What does he suggest be done to improve the situation?

2. What is Bigler's thesis in this essay? Where in the essay is his thesis most clearly presented?

3. Does Bigler give his readers any reasons why the disabled are not being hired as often as they should be? Does the success of his thesis depend upon his providing such reasons? Explain.

4. Bigler frames his essay with references to a particular job interview. Discuss the way Bigler connects the beginning and ending of his essay. Has he employed an effective strategy in this regard? Explain.

5. What are the "cosmetic acts" that Bigler refers to in paragraph 8? Why does he use this particular term? (Glossary: *Diction*)

6. What audience(s) would seem to be most interested in what Bigler has to say in his essay? Explain.

Vocabulary

Refer to your dictionary to define the following words as they are used in this selection. Then use each word in a sentence of your own.

worrisome (2)   forthright (7)
seminars (5)   proclamations (8)
enhance (6)   self-esteem (9)

Suggested Writing Assignments

1. Write an essay in which you use as your thesis the formula "Give us _____, not _____." You may use one of the following topics or create one of your own:

   Give us peace, not more arms.

   Give us results, nor more red tape.

Give us action, not talk.

Give us jobs, not welfare.

Give us choices, not rules.

Give us answers, not excuses.

Give us opportunities, not promises.

Give us better government, not more taxes.

2. One year after Eric Bigler's essay was published, he was still not employed in a full-time position. Develop a thesis and write an essay of your own as to why the disabled have a difficult time gaining employment despite their personal talents and educational backgrounds.

ANXIETY: CHALLENGE BY ANOTHER NAME

James Lincoln Collier

*James Lincoln Collier is a free-lance writer with
over six hundred articles to his credit. He was born
in New York in 1928 and graduated from Hamilton
College in 1950. Among his many books are* Rock
Star *(1970),* It's Murder at St. Basket's *(1972),* My
Brother Sam Is Dead *(1974),* Rich and Famous
(1975), Give Dad My Best *(1976), and* Duke Ellington *(1987). Collier's best-known book is* The
Making of Jazz: A Comprehensive History *(1978),
still regarded as the best general history of the subject. As you read the following essay, pay particular
attention to Collier's thesis, where it is placed in the
essay, and how well he supports it.*

Between my sophomore and junior years at college, a chance 1
came up for me to spend the summer vacation working on
a ranch in Argentina. My roommate's father was in the cattle
business, and he wanted Ted to see something of it. Ted said he
would go if he could take a friend, and he chose me.

The idea of spending two months on the fabled Argentine 2
Pampas was exciting. Then I began having second thoughts. I had
never been very far from New England, and I had been homesick
my first few weeks at college. What would it be like in a strange
country? What about the language? And besides, I had promised
to teach my younger brother to sail that summer. The more I
thought about it, the more the prospect daunted me. I began
waking up nights in a sweat.

In the end I turned down the proposition. As soon as Ted asked 3
somebody else to go, I began kicking myself. A couple of weeks
later I went home to my old summer job, unpacking cartons at
the local supermarket, feeling very low. I had turned down something I wanted to do because I was scared, and had ended up

feeling depressed. I stayed that way for a long time. And it didn't help when I went back to college in the fall to discover that Ted and his friend had had a terrific time.

In the long run that unhappy summer taught me a valuable 4 lesson out of which I developed a rule for myself: *do what makes you anxious; don't do what makes you depressed.*

I am not, of course, talking about severe states of anxiety or 5 depression, which require medical attention. What I mean is that kind of anxiety we call stage fright, butterflies in the stomach, a case of nerves—the feelings we have at a job interview, when we're giving a big party, when we have to make an important presentation at the office. And the kind of depression I am referring to is that downhearted feeling of the blues, when we don't seem to be interested in anything, when we can't get going and seem to have no energy.

I was confronted by this sort of situation toward the end of my 6 senior year. As graduation approached, I began to think about taking a crack at making my living as a writer. But one of my professors was urging me to apply to graduate school and aim at a teaching career.

I wavered. The idea of trying to live by writing was scary—a lot 7 more scary than spending a summer on the Pampas, I thought. Back and forth I went, making my decision, unmaking it. Suddenly, I realized that every time I gave up the idea of writing, that sinking feeling went through me; it gave me the blues.

The thought of graduate school wasn't what depressed me. It 8 was giving up on what deep in my gut I really wanted to do. Right then I learned another lesson. To avoid that kind of depression meant, inevitably, having to endure a certain amount of worry and concern.

The great Danish philosopher Søren Kierkegaard believed that 9 anxiety always arises when we confront the possibility of our own development. It seems to be a rule of life that you can't advance without getting that old, familiar, jittery feeling.

Even as children we discover this when we try to expand our- 10 selves by, say, learning to ride a bike or going out for the school play. Later in life we get butterflies when we think about having that first child, or uprooting the family from the old hometown to find a better opportunity halfway across the country. Any time, it seems, that we set out aggressively to get something we want, we meet up with anxiety. And it's going to be our traveling companion, at least part of the way, into any new venture.

When I first began writing magazine articles, I was frequently required to interview big names—people like Richard Burton, Joan Rivers, sex authority William Masters, baseball-great Dizzy Dean. Before each interview I would get butterflies and my hands would shake. 11

At the time, I was doing some writing about music. And one person I particularly admired was the great composer Duke Ellington. Onstage and on television, he seemed the very model of the confident, sophisticated man of the world. Then I learned that Ellington still got stage fright. If the highly honored Duke Ellington, who had appeared on the bandstand some 10,000 times over 30 years, had anxiety attacks, who was I to think I could avoid them? 12

I went on doing those frightening interviews, and one day, as I was getting onto a plane for Washington to interview columnist Joseph Alsop, I suddenly realized to my astonishment that I was looking forward to the meeting. What had happened to those butterflies? 13

Well, in truth, they were still there, but there were fewer of them. I had benefited, I discovered, from a process psychologists call "extinction." If you put an individual in an anxiety-provoking situation often enough, he will eventually learn that there isn't anything to be worried about. 14

Which brings us to a corollary to my basic rule: *you'll never eliminate anxiety by avoiding the things that caused it.* I remember how my son Jeff was when I first began to teach him to swim at the lake cottage where we spent our summer vacations. He resisted, and when I got him into the water he sank and sputtered and wanted to quit. But I was insistent. And by summer's end he was splashing around like a puppy. He had "extinguished" his anxiety the only way he could—by confronting it. 15

The problem, of course, is that it is one thing to urge somebody else to take on those anxiety-producing challenges; it is quite another to get ourselves to do it. 16

Some years ago I was offered a writing assignment that would require three months of travel through Europe. I had been abroad a couple of times on the usual "If it's Tuesday this must be Belgium" trips, but I hardly could claim to know my way around 17 the continent. Moreover, my knowledge of foreign languages was limited to a little college French.

I hesitated. How would I, unable to speak the language, totally 18 unfamiliar with local geography or transportation systems, set up interviews and do research? It seemed impossible, and with considerable regret I sat down to write a letter begging off. Halfway through, a thought—which I subsequently made into another corollary to my basic rule—ran through my mind: *you can't learn if you don't try.* So I accepted the assignment.

There were some bad moments. But by the time I had finished 19 the trip I was an experienced traveler. And ever since, I have never hesitated to head for even the most exotic of places, without guides or even advanced bookings, confident that somehow I will manage.

The point is that the new, the different, is almost by definition 20 scary. But each time you try something, you learn, and as the learning piles up, the world opens to you.

I've made parachute jumps, learned to ski at 40, flown up the 21 Rhine in a balloon. And I know I'm going to go on doing such things. It's not because I'm braver or more daring than others. I'm not. But I don't let the butterflies stop me from doing what I want. Accept anxiety as another name for challenge and you can accomplish wonders.

Questions for Study and Discussion

1. What is Collier's thesis in this essay? Based on your own experiences, do you think that Collier's thesis is a valid one? Explain.
2. What is the process known to psychologists as "extinction"?
3. Collier provides some rules for himself. What are these rules? He says that his second and third rules are corollaries to a basic rule. What does Collier mean?
4. What do you think Collier's purpose was in writing this essay? (Glossary: *Purpose*) Explain.
5. Identify the figure of speech that Collier uses toward the end of paragraph 10. (Glossary: *Figures of Speech*)

6. Explain how paragraphs 17–19 function within the context of Collier's essay. (Glossary: *Illustration*)

Vocabulary

Refer to your dictionary to define the following words as they are used in this selection. Then use each word in a sentence of your own.

daunted (2)	butterflies (5)
proposition (3)	crack (6)
anxiety (5)	venture (10)
depression (5)	corollary (15)

Suggested Writing Assignments

1. Building on your own experiences and the reading you have done, write an essay in which you use as your thesis either Collier's basic rule or one of his corollaries to that basic rule.
2. Write an essay in which you use any of the following as your thesis:

   Good manners are a thing of the past.

   We need rituals in our lives.

   To tell a joke well is an art.

   We are a drug-dependent society.

   Losing weight is a breeze.

2

UNITY

A well-written essay should be unified; that is, everything in it should be related to its thesis, or main idea. The first requirement for unity is that the thesis itself be clear, either through a direct statement, called the *thesis statement*, or by implication. The second requirement is that there be no digressions, no discussion or information that is not shown to be logically related to the thesis. A unified essay stays within the limits of its thesis.

Here, for example, is a short essay called "Over-Generalizing" about the dangers of making generalizations. As you read, notice how carefully author Stuart Chase sticks to his point.

One swallow does not make a summer, nor can two or three cases often support a dependable generalization. Yet all of us, including the most polished eggheads, are constantly falling into this mental peopletrap. It is the commonest, probably the most seductive, and potentially the most dangerous, of all the fallacies.

You drive through a town and see a drunken man on the sidewalk. A few blocks further on you see another. You turn to your companion: "Nothing but drunks in this town!" Soon you are out in the country, bowling along at fifty. A car passes you as if you were parked. On a curve a second whizzes by. Your companion turns to you: "All the drivers in this state are crazy!" Two thumping generalizations, each built on two cases. If we stop to think, we usually recognize the exaggeration and the unfairness of such generalizations. Trouble comes when we do not stop to think—or when we build them on a prejudice.

This kind of reasoning has been around for a long time. Aristotle was aware of its dangers and called it "reasoning by example," meaning too few examples. What it boils down to is failing to count your swallows before announcing that summer is here. Driving from my home to New Haven the other day, a distance of about forty miles, I caught myself saying: "Every time I look around I see a new ranch-type house going up." So on the return trip I counted them; there were exactly five under construction. And how many times had I "looked around"? I suppose I had glanced to right and left—as one must at side roads and so forth in driving—several hundred times.

In this fallacy we do not make the error of neglecting facts   4
altogether and rushing immediately to the level of opinion. We start at the fact level properly enough, but *we do not stay there.* A case of two and up we go to a rousing oversimplification about drunks, speeders, ranch-style houses—or, more seriously, about foreigners, Negroes, labor leaders, teen-agers.

Why do we over-generalize so often and sometimes so dis-   5
astrously? One reason is that the human mind is a generalizing machine. We would not be people without this power. The old academic crack: "All generalizations are false, including this one," is only a play on words. We *must* generalize to communicate and to live. But we should beware of beating the gun; of not waiting until enough facts are in to say something useful. Meanwhile it is a plain waste of time to listen to arguments based on a few handpicked examples.

Everything in the essay relates to Chase's thesis statement, which is included in the essay's first sentence: ". . . nor can two or three cases often support a dependable generalization." Paragraphs 2 and 3 document the thesis with examples; paragraph 4 explains how over-generalizing occurs; paragraph 5 analyzes why people over-generalize; and, for a conclusion, Chase restates his thesis in different words. An essay may be longer, more complex, and more wide-ranging than this one, but to be effective it must also avoid digressions and remain close to the author's main idea.

THE MEANINGS OF A WORD

Gloria Naylor

American novelist and essayist Gloria Naylor was born in 1950 in New York City. She worked first as a missionary for the Jehovah's Witnesses from 1967 to 1975, then as a telephone operator until 1981. That year she graduated from Brooklyn College of the City of New York and began graduate work in African American studies at Yale University. She has published several novels on the "black experience": The Women of Brewster Place *(1982),* Linden Hills *(1985),* Mama Day *(1988), and* Bailey's Cafe *(1992). The following essay first appeared in the* New York Times *in 1986. In it Naylor examines the ways in which words can take on meaning depending on who uses them and to what purpose.*

Language is the subject. It is the written form with which I've managed to keep the wolf away from the door and, in diaries, to keep my sanity. In spite of this, I consider the written word inferior to the spoken, and much of the frustration experienced by novelists is the awareness that whatever we manage to capture in even the most transcendent passages falls far short of the richness of life. Dialogue achieves its power in the dynamics of a fleeting moment of sight, sound, smell, and touch. 1

I'm not going to enter the debate here about whether it is language that shapes reality or vice versa. That battle is doomed to be waged whenever we seek intermittent reprieve from the chicken and egg dispute. I will simply take the position that the spoken word, like the written word, amounts to a nonsensical arrangement of sounds or letters without a consensus that assigns "meaning." And building from the meanings of what we hear, we order reality. Words themselves are innocuous; it is the consensus that gives them true power. 2

I remember the first time I heard the word *nigger*. In my third-grade class, our math tests were being passed down the rows, and as I handed the papers to a little boy in back of me, I remarked that once again he had received a much lower mark than I did. He snatched his test from me and spit out that word. Had he called me a nymphomaniac or a necrophiliac, I couldn't have been more puzzled. I didn't know what a nigger was, but I knew that whatever it meant, it was something he shouldn't have called me. This was verified when I raised my hand, and in a loud voice repeated what he had said and watched the teacher scold him for using a "bad" word. I was later to go home and ask the inevitable question that every black parent must face—"Mommy, what does *nigger* mean?"

And what exactly did it mean? Thinking back, I realize that this could not have been the first time the word was used in my presence. I was part of a large extended family that had migrated from the rural South after World War II and formed a close-knit network that gravitated around my maternal grandparents. Their ground-floor apartment in one of the buildings they owned in Harlem was a weekend mecca for my immediate family, along with countless aunts, uncles, and cousins who brought along assorted friends. It was a bustling and open house with assorted neighbors and tenants popping in and out to exchange bits of gossip, pick up an old quarrel, or referee the ongoing checkers game in which my grandmother cheated shamelessly. They were all there to let down their hair and put up their feet after a week of labor in the factories, laundries, and shipyards of New York.

Amid the clamor, which could reach deafening proportions—two or three conversations going on simultaneously, punctuated by the sound of a baby's crying somewhere in the back rooms or out on the street—there was still a rigid set of rules about what was said and how. Older children were sent out of the living room when it was time to get into the juicy details about "you-know-who" up on the third floor who had gone and gotten herself "p-r-e-g-n-a-n-t!" But my parents, knowing that I could spell well beyond my years, always demanded that I follow the others out to play. Beyond sexual misconduct and death, everything else was considered harmless for our young ears. And so among the anecdotes of the triumphs and disappointments in the various workings of their lives, the word *nigger* was used in my presence, but it was set within contexts and inflections that caused it to register in my mind as something else.

In the singular, the word was always applied to a man who had 6 distinguished himself in some situation that brought their approval for his strength, intelligence, or drive:

"Did Johnny *really* do that?" 7

"I'm telling you, that nigger pulled in $6,000 of overtime last 8 year. Said he got enough for a down payment on a house."

When used with a possessive adjective by a woman—"my 9 nigger"—it became a term of endearment for her husband or boyfriend. But it could be more than just a term applied to a man. In their mouths it became the pure essence of manhood—a disembodied force that channeled their past history of struggle and present survival against the odds into a victorious statement of being: "Yeah, that old foreman found out quick enough—you don't mess with a nigger."

In the plural, it became a description of some group within the 10 community that had overstepped the bounds of decency as my family defined it. Parents who neglected their children, a drunken couple who fought in public, people who simply refused to look for work, those with excessively dirty mouths or unkempt households were all "trifling niggers." This particular circle could forgive hard times, unemployment, the occasional bout of depression— they had gone through all of that themselves—but the unforgivable sin was a lack of self-respect.

A woman could never be a "nigger" in the singular, with its 11 connotation of confirming worth. The noun *girl* was its closest equivlent in that sense, but only when used in direct address and regardless of the gender doing the addressing. *Girl* was a token of respect for a woman. The one-syllable word was drawn out to sound like three in recognition of the extra ounce of wit, nerve, or daring that the woman had shown in the situation under discussion.

"G-i-r-l, stop. You mean you said that to his face?" 12

But if the word was used in a third-person reference or short- 13 ened so that it almost snapped out of the mouth, it always involved some element of communal disapproval. And age became an important factor in these exchanges. It was only between individuals of the same generation, or from any older person to a younger (but never the other way around), that *girl* would be considered a compliment.

I don't agree with the argument that use of the word *nigger* at   14
this social stratum of the black community was an internalization of racism. The dynamics were the exact opposite: the people in my grandmother's living room took a word that whites used to signify worthlessness or degradation and rendered it impotent. Gathering there together, they transformed *nigger* to signify the varied and complex human beings they knew themselves to be. If the word was to disappear totally from the mouths of even the most liberal of white society, no one in that room was naive enough to believe it would disappear from white minds. Meeting the word head-on, they proved it had absolutely nothing to do with the way they were determined to live their lives.

So there must have been dozens of times that *nigger* was   15
spoken in front of me before I reached the third grade. But I didn't "hear" it until it was said by a small pair of lips that had already learned it could be a way to humiliate me. That was the word I went home and asked my mother about. And since she knew that I had to grow up in America, she took me in her lap and explained.

Questions for Study and Discussion

1. How does Naylor explain her preference for the spoken word over the written word? What does she mean by "context"?

2. What are the two meanings of the word "nigger" as Naylor uses it in her essay? Where in the essay is the clearest definition of each use of the word presented?

3. Naylor said she must have heard the word "nigger" many times while she was growing up; yet she "heard" it for the first time when she was in the third grade. How does she explain this seeming contradiction?

4. Naylor gives a detailed narration of her family and its life-style in paragraphs 4 and 5. What kinds of detail does she include in her brief story? How does this narration contrib-

ute to your understanding of the word "nigger" as used by her family? Why do you suppose she offers so little in the way of a definition of the other use of the word "nigger"? What is the effect on you as a reader? Explain.

5. Would you characterize Naylor's tone as angry, objective, cynical, or something else? (Glossary: *Tone*) Cite examples of her diction to support your answer. (Glossary: *Diction*)

6. What is the meaning of Naylor's last sentence? How well does it work as an ending for her essay? (Glossary: *Endings*)

Vocabulary

Refer to your dictionary to define the following words as they are used in this selection. Then use each word in a sentence of your own.

transcendent (1)	anecdotes (5)
consensus (2)	inflections (5)
innocuous (2)	unkempt (10)
nymphomaniac (3)	trifling (10)
necrophiliac (3)	internalization (14)
mecca (4)	impotent (14)
clamor (5)	

Suggested Writing Assignments

1. Write a short essay in which you define a word that has more than one meaning, depending on one's point of view. For example, wife, macho, liberal, success, and marriage.

2. Naylor disagrees with the notion that use of the word "nigger" in the African American community can be taken as an "internalization of racism." Reexamine her essay and discuss in what ways her definition of the word "nigger" affirms or denies her position. Draw on your own experiences, observations, and reading to add support to your answer.

WHY "MODEL MINORITY" DOESN'T FIT

Diane Yen-Mei Wong

Diane Yen-Mei Wong writes about Asian American issues in a column that appears in the Hawaii Herald. *She currently lives in Oakland, California. In the following selection, which appeared in* USA Weekend *in January 1994, she discusses the dangers of stereotypes and how personal experience has forced her to reevaluate her own ethnic community.*

I stopped by a peaceful lake on one of Seattle's rare sunny days to watch a wonderfully multiracial, multiethnic parade of people walk, jog, bicycle and skate along the bike path. For them, life looked good and the whole weekend lay ahead. The irony did not escape me.

Just a few hours before, I had been inside a windowless courtroom listening to a judge render a final sentence of 70 years in prison to a Vietnamese-American man, Dung Hoang Le, barely out of his teens. He had fatally stabbed my best friend's mother, Mayme Lui, a petite septuagenarian Chinese-American widow. He had mutilated her body to wrench off a jade bracelet, then attempted to extort money from her family as he led them to believe she was still alive.

He needed money fast. He had just wrecked his cousin's car and discovered his girlfriend was pregnant. Without a job or marketable skills, he was at a critical juncture. Rather than earn money through hard work, he chose crime. This decision changed our lives forever.

I used to see my friend's mother whenever I was visiting in town; we laughed and talked and ate. Now I try to comfort the family as they negotiate their lives around her absence. I am haunted by frequent nightmares of the terror and pain she must have felt. But this man's act also has compelled me to rethink how I view my own community of Asian Americans.

For more than two decades, I have argued that the diverse Asian-American community cannot be stereotyped. One of the

42

most troubling and persistent images is that we are a "model minority," people who have succeeded when other people of color have not. We are held up as proof that racial discrimination either does not exist or, if it does, is not much of a handicap. I have argued that this stereotype negates the existence of the large segments of our ethnic communities that live in poverty, have little or no education, and work in sweatshops for less than the minimum wage or in family-owned businesses for no wages.

Violence in the Asian-American community, like violence in 6 many other communities, is growing at such an alarming rate that several cities, including Seattle, have assigned special units to investigate crimes committed by Asian-American gangs. City officials in Seattle say that from 1988 to 1993, for example, the number of Asian-Pacific Islander youths involved in gangs increased eightfold.

Despite this reality, too many Asian Americans and others cling 7 to the mythical model-minority image. They want to believe that crime, especially violent crime, happens in other communities, not in one that spawns valedictorians and scientists and espouses respect for authority and close family ties.

The model-minority mantra, however, no matter how frequently 8 repeated, cannot protect us against the intensifying violence perpetrated by our own.

I have heard "experts" say that some immigrants and refugees 9 may commit crimes because of cultural unfamiliarity or a lack of sophistication about the American way of life. Some say there is a heightened sense of detachment adopted by refugees dulled by the horror of seeing so many deaths in war.

Even if true, these arguments do not explain why many other 10 people facing similar circumstances do not extort, kidnap and murder. Surely killing someone for money is not an acceptable act in any country.

And it may get worse. As the interaction among the different 11 Asian-American ethnic groups grows, crimes increasingly will cross ethnic lines.

A Chinese-American wedding reception becomes the target of 12 non-Chinese-American criminals whose eyes see not the ethnicity of the newlyweds but only the jade and gold jewelry worn just for the special occasion. Is it any wonder that some wedding parties now include security guards?

At the sentencing, I happened to sit next to a small, elderly well-   13
to-do and prominent Chinese American. I found myself wondering how much of her interest in the outcome was related to how
unsafe she felt now that her ethnicity no longer could protect her.

Asian Americans have been considered different from other   14
minorities. We are supposed to be harmless and somehow exotic,
the least offensive minority group to have around if one must
have any around at all. Tragically, it may be the rising crime rate
within our own "model-minority" community that finally proves,
once and for all, that we are more like everyone else than some of
us ever thought.

Questions for Study and Discussion

1. Reread paragraphs 1–3. Why does Wong use them to begin
   her essay? (Glossary: *Beginnings and Endings*) In what way
   do they help unify the essay?
2. What is Wong's thesis? (Glossary: *Thesis*) Where is it stated?
   What does Wong gain by stating her thesis where she does?
3. Who is Wong's audience? (Glossary: *Audience*) Explain your
   answer.
4. Why does Wong think that the "model minority" stereotype
   of the Asian American community is harmful? Identify how
   she illustrates her argument. (Glossary: *Illustration*)
5. Why does Wong think violence in the Asian American community might get worse? Do you agree with her assessment? Why or why not?
6. What purpose does paragraph 13 serve? How does it help
   Wong unify her essay?

Vocabulary

Refer to your dictionary to define the following words as they
are used in this selection. Then use each word in a sentence of
your own.

render (2)   valedictorians (7)
septuagenarian (2)   espouses (7)
extort (2)   mantra (8)

Suggested Writing Assignments

1. Write an essay in which you explore how a personal experience changed your thinking about a particular subject. It can be about any subject you choose—how you view your peers or another group of people, an issue in current events, political beliefs, etc. Write a unified essay in which you incorporate your revised opinion or belief into the thesis statement. Make sure that each paragraph contributes to your exploration of how and why your thinking has changed.

2. Write a unified essay using the following sentence as a thesis: "Ethnic stereotypes, whether positive or negative, are harmful."

DON'T LET STEREOTYPES
WARP YOUR JUDGMENTS

Robert L. Heilbroner

*The economist Robert L. Heilbroner was educated
at Harvard and at the New School for Social Research, where he has been the Norman Thomas
Professor of Economics since 1972. He has written*
The Future as History *(1960),* A Primer of Government Spending: Between Capitalism and So-
cialism *(1970), and* An Inquiry into the Human
Prospect *(1974). "Don't Let Stereotypes Warp Your
Judgments" first appeared in* Reader's Digest, *and
it is a particularly timely essay for people who are
seeking understanding and respect for all in a culturally diverse, pluralistic society. As you read this
essay, pay specific attention to its unity—the relationships of the paragraphs to the thesis.*

Is a girl called Gloria apt to be better-looking than one called
Bertha? Are criminals more likely to be dark than blond? Can
you tell a good deal about someone's personality from hearing his
voice briefly over the phone? Can a person's nationality be pretty
accurately guessed from his photograph? Does the fact that
someone wears glasses imply that he is intelligent?

The answer to all these questions is obviously, "No."

Yet, from all the evidence at hand, most of us believe these
things. Ask any college boy if he'd rather take his chances with a
Gloria or a Bertha, or ask a college girl if she'd rather blinddate a
Richard or a Cuthbert. In fact, you don't have to ask: college
students in questionnaires have revealed that names conjure up
the same images in their minds as they do in yours—and for as
little reason.

Look into the favorite suspects of persons who report "suspicious characters" and you will find a large percentage of them to
be "swarthy" or "dark and foreign-looking"—despite the testi-

mony of criminologists that criminals do *not* tend to be dark, foreign or "wild-eyed." Delve into the main asset of a telephone stock swindler and you will find it to be a marvelously confidence-inspiring telephone "personality." And whereas we all think we know what an Italian or a Swede looks like, it is the sad fact that when a group of Nebraska students sought to match faces and nationalities of 15 European countries, they were scored wrong in 93 percent of their identifications. Finally, for all the fact that horn-rimmed glasses have now become the standard television sign of an "intellectual," optometrists know that the main thing that distinguishes people with glasses is just bad eyes.

Stereotypes are a kind of gossip about the world, a gossip that makes us prejudge people before we ever lay eyes on them. Hence it is not surprising that stereotypes have something to do with the dark world of prejudice. Explore most prejudices (note that the word means prejudgment) and you will find a cruel stereotype at the core of each one. 5

For it is the extraordinary fact that once we have typecast the world, we tend to see people in terms of our standardized pictures. In another demonstration of the power of stereotypes to affect our vision, a number of Columbia and Barnard students were shown 30 photographs of pretty but unidentified girls, and asked to rate each in terms of "general liking," "intelligence," "beauty" and so on. Two months later, the same group were shown the same photographs, this time with fictitious Irish, Italian, Jewish and "American" names attached to the pictures. Right away the ratings changed. Faces which were now seen as representing a national group went down in looks and still farther down in likability, while the "American" girls suddenly looked decidedly prettier and nicer. 6

Why is it that we stereotype the world in such irrational and harmful fashion? In part, we begin to type-cast people in our childhood years. Early in life, as every parent whose child has watched a TV Western knows, we learn to spot the Good Guys from the Bad Guys. Some years ago, a social psychologist showed very clearly how powerful these stereotypes of childhood vision are. He secretly asked the most popular youngsters in an elementary school to make errors in their morning gym exercises. Afterwards, he asked the class if anyone had noticed any mistakes during gym period. Oh, yes, said the children. But it was the 7 *unpopular* members of the class—the "bad guys"—they remembered as being out of step.

We not only grow up with standardized pictures forming inside 8
of us, but as grown-ups we are constantly having them thrust
upon us. Some of them, like the half-joking, half-serious stereotypes of mothers-in-law, or country yokels, or psychiatrists, are
dinned into us by the stock jokes we hear and repeat. In fact,
without such stereotypes, there would be a lot fewer jokes. Still
other stereotypes are perpetuated by the advertisements we read,
the movies we see, the books we read.

And finally, we tend to stereotype because it helps us make 9
sense out of a highly confusing world, a world which William
James once described as "one great, blooming, buzzing confusion." It is a curious fact that if we don't *know* what we're looking
at, we are often quite literally unable to *see* what we're looking at.
People who recover their sight after a lifetime of blindness actually cannot at first tell a triangle from a square. A visitor to a
factory sees only noisy chaos where the superintendent sees a perfectly synchronized flow of work. As Walter Lippmann has said,
"For the most part we do not first see, and then define; we define
first, and then we see."

Stereotypes are one way in which we "define" the world in 10
order to see it. They classify the infinite variety of human beings
into a convenient handful of "types" towards whom we learn to
act in stereotyped fashion. Life would be a wearing process if we
had to start from scratch with each and every human contact.
Stereotypes economize on our mental effort by covering up the
blooming, buzzing confusion with big recognizable cut-outs.
They save us the "trouble" of finding out what the world is like—
they give it its accustomed look.

Thus the trouble is that stereotypes make us mentally lazy. As 11
S. I. Hayakawa, the authority on semantics, has written: "The
danger of stereotypes lies not in their existence, but in the fact
that they become for all people some of the time, and for some
people all the time, *substitutes for observation*." Worse yet, stereotypes get in the way of our judgment, even when we do observe the world. Someone who has formed rigid preconceptions
of all Latins as "excitable," or all teenagers as "wild," doesn't alter
his point of view when he meets a calm and deliberate Genoese,
or a serious-minded high school student. He brushes them aside

as "exceptions that prove the rule." And, of course, if he meets someone true to type, he stands triumphantly vindicated. "They're all like that," he proclaims, having encountered an excited Latin, an ill-behaved adolescent.

Hence, quite aside from the injustice which stereotypes do to others, they impoverish ourselves. A person who lumps the world into simple categories, who type-casts all labor leaders as "racketeers," all businessmen as "reactionaries," all Harvard men as "snobs," and all Frenchmen as "sexy," is in danger of becoming a stereotype himself. He loses his capacity to be himself—which is to say, to see the world in his own absolutely unique, inimitable and independent fashion. 12

Instead, he votes for the man who fits his standardized picture of what a candidate "should" look like or sound like, buys the goods that someone in his "situation" in life "should" own, lives the life that others define for him. The mark of the stereotype person is that he never surprises us, that we do indeed have him "typed." And no one fits this strait-jacket so perfectly as someone whose opinions about *other people* are fixed and inflexible. 13

Impoverishing as they are, stereotypes are not easy to get rid of. The world we type-cast may be no better than a Grade B movie, but at least we know what to expect of our stock characters. When we let them act for themselves in the strangely unpredictable way that people do act, who knows but that many of our fondest convictions will be proved wrong? 14

Nor do we suddenly drop our standardized pictures for a blinding vision of the Truth. Sharp swings of ideas about people often just substitute one stereotype for another. The true process of change is a slow one that adds bits and pieces of reality to the pictures in our heads, until gradually they take on some of the blurriness of life itself. Little by little, we learn not that Jews and Negroes and Catholics and Puerto Ricans are "just like everybody else"—for that, too, is a stereotype—but that each and every one of them is unique, special, different and individual. Often we do not even know that we have let a stereotype lapse until we hear someone saying, "all so-and-so's are like such-and-such," and we hear ourselves saying, "Well—maybe." 15

Can we speed the process along? Of course we can. 16

First, we can become *aware* of the standardized pictures in our heads, in other people's heads, in the world around us. 17

Second, we can become suspicious of all judgments that we   18
allow exceptions to "prove." There is no more chastening thought
than that in the vast intellectual adventure of science, it takes but
one tiny exception to topple a whole edifice of ideas.

Third, we can learn to be chary of generalizations about people.   19
As F. Scott Fitzgerald once wrote: "Begin with an individual, and
before you know it you have created a type; begin with a type, and
you find you have created—nothing."

Most of the time, when we type-cast the world, we are not in   20
fact generalizing about people at all. We are only revealing the
embarrassing facts about the pictures that hang in the gallery of
stereotypes in our own heads.

Questions for Study and Discussion

1. What is Heilbroner's main point, or thesis, in this essay?
   (Glossary: *Thesis*)

2. Study paragraphs 6, 8, and 15. Each paragraph illustrates
   Heilbroner's thesis. How? What does each paragraph contribute to support the thesis?

3. Transitional devices indicate relationships between paragraphs and thus help to unify the essay. Identify three transitions in this essay. Explain how they help to unify the
   essay. (Glossary: *Transitions*)

4. What are the reasons Heilbroner gives for why we stereotype individuals? What are some of the dangers of stereotypes, according to Heilbroner? How does he say we can rid
   ourselves of stereotypes?

5. Heilbroner uses the word *picture* in his discussion of stereotypes. Why is this an appropriate word in this discussion?
   (Glossary: *Diction*)

Vocabulary

Refer to your dictionary to define the following words as they
are used in this selection. Then use each word in a sentence of
your own.

irrational (7)   impoverish (12)
perpetuated (8)   chastening (18)
infinite (10)   edifice (18)
preconceptions (11)   chary (19)
vindicated (11)

Suggested Writing Assignments

1. Write an essay in which you attempt to convince your readers that it is not in their best interests to perform a particular act—for example, smoke, take stimulants to stay awake, go on a crash diet, or make snap judgments. In writing your essay, follow Heilbroner's lead: first identify the issue; then explain why it is a problem; and, finally, offer a solution or some advice. Remember to unify the various parts of your essay.

2. Have you ever been considered as a stereotype—a student, or a member of a particular sex, class, ethnic, national, or racial group? Write a unified essay that examines how stereotyping has affected you, how it has perhaps changed you, and how you regard the process.

3

ORGANIZATION

In an essay, ideas and information cannot be presented all at once; they have to be arranged in some order. That order is the essay's organization.

The pattern of organization in an essay should be suited to the writer's subject and purpose. For example, if you are writing about your experience working in a fast-food restaurant, and your purpose is to tell about the activities of a typical day, you might present those activities in chronological order. If, on the other hand, you wish to argue that working in a bank is an ideal summer job, you might proceed from the least rewarding to the most rewarding aspect of this job; this is called "climactic" order.

Some often-used patterns of organization are time order, space order, and logical order. Time order, or chronological order, is used to present events as they occurred. A personal narrative, a report of a campus incident, or an account of a historical event can be most naturally and easily related in chronological order. The description of a process, such as the refinishing of a table, the building of a stone wall, or the way to serve a tennis ball, almost always calls for a chronological organization. Of course, the order of events can sometimes be rearranged for special effect. For example, an account of an auto accident may begin with the collision itself and then go back in time to tell about the events leading up to it. One essay that is a model of chronological order is Dick Gregory's "Shame" (pp. 227–30).

Space order is used when describing a person, place, or thing. This organizational pattern begins at a particular point and moves in some direction, such as left to right, top to bottom, east to west, outside to inside, front to back, near to far, around, or over. In describing a house, for example, a writer could move from top to bottom, from outside to inside, or in a circle around the outside.

Logical order can take many forms depending on the writer's purpose. These include: general to specific, most familiar to least familiar, and smallest to biggest. Perhaps the most common type of logical order is order of importance. Notice how the writer uses this order in the following paragraph:

> The Egyptians have taught us many things. They were excellent farmers. They knew all about irrigation. They built temples which were afterwards copied by the Greeks and which served as the earliest models for the churches in which we worship nowadays. They invented a calendar which proved such a useful instrument for the purpose of measuring time that it has survived with a few changes until today. But most important of all, the Egyptians learned how to preserve speech for the benefit of future generations. They invented the art of writing.

By organizing the material according to the order of increasing importance, the writer places special emphasis on the final sentence. In writing a descriptive essay you can move from the least striking to the most striking detail, so as to keep your reader interested and involved in the description. In an explanatory essay you can start with the point that readers will find least difficult to understand and move on to the most difficult; that's how teachers organize many courses. Or, in writing an argumentative essay, you can move from your least controversial point to the most controversial, preparing your reader gradually to accept your argument.

REACH OUT AND WRITE SOMEONE

Lynn Wenzel

Lynn Wenzel has been published in many major newspapers and magazines, including Ms., *News-week, the* New York Times, Newsday, *and* Down East: The Magazine of Maine. *Her book* I Hear America Singing: A Nostalgic Tour of Popular Sheet Music *appeared in 1989. Wenzel was gradu-ated magna cum laude from William Paterson College and makes her home in Maywood, New Jersey. As you read her essay, pay particular atten-tion to the way she has organized her examples to illustrate the importance of letter writing.*

Everyone is talking about the breakup of the telephone company. Some say it will be a disaster for poor people and a bonanza for large companies while others fear a personal phone bill so exorbitant that—horror of horrors—we will all have to start writing letters again.

It's about time. One of the many talents lost in this increasingly technological age is that of putting pen to paper in order to com-municate with family, friends and lovers.

Reading, and enjoying it, may not be the strong suit of our young but writing has truly become a lost art. I am not talking about creative writing because this country still has its full share of fine fiction and poetry writers. There will always be those spe-cial few who need to transform experiences into short stories or poetry.

No, the skill we have lost is that of letter writing. When was the last time the mailbox contained anything more than bills, politi-cal and fund-raising appeals, advertisements, catalogs, maga-zines or junk mail?

Once upon a time, the only way to communicate from a dis-tance was through the written word. As the country expanded and people moved west, they knew that when they left mother, father, sister, brother, it was very probably the last time they would see them again. So daughters, pioneering in Indiana or Michigan, wrote home with the news that their first son had been born dead, but the second child was healthy and growing and they also had a house and barn. By the time the letter reached east, another child might have been born, yet it was read over and again, then smoothed out and slipped into the family Bible or keepsake box.

Letters were essential then. Imagine John Adams fomenting rev-   6
olution and forming a new government without Abigail's letters to sustain him. Think of Elizabeth Barrett and Robert Browning without their written declarations of love; of all the lovers who, parted against their will, kept hope alive through letters often passed by hand or mailed in secret.

And what of history? Much of our knowledge of events and of   7
the people who lived them is based on such commonplace communication. Harry Truman's letters to Bess, Mamie and Ike's correspondence and Eleanor Roosevelt's letters to some of her friends all illuminate actions and hint at intent. F. Scott Fitzgerald's letters to his daughter, Scottie, which were filled with melancholy over his wife's mental illness, suggest in part the reason why his last years were so frustratingly uncreative. Without letters we would have history—dry facts and dates of wars, treaties, elections, revolutions. But the causes and effects might be left unclear.

We would also know little about women's lives. History, until   8
recently, neglected women's contributions to events. Much of what we now know about women in history comes from letters found, more often than not, in great-grandmother's trunk in the attic, carefully tied with ribbon, or stored, yellowed and boxed, in a carton in the archives of a "women's college." These letters have helped immensely over the past ten years to create a verifiable women's history which is now taking its rightful place alongside weighty tomes about men's contributions to the changing world.

The story of immigration often begins with a letter. Millions   9
of brave souls, carrying their worldly possessions in one bag, stepped off a ship and into American life on the strength of a note saying, "Come. It's better here."

To know how important the "art" of letter writing was, we have   10
only to look at the accouterments our ancestors treasured and considered necessary: inkstands of silver, gold or glass, crafted to occupy a prominent place on the writing table; hot wax for a

personal seal; the seals themselves, sometimes ornately carved in silver; quills, and then fountain pens. These were not luxuries but necessities.

Perhaps most important of all, letter writing required *thinking*   11
before putting pen to paper. No hurried telephone call can ever replace the thoughtful, intelligent correspondence between two people, the patching up of a friendship, the formal request for the pleasure of someone's company, or a personal apology. Once written and sent, the writer can never declare, "But I never said that." Serious letter writing demands thought, logic, organization and sincerity because words, once written, cannot be taken back. These are qualities we must not lose, but ones we should polish and bring to luster.

What, after all, will we lose: our lover's letters tied with an old   12
hair ribbon, written from somewhere far away; our children's first scribbled note from summer camp; the letters friends sent us as we scattered after college; letters we sent our parents telling them how much they meant to us? Without letters, what will we save, laugh about, read out loud to each other 20 years from now on a snowy afternoon in front of a fire?

Telephone bills.   13

And that is the saddest note of all.   14

Questions for Study and Discussion

1. What is Wenzel's thesis in this essay? Where is it stated? (Glossary: *Thesis*)

2. Why does Wenzel concentrate on letter writing in her essay and not on other kinds of writing?

3. What role has letter writing played in our understanding of history, according to Wenzel?

4. In what ways is writing a letter different from making a phone call? What can letter writing do to help us develop as human beings?

5. Which of the three patterns of organization has Wenzel used in presenting her examples of the importance of letter writing? Support your answer with examples.

6. How effective do you find the beginning and ending of Wenzel's essay? Explain. (Glossary: *Beginnings and Endings*)

Vocabulary

Refer to your dictionary to define the following words as they are used in this selection. Then use each word in a sentence of your own.

exorbitant (1)   accouterments (10)
fomenting (6)   seal (10)
tomes (8)

Suggested Writing Assignments

1. Write a personal letter to a friend or relative with whom you haven't been in contact for some while. Draft and re-draft the letter carefully, making it as thoughtful and interesting as you can. Send the letter and report back to your class or instructor on the response that the letter elicited.

2. Think of a commonplace subject that people might take for granted but that you find interesting. Write an essay on that subject, using one of the following types of logical order:

   least important to most important
   most familiar to least familiar
   smallest to biggest
   oldest to newest
   easiest to understand to most difficult to understand
   good news to bad news
   general to specific

MADE TO ORDER BABIES

Geoffrey Cowley

Raised in Salt Lake City, Geoffrey Cowley earned a B.A. in English from Lewis & Clark College in Portland, Oregon, and an M.A. in English from the University of Washington, in Seattle. A newspaper and feature writer, Cowley joined Newsweek *in 1988, and since 1990 has been the magazine's health and medicine editor. His medical cover stories for* Newsweek *have covered such topics as AIDS, Chronic Fatigue Syndrome, Prozac, Halcion, and tuberculosis. Cowley is credited with breaking the story in 1992 that doctors were studying AIDS-like illnesses in people not infected with HIV. The article touched off a global investigation that is ongoing. In the following article, which first appeared in* Newsweek *in 1990, Cowley explores some of the moral and ethical dimensions of prenatal testing. He concludes that "failing to think, as a society, about the appropriate uses of the new tests would be a grave mistake."*

For centuries, Jewish communities lived Job-like with the   1
knowledge that many of their babies would thrive during infancy, grow demented and blind as toddlers and die by the age of 5. Joseph Ekstein, a Hasidic rabbi in Brooklyn, lost four children to Tay-Sachs disease over three decades, and his experience was not unusual. Some families were just unlucky.

Today, the curse of Tay-Sachs is being lifted—not through bet-   2
ter treatments (the hereditary disease is as deadly as ever) but through a new cultural institution called Chevra Dor Yeshorim, the "Association of an Upright Generation." Thanks largely to Rabbi Ekstein's efforts, Orthodox teenagers throughout the world now line up at screening centers to have their blood tested for evidence of the Tay-Sachs gene. Before getting engaged, prospec-

tive mates simply call Chevra Dor Yeshorim and read off the code numbers assigned to their tests results.

If the records show that neither person carries the gene, or that just one does, the match is judged sound. But if both happen to be carriers (meaning any child they conceive will have a one-in-four chance of suffering the fatal disease), marriage is virtually out of the question. Even if two carriers wanted to wed, few rabbis would abet them. "It's a rule of thumb that engagements won't occur until compatibility is established," says Rabbi Jacob Horowitz, codirector of the Brooklyn-based program. "Each day, we could stop many marriages worldwide."

Marriage isn't the only institution being reshaped by modern genetics; a host of new diagnostic tests could soon change every aspect of creating a family. Physicians can now identify some 250 genetic defects, not only in the blood of a potential parent but in the tissue of a developing fetus. The result is that, for the first time in history, people are deciding, rather than wondering, what kind of children they will bear.

Choosing to avoid a horrible disease may be easy, at least in principle, but that's just one of many options 21st century parents could face. Already, conditions far less grave than Tay-Sachs have been linked to specific genes, and the science is still exploding. Researchers are now at work on a massive $3 billion project to decipher the entire human genetic code. By the turn of the century, knowledge gained through this Human Genome Initiative could enable doctors to screen fetuses—even test-tube embryos—for traits that have nothing to do with disease. "Indeed," says Dr. Paul Berg, director of the Beckman Center for Molecular and Genetic Medicine at Stanford, "we should be able to locate which [gene] combinations affect kinky hair, olive skin and pointy teeth."

How will such knowledge be handled? How should it be handled? Are we headed for an age in which having a child is morally analogous to buying a car? There is already evidence that couples are using prenatal tests to identify and abort fetuses on the basis of sex, and there is no reason to assume the trend will stop there. "We should be worried about the future and where this might take us," says George Annas, a professor of health law at Boston University's School of Medicine. "The whole definition of normal could well be changed. The issue becomes not the ability of the child to be happy but rather our ability to be happy with the child."

So far, at least, the emphasis has been on combating serious   7
hereditary disorders. Everyone carries four to six genes that are harmless when inherited from one parent but can be deadly when inherited from both. Luckily, most of these mutations are rare enough that carriers are unlikely to cross paths. But some have become common within particular populations. Five percent of all whites carry the gene for cystic fibrosis, for example, and one in 2,000 is born with the disease. Seven percent of all blacks harbor the mutation for sickle-cell anemia, and one in 500 is afflicted. Asian and Mediterranean people are particularly prone to the deadly blood disease thalassemia, just as Jews are to Tay-Sachs.

When accommodating the disability means watching a toddler   8
die of Tay-Sachs or thalassemia, few couples hesitate to abort, and only the most adamant pro-lifer would blame them. But few of the defects for which fetuses can be screened are so devastating. Consider Huntington's disease, the hereditary brain disorder that killed the folk singer Woody Guthrie. Huntington's relentlessly destroys its victim's mind, and anyone who inherits the gene eventually gets the disease. Yet Huntington's rarely strikes anyone under 40, and it can remain dormant into a person's 70s. What does a parent do with the knowledge that a fetus has the gene? Is some life better than none?

Most carriers think not. . . .   9

As more abnormalities are linked to genes, the dilemmas can   10
only get stickier. Despite all the uncertainties, a positive test for Down or Huntington's leaves no doubt that the condition will set in. But not every disease-related gene guarantees ill health. Those associated with conditions like alcoholism, Alzheimer's disease and manic-depressive illness signal only a susceptibility. Preventing such conditions would thus require aborting kids who might never have suffered. And because one gene can have more than one effect, the effort could have unintended consequences. There is considerable evidence linking manic-depressive illness to artistic genius, notes Dr. Melvin Konner, an anthropologist and nonpracticing physician at Emory University. "Doing away with the gene would destroy the impetus for much human creativity."

The future possibilities are even more troubling when you con-   11
sider that mere imperfections could be screened for as easily as

serious diseases. Stuttering, obesity and reading disorders are all traceable to genetic markers, notes Dr. Kathleen Nolan of The Hastings Center, a biomedical think tank in suburban New York. And many aspects of appearance and personality are under fairly simple genetic control. Are we headed for a time when straight teeth, a flat stomach and a sense of humor are standards for admission into some families? It's not inconceivable. "I see people in my clinic occasionally who have a sort of new-car mentality," says Dr. Francis Collins, a University of Michigan geneticist who recently helped identify the gene for cystic fibrosis. "It's got to be perfect, and if it isn't you take it back to the lot and get a new one."

At the moment, gender is the only nonmedical condition for which prenatal tests are widely available. There are no firm figures on how often people abort to get their way, but physicians say many patients use the tests for that purpose. The requests have traditionally come from Asians and East Indians expressing a cultural preference for males. But others are now asking, too. "I've found a high incidence of sex selection coming from doctors' families in the last two years," says Dr. Lawrence D. Platt, a geneticist at the University of Southern California—"much higher than ethnic requests. Once there is public awareness about the technology, other people will use the procedure as well."   12

Those people will find their physicians increasingly willing to help. A 1973 survey of American geneticists found that only 1 percent considered it morally acceptable to help parents identify and abort fetuses of the undesired sex. Last year University of Virginia ethicist John C. Fletcher and Dr. Mark I. Evans, a geneticist at Wayne State University, conducted a similar poll and found that nearly 20 percent approved. Meanwhile, 62 percent of the geneticists questioned in a 1985 survey said they would screen fetuses for a couple who had four healthy daughters and wanted a son.   13

Right or wrong, the new gender option has set an important precedent. If parents will screen babies for one nonmedical condition, there is no reason to assume they won't screen them for others. Indeed, preliminary results from a recent survey of 200 New England couples showed that while only 1 percent would abort on the basis of sex, 11 percent would abort to save a child from obesity. As Dr. Robin Dawn Clark, head of clinical genetics at Loma Linda Medical Center observes, the temptation will be to select for "other features that are honored by society."   14

The trend toward even greater control could lead to bizarre, 15
scifi scenarios. But it seems unlikely that prenatal swimsuit competitions will sweep the globe anytime soon: most of the globe has yet to reap the benefits of 19th-century medicine. Even in America, many prospective parents are still struggling to obtain basic health insurance. If the masses could suddenly afford cosmetic screening tests, the trauma of abortion would remain a powerful deterrent. And while [geneticist] John Buster's dream of extracting week-old embryos for a quick gene check could ease the trauma, it seems a safe bet many women would still opt to leave their embryos alone.

The more immediate danger is that the power to predict chil- 16
dren's medical futures will diminish society's tolerance for serious defects. Parents have already sued physicians for "wrongful life" after giving birth to disabled children, claiming it was the doctor's responsibility to detect the defect in the womb. The fear of such suits could prompt physicians to run every available test, however remote the possibility of spotting a medical problem. Conversely, parents who are content to forgo all the genetic fortune-telling could find themselves stigmatized for their backward ways. When four-cell embryos can be screened for hereditary diseases, failing to ensure a child's future health could become the same sort of offense that declining heroic measures for a sick child is today.

In light of all the dangers, some critics find the very practice of 17
prenatal testing morally questionable. "Even at the beginning of the journey the eugenics question looms large," says Jeremy Rifkin, a Washington activist famous for his opposition to genetic tinkering. "Screening is eugenics." Perhaps, but its primary effect so far has been to bring fewer seriously diseased children into the world. In Britain's Northeast Thames region, the number of Indian and Cypriot children born with thalassemia fell by 78 percent after prenatal tests became available in the 1970s. Likewise, carrier and prenatal screening have virtually eliminated Tay-Sachs from the United States and Canada.

Failing to think, as a society, about the appropriate uses of the 18
new tests would be a grave mistake. They're rife with potential for abuse, and the coming advances in genetic science will make them more so. But they promise some control over diseases that have caused immense suffering and expense. Society need only

remember that there are no perfect embryos but many ways to be a successful human being.

Questions for Study and Discussion

1. To study the organization of Cowley's essay, it is useful to divide it into three-paragraph blocks. Summarize what Cowley says in each block (1–3, 4–6, and so on). What form of organization does Cowley use? Is it effective? Why or why not?
2. How does Cowley's title affect the way you read the essay? (Glossary: *Title*) Do you think it is an appropriate title? Explain.
3. What is Cowley's purpose? (Glossary: *Purpose*) How does he organize his essay to communicate his purpose?
4. Note where Cowley inserts quotes from medical experts into his essay. Comment on his choice of placement of the quotes. What does he gain by using them?
5. Summarize the benefits and dangers of prenatal testing.
6. What does Cowley accomplish in the fifth block (paragraphs 13–15)? What is its importance relative to the rest of the essay? Why does Cowley place it near the end?
7. What is Cowley's tone? (Glossary: *Tone*) Support your answer.

Vocabulary

Refer to your dictionary to define the following words as they are used in this selection. Then use each word in a sentence of your own.

abet (3)	ethicist (13)
analogous (6)	stigmatized (16)
prenatal (6)	eugenics (17)
adamant (8)	rife (18)
impetus (10)	

Suggested Writing Assignments

1. Write a short, well-organized essay in which you either support or oppose the use of prenatal testing of fetuses for all but the most severe conditions. Organize your essay by beginning with the point that you believe is of the least importance or has the least impact and ending with your strongest point.

2. Imagine you are writing in the year 2050. How have eugenics developed in the past fifty years or so? What procedures gained widespread acceptance? Has there been a backlash if "cosmetic" eugenics increased? Have genetic diseases been wiped out? How have the prenuptial proceedings changed for couples? Write an essay, organized chronologically, in which you discuss the five most important changes in eugenics since 2000. Use your creativity, but make sure your essay makes chronological sense.

THE CORNER STORE

Eudora Welty

Eudora Welty is perhaps one of the most honored and respected writers at work today. She was born in 1909 in Jackson, Mississippi, where she has lived most of her life. Her published works include many short stories, now available as her Collected Stories *(1980); five novels; a collection of her essays,* The Eye of the Story *(1975); and a memoir,* One Writer's Beginnings *(1987). In 1973 her novel* The Optimist's Daughter *won the Pulitzer prize for fiction. Welty's description of the corner store, taken from an essay about growing up in Jackson, will recall for many readers the neighborhood store where they grew up.*

Our Little Store rose right up from the sidewalk; standing in a street of family houses, it alone hadn't any yard in front, any tree or flower bed. It was a plain frame building covered over with brick. Above the door, a little railed porch ran across on an upstairs level and four windows with shades were looking out. But I didn't catch on to those.

Running in out of the sun, you met what seemed total obscurity inside. There were almost tangible smells—licorice recently sucked in a child's cheek, dill pickle brine that had leaked through a paper sack in a fresh trail across the wooden floor, ammonia-loaded ice that had been hoisted from wet croker sacks and slammed into the icebox with its sweet butter at the door, and perhaps the smell of still untrapped mice.

Then through the motes of cracker dust, cornmeal dust, the Gold Dust of the Gold Dust Twins that the floor had been swept out with, the realities emerged. Shelves climbed to high reach all the way around, set out with not too much of any one thing but a lot of things—lard, molasses, vinegar, starch, matches, kerosene, Octagon soap (about a year's worth of octagon-shaped coupons cut out and saved brought a signet ring addressed to you in the mail). It was up to you to remember what you came for, while your eye traveled from cans of sardines to tin whistles to ice cream salt to harmonicas to flypaper (over your head, batting around on a thread beneath the blades of the ceiling fan, stuck with its testimonial catch).

Its confusion may have been in the eye of its beholder. En- 4
chantment is cast upon you by all those things you weren't sup-posed to have need for, to lure you close to wooden tops you'd outgrown, boys' marbles and agates in little net pouches, small rubber balls that wouldn't bounce straight, frail, frazzly kite string, clay bubble pipes that would snap off in your teeth, the stiffest scissors. You could contemplate those long narrow boxes of sparklers gathering dust while you waited for it to be the Fourth of July or Christmas, and noisemakers in the shape of tin frogs for somebody's birthday party you hadn't been invited to yet, and see that they were all marvelous.

You might not have even looked for Mr. Sessions when he came 5
around his store cheese (as big as a doll's house) and in front of the counter looking for you. When you'd finally asked him for, and received from him in its paper bag, whatever single thing it was that you had been sent for, the nickel that was left over was yours to spend.

Down at a child's eye level, inside those glass jars with mouths 6
in their sides through which the grocer could run his scoop or a child's hand might be invited to reach for a choice, were wine-balls, all-day suckers, gumdrops, peppermints. Making a row under the glass of a counter were the Tootsie Rolls, Hershey bars, Goo Goo Clusters, Baby Ruths. And whatever was the name of those pastilles that came stacked in a cardboard cylinder with a cardboard lid? They were thin and dry, about the size of tiddledy-winks, and in the shape of twisted rosettes. A kind of chocolate dust came out with them when you shook them out in your hand. Were they chocolate? I'd say, rather, they were brown. They didn't taste of anything at all, unless it was wood. Their attraction was the number you got for a nickel.

Making up your mind, you circled the store around and 7
around, around the pickle barrel, around the tower of Cracker-jack boxes; Mr. Sessions had built it for us himself on top of a packing case like a house of cards.

If it seemed too hot for Crackerjacks, I might get a cold drink. 8
Mr. Sessions might have already stationed himself by the cold-
drinks barrel, like a mind reader. Deep in ice water that looked
black as ink, murky shapes—that would come up as Coca-Colas,
Orange Crushes, and various flavors of pop—were all swimming
around together. When you gave the word, Mr. Sessions plunged
his bare arm in to the elbow and fished out your choice, first try.
I favored a locally bottled concoction called Lake's Celery. (What
else could it be called? It was made by a Mr. Lake out of celery. It
was a popular drink here for years but was not known universally,
as I found out when I arrived in New York and ordered one in the
Astor bar.) You drank on the premises, with feet set wide apart to
miss the drip, and gave him back his bottle and your nickel.

But he didn't hurry you off. A standing scales was by the door, 9
with a stack of iron weights and a brass slide on the balance arm,
that would weigh you up to three hundred pounds. Mr. Sessions,
whose hands were gentle and smelled of carbolic, would lift you
up and set your feet on the platform, hold your loaf of bread for
you, and taking his time while you stood still for him, he would
make certain of what you weighed today. He could even remember what you weighed the last time, so you could subtract and
announce how much you'd gained. That was goodbye.

Questions for Study and Discussion

1. Which of the three patterns of organization has Welty used
   in this essay: chronological, spatial, or logical? If she has
   used more than one, where precisely has she used each
   type?
2. What is the dominant impression that Welty creates in her
   description of the corner store? (Glossary: *Dominant Impression*) How does Welty create this dominant impression?
3. What does Welty mean when she writes that the store's
   "confusion may have been in the eye of its beholder" (4)?
   What factors might lead one to become confused?
4. What impression of Mr. Sessions does Welty create? What
   details contribute to this impression?

5. Welty places certain pieces of information in parentheses in this essay. Why are they in parentheses? What, if anything, does this information add to our understanding of the corner store? Might this information be left out? Explain.

6. Comment on Welty's ending. Is it too abrupt? Why or why not? (Glossary: *Beginnings and Endings*)

Vocabulary

Refer to your dictionary to define the following words as they are used in this selection. Then use each word in a sentence of your own.

frame (1)	signet (3)
tangible (2)	agates (4)
brine (2)	concoction (8)
motes (3)	scales (9)

Suggested Writing Assignments

1. Describe your neighborhood store or supermarket. Gather a large quantity of detailed information from memory and from an actual visit to the store if that is still possible. Once you have gathered your information, try to select those details that will help you create a dominant impression of the store. Finally, organize your examples and illustrations according to some clear organizational pattern.

2. Write an essay on one of the following topics:

   local restaurants
   reading materials
   television shows
   ways of financing a college education
   types of summer employment

   Be sure to use an organizational pattern that is well thought out and suited to both your material and your purpose.

4

BEGINNINGS AND ENDINGS

"Begin at the beginning and go on till you come to the end: then stop," advised the King of Hearts in *Alice in Wonderland*. "Good advice, but more easily said than done," you might be tempted to reply. Certainly, no part of writing essays can be more daunting than coming up with effective beginnings and endings. In fact, many writers feel these are the most important parts of any piece of writing regardless of its length. Even before coming to your introduction proper, your readers will usually know something about your intentions from your title. Titles like "The Case against Euthanasia," "How to Buy a Used Car," or "What Is a Migraine Headache?" indicate both your subject and approach and prepare your readers for what is to follow.

But what makes for an effective beginning? Not unlike a personal greeting, a good beginning should catch a reader's interest and then hold it. The experienced writer realizes that most readers would rather do almost anything than make a commitment to read, so the opening or "lead," as journalists refer to it, requires a lot of thought and much revising to make it right and to keep the reader's attention from straying. The inexperienced writer knows that the beginning is important but tries to write it first and to perfect it before moving on to the rest of the essay. Although there are no "rules" for writing introductions, we can offer one bit of general advice: wait until the writing process is well underway or almost completed before focusing on your lead. Following this advice will keep you from spending too much time on an introduction that you will probably revise. More importantly, once you actually see how your essay develops, you will know better how to introduce it to your reader.

In addition to capturing your reader's attention, a good beginning frequently introduces your thesis and either suggests or actually reveals the structure of the composition. Keep in mind that the best beginning is not necessarily the most catchy or the most shocking but the one most appropriate for the job you are trying to do.

Beginnings

The following examples from published essays show you some effective beginnings:

Short Generalization

> It is a miracle that New York works at all.
>
> E. B. White

Startling Claim

> It is possible to stop most drug addiction in the United States within a very short time.
>
> Gore Vidal

Rhetorical Questions

> Just how interconnected *is* the animal world? Is it true that if we change any part of that world we risk unduly damaging life in other, larger parts of it?
>
> Matthew Douglas

Humor/Apt Quotation

> The right to pursue happiness is issued to Americans with their birth certificates, but no one seems quite sure which way it ran. It may be we are issued a hunting license but offered no game. Jonathan Swift seemed to think so when he attacked the idea of happiness as "the possession of being well-deceived," the felicity of being "a fool among knaves." For Swift saw society as Vanity Fair, the land of false goals.
>
> John Ciardi

Startling Fact

> Charles Darwin and Abraham Lincoln were born on the same day—February 12, 1809. They are also linked in another curious way—for both must simultaneously play, and for similar reasons, the role of man and legend.
>
> Stephen Jay Gould

Dialogue

"This would be excellent, to go in the ocean with this thing," says Dave Gembutis, fifteen.

He is looking at a $170 Sea Cruiser raft.

"Great," says his companion, Dan Holmes, also fifteen.

This is at Herman's World of Sporting Goods, in the middle of the Woodfield Mall in Schaumburg, Illinois.

Bob Greene

Statistics/Question

In the 40 years from 1939 to 1979 white women who work full time have with monotonous regularity made slightly less than 60 percent as much as white men. Why?

Lester C. Thurow

Irony

In Moulmein, in lower Burma, I was hated by large numbers of people—the only time in my life that I have been important enough for this to happen to me.

George Orwell

There are many more excellent ways to begin an essay, but there are also some ways of beginning that should be avoided. Some of these follow:

Apology

I am a college student and do not consider myself an expert on the computer industry, but I think that many computer companies make false claims about just how easy it is to learn to use a computer.

Complaint

I'd rather write about a topic of my own choice than the one that is assigned, but here goes.

Webster's Dictionary

Webster's New Collegiate Dictionary defines the verb *to snore* as follows: "to breathe during sleep with a rough hoarse noise due to vibration of the soft palate."

Platitude

America is the land of opportunity and no one knows it better than Madonna.

Reference to Title

As you can see from my title, this essay is about why we should continue to experiment with human heart transplants.

Endings

An effective ending does more than simply indicate where the writer stopped writing. A conclusion may summarize; may inspire the reader to further thought or even action; may return to the beginning by repeating key words, phrases, or ideas; or may surprise the reader by providing a particularly convincing example to support a thesis. Indeed, there are, as with beginnings, many ways to write a conclusion, but the effectiveness of any choice really must be measured by how appropriately it fits what has gone before it. In the following conclusion to a long chapter on weasel words, a form of deceptive advertising language, writer Paul Stevens summarizes the points that he has made:

> A weasel word is a word that's used to imply a meaning that cannot be truthfully stated. Some weasels imply meanings that are not the same as their actual definition, such as "help," "like," or "fortified." They can act as qualifiers and/or comparatives. Other weasels, such as "taste" and "flavor," have no definite meanings, and are simply subjective opinions offered by the manufacturer. A weasel of omission is one that implies a claim so strongly that it forces you to supply the bogus fact. Adjectives are weasels used to convey feelings and emotions to a greater extent than the product itself can.
>
> In dealing with weasels, you must strip away the innuendos and try to ascertain the facts, if any. To do this, you need to ask questions such as: How? Why? How many? How much? Stick to basic definitions of words. Look them up if you have to. Then, apply the strict definition to the text of the advertisement or commercial. "Like" means similar to, but not the same as. "Virtually" means the same in essence, but not in fact.

Above all, never underestimate the devious qualities of a weasel. Weasels twist and turn and hide in dark shadows. You must come to grips with them, or advertising will rule you forever.

My advise to you is: Beware of weasels. They are nasty and untrainable, and they attack pocketbooks.

If you are having trouble with your conclusion—and this is not an uncommon problem—it may be because of problems with your essay itself. Frequently, writers do not know when to end because they are not sure about their overall purpose in the first place. For example, if you are taking a trip and your purpose is to go to Chicago, you'll know when you get there and will stop. But if you don't really know where you are going, it's very difficult to know when to stop.

It's usually a good idea in your conclusion to avoid such over-worked expressions as "In conclusion," "In summary," "I hope I have shown," or "Finally." Your conclusion should also do more than simply repeat what you've said in your opening paragraph. The most satisfying essays are those in which the conclusion provides an interesting way of wrapping up ideas introduced in the beginning and developed throughout.

Advertisements for Oneself

Lance Morrow

Lance Morrow was born in Lewisburg, Pennsylvania, in 1935. He graduated from Harvard, and a career in journalism led him to Time *magazine in 1965. He won a National Magazine Award for his essays in 1981. He has published three books, including* Fishing in the Tiber *(1988), a collection of his essays. Morrow now lives in New York City and continues as a senior writer for* Time. *In the following essay, he considers different aspects of self-advertising through personal ads.*

I t is an odd and compact art form, and somewhat unnatural. A person feels quite uncomfortable composing a little song of himself for the classifieds. The personal ad is like haiku of self-celebration, a brief solo played on one's own horn. Someone else should be saying these things. It is for others to pile up the extravagant adjectives ("sensitive, warm, witty, vibrant, successful, handsome, accomplished, incredibly beautiful, cerebral, and sultry") while we stand demurely by. But someone has to do it. One competes for attention. One must advertise. One must chum the waters and bait the hook, and go trolling for love and laughter, for caring and sharing, for long walks and quiet talks, for Bach and brie. Nonsmokers only. Photo a must.

There are poetic conventions and clichés and codes in composing a personal ad. One specifies DWF (divorced white female), SBM (single black male), GWM (gay white male) and so on, to describe marital status, race, sex. Readers should understand the euphemisms. "Zaftig" or "Rubenesque," for example, usually means fat. "Unpretentious" is liable to mean boring. "Sensuous" means the party likes sex.

Sometimes the ads are quirkily self-conscious. "Ahem," began one suitor in the *New York Review of Books.* "Decent, soft-spoken sort, sanely silly, philosophish, seeks similar." Then he started to hit his stride: "Central Jersey DM WASP professional, 38, 6'2", slow hands, student of movies and Marx, gnosis and news, craves womanish companionship. . . ."

The sociology of personals has changed in recent years. One reason that people still feel uncomfortable with the form is that during the sixties and early seventies personal ads had a slightly sleazy connotation. They showed up in the back of underground newspapers and sex magazines, the little billboards through which wife swappers and odd sexual specialists communicated. In the past several years, however, personal ads have become a popular and reputable way of shopping for new relationships. The *Chicago Tribune* publishes them. So does the conservative *National Review,* although a note from the publisher advises, "*NR* extends maximum freedom in this column, but *NR*'s maximum freedom may be another man's straitjacket. *NR* reserves the right to reject any copy deemed unsuitable." *National Review* would likely have turned down a West Coast entreaty: "Kinky Boy Scout seeks Kinky Girl Scout to practice knots. Your rope or mine?" *National Review*'s personals are notably chaste, but so are those in most other magazines. The emphasis is on "traditional values," on "long-term relationships" and "nest building." The sexual revolution has cooled down to a domestic room temperature. The raciest item might call for a woman with "Dolly Parton-like figure." One ad in Los Angeles stated: "Branflake patent holder tired of money and what it can buy seeks intellectual stimulation from big-bosomed brunette. Photo please." The *Village Voice* rejected the language of a man who wanted a woman with a "big ass." A few days later the man returned with an ad saying he sought a "callipygian" woman.

Every week *New York* magazine publishes five or six pages of personals. The *New York Review of Books* publishes column after column of some of the most entertaining personals. Many of them are suffused with a soft-focus romanticism. Firelight plays over the fantasy. Everyone seems amazingly successful. The columns are populated by Ph.D.s. Sometimes one encounters a millionaire. Occasionally a satirical wit breaks the monotony: "I am DWM, wino, no teeth, smell bad, age 40—look 75. Live in good cardboard box in low-traffic alley. You are under 25, tall, sophisticated, beautiful, talented, financially secure, and want more out of life. Come fly with me."

Humor helps, especially in a form that usually gives off a flat glare of one-dimensional optimism. It is hard not to like the "well read, well shaped, well disposed widow, early sixties, not half bad in the dusk with the light behind me." She sought a "companionable, educated, professional man of wit and taste," and she probably deserved him. Her self-effacement is fairly rare in personals. The ads tend sometimes to be a little nervous and needing, and anxiously hyperbolic. Their rhetoric tends to get overheated and may produce unintended effects. A man's hair stands on end a bit when he encounters "Alarmingly articulate, incorrigibly witty, overeducated, but extremely attractive NYC woman." A female reader of *New York* magazine might enjoy a chuckling little shudder at this: "I am here! A caring, knowing, daffy, real, tough, vulnerable, and handsome brown-eyed psychoanalyst." One conjures up the patient on the couch and a Freudian in the shape of Daffy Duck shouting: "You're desPICable!"

The struggle is composing one's ad is to be distinctive and relentlessly self-confident. What woman could resist the "rugged rascal with masculine determined sensual viewpoint"? An ad should not overreach, however, like the woman who began: "WANTED: One Greek god of refined caliber."

Not all the ads are jaunty or dewy-eyed. One begins: "Have herpes?" Some are improbably specialized: "Fishing Jewish woman over 50 seeks single man to share delights of angling." Or: "Literate snorkeler . . . have room in my life for one warm, secure, funny man."

Anyone composing a personal ad faces an inherent credibility problem. While we are accustomed to the self-promotions of politicians, say, we sense something bizarre when ordinary people erupt in small rhapsodies of self-celebration that are occasioned by loneliness and longing. One is haunted by almost piteous cries that come with post-office-box number attached: "Is there anyone out there? Anyone out there for me?"

Composing an ad with oneself as the product is an interesting psychological exercise, and probably good training in self-assertion. Truth will endure a little decorative writing, perhaps. The personals are a form of courtship that is more efficient, and easier on the liver, than sitting in bars night after night, hoping for a lucky encounter. Yet one feels sometimes a slightly disturbed and forlorn vibration in those columns of chirpy pleading. It is inorganic courtship. There is something severed, a lost connection. One may harbor a buried resentment that there are not parents and aunts and churches and cotillions to arrange the meetings in more seemly style.

That, of course, may be mere sentimentalism. Whatever works. ₁₁ Loneliness is the Great Satan. Jane Austen, who knew everything about courtship, would have understood the personals columns perfectly. Her novel *Emma*, in fact, begins, "Emma Woodhouse, handsome, happy, clever, and rich, with a comfortable home and happy disposition." The line might go right into the *New York Review of Books*.

Questions for Study and Discussion

1. How does Morrow's opening paragraph work to introduce both the tone and the topic of his essay? (Glossary: *Tone*) Pay close attention to his diction. (Glossary: *Diction*) How effectively does he introduce the reader to the world of the personals? Explain your answer.

2. How has the sociology of the personals changed in recent years?

3. What is Morrow's purpose in this essay? (Glossary: *Purpose*) Does he achieve his purpose?

4. Morrow states: "Anyone composing a personal ad faces an inherent credibility problem." What does he mean? What does Morrow see as a positive point to composing a personal? What is negative about it?

5. In your opinion, what is Morrow's attitude toward his subject? (Glossary: *Attitude*) Support your answer with examples from the essay.

6. Why does Morrow quote Jane Austen at the end of the essay? In what way does the quote support his purpose in the essay?

Vocabulary

Refer to your dictionary to define the following words as they are used in this selection. Then use each word in a sentence of your own.

haiku (1)	suffused (5)
cerebral (1)	self-effacement (6)
sultry (1)	hyperbolic (6)
euphemisms (2)	incorrigibly (6)
gnosis (3)	cotillions (10)
callipygian (4)	

Suggested Writing Assignments

1. A personal ad is an excellent example of a writing form where good beginnings and endings are crucial. Try writing your own personal (or one on behalf of a friend) according to the conventions described by Morrow. Make it a little longer than most of those seen in a typical newspaper—you won't pay by the line, after all—and work on catching the reader's attention. Consider what impression you want to leave the reader with at the end.

2. "Personals are a good way to find a romantic partner." Write an essay in which you agree or disagree with this statement. Imagine you are writing for an audience that generally disagrees with you. If you are to persuade them, you will have to catch their attention right away, and you will have to have a convincing conclusion, so carefully construct your beginning and ending.

OF MY FRIEND HECTOR AND MY ACHILLES HEEL

Michael T. Kaufman

The writer of the "About New York" column for the New York Times, Michael T. Kaufman was born in 1938 in Paris and grew up in the United States. He studied at the Bronx High School of Science, City College of New York, and Columbia University. He began his career at the New York Times as a reporter and feature writer and before assuming his present position, served as bureau chief in Ottawa and Warsaw. In the following article, which appeared in the New York Times in 1992, Kaufman uses the story of his childhood friend Hector Elizondo to reflect on his own "prejudice and stupidity."

This story is about prejudice and stupidity. My own. 1

It begins in 1945 when I was a 7-year-old living on the fifth floor 2
of a tenement walkup on 107th Street between Columbus and
Manhattan Avenues in New York City. The block was almost
entirely Irish and Italian, and I believe my family was the only
Jewish one around.

One day a Spanish-speaking family moved into one of the four 3
apartments on our landing. They were the first Puerto Ricans I
had met. They had a son who was about my age named Hector,
and the two of us became friends. We played with toy soldiers and
I particularly remember how, using rubber bands and wood from
orange crates, we made toy pistols that shot off little squares we
cut from old linoleum.

We visited each other's home and I know that at the time I liked 4
Hector and I think he liked me. I may even have eaten my first
avocado at his house.

About a year after we met, my family moved to another part of 5
Manhattan's West Side and I did not see Hector again until I entered Booker T. Washington Junior High School as an 11-year-old.

The Special Class

The class I was in was called 7SP-1; the SP was for special.   6
Earlier, I recall, I had been in the IGC class, for "intellectually
gifted children." The SP class was to complete the seventh, eighth
and ninth grades in two years and almost all of us would then go
to schools like Bronx Science, Stuyvesant or Music and Art,
where admission was based on competitive exams. I knew I was
in the SP class and the IGC class. I guess I also knew that other
people were not.

Hector was not. He was in some other class, maybe even 7-2,   7
the class that was held to be the next-brightest, or maybe 7-8. I
remember I was happy to see him whenever we would meet, and
sometimes we played punchball during lunch period. Mostly, of
course, I stayed with my own classmates, with other Intellectually
Gifted Children.

Sometimes children from other classes, those presumably not   8
so intellectually gifted, would tease and taunt us. At such times I
was particularly proud to have Hector as a friend. I assumed that
he was tougher than I and my classmates and I guess I thought
that if necessary he would come to my defense.

Different High Schools

For high school, I went uptown to Bronx Science. Hector, I   9
think, went downtown to Commerce. Sometimes I would see him
in Riverside Park, where I played basketball and he worked out
on the parallel bars. We would acknowledge each other, but by
this time the conversations we held were perfunctory—sports,
families, weather.

After I finished college, I would see him around the neighbor-   10
hood pushing a baby carriage. He was the first of my contemporaries to marry and to have a child.

A few years later, in the 60's, married and with children of my   11
own, I was once more living on the West Side, working until late
at night as a reporter. Some nights as I took the train home I
would see Hector in the car. A few times we exchanged nods, but
more often I would pretend that I didn't see him, and maybe he
also pretended he didn't see me. Usually he would be wearing a
knitted watch cap, and from that I deduced that he was probably
working on the docks as a longshoreman.

I remember quite distinctly how I would sit on the train and think about how strange and unfair fate had been with regard to the two of us who had once been playmates. Just because I had become an intellectually gifted adult or whatever and he had become a longshoreman or whatever, was that any reason for us to have been left with nothing to say to each other? I thought it was wrong and unfair, but I also thought that conversation would be a chore or a burden. That is pretty much what I thought about Hector, if I thought about him at all, until one Sunday in the mid-70's, when I read in the drama section of this newspaper that my childhood friend, Hector Elizondo, was replacing Peter Falk in the leading role in "The Prisoner of Second Avenue." 12

Since then, every time I have seen this versatile and acclaimed actor in movies or on television I have blushed for my assumptions. I have replayed the subway rides in my head and tried to fathom why my thoughts had led me where they did. 13

In retrospect it seems far more logical that the man I saw on the train, the man who had been my friend as a boy, was coming home from an Off Broadway theater or perhaps from a job as a waiter while taking acting classes. So why did I think he was a longshoreman? Was it just the cap? Could it be that his being Puerto Rican had something to do with it? Maybe that reinforced the stereotype I concocted, but it wasn't the root of it. 14

When It Got Started

No, the foundation was laid when I was 11, when I was in 7SP-1 and he was not, when I was in the IGC class and he was not. 15

I have not seen him since I recognized how I had idiotically kept tracking him for years and decades after the school system had tracked both of us. I wonder now if my experience was that unusual, whether social categories conveyed and absorbed before puberty do not generally tend to linger beyond middle age. And I wonder, too, that if they affected the behavior of someone like myself who had been placed on the upper track, how much more damaging it must have been for someone consigned to the lower. 16

I have at times thought of calling him, but kept from doing it because how exactly does one apologize for thoughts that were never expressed? And there was still the problem of what to say. "What have you been up to for the last 40 years?" Or "Wow, was 17

I wrong about you!" Or maybe just, "Want to come over and help me make a linoleum gun?"

Questions for Study and Discussion

1. If you are unfamiliar with the Greek myth of Hector and Achilles, look it up in a book on mythology. Why does Kaufman allude to Hector and Achilles in his title? (Glossary: *Allusion*)

2. How do Kaufman's first two sentences affect how the reader views the rest of the essay? Did they catch your attention? Why or why not?

3. How does Kaufman organize his essay? (Glossary: *Organization*)

4. What is Kaufman's purpose in the essay? How does his organization of the essay help him express his purpose? (Glossary: *Purpose*)

5. Why did Kaufman ignore Hector after he graduated from college? What does this tell him about society in general?

6. Why is Kaufman's ending effective? What point does he want to emphasize with the ending he uses?

Vocabulary

Refer to your dictionary to define the following words as they are used in this selection. Then use each word in a sentence of your own.

intellectually (6)   acclaimed (13)
perfunctory (9)   concocted (14)
contemporaries (10)

Suggested Writing Assignments

1. Kaufman's essay is a deeply personal one. Use it as a model to write an essay about a time or an action in your life that you are not proud of. What happened? Why did it happen?

What would you do differently if you could? Be sure to catch the reader's attention in the beginning and to end your essay with a thought-provoking conclusion.

2. Everyone has childhood friends that we either have lost track of or don't communicate with as often as we would like. Choose an old friend that you have lost track of and would like to see again. Write an essay about your relationship. What made your friend special to you as a child? Why did you lose touch? What does the future hold? Organize your essay chronologically.

EVEN YOU CAN GET IT

Bruce Lambert

Bruce Lambert was born in 1943, in Albany, New York, and attended Hamilton College, where he prepared for a career in journalism. Lambert covered government and political issues for several New York newspapers until 1984 when he began to focus on the issue of AIDS. In 1988 the New York Times *assigned Lambert to cover the AIDS story exclusively. He first published the following article on March 11 and 12, 1989. In it he alerts heterosexuals that they should not become complacent about protecting themselves from the dangers of AIDS. Notice how Lambert catches our attention with his surprising opening line and how his conclusion captures the "determined optimism" of Alison's struggle.*

A lison L. Gertz wasn't supposed to get AIDS.   1

She has never injected drugs or had a blood transfusion, and   2
she describes herself as "not at all promiscuous." But she does say
she had a single sexual encounter—seven years ago—with a male
acquaintance who, she has since learned, has died of AIDS.

Though AIDS has hit hardest among gay men and poor intra-   3
venous drug users, it also afflicts people like Ms. Gertz.

"People think this can't happen to them," she said in an inter-   4
view at her Manhattan apartment. "I never thought I could have
AIDS."

Going Public

She is 23 years old, affluent, college-educated and a profes-   5
sional from a prominent family. She grew up on Park Avenue.

Now Ms. Gertz and her family are going public because they   6
have a message. A message for heterosexuals who could make a

84

potentially fatal mistake if they dismiss the threat of AIDS. A message for doctors who may miss a diagnosis; she spent three weeks undergoing exhaustive hospital tests for all other conceivable causes of her illness before AIDS was discovered. And a message asking for greater public support on AIDS issues.

"I decided when I was in the hospital I would give as much time   7
as I can to help people who are going through this, and warn others of the danger," she said. "I want to make a condom commercial, do speaking engagements, whatever I can.

"All the AIDS articles are about homosexuals or poor people on   8
drugs, and unfortunately a lot of people just flip by them," she said. "They think it doesn't apply to them."

But she added: "They can't turn the page on me. I could be one   9
of them, or their daughter. They have to deal with this."

Statistics show that the number of AIDS cases is rising alarm-   10
ingly among heterosexuals who get the virus by sharing needles for drugs and then pass it to their sex partners and babies.

Although there is no evidence that AIDS is spreading rampantly   11
among other heterosexuals in this country—as it is in Haiti and parts of Africa—cases like Ms. Gertz's do exist. About four percent of all newly reported AIDS cases stem from heterosexual intercourse, and that rate has been remaining steady.

New York City has recorded 524 cases in which women got ac-   12
quired immune deficiency syndrome through sexual intercourse. The men they were with were infected through either drug use or sexual contact with other men. Another 83 cases were of women from Haiti or Africa.

"It Took Only One Time for Me"

"I want to talk to these kids who think they're immortal," Ms.   13
Gertz said. "I want to tell them: I'm heterosexual, and it took only one time for me."

Ms. Gertz is certain how it happened. "It was one romantic   14
night," she said. "There were roses and champagne and everything. That was it. I only slept with him once."

Ms. Gertz has since learned that the man was bisexual and that   15
he has died of AIDS. Had she known his past then, she said, she doubts it would have made a difference. "At that point they weren't publicizing AIDS," she said. "It wasn't an issue then."

AIDS is no respecter of wealth or social status. Ms. Gertz is a   16
granddaughter of a founder of the old Gertz department stores in
Queens and on Long Island. Her father, Jerrold E. Gertz, is a real-
estate executive; her mother, Carol, is the co-founder of Tennis
Lady, a national chain of high-fashion shops. Ms. Gertz went
to Horace Mann, an exclusive private school in the Bronx, then
studied art at Parsons School of Design in Manhattan.

"Probably Just a Bug"

When AIDS struck, Ms. Gertz said, "I was just, as they say, start-   17
ing out in life." Her goals had been simple: "I wanted a house and
kids and animals and to paint my paintings.

She had recently signed on with an art agent, embarking on a   18
career as an illustrator. She had also quit her pack-a-day smoking
habit and joined a health club "to get really healthy," she said.

Then fever and a spell of diarrhea hit last summer. A doctor told   19
her it was "probably just a bug," she said. But the symptoms persisted, so she checked into Lenox Hill Hospital.

When her doctor told her the diagnosis, he had tears in his   20
eyes. "I said 'Oh, my God. I'm going to die,'" she recalled. "And as
I said it, I thought to myself, 'No I'm not. Why am I saying this?'
I thought my life was over. 'I'm 22, I'm never going to have sex
again. I'm never going to have children.'"

Determined to Keep Going

From that initial shock, Ms. Gertz bounced back with the ebul-   21
lience so well known to her friends—they call her Ali for short—
and with the fervor of activism that runs in the family. Recovering
from her first treatment, she returned to her apartment, her pets
(a dog, Saki; a cat, Sambucca, and tropical fish) and a new course
in life.

"It's a dreadful disease, but it's also a gift," she said. "I've always   22
been positive, optimistic. I thought, 'What can I do with it? I like
to think I'm here for a purpose. If I die, I would like to have left
something, to make the world a little bit better before I go, to help
people sick like me and prevent others from getting this. It would
make it all worthwhile."

She and friends are organizing a fall theater performance and   23
dinner-dance to raise money for an AIDS newsletter and other

AIDS services. Her parents and their friends are planning a spring benefit for an organization they are forming called Concerned Parents and Friends for AIDS Research.

To keep her functioning normally, Ms. Gertz each day takes 24 AZT, Acyclovir and Bactrim pills, which fight the virus and opportunistic diseases. "We just have to keep her healthy until there's a breakthrough and they find a cure," her mother said.

"I Started to Cry Softly"

"I'm not afraid of death, but I am afraid of pain," Ms. Gertz 25 said. She is learning psychological and behavioral techniques to withstand it, and doctors have promised medication if she needs it. "As far as dying goes, it's okay," she said. "There's no point in thinking about it now."

But her frequent high spirits do not erase her pain. While 26 watching a soap opera love scene one day, she said, "I started to cry softly."

"I've made a conscious effort not to cry in front of people," she 27 added. "But I do give myself a certain amount of time each month to be miserable, to cry and to vent."

Ms. Gertz is an only child. Her illness "was an enormous shock," 28 her father said. "AIDS was the furthest thing from my mind. I used to suspect they magnified the statistics to get research money." Now he's giving and raising money himself and feels "anger at AIDS happening to anyone."

"It certainly turned our lives around," Mrs. Gertz said. "It changes 29 your perspective on what's important." For her, every day starts with a morning call to her daughter's apartment, a block away.

One of Ms. Gertz's first concerns was not for herself. "I was 30 worried about my previous boyfriends," she said. "I didn't want them to be sick." Two past boyfriends have been tested, she said and "both of them are O.K."

Her current boyfriend "is wonderful," she said. "He's stood by 31 me." But AIDS has changed their relationship. "Yes, you can have safe sex. I know all the facts, and so does he. But still, in the back of his mind, he is scared, so we don't sleep together any more, and that's rough."

Ms. Gertz has not felt ostracized as many AIDS patents have. 32 But there have been a few exceptions.

"The nurses told me this one resident doctor, a woman, insisted   33
that I must have used IV drugs or must have had anal sex," Ms.
Gertz said. She interprets the doctor's own possible risk by regarding the patient as different.

Loss of a Friend

"And one friend I lost," Ms. Gertz said. "She left. She deserted   34
me." That, too, she understands. "She was with me at Studio 54
during those earlier years, and she was much more sexually
active than I was. It wasn't my mortality she was facing; it was her
own. She just couldn't handle it."

Health insurance is a problem that has made her financially de-   35
pendent on her parents. "I think the insurance company owes me
about $50,000," she said. "I haven't gotten one dime. They're try-
ing to prove I knew I had this before I signed up for the policy two
years before."

That angers Ms. Gertz because of the dozens of exhaustive,   36
sometimes painful, tests she underwent to find what was wrong.

The Gertz family praises the hospital staff and their doctors,   37
but it does regret that AIDS wasn't checked earlier, Mrs. Gertz said,
"Because of her background, nobody thought this was a possibility."

"It stands to reason you're going to see more people like Ali,"   38
her mother said, since AIDS symptoms may not show up for 10 or
12 years.

Indeed, such cases are appearing.   39

Dr. Jody Robinson, an internist in Washington who has written   40
on AIDS, said that other cases like Ms. Gertz's are "out there."

"How many is a tremendous unknown," he said. "It may not   41
be an overwhelming number, but what will it be five or six years
from now?"

The danger, he said, is that because experts have said there has   42
not been an explosive outbreak among heterosexuals, people
have become complacent.

"The common wisdom has gone back to the idea that AIDS is   43
really the gay plague and disease of IV drug users that it was set
out to be in the first place, and the warning on heterosexual
spread was a false alarm," he said.

Alison Gertz struggles against AIDS with the benefit of a num-   44
ber of factors unknown to most patients—she has a determined

optimism bolstered by the love of family and friends, financial aid and first-class medical care.

Gathered on a sofa for photographs, the Gertz family was all   45 hugs and smiles. "I never felt from the beginning that this was anything to be hidden or ashamed of," Mrs. Gertz said. After a few pictures were taken, she wondered aloud. "Should we be looking so happy for such a serious subject?"

For a few seconds the family managed sober expressions for   46 the camera. But soon, for at least one more day, the smiles broke through again.

Questions for Study and Discussion

1. How would you describe Lambert's beginning? How did you react to it? Did you think his beginning was effective? Why or why not?

2. How did Alison Gertz get AIDS? Did it surprise you that a heterosexual female contracted AIDS?

3. In paragraph 22 Alison Gertz says, "It's a dreadful disease, but it's also a gift." What does Alison mean by this?

4. Who is Alison Gertz' audience? (Glossary: *Audience*) What is her message for this audience? How likely is her audience to hear her message? Explain.

5. What is Lambert's attitude towards AIDS? What in his essay led you to this conclusion?

6. How has Lambert organized his essay? What function do the running titles serve with his overall organizational plan?

Vocabulary

Refer to your dictionary to define the following words as they are used in this selection. Then use each word in a sentence of your own.

promiscuous (2)	embark (18)
affluent (5)	ebullience (21)
rampant (11)	fervor (21)

optimistic (22)   ostracized (32)
opportunistic (24)   bolster (44)

Suggested Writing Assignments

1. How knowledgeable is the American public about AIDS? Do you think we know all the facts? How has the media worked to inform society of hazards and untruths about AIDS? Write an essay in which you discuss what responsibility you believe the media has to keep the public informed.

2. American pop-singer Madonna has recently come under fire for the "lurid" content of some of her videos and stage shows. Madonna explains that her sexual overtones will encourage children to go to their parents and discuss things such as safe sex and premarital sex. How do you react to her reasoning? Is her approach for bringing these topics into the open a reasonable one? Write an essay in which you discuss the role of sex education in our fight against AIDS.

HOW TO TAKE A JOB INTERVIEW

Kirby W. Stanat

A former personnel recruiter and placement officer at the University of Wisconsin—Milwaukee, Kirby W. Stanat has helped thousands of people get jobs. His book Job Hunting Secrets and Tactics *(1977) tells readers what they need to know in order to get the jobs they want. In this selection Stanat analyzes the campus interview, a process that hundreds of thousands of college students undergo each year as they seek to enter the job market. Notice how Stanat begins and how the "snap" of his ending echoes back through his essay.*

To succeed in campus job interviews, you have to know where that recruiter is coming from. The simple answer is that he is coming from corporate headquarters. 1

That may sound obvious, but it is a significant point that too many students do not consider. The recruiter is not a free spirit as he flies from Berkeley to New Haven, from Chapel Hill to Boulder. He's on an invisible leash to the office, and if he is worth his salary, he is mentally in corporate headquarters all the time he's on the road. 2

If you can fix that in your mind—that when you walk into that bare-walled cubicle in the placement center you are walking into a branch office of Sears, Bendix or General Motors—you can avoid a lot of little mistakes and maybe some big ones. 3

If, for example, you assume that because the interview is on campus the recruiter expects you to look and act like a student, you're in for a shock. A student is somebody who drinks beer, wears blue jeans and throws a Frisbee. No recruiter has jobs for student Frisbee whizzes. 4

A cool spring day in late March, Sam Davis, a good recruiter who has been on the college circuit for years, is on my campus talking to candidates. He comes out to the waiting area to meet 5

the student who signed up for an 11 o'clock interview. I'm standing in the doorway of my office taking in the scene.

Sam calls the candidate: "Sidney Student." There sits Sidney.   6
He's at a 45 degree angle, his feet are in the aisle, and he's almost
lying down. He's wearing well-polished brown shoes, a tasteful
pair of brown pants, a light brown shirt, and a good looking tie.
Unfortunately, he tops off this well-coordinated outfit with his
Joe's Tavern Class A Softball Championship jacket, which has a
big woven emblem over the heart.

If that isn't bad enough, in his left hand is a cigarette and in his   7
right hand is a half-eaten apple.

When Sam calls his name, the kid is caught off guard. He   8
ditches the cigarette in an ashtray, struggles to his feet, and trans-
fers the apple from the right to the left hand. Apple juice is everywhere, so Sid wipes his hand on the seat of his pants and shakes
hands with Sam.

Sam, who by now is close to having a stroke, gives me that   9
what-do-I-have-here look and has the young man follow him into
the interviewing room.

The situation deteriorates even further—into pure Laurel and   10
Hardy. The kid is stuck with the half-eaten apple, doesn't know
what to do with it, and obviously is suffering some discomfort. He
carries the apple into the interviewing room with him and places
it in the ashtray on the desk—right on top of Sam's freshly lit
cigarette.

The interview lasts five minutes. . . .   11

Let us move in for a closer look at how the campus recruiter   12
operates.

Let's say you have a 10 o'clock appointment with the recruiter   13
from the XYZ Corporation. The recruiter gets rid of the candidate
in front of you at about 5 minutes to 10, jots down a few notes
about what he is going to do with him or her, then picks up your
résumé or data sheet (which you have submitted in advance). . . .

Although the recruiter is still in the interview room and you are   14
still in the lobby, your interview is under way. You're on. The recruiter will look over your sheet pretty carefully before he goes
out to call you. He develops a mental picture of you.

He thinks, "I'm going to enjoy talking with this kid," or "This   15
one's going to be a turkey." The recruiter has already begun to
make a screening decision about you.

His first impression of you, from reading the sheet, could come   16
from your grade point. It could come from misspelled words. It
could come from poor erasures or from the fact that necessary information is missing. By the time the recruiter has finished reading your sheet, you've already hit the plus or minus column.

Let's assume the recruiter got a fairly good impression from   17
your sheet.

Now the recruiter goes out to the lobby to meet you. He almost   18
shuffles along, and his mind is somewhere else. Then he calls
your name, and at that instant he visibly clicks into gear. He just
went to work.

As he calls your name he looks quickly around the room, wait-   19
ing for somebody to move. If you are sitting on the middle of your
back, with a book open and a cigarette going, and if you have to
rebuild yourself to stand up, the interest will run right out of the
recruiter's face. You, not the recruiter, made the appointment for
10 o'clock, and the recruiter expects to see a young professional
come popping out of that chair like today is a good day and you're
anxious to meet him.

At this point, the recruiter does something rude. He doesn't   20
walk across the room to meet you halfway. He waits for you to
come to him. Something very important is happening. He wants
to see you move. He wants to get an impression about your posture, your stride, and your briskness.

If you slouch over to him, sidewinderlike, he is not going to   21
be impressed. He'll figure you would probably slouch your way
through your workdays. He wants you to come at him with lots of
good things going for you. If you watch the recruiter's eyes, you
can see the inspection. He glances quickly at shoes, pants, coat,
shirt; dress, blouse, hose—the whole works.

After introducing himself, the recruiter will probably say,   22
"Okay, please follow me," and he'll lead you into his interviewing
room.

When you get to the room, you may find that the recruiter will   23
open the door and gesture you in—with him blocking part of the
doorway. There's enough room for you to get past him, but it's a
near thing.

As you scrape past, he gives you a closeup inspection. He looks   24
at your hair; if it's greasy, that will bother him. He looks at your
collar; if it's dirty, that will bother him. He looks at your shoul-

ders; if they're covered with dandruff, that will bother him. If you're a man, he looks at your chin. If you didn't get a close shave, that will irritate him. If you're a woman, he checks your makeup. If it's too heavy, he won't like it.

Then he smells you. An amazing number of people smell bad. 25 Occasionally a recruiter meets a student who smells like a canal horse. That student can expect an interview of about four or five minutes.

Next the recruiter inspects the back side of you. He checks your 26 hair (is it combed in front but not in back?), he checks your heels (are they run down?), your pants (are they baggy?), your slip (is it showing?), your stockings (do they have runs?).

Then he invites you to sit down. 27

At this point, I submit, the recruiter's decision on you is 75 to 80 28 percent made.

Think about it. The recruiter has read your résumé. He knows 29 who you are and where you are from. He knows your marital status, your major and your grade point. And he knows what you have done with your summers. He has inspected you, exchanged greetings with you and smelled you. There is very little additional hard information that he must gather on you. From now on it's mostly body chemistry.

Many recruiters have argued strenuously with me that they 30 don't make such hasty decisions. So I tried an experiment. I told several recruiters that I would hang around in the hall outside the interview room when they took candidates in.

I told them that as soon as they had definitely decided not to 31 recommend (to department managers in their companies) the candidate they were interviewing, they should snap their fingers loud enough for me to hear. It went like this.

First candidate: 38 seconds after the candidate sat down: Snap! 32

Second candidate: 1 minute, 42 seconds: Snap! 33

Third candidate: 45 seconds: Snap! 34

One recruiter was particularly adamant, insisting that he didn't 35 rush to judgment on candidates. I asked him to participate in the snapping experiment. He went out in the lobby, picked up his first candidate of the day, and headed for an interview room.

As he passed me in the hall, he glared at me. And his fingers 36 went "Snap!"

Questions for Study and Discussion

1. Explain the appropriateness of the beginning and ending of Stanat's essay.

2. What are Stanat's purpose and thesis in telling the reader how the recruitment process works? (Glossary: *Purpose* and *Thesis*)

3. In paragraphs 12–29 Stanat explains how the campus recruiter works. Make a list of the steps in that process.

4. Why do recruiters pay so much attention to body language when they interview job candidates?

5. What specifically have you learned from reading Stanat's essay? Do you feel that the essay is useful in preparing someone for a job interview? Explain.

6. Stanat's tone—his attitude toward his subject and audience—in this essay is informal. What in his sentence structure and diction creates this informality? Cite examples. How might the tone be made more formal for a different audience?

Vocabulary

Refer to your dictionary to define the following words as they are used in this selection. Then use each word in a sentence of your own.

cubicle (3)   résumé (13)
deteriorates (10)   adamant (35)

Suggested Writing Assignments

1. Stanat's purpose is to offer practical advice to students interviewing for jobs. Determine a subject about which you could offer advice to a specific audience. Present your advice in the form of an essay, being careful to provide an attention-grabbing beginning and a convincing conclusion.

2. Stanat gives us an account of the interview process from the viewpoint of the interviewer. If you have ever been inter-

viewed and remember the experience well, write an essay on your feelings and thoughts as the interview took place. What were the circumstances of the interview? What questions were asked of you, how did you feel about them, and how comfortable was the process? How did the interview turn out? What precisely, if anything, did you learn from the experience? What advice would you give anyone about to be interviewed?

5

PARAGRAPHS

Within an essay, the paragraph is the most important unit of thought. Like the essay, it has its own main idea, often stated directly in a topic sentence. Like a good essay, a good paragraph is unified: it avoids digressions and develops its main idea. Paragraphs use many of the rhetorical techniques that essays use, techniques such as classification, comparison and contrast, and cause and effect. Consider the following three paragraphs:

> I've learned from experience that good friendships are based on a delicate balance. When friends are on a par, professionally and personally, it's easier for them to root for one another. It's taken me a long time to realize that not all my "friends" wish me well. Someone who wants what you have may not be able to handle your good fortune: If you find yourself apologizing for your hard-earned raise or soft-pedaling your long-awaited promotion, it's a sure sign that the friendship is off balance. Real friends are secure enough in their own lives to share each other's successes—not begrudge them.
>
> Stephanie Mansfield

> Most stories of illegal drugs overshadow Americans' struggles with alcohol, tobacco, food, and nonprescription drugs—our so-called legal addictions. The problem of substance abuse is far more complex and far more pervasive than any of us really knows or is willing to admit. In 1990, for example, 14,000 deaths were attributed to cocaine and heroin. In that same year, 390,000 deaths were attributed to tobacco and 90,000 to alcohol. It's not surprising then that many sociologists believe we are a nation of substance abusers—drinkers, smokers, eaters, and pill poppers. Although the statistics are alarming, they do not begin to suggest the heavy toll of substance abuse on Americans and their families. Loved ones die, relationships are fractured, children are abandoned, job productivity falters, and the dreams of young people are extinguished.
>
> Alfred Rosa and Paul Eschholz

Many rock musicians consciously work to maintain the aura of mystery surrounding themselves. Typically, they walk on stage and proceed to sneer at or completely ignore the audience. If a star is especially articulate, he may yell, "A-a-all ri-i-ight! Gonna rock to-o- ni-i-ight!" He cannot use the vocabulary of the common man, for fear of being mistakenly identified as such. Besides, a few well-timed thrusts of the hips communicate the message just as well. The audience responds wildly to this invitation, and the concert is off to a good start. The performer has successfully gauged the mood of the spectators; now his task is to manipulate it, through his choice of material and through such actions as dancing, prancing, foot-stomping, and unearthly screaming. His movements, gestures, and often, his bizarre clothing, high heels, and make-up deliberately violate accepted standards of conduct and appearance. He can afford to take chances and to risk offending people; after all, as every good student of mythology knows, deities are not bound by the same restrictions as mere mortals. The Dionysus figure on the stage tempts us to follow him into the never-never land where inhibitions are nonexistent.

Jennifer McBride Young

Many writers find it helpful to think of the paragraph as a very small, compact essay. Here is a paragraph from an essay on testing:

Multiple-choice questions distort the purposes of education. Picking one answer among four is very different from thinking a question through to an answer of one's own, and far less useful in life. Recognition of vocabulary and isolated facts makes the best kind of multiple-choice questions, so these dominate the tests, rather than questions that test the use of knowledge. Because schools want their children to perform well, they are often tempted to teach the limited sorts of knowledge most useful on the tests.

This paragraph, like all well-written paragraphs, has several distinguishing characteristics: it is unified, coherent, and adequately developed. It is unified in that every sentence and every idea relate to the main idea, stated in the topic sentence, "Multiple-choice questions distort the purposes of education." It is coherent in that the sentences and ideas are arranged logically and the relationships among them are made clear by the use of effective transitions. Finally, the paragraph is adequately developed in that it presents a short but persuasive argument supporting its main idea.

How much development is "adequate" development? The answer depends on many things: how complicated or controversial the main idea is; what readers already know and believe; how much space the writer is permitted. Everyone, or nearly everyone, agrees that the earth circles around the sun; a single sentence would be enough to make that point. A writer trying to argue that affirmative action has outlived its usefulness, however, would need many sentences, indeed many paragraphs, to develop that idea convincingly.

Here is another model of an effective paragraph. As you read this paragraph about the resourcefulness of pigeons in evading attempts to control them, pay particular attention to its controlling idea, unity, development, and coherence.

> Pigeons [and their human friends] have proved remarkably resourceful in evading nearly all the controls, from birth-control pellets to carbide shells to pigeon apartment complexes, that pigeon-haters have devised. One of New York's leading museums once put large black rubber owls on its wide ledges to discourage the large number of pigeons that roosted there. Within the day the pigeons had gotten over their fear of owls and were back perched on the owls' heads. A few years ago San Francisco put a sticky coating on the ledges of some public buildings, but the pigeons got used to the goop and came back to roost. The city then tried trapping, using electric owls, and periodically exploding carbide shells outside a city building, hoping the noise would scare the pigeons away. It did, but not for long, and the program was abandoned. More frequent explosions probably would have distressed the humans in the area more than the birds. Philadelphia tried a feed that makes pigeons vomit, and then, they hoped, go away. A New York firm claimed it had a feed that made a pigeon's nervous system send "danger signals" to · the other members of its flock.

The controlling idea is stated at the beginning in a topic sentence. Other sentences in the paragraph support the controlling idea with examples. Since all the separate examples illustrate how pigeons have evaded attempts to control them, the paragraph is unified. Since there are enough examples to convince the reader of the truth of the topic statement, the paragraph is adequately developed. Finally, the regular use of transitional words and phrases such as *once, within the day, a few years ago,* and *then,* lends the paragraph coherence.

How long should a paragraph be? In modern essays most paragraphs range from 50 to 250 words, but some run a full page or more and others may be only a few words long. The best answer is that a paragraph should be long enough to develop its main idea adequately. Some authors, when they find a paragraph running very long, may break it into two or more paragraphs so that readers can pause and catch their breath. Other writers forge ahead, relying on the unity and coherence of their paragraph to keep their readers from getting lost.

Articles and essays that appear in magazines and newspapers often have relatively short paragraphs, some of only one or two sentences. The reason for this is that they are printed in very narrow columns, which make paragraphs of average length appear very long. But often you will find that these journalistic "paragraphs" could be joined together into a few longer, more normal paragraphs. Longer, more normal paragraphs are the kind you should use in all but journalistic writing.

SIMPLICITY

William Zinsser

William Zinsser was born in New York City in 1922. After graduating from Princeton University, he worked for the New York Herald Tribune, *first as a feature writer and later as its drama editor and film critic. Zinsser has written a number of books, including* Pop Goes America *(1966),* The Lunacy Boom *(1970),* Writing with a Word Processor *(1983),* Willie and Dwike: An American Profile *(1984), and* Writing to Learn *(1988), as well as other social and cultural commentaries. In this selection from his popular book* On Writing Well, *Zinsser, reminding us of Thoreau before him, exhorts the writer to "Simplify, simplify." Notice that Zinsser's paragraphs are unified and logically developed, and consequently work well together to support his thesis.*

Clutter is the disease of American writing. We are a society strangling in unnecessary words, circular constructions, pompous frills and meaningless jargon. 1

Who can understand the viscous language of everyday American commerce: the memo, the corporation report, the business letter, the notice from the bank explaining its latest "simplified" statement? What member of an insurance or medical plan can decipher the brochure explaining his costs and benefits? What father or mother can put together a child's toy from the instructions on the box? Our national tendency is to inflate and thereby sound important. The airline pilot who announces that he is presently anticipating experiencing considerable precipitation wouldn't think of saying it may rain. The sentence is too simple—there must be something wrong with it. 2

But the secret of good writing is to strip every sentence to its cleanest components. Every word that serves no function, every long word that could be a short word, every adverb that carries 3

101

the same meaning that's already in the verb, every passive construction that leaves the reader unsure of who is doing what—these are the thousand and one adulterants that weaken the strength of a sentence. And they usually occur in proportion to education and rank.

During the 1960s the president of my university wrote a letter   4
to mollify the alumni after a spell of campus unrest. "You are probably aware," he began, "that we have been experiencing very considerable potentially explosive expressions of dissatisfaction on issues only partially related." He meant the students had been hassling them about different things. I was far more upset by the president's English than by the students' potentially explosive expressions of dissatisfaction. I would have preferred the presidential approach taken by Franklin D. Roosevelt when he tried to convert into English his own government's memos, such as this blackout order of 1942:

> Such preparations shall be made as will completely obscure all Federal buildings and non-Federal buildings occupied by the Federal government during an air raid for any period of time from visibility by reason of internal or external illumination.

"Tell them," Roosevelt said, "that in buildings where they have to keep the work going to put something across the windows."

Simplify, simplify. Thoreau said it, as we are so often reminded,   5
and no American writer more consistently practiced what he preached. Open *Walden* to any page and you will find a man saying in a plain and orderly way what is on his mind:

> I went to the woods because I wished to live deliberately, to front only the essential facts of life, and see if I could not learn what it had to teach, and not, when I came to die, discover that I had not lived.

How can the rest of us achieve such enviable freedom from   6
clutter? The answer is to clear our heads of clutter. Clear thinking becomes clear writing; one can't exist without the other. It's impossible for a muddy thinker to write good English. You may get away with it for a paragraph or two, but soon the reader will be lost, and there's no sin so grave, for the reader will not easily be lured back.

Who is this elusive creature, the reader? The reader is someone   7
with an attention span of about 30 seconds—a person assailed by
other forces competing for attention. At one time these forces
weren't so numerous: newspapers, radio, spouse, home, children.
Today they also include a "home entertainment center" (TV, VCR,
tapes, CDs), pets, a fitness program, a yard and all the gadgets
that have been bought to keep it spruce, and that most potent of
competitors, sleep. The person snoozing in a chair with a magazine or a book is a person who was being given too much unnecessary trouble by the writer.

It won't do to say that the reader is too dumb or too lazy to keep   8
pace with the train of thought. If the reader is lost, it's usually because the writer hasn't been careful enough. The carelessness can
take any number of forms. Perhaps a sentence is so excessively
cluttered that the reader, hacking through the verbiage, simply
doesn't know what it means. Perhaps a sentence has been so
shoddily constructed that the reader could read it in several ways.
Perhaps the writer has switched pronouns in midsentence, or has
switched tenses, so the reader loses track of who is talking or
when the action took place. Perhaps Sentence B is not a logical
sequel to Sentence A—the writer, in whose head the connection is
clear, hasn't bothered to provide the missing link. Perhaps the
writer has used an important word incorrectly by not taking the
trouble to look it up. The writer may think "sanguine" and "sanguinary" mean the same thing, but the difference is a bloody big
one. The reader can only infer (speaking of big differences) what
the writer is trying to imply.

Faced with such obstacles, readers are at first tenacious. They   9
blame themselves—they obviously missed something, and they
go back over the mystifying sentence, or over the whole paragraph, piecing it out like an ancient rune, making guesses and
moving on. But they won't do this for long. The writer is making
them work too hard, and they will look for one who is better at
the craft.

Writers must therefore constantly ask: What am I trying to say?   10
Surprisingly often they don't know. Then they must look at what
they have written and ask: Have I said it? Is it clear to someone
encountering the subject for the first time? If it's not, some fuzz
has worked its way into the machinery. The clear writer is someone clearheaded enough to see this stuff for what it is: fuzz.

I don't mean that some people are born clearheaded and are   11
therefore natural writers, whereas others are naturally fuzzy and
will never write well. Thinking clearly is a conscious act that
writers must force upon themselves, just as if they were working
on any other project that requires logic: adding up a laundry list
or doing an algebra problem. Good writing doesn't come naturally, though most people obviously think it does. The professional writer is constantly being bearded by strangers who say
they'd like to "try a little writing sometime"—meaning when they
retire from their real profession, which is difficult, like insurance
or real estate. Or they say, "I could write a book about that." I
doubt it.

Writing is hard work. A clear sentence is no accident. Very few   12
sentences come out right the first time, or even the third time.
Remember this in moments of despair. If you find that writing
is hard, it's because it *is* hard. It's one of the hardest things people do.

Questions for Study and Discussion

1. What exactly does Zinsser mean by clutter? How does Zinsser feel that we can free outselves of clutter?

2. In paragraph 3 Zinsser lists a number of "adulterants" that
weaken English sentences and claims that "they usually occur in proportion to education and rank." Why do you suppose this is true?

3. What is the relationship between thinking and writing for
Zinsser?

4. In paragraph 10, Zinsser says that writers must constantly
ask themselves some questions. What are these and why are
they important?

5. How do Zinsser's first and last paragraphs serve to introduce and conclude his essay? (Glossary: *Beginnings and
Endings.*)

6. What is the function of paragraphs 4 and 5 in the context
of the essay?

7. How do the questions in paragraph 2 further Zinsser's purpose? (Glossary: *Rhetorical Question*)

Vocabulary

Refer to your dictionary to define the following words as they
are used in this selection. Then use each word in a sentence of
your own.

pompous (1)   enviable (6)
decipher (2)   tenacious (9)
adulterants (3)   bearded (11)
mollify (4)

Suggested Writing Assignments

1. The following pages show a passage from the final manuscript for Zinsser's essay. Carefully study the manuscript
and Zinsser's changes, and then write several well-developed
paragraphs analyzing the ways he has eliminated clutter.

is too dumb or too lazy to keep pace with the ~~writer's~~ train

of thought. My sympathics are ~~entirely~~ with him. ~~He's not~~

~~so dumb.~~ (If the reader is lost, it is generally because the

writer ~~of the article~~ has not been careful enough to keep

him on the ~~proper~~ path.

This carelessness can take any number of ~~different~~ forms.

Perhaps a sentence is so excessively ~~long and~~ cluttered that

the reader, hacking his way through ~~all~~ the verbiage, simply

doesn't know what *it* ~~the writer~~ means. Perhaps a sentence has

been so shoddily constructed that the reader could read it in

any of *several* ~~two or three different~~ ways. ~~He thinks he knows what~~

~~the writer is trying to say, but he's not sure.~~ Perhaps the

writer has switched pronouns in mid-sentence, or ~~perhaps he~~

has switched tenses, so the reader loses track of who is

talking ~~to whom~~ or ~~exactly~~ when the action took place. Perhaps Sentence B is not a logical sequel to Sentence A -- the writer, in whose head the connection is ~~perfectly~~ clear, has not bothered to provide ~~given enough thought to providing~~ the missing link. Perhaps the writer has used an important word incorrectly by not taking the trouble to look it up ~~and make sure.~~ He may think that "sanguine" and "sanguinary" mean the same thing, but ~~I can assure you that~~ (the difference is a bloody big one ~~to the reader.~~ The reader ~~He~~ can only ~~try to~~ infer ~~what~~ (speaking of big differences) what the writer is trying to imply.

Faced with these ~~such a variety of~~ obstacles, the reader is at first a remarkably tenacious bird. He ~~tends to~~ blames ~~blame~~ himself. ~~He~~ obviously missed something, ~~he thinks,~~ and he goes back over the mystifying sentence, or over the whole paragraph, piecing it out like an ancient rune, making guesses and moving on. But he won't do this for long. ~~He will soon run out of patience.~~ (The writer is making him work too hard ~~-- harder than he should have to work --~~ and the reader will look for one ~~a writer~~ who is better at his craft.

The writer must therefore constantly ask himself: What am I trying to say ~~in this sentence?~~ (Surprisingly often, he doesn't know.) ~~And~~ Then he must look at what he has ~~just~~ written and ask: Have I said it? Is it clear to someone encountering ~~who is coming upon~~ the subject for the first time? If it's not, ~~clear,~~ it is because some fuzz has worked its way into the machinery. The clear writer is a person ~~who is~~ clear-headed enough to see this stuff for what it is: fuzz.

I don't mean ~~to suggest~~ that some people are born clear-headed and are therefore natural writers, whereas others ~~other people~~ are naturally fuzzy and will ~~therefore~~ never write

well. Thinking clearly is ~~an entirely~~ conscious act that the
writer must ~~keep forcing~~ **force** upon himself, just as if he were
~~starting out~~ **embarking** on any other ~~kind of~~ project that ~~calls for~~ **requires** logic:
adding up a laundry list or doing an algebra problem ~~or playing~~
~~chess.~~ Good writing doesn't ~~just~~ come naturally, though most
people obviously think ~~it's as easy as walking.~~ **it does.** The professional

2. If what Zinsser writes about clutter is an accurate assessment, we should easily find numerous examples of clutter all around us. During the next few days, make a point of looking for clutter in the written materials you come across. Choose one example that you find—an article, an essay, a form letter, or a chapter from a textbook, for example—and write an extended analysis explaining how it might have been written more simply. Develop your paragraphs well, make sure they are coherent, and try not to "clutter" your own writing.

BILINGUALISM'S GOAL

Barbara Mujica

Barbara Mujica was born in Altoona, Pennsylvania, in 1943. After receiving degrees at UCLA (A.B., 1964) and New York University (Ph.D., 1974), she joined the faculty at Georgetown University in 1974. She is currently Professor of Hispanic Literatures, Cultures, and Language at Georgetown. Her recent writings include a novel, The Deaths of Don Bernardo, *and she is editor-in-chief of* Verbena: Bilingual Review of the Arts. *In the following selection, Mujica considers how bilingual education can help and hinder children of Hispanic families.*

Mine is a Spanish-speaking household. We use Spanish exclusively. I have made an effort not only to encourage use of the language but also to familiarize my children with Hispanic culture. I use books from Latin America to teach them to read and write, and I try to maintain close contacts with Spanish-speaking relatives. Instilling in my children a sense of family and ethnic identity is my role; it is not the role of the school system.

The public schools, supported by public funds, have the responsibility to teach skills needed in public life—among them the use of the English language. They also must inculcate an appreciation of all the cultures that have contributed to this country's complex social weave. To set one ethnic group apart as more worthy of attention than others is unjust, and might breed resentment against that group.

I differ with educators who advocate bilingual education programs whose goal is to preserve the Spanish language and culture among children of Hispanic families. These professionals argue that in an English-speaking environment, Spanish-speaking children often feel alienated and that this causes them to become withdrawn and hostile. To prevent this reaction, they say, the home environment must be simulated at school.

Imagine how much more alienated these youngsters will feel, 4
however, if they are kept in special bilingual programs separate
from the general student body, semester after semester. How much
more uncomfortable they will feel if they are maintained in ghettos
in the school. Youngsters feel a need to conform. They imitate
each other in dress and in habit. To isolate Spanish-speaking children from their English-speaking peers may prove more psychologically damaging than hurling them into an English-speaking
environment with no transition courses at all.

The purpose of bilingual education must be to teach English to 5
non-English-speaking youngsters so that they will be able to function in regular classes.

The term "bilingual education" encompasses a huge variety of 6
programs ranging from total immersion to special classes for foreigners to curricula that offer courses in mathematics and history
in the child's native language. The most effective bilingual education programs have as their goal the gradual incorporation of
non-English-speaking students into regular programs in which
English is used.

Not all children of Spanish-speaking parents need bilingual 7
education. Many Spanish-speaking parents oppose the placement of their children in special programs; the wishes of these
parents should be respected. Furthermore, very young children
are able to learn a foreign language rapidly; bilingual programs
for the nursery, kindergarten and early primary years should be
kept to a minimum. Older children who have done part of their
schooling in a foreign country often need to be eased into an
English-speaking curriculum more gently. For them, it is helpful to offer certain subjects in their native tongues until they have
learned English; otherwise, they may feel so lost and frustrated
that they will drop out of school. High school dropouts have less
chance than others of finding satisfying careers and are more
likely to find themselves in trouble and unemployed.

Hispanics are now the fastest-growing minority in the United 8
States. According to the Population Reference Bureau, a private
organization, Hispanics, counted at 14.6 million in the 1980 cen-
sus, may well number 47 million by the year 2020. Yet, they are
notoriously underrepresented in the arts, sciences, professions
and politics. Economically, as a group, they tend to lag behind
non-Hispanics. According to March 1983 Federal figures, the

median income for Hispanics is $16,227; for non-Hispanics, $23,907. Certainly, part of the remedy is educational programs that give young people the preparation and confidence necessary to pursue satisfying careers.

To get better jobs, young people must be fluent in English. 9 Without English, they will be stuck in menial positions. Without English, they will be unable to acquire advanced degrees. Without English, they will be unable to protest to the proper authorities if they are abused. Non-English-speaking individuals are vulnerable to not only economic but also political exploitation. Too often, politicians who speak their language claim unjustly to represent their interests.

The primary goal of bilingual education must be mainstream- 10 ing of non-English-speaking children through the teaching of English. But while the schools teach my children English, I will continue to teach them Spanish at home, because Spanish is part of their heritage. Ethnic identity, like religion, is a family matter.

Questions for Study and Discussion

1. What is Mujica's purpose in this essay? (Glossary: *Purpose*)

2. Why does Mujica use the sentence, "Mine is a Spanish-speaking household," to begin her essay? (Glossary: *Beginnings and Endings*) Why is this fact so important to her purpose?

3. Although most of the paragraphs in the selection are short, paragraph 5 is a single sentence. What does Mujica accomplish by using a one-sentence paragraph?

4. Examine the structure of paragraph 7. Identify the topic sentence and the elements that make it a coherent, developed paragraph. What function does it serve in the framework of Mujica's essay as a whole?

5. Why is bilingual education of particular importance to Hispanics?

6. What, according to Mujica, is bilingualism's goal? How can it best be achieved?

Vocabulary

Refer to your dictionary to define the following words as they are used in this selection. Then use each word in a sentence of your own.

instilling (1)	curricula (6)
inculcate (2)	notoriously (8)
advocate (3)	menial (9)

Suggested Writing Assignments

1. Mujica concludes her essay by saying "Ethnic identity, like religion, is a family matter." Write an essay in which you outline her meaning in this statement, then go on to support or oppose it. Make sure that each paragraph in your essay has a topic sentence that is adequately developed, is coherent, and is important to the essay as a whole.

2. If you have studied a different language in school, write an essay about your experiences learning a second language. Why did you study it? What did it take to learn it? How would your experience have been different if you lived in the country where they speak this language and you had to go to school and learn in this language? Make sure that you organize your essay logically, and have paragraphs that are coherent and adequately developed.

"I Just Wanna Be Average"

Mike Rose

Born in Altoona, Pennsylvania, to immigrant parents, Mike Rose moved to California in the early fifties. A graduate of Loyola University in Los Angeles, Rose is now director of UCLA Writing Programs. He has written a number of books and articles on language and literacy. He is best known for his book Lives on the Boundary: The Struggles and Achievements of America's Underprepared, *which the National Council of Teachers of English recognized with its highest award in 1989. In the following selection from that semiautobiographical work, Rose explains how his high school English teacher, Jack MacFarland, picked him up out of the doldrums of "scholastic indifference."*

Jack MacFarland couldn't have come into my life at a better time. My father was dead, and I had logged up too many years of scholastic indifference. Mr. MacFarland had a master's degree from Columbia and decided, at twenty-six, to find a little school and teach his heart out. He never took any credentialing courses, couldn't bear to, he said, so he had to find employment in a private system. He ended up at Our Lady of Mercy teaching five sections of senior English. He was a beatnik who was born too late. His teeth were stained, he tucked his sorry tie in between the third and fourth buttons of his shirt, and his pants were chronically wrinkled. At first, we couldn't believe this guy, thought he slept in his car. But within no time, he had us so startled with work that we didn't much worry about where he slept or if he slept at all. We wrote three or four essays a month. We read a book every two to three weeks, starting with the *Iliad* and ending up with Hemingway. He gave us a quiz on the reading every other day. He brought a prep school curriculum to Mercy High.

MacFarland's lectures were crafted, and as he delivered them he would pace the room jiggling a piece of chalk in his cupped

112

hand, using it to scribble on the board the names of all the writers and philosophers and plays and novels he was weaving into his discussion. He asked questions often, raised everything from Zeno's paradox to the repeated last line of Frost's "Stopping by Woods on a Snowy Evening." He slowly and carefully built up our knowledge of Western intellectual history—with facts, with connections, with speculations. We learned about Greek philosophy, about Dante, the Elizabethan world view, the Age of Reason, existentialism. He analyzed poems with us, had us reading sections from John Ciardi's *How Does a Poem Mean?*, making a potentially difficult book accessible with his own explanations. We gave oral reports on poems Ciardi didn't cover. We imitated the styles of Conrad, Hemingway, and *Time* magazine. We wrote and talked, wrote and talked. The man immersed us in language.

Even MacFarland's barbs were literary. If Jim Fitzsimmons, 3 hung over and irritable, tried to smart-ass him, he'd rejoin with a flourish that would spark the indomitable Skip Madison—who'd lost his front teeth in a hapless tackle—to flick his tongue through the gap and opine, "good chop," drawing out the single "o" in stinging indictment. Jack MacFarland, this tobacco-stained intellectual, brandished linguistic weapons of a kind I hadn't encountered before. Here was this *egghead*, for God's sake, keeping some pretty difficult people in line. And from what I heard, Mike Dweetz and Steve Fusco and all the notorious Voc. Ed. crowd settled down as well when MacFarland took the podium. Though a lot of guys groused in the schoolyard, it just seemed that giving trouble to this particular teacher was a silly thing to do. Tomfoolery, not to mention assault, had no place in the world he was trying to create for us, and instinctively everyone knew that. If nothing else, we all recognized MacFarland's considerable intelligence and respected the hours he put into his work. It came to this: The troublemaker would look foolish rather than daring. Even Jim Fitzsimmons was reading *On the Road* and turning his incipient alcoholism to literary ends.

There were some lives that were already beyond Jack MacFar- 4 land's ministrations, but mine was not. I started reading again as I hadn't since elementary school. I would go into our gloomy little bedroom or sit at the dinner table while, on the television, Danny McShane was paralyzing Mr. Moto with the atomic drop, and work slowly back through *Heart of Darkness*, trying to catch the words in Conrad's sentences. I certainly was not MacFarland's best student; most of the other guys in College Prep, even my fellow slackers, had better backgrounds than I did. But I worked very hard, for MacFarland had hooked me. He tapped my old interest in reading and creating stories. He gave me a way to feel special by using my mind. And he provided a role model that wasn't shaped on physical prowess alone, and something inside me that I wasn't quite aware of responded to that. Jack MacFarland established a literacy club, to borrow a phrase of Frank Smith's, and invited me—invited all of us—to join.

There's been a good deal of research and speculation suggesting that the acknowledgment of school performance with extrinsic rewards—smiling faces, stars, numbers, grades—diminishes the intrinsic satisfaction children experience by engaging in reading or writing or problem solving. While it's certainly true that we've created an educational system that encourages our best and brightest to become cynical grade collectors and, in general, have developed an obsession with evaluation and assessment, I must tell you that venal though it may have been, I loved getting good grades from MacFarland. I now know how subjective grades can be, but then they came tucked in the back of essays like bits of scientific data, some sort of spectroscopic readout that said, objectively and publicly, that I had made something of value. I suppose I'd been mediocre for too long and enjoyed a public redefinition. And I suppose the workings of my mind, such as they were, had been private for too long. My linguistic play moved into the world; like the intergalactic stories I told years before on Frank's berry-splattered truck bed, these papers with their circled, red B-pluses and A-minuses linked my mind to something outside it. I carried them around like a club emblem.

One day in the December of my senior year, Mr. MacFarland asked me where I was going to go to college. I hadn't thought much about it. Many of the students I teach today spent their last year in high school with a physics text in one hand and the Stanford catalog in the other, but I wasn't even aware of what "entrance requirements" were. My folks would say that they wanted me to go to college and be a doctor, but I don't know how seriously I ever took that; it seemed a sweet thing to say, a bit of supportive family chatter, like telling a gangly daughter she's graceful. The reality of higher education wasn't in my scheme of things: No one in the family had gone to college; only two of my uncles had completed high school. I figured I'd get a night job and go to the local junior college because I knew that Snyder and Company were going there to play ball. But I hadn't even prepared for that. When I finally said, "I don't know," MacFarland looked down at me—I was seated in his office—and said, "Listen, you can write."

My grades stank. I had A's in biology and a handful of B's in a   7
few English and social science classes. All the rest were C's—or worse. MacFarland said I would do well in his class and laid down the law about doing well in the others. Still, the record for my first three years wouldn't have been acceptable to any four-year school. To nobody's surprise, I was turned down flat by USC and UCLA. But Jack MacFarland was on the case. He had received his bachelor's degree from Loyola University, so he made calls to old professors and talked to somebody in admissions and wrote me a strong letter. Loyola finally accepted me as a probationary student. I would be on trial for the first year, and if I did okay, I would be granted regular status. MacFarland also intervened to get me a loan, for I could never have afforded a private college without it. Four more years of religion classes and four more years of boys at one school, girls at another. But at least I was going to college. Amazing.

Questions for Study and Discussion

1. Why do you think Rose chose the title "I Just Wanna Be Average"? (Glossary: *Title*) How does it relate to the essay?
2. Describe Jack MacFarland. How does his appearance contrast with his ability as a teacher?
3. Rose's paragraphs are long and full of information, but they are very coherent. Summarize in one sentence the topics of each of the seven paragraphs.
4. Analyze the transitions between paragraphs 2 and 3 and between 3 and 4. (Glossary: *Transitions*) What techniques does Rose use to smoothly introduce the reader to different aspects of his relationship with Jack MacFarland?

5. Rose introduces the reader to some of his classmates, quickly establishes their personalities, and names them in full: Jim Fitzsimmons, Skip Madison, Mike Dweetz. Why does he do this? How does it help him describe MacFarland?

6. Why does Rose have difficulty getting into college? How does he finally make it?

Vocabulary

Refer to your dictionary to define the following words as they are used in this selection. Then use each word in a sentence of your own.

beatnik (1)	linguistic (3)
curriculum (1)	incipient (3)
paradox (2)	ministrations (4)
existentialism (2)	extrinsic (5)
rejoin (3)	spectroscopic (5)
indomitable (3)	gangly (6)

Suggested Writing Assignments

1. Pick a good teacher that you have had. Identify what about him or her was of importance and how he or she influenced your life. Write an essay about the teacher using this essay as a model. Make sure that each paragraph accomplishes a specific purpose and that each paragraph is coherent enough to be readily summarized.

2. Write an essay about the process you went through to get into college. Did you visit different schools? Did your parents pressure you to go? Have you always wanted to go to college, or did you make the decision later in high school, like Rose? Did any particular teacher(s) help you? Make sure that you develop your paragraphs fully and that you have effective transitions between paragraphs.

6

TRANSITIONS

Transitions are words and phrases that are used to signal the relationships between ideas in an essay and to join the various parts of an essay together. Writers use transitions to relate ideas within sentences, between sentences, and between paragraphs. Perhaps the most common type of transition is the so-called transitional expression. Following is a list of transitional expressions categorized according to their functions.

ADDITION: and, again, too, also, in addition, further, furthermore, moreover, besides

CAUSE AND EFFECT: therefore, consequently, thus, accordingly, as a result, hence, then, so

COMPARISON: similarly, likewise, by comparison

CONCESSION: to be sure, granted, of course, it is true, to tell the truth, certainly, with the exception of, although this may be true, even though, naturally

CONTRAST: but, however, in contrast, on the contrary, on the other hand, yet, nevertheless, after all, in spite of

EXAMPLE: for example, for instance

PLACE: elsewhere, here, above, below, farther on, there, beyond, nearby, opposite to, around

RESTATEMENT: that is, as I have said, in other words, in simpler terms, to put it differently, simply stated

SEQUENCE: first, second, third, next, finally

SUMMARY: in conclusion, to conclude, to summarize, in brief, in short

TIME: afterward, later, earlier, subsequently, at the same time, simultaneously, immediately, this time, until now, before, meanwhile, shortly, soon, currently, when, lately, in the meantime, formerly

Besides transitional expressions, there are two other important ways to make transitions: by using pronoun reference and by repeating key words and phrases. This paragraph begins with the phrase "Besides transitional expressions": the phrase contains the transitional word *besides* and also repeats an earlier idea. Thus the reader knows that this discussion is moving toward a new but related idea. Repetition can also give a word or idea emphasis: "Foreigners look to America as a land of freedom. Freedom, however, is not something all Americans enjoy."

Pronoun reference avoids monotonous repetition of nouns and phrases. Without pronouns, these two sentences are wordy and tiring to read: "Jim went to the concert, where he heard some of Beethoven's music. Afterwards, Jim bought a recording of some of Beethoven's music." A more graceful and readable passage results if two pronouns are substituted in the second sentence: "Afterwards, he bought a recording of it." The second version has another advantage in that it is now more tightly related to the first sentence. The transition between the two sentences is smoother.

In the following example, notice how Rachel Carson uses transitional expressions, repetition of words and ideas, and pronoun reference:

> Under primitive agricultural conditions the farmer had few insect problems. *These* arose with the intensification of agriculture—the devotion of immense acreages to a single crop. *Such a system* set the stage for explosive increases in specific insect populations. Single-crop farming does not take advantage of the principles by which nature works; *it* is agriculture as an engineer might conceive it to be. Nature has introduced great variety into the landscape, but man has displayed a passion for simplifying *it*. *Thus he* undoes the built-in checks and balances by which nature holds the species within bounds. One important natural *check* is a limit on the amount of suitable habitat for each species. *Obviously*

Margin annotations:
- *pronoun reference*
- *repeated key idea*
- *pronoun reference*
- *pronoun reference*
- *repeated key word*
- *transitional expression; pronoun reference*

then, an insect that lives on wheat can build up its population to much higher levels on a farm devoted to wheat than on one in which wheat is intermingled with other crops to which the insect is not adapted.

repeated key idea

The same thing happens in other situations. A generation or more ago, the towns of large areas of the United States lined their streets with the noble elm tree. *Now* the beauty *they* hopefully created is threatened with complete destruction as disease sweeps through the elms, carried by a beetle that would have only limited chance to build up large populations and to spread from tree to tree if the elms were only occasional trees in a richly diversified planting.

Carson's transitions in this passage enhance its *coherence*—that quality of good writing that results when all sentences, paragraphs and longer divisions of an essay are effectively and naturally connected.

WHY I WANT TO HAVE A FAMILY

Lisa Brown

When she wrote the following essay, Lisa Brown was a junior majoring in American Studies at the University of Texas. In her essay, which was published as a "My Turn" column in the October 1984 issue of Newsweek on Campus, *she uses a variety of transitional devices to put together a coherent argument—that many women in their drive to success have overlooked the potential for fulfillment inherent in good relationships and family life.*

For years the theory of higher education operated something like this: men went to college to get rich, and women went to college to marry rich men. It was a wonderful little setup, almost mathematical in its precision. To disturb it would have been to rock an American institution. 1

During the '60s, though, this theory lost much of its luster. As the nation began to recognize the idiocy of relegating women to a secondary role, women soon joined men in what once were male-only pursuits. This rebellious decade pushed women toward independence, showed them their potential and compelled them to take charge of their lives. Many women took the opportunity and ran with it. Since then feminine autonomy has been the rule, not the exception, at least among college women. 2

That's the good news. The bad news is that the invisible push has turned into a shove. Some women are downright obsessive about success, to the point of becoming insular monuments to selfishness and fierce bravado, the condescending sort that hawks: "I don't need *anybody.* So there." These women dismiss children and marriage as unbearably outdated and potentially harmful to their up-and-coming careers. This notion of independence smacks of egocentrism. What do these women fear? Why can't they slow down long enough to remember that relationships and a family life are not inherently awful things? 3

Granted that for centuries women were on the receiving end of   4
some shabby treatment. Now, in an attempt to liberate college
women from the constraints that forced them almost exclusively
into teaching or nursing as a career outside the home—always
subject to the primary career of motherhood—some women have
gone too far. Any notion of motherhood seems to be regarded as
an unpleasant reminder of the past, when homemakers were
imprisoned by husbands, tots and household chores. In short,
many women consider motherhood a time-consuming obstacle
to the great joy of working outside the home.

The rise of feminism isn't the only answer. Growing up has   5
something to do with it, too. Most people find themselves in a
bind as they hit their late 20s: they consider the ideals they grew
up with and find that these don't necessarily mix with the ones
they've acquired. The easiest thing to do, it sometimes seems,
is to throw out the precepts their parents taught. Growing up,
my friends and I were enchanted by the idea of starting new
traditions. We didn't want self-worth to be contingent upon
whether there was a man or child around the house to make us
feel wanted.

I began to reconsider my values after my sister and a friend had   6
babies. I was entertained by their pregnancies and fascinated by
the births; I was also thankful that I wasn't the one who had to
change the diapers every day. I was a doting aunt only when I
wanted to be. As my sister's and friend's lives changed, though,
my attitude changed. I saw their days flip-flop between frustration and joy. Though these two women lost the freedom to run off
to the beach or to a bar, they gained something else—an abstract
happiness that reveals itself when they talk about Jessica's or
Amanda's latest escapade or vocabulary addition. Still in their
20s, they shuffle work and motherhood with the skill of poker
players. I admire them, and I marvel at their kids. Spending time
with the Jessicas and Amandas of the world teaches us patience
and sensitivity and gives us a clue into our own pasts. Children
are also reminders that there is a future and that we must work
to ensure its quality.

Now I feel challenged by the idea of becoming a parent. I want   7
to decorate a nursery and design Halloween costumes; I want to
answer my children's questions and help them learn to read. I
want to be unselfish. But I've spent most of my life working in the

opposite direction: toward independence, no emotional or financial strings attached. When I told a friend—one who likes kids but never, ever wants them—that I'd decided to accommodate motherhood, she accused me of undermining my career, my future, my life. "If that's all you want, then why are you even in college?" she asked.

The answer's simple: I want to be a smart mommy. I have solid career plans and look forward to working. I make a distinction between wanting kids and wanting nothing but kids. And I've accepted that I'll have to give up a few years of full-time work to allow time for being pregnant and buying Pampers. As for undermining my life, I'm proud of my decision because I think it's evidence that the women's movement is working. While liberating women from the traditional childbearing role, the movement has given respectability to motherhood by recognizing that it's not a brainless task like dishwashing. At the same time, women who choose not to have children are not treated as oddities. That certainly wasn't the case even 15 years ago. While the graying, middle-aged bachelor was respected, the female equivalent—tagged a spinster—was automatically suspect.   8

Today, women have choices: about careers, their bodies, children. I am grateful that women are no longer forced into motherhood as a function of their biology; it's senseless to assume that having a uterus qualifies anyone to be a good parent. By the same token, it is ridiculous for women to abandon all maternal desire because it might jeopardize personal success. Some women make the decision to go childless without ever analyzing their true needs or desires. They forget that motherhood can add to personal fulfillment.   9

I wish those fiercely independent women wouldn't look down upon those of us who, for whatever reason, choose to forgo much of the excitement that runs in tandem with being single, liberated and educated. Excitement also fills a family life; it just comes in different ways.   10

I'm not in college because I'll learn how to make tastier pot roast. I'm a student because I want to make sense of the world and of myself. By doing so, I think I'll be better prepared to be a mother to the new lives that I might bring into the world. I'll also be a better me. It's a package deal I don't want to turn down.   11

Questions for Study and Discussion

1. What is Brown arguing for in this essay? What does she say prompted a change in her attitude? (Glossary: *Attitude*)
2. Against what group is Brown arguing? What does she find wrong with the beliefs of that group?
3. What reasons does she provide for wanting to have a family?
4. Identify Brown's use of transitions in paragraphs 2, 3, 4, 6, 8, and 9. How do these help you as a reader to follow her point?
5. What are the implications for you of Brown's last two sentences in paragraph 6: "Spending time with the Jessicas and Amandas of the world teaches us patience and sensitivity and gives us a clue into our pasts. Children are also the reminders that there is a future and that we must work to ensure its quality"?
6. For what audience do you think this essay is intended? Do you think men would be as interested as women in the author's viewpoint? Explain. (Glossary: *Audience*)

Vocabulary

Refer to your dictionary to define the following words as they are used in this selection. Then use each word in a sentence of your own.

relegating (2)	precepts (5)
autonomy (2)	contingent (5)
insular (3)	doting (6)
bravado (3)	tandem (10)

Suggested Writing Assignments

1. Write an essay in which you argue any one of the following positions with regard to the women's movement: it has gone too far; it is out of control; it is misdirected; it hasn't gone far enough or done enough; it needs to reach more women and men; it should lower its sights; a position of your own

different from the above. Whichever position you argue, be sure that you provide sufficient evidence to support your point of view.

2. Fill in the following statement and write an argument in support of it:

The purpose of a college education is to _____
_____ .

How I Got Smart

Steve Brody

Steve Brody is a retired high school English teacher who enjoys writing about the lighter side of teaching. He was born in Chicago in 1915 and received his bachelor's degree in English from Columbia University. In addition to his articles in educational publications, Brody has published many newspaper articles on travel and a humorous book about golf, How to Break Ninety Before You Reach It *(1979). As you read his account of how love made him smart, notice the way he uses transitional words and expressions to unify his essay and make it a seamless whole.*

A common misconception among youngsters attending school is that their teachers were child prodigies. Who else but a bookworm, prowling the libraries and disdaining the normal youngster's propensity for play rather than study, would grow up to be a teacher anyway?

I tried desperately to explain to my students that the image they had of me as an ardent devotee of books and homework during my adolescence was a bit out of focus. Au contraire! I hated compulsory education with a passion. I could never quite accept the notion of having to go to school while the fish were biting.

Consequently, my grades were somewhat bearish. That's how my father, who dabbled in the stock market, described them. Presenting my report card for my father to sign was like serving him a subpoena. At midterm and other sensitive periods, my father kept a low profile.

But in my sophomore year, something beautiful and exciting happened. Cupid aimed his arrow and struck me squarely in the heart. All at once, I enjoyed going to school, if only to gaze at the lovely face beneath the raven tresses in English II. My princess sat near the pencil sharpener, and that year I ground up enough pencils to fuel a campfire.

Alas, Debbie was far beyond my wildest dreams. We were sep- 5
arated not only by five rows of desks, but by about 50 I.Q. points.
She was the top student in English II, the apple of Mrs. Larrivee's
eye. I envisioned how eagerly Debbie's father awaited her report
card.

Occasionally, Debbie would catch me staring at her, and she 6
would flash a smile—an angelic smile that radiated enlighten-
ment and quickened my heartbeat. It was a smile that signaled
hope and made me temporarily forget the intellectual gulf that
separated us.

I schemed desperately to bridge that gulf. And one day, as I was 7
passing the supermarket, an idea came to me.

A sign in the window announced that the store was offering 8
the first volume of a set of encyclopedias at the introductory price
of 29 cents. The remaining volumes would cost $2.49 each, but it
was no time to be cynical.

I purchased Volume I—Aardvark to Asteroid—and began my 9
venture into the world of knowledge. I would henceforth become
a seeker of facts. I would become chief egghead in English II and
sweep the princess off her feet with a surge of erudition. I had it
all planned.

My first opportunity came one day in the cafeteria line. I looked 10
behind me and there she was.

"Hi," she said. 11

After a pause, I wet my lips and said, "Know where anchovies 12
come from?"

She seemed surprised. "No, I don't." 13

I breathed a sigh of relief. "The anchovy lives in salt water and 14
is rarely found in fresh water." I had to talk fast, so that I could get
all the facts in before we reached the cash register. "Fishermen
catch anchovies in the Mediterranean Sea and along the Atlantic
coast near Spain and Portugal."

"How fascinating," said Debbie. 15

"The anchovy is closely related to the herring. It is thin and 16
silvery in color. It has a long snout and a very large mouth."

"Incredible." 17

"Anchovies are good in salads, mixed with eggs, and are often 18
used as appetizers before dinner, but they are salty and cannot be
digested too rapidly."

Debbie shook her head in disbelief. It was obvious that I had 19
made quite an impression.

A few days later, during a fire drill, I sidled up to her and asked,   20
"Ever been to the Aleutian Islands?"

"Never have," she replied.   21

"Might be a nice place to visit, but I certainly wouldn't want to   22
live there," I said.

"Why not?" said Debbie, playing right into my hands.   23

"Well, the climate is forbidding. There are no trees on any of the   24
100 or more islands in the group. The ground is rocky and very
little plant life can grow on it."

"I don't think I'd even care to visit," she said.   25

The fire drill was over and we began to file into the building, so   26
I had to step it up to get the natives in. "The Aleuts are short and
sturdy and have dark skin and black hair. They subsist on fish,
and they trap blue fox, seal and otter for their valuable fur."

Debbie's hazel eyes widened in amazement. She was undoubt-   27
edly beginning to realize that she wasn't dealing with an ordinary
lunkhead. She was gaining new and valuable insights instead of
engaging in the routine small talk one would expect from most
sophomores.

Luck was on my side, too. One day I was browsing through the   28
library during my study period. I spotted Debbie sitting at a table,
absorbed in a crossword puzzle. She was frowning, apparently
stumped on a word. I leaned over and asked if I could help.

"Four-letter word for Oriental female servant," Debbie said.   29

"Try *amah*," I said, quick as a flash.   30

Debbie filled in the blanks, then turned to stare at me in amaze-   31
ment. "I don't believe it," she said. "I just don't believe it."

And so it went, that glorious, amorous, joyous sophomore year.   32
Debbie seemed to relish our little conversations and hung on my
every word. Naturally, the more I read, the more my confidence
grew. I expatiated freely on such topics as adenoids, air brakes,
and arthritis.

In the classroom, too, I was gradually making my presence felt.   33
Among my classmates, I was developing a reputation as a wheeler-
dealer in data. One day, during a discussion of Coleridge's "The
Ancient Mariner," we came across the word *albatross*.

"Can anyone tell us what an albatross is?" asked Mrs. Larrivee.   34

My hand shot up. "The albatross is a large bird that lives mostly   35
in the ocean regions below the equator, but may be found in the
north Pacific as well. The albatross measures as long as four feet
and has the greatest wingspread of any bird. It feeds on the sur-

face of the ocean, where it catches shellfish. The albatross is a very voracious eater. When it is full it has trouble getting into the air again."

There was a long silence in the room. Mrs. Larrivee couldn't quite believe what she had just heard. I sneaked a peek at Debbie and gave her a big wink. She beamed proudly and winked back. 36

It was a great feeling, having Debbie and Mrs. Larrivee and my peers according me respect and paying attention when I spoke. 37

My grades edged upward and my father no longer tried to avoid me when I brought home my report card. I continued reading the encyclopedia diligently, packing more and more into my brain. 38

What I failed to perceive was that Debbie all this while was going steady with a junior from a neighboring school—a hockey player with a C+ average. The revelation hit me hard, and for a while I felt like disgorging and forgetting everything I had learned. I had saved enough money to buy Volume II—Asthma to Bullfinch—but was strongly tempted to invest in a hockey stick instead. 39

How could she lead me on like that—smiling and concurring and giving me the impression that I was important? 40

I felt not only hurt, but betrayed. Like Agamemnon, but with less dire consequences, thank God. 41

In time I recovered from my wounds. The next year Debbie moved from the neighborhood and transferred to another school. Soon she became no more than a fleeting memory. 42

Although the original incentive was gone, I continued pouring over the encyclopedias, as well as an increasing number of other books. Having savored the heady wine of knowledge, I could not now alter my course. For: 43

> "A little knowledge is a dangerous thing:
> Drink deep, or taste not the Pierian spring."

So wrote Alexander Pope, Volume XIV, Paprika to Pterodactyl. 44

Questions for Study and Discussion

1. Why didn't Brody stop reading the volumes of the encyclopedias when he discovered that Debbie had a steady boyfriend?

2. If you find Brody's narrative humorous, try to explain the sources of his humor. For example, what humor resides in the choice of examples Brody uses?

3. How are paragraphs 2 and 3, 3 and 4, 5 and 6, 31 and 32, and 43 and 44 linked? Identify the transitions that Brody uses in paragraph 35.

4. Brody refers to Coleridge's "The Ancient Mariner" in paragraph 33 and Agamemnon in paragraph 41, and he quotes Alexander Pope in paragraph 43. Use an encyclopedia to explain Brody's allusions. (Glossary: *Allusion*)

5. Comment on the effectiveness of the beginning and ending of Brody's essay. (Glossary: *Beginnings and Endings*)

6. Brody could have told his story using far less dialogue than he did. What, in your opinion, would have been gained or lost had he done so? (Glossary: *Dialogue*)

Vocabulary

Refer to your dictionary to define the following words as they are used in this selection. Then use each word in a sentence of your own.

misconception (1)	forbidding (24)
prodigies (1)	subsist (26)
devotee (2)	amorous (32)
bearish (3)	expatiated (32)
dabbled (3)	adenoids (32)
surge (9)	voracious (35)
erudition (9)	disgorging (39)
snout (16)	savored (43)
sidled (20)	

Suggested Writing Assignments

1. One serious thought that arises as a result of reading Brody's essay is that perhaps we learn best when we are sufficiently motivated to do so. And once motivated, the desire to learn seems to feed on itself: "Having savored the heady wine of knowledge, I could not now alter my course" (43).

Write an essay in which you explore this same subject using your own experiences.

2. In *The New York Times Complete Manual of Home Repair,* Bernard Gladstone gives directions for applying blacktop sealer to a driveway. His directions appear below in scrambled order. First, carefully read all of Gladstone's sentences. Next, arrange the sentences in what seems to you the correct sequence, paying attention to transitional devices. Be prepared to explain the reasons for your particular arrangement of the sentences.

1. A long-handled pushbroom or roofing brush is used to spread the coating evenly over the entire area.
2. Care should be taken to make certain the entire surface is uniformly wet, though puddles should be swept away if water collects in low spots.
3. Greasy areas and oil slicks should be scraped up, then scrubbed thoroughly with a detergent solution.
4. With most brands there are just three steps to follow.
5. In most cases one coat of sealer will be sufficient.
6. The application of blacktop sealer is best done on a day when the weather is dry and warm, preferably while the sun is shining on the surface.
7. This should not be applied until the first coat is completely dry.
8. First sweep the surface absolutely clean to remove all dust, dirt and foreign material.
9. To simplify spreading and to assure a good bond, the surface of the driveway should be wet down thoroughly by sprinkling with a hose.
10. However, for surfaces in poor condition a second coat may be required.
11. The blacktop sealer is next stirred thoroughly and poured on while the surface is still damp.
12. The sealer should be allowed to dry overnight (or longer if recommended by the manufacturer) before normal traffic is resumed.

FACING VIOLENCE

Michael T. Kaufman

Warsaw Bureau Chief of the New York Times, *Michael T. Kaufman was born in 1938 in Paris and grew up in the United States. He studied at the Bronx High School of Science, City College of New York, and Columbia University. He began his career at the* New York Times *as a reporter and feature writer and before assuming his present position, served as bureau chief in Ottawa, Canada. The following article appeared in the* New York Times Magazine. *In it Kaufman reflects on our reluctance to deal with the realities of violence, preferring instead the superficial and vicarious version we get on television. As you read Kaufman's essay, notice how he makes smooth transitions from one paragraph to the next with transitional expressions, pronoun references, and the repetition of key ideas.*

Almost 20 years ago, when my oldest son was very young, I   1
tried to shield the boy from violence and aggression, these alleged attributes of manliness. My wife and I had agreed to raise our children in an atmosphere of nonviolence, without playthings that simulated weapons. Then my uncle came to visit us from Israel. My uncle, unlike his wife and children, had survived Auschwitz, and he was surprised that my son had no toy guns. I tried to explain, but, asserting the moral authority of a war victim and survivor, he took my son off to Macy's to buy the biggest, noisiest toy machine gun he could find. My uncle said that if people do not go bang bang when they are young they go bang bang when they grow up.

Since then, we have lived in Africa and in Asia and I have seen   2
and heard bang bang. I am not sure I fully understand what my uncle meant, but I no longer think that exposure to the symbols of death and violence causes little boys to grow up ethically impaired. In fact, now that I am living in North American civiliza-

tion, where enormous energies are spent rendering death and violence either fictional or abstract, I think the greatest moral pitfall is not that we witness too much bang bang, but that, for the most part, we perceive it vicariously. We shield ourselves from real death and pain while paying to see these same things, sanitized and stylized, in the movies.

This idea crystallized in my mind after a conversation I had a   3 short while ago with Jack Troake, a thoughtful man who, like his father, grandfather and great-grandfather, makes his living by fishing from his home port of Twillingate, Newfoundland. Like his ancestors and neighbors, he also used to spend the icebound winter months hunting gray skin seals, but he does so no longer. The market for seal pelts in Europe and the United States has been destroyed because of protests launched abroad by animal-rights groups. The original protests were against the clubbing of baby white-furred seal pups, a hunt that Jack Troake never joined. Then the outcry spread to include all seals. Last year, a British supermarket chain declared it would no longer stock Canadian fish because of someone's belief that some fishermen either now hunt seals or once did.

As we sat on Mr. Troake's radar-equipped boat watching his   4 sons mend nets, he made it clear that he was flabbergasted and insulted by what he assumed to be the view of some foreigners that he and his neighbors were barbarians. "Look old boy, there's no doubt about it, I make my living killing things. We kill mackerel and cod and we used to kill seals. Now, there seems to be a bunch of people who do not like that. I imagine them sitting eating lamb chops and steak and chicken, thinking they all come neatly wrapped in plastic from some food factory. I wonder whether they have ever seen anything die or anything born, except on television and in the movies. But, to tell you the truth, old boy, I really feel sorry for those people who are so upset about this old Christian."

Me too. I left Twillingate, and in a motel that night I watched   5 the footage from Beirut. As I remember now, it contained what have become the current visual clichés of violence. Men firing bazookas around a corner at something. Smoke and rubble. Women with shopping bags walking fast across a street. Adolescent gunmen smiling into the camera from the backs of trucks. It conveyed a sense of destruction, but it stopped short of being horrible.

I knew the images were authentic, but they did not seem real. They blurred into an already crowded memory bank of two-dimensional violence: Dirty Harry, the A Team, Beirut, Belfast, El Salvador, car crashes. And I thought how I, bombarded with such pictures of death, had, two years ago, backed away from the real drama of death when it touched me as something more than a witness. I had sent my own mother to die in a nursing home, among death specialists. I did not hold her as her life ebbed. Later, I consoled myself with the thought that this is what people do in a technological culture, and that, anyway, the room was clean and the doctors said she did not suffer greatly.

I recall how we used to hear that the images of the Vietnam War, shown on television, sensitized the nation. Perhaps. I can recall the naked little girl running from napalm, and the man being shot by a police official in Saigon. But everything else has been jumbled in memory, and what remains are mostly recollections of what I now think of as my skin-deep shock and my pious responses. There were too many images. The only people I hear talking about Vietnam now are the ones who were there. 6

What I do remember is the first dead man I ever saw, a man shot and bleeding on dirty stairs in New York. I remember victims of massacres in Zaire and Rhodesia, and I can recall where each of those bodies lay. I remember an Afghan freedom fighter in a hospital in Peshawar, his leg lost in a land-mine explosion. He had his rifle with him, and his 7-year-old son was on his bed touching the man's stump. The father was talking about returning to fight Soviet forces; he hoped that his son would continue the fight. For that small boy, perhaps, the moment was indeed too much bang bang, but I am no longer sure. 7

As for little boys playing with toy guns, I don't think it matters much, one way or the other. What does matter, it seems to me, is that at some time in their formative years, maybe in high school, our children should bear witness to the everyday violence they could see, say, in an emergency ward of a big city hospital. I know it sounds extreme, but maybe our children could learn something valuable if they were taken for a day or two to visit a police station or an old-age home. It might serve as an antidote for the unreal violence on all our screens. 8

What would be learned, I think, is that, up close and in three dimensions, the dead, the dying and the suffering are always to 9 some extent "us." On the screens they always seem to be "them." I don't understand it, really, any more than my uncle's view of bang bang, but I know that as long as men die and men kill it is wrong to turn away too much. Also, I am certain that I would prefer to be judged by the hunter Jack Troake than by anyone who would judge him harshly.

Questions for Study and Discussion

1. What is Kaufman's thesis? (Glossary *Thesis*) Where is it stated? Is it stated in more than one place?
2. What did Kaufman's uncle have to say about guns? Why do you suppose Kaufman has difficulty understanding him? Do you? Explain.
3. Does Kaufman develop his thesis using emotional appeals or thoughtful examples? Cite examples from the text to support your answer.
4. What exactly are the "visual clichés" Kaufman refers to in paragraph 5? Why do you suppose he thinks they fall short of being "horrible"?
5. In paragraph 5, Kaufman relates the deeply personal tale of his mother's death. What is the effect of this incident on the you? What would have been gained or lost had he left it out?
6. Reread the first sentences in paragraphs 1–7. What do they have in common? How do they work to make the transition from paragraph to paragraph?
7. Why do you suppose Kaufman would "prefer to be judged by the hunter Jack Troake than by anyone who would judge him harshly"? Explain.

Vocabulary

Refer to your dictionary to define the following words as they are used in this selection. Then use each word in a sentence of your own.

alleged (1)   flabbergasted (4)
impaired (2)   sensitized (6)
vicariously (2)   antidote (8)

Suggested Writing Assignments

1. Kaufman believes that "We shield ourselves from real death and pain while paying to see these same things, sanitized and stylized, in the movies." Using examples from your own experience or observation, write an essay in which you agree or disagree with Kaufman's assessment of civilization in America.

2. In paragraph 8, Kaufman offers a solution to the problem of un-faced violence. How realistic is his solution? How necessary is it? In your own words, defend or attack Kaufman's solution.

7

EFFECTIVE SENTENCES

Each of the following paragraphs describes the city of Vancouver. Although the content of both paragraphs is essentially the same, the first paragraph is written in sentences of nearly the same length and pattern and the second paragraph in sentences of varying length and pattern.

Water surrounds Vancouver on three sides. The snow-crowned Coast Mountains ring the city on the northeast. Vancouver has a floating quality of natural loveliness. There is a curved beach at English Bay. This beach is in the shape of a half moon. Residential high rises stand behind the beach. They are in pale tones of beige, blue, and ice-cream pink. Turn-of-the-century houses of painted wood frown upward at the glitter of office towers. Any urban glare is softened by folds of green lawns, flowers, fountains, and trees. Such landscaping appears to be unplanned. It links Vancouver to her ultimate treasure of greenness. That treasure is thousand-acre Stanley Park. Surrounding stretches of water dominate. They have image-evoking names like False Creek and Lost Lagoon. Sailboats and pleasure craft skim blithely across Burrard Inlet. Foreign freighters are out in English Bay. They await their turn to take on cargoes of grain.

Surrounded by water on three sides and ringed to the northeast by the snow-crowned Coast Mountains, Vancouver has a floating quality of natural loveliness. At English Bay, the half-moon curve of beach is backed by high rises in pale tones of beige, blue, and ice-cream pink. Turn-of-the-century houses of painted wood frown upward at the glitter of office towers. Yet any urban glare is quickly softened by folds of green lawns, flowers, fountains, and trees that in a seemingly unplanned fashion link Vancouver to her ultimate treasure of greenness—thousand-acre Stanley Park. And always it is the surrounding stretches of water that dominate, with their image-evoking names like False Creek and Lost Lagoon. Sailboats and pleasure craft skim blithely across Burrard Inlet, while out in English Bay foreign freighters await their turn to take on cargoes of grain.

The difference between these two paragraphs is dramatic. The first is monotonous because of the sameness of the sentences and because the ideas are not related to one another in a meaningful way. The second paragraph is much more interesting and readable; its sentences vary in length and are structured to clarify the relationships among the ideas. Sentence variety, an important aspect of all good writing, should not be used for its own sake, but rather to express ideas precisely and to emphasize the most important ideas within each sentence. Sentence variety includes the use of subordination, the periodic and loose sentence, the dramatically short sentence, the active and passive voice, and coordination.

Subordination, the process of giving one idea less emphasis than another in a sentence, is one of the most important characteristics of an effective sentence and a mature prose style. Writers subordinate ideas by introducing them either with subordinating conjunctions (*because, if, as though, while, when, after, in order that*) or with relative pronouns (*that, which, who, whomever, what*). Subordination not only deemphasizes some ideas, but also highlights others that the writer feels are more important.

Of course, there is nothing about an idea—*any* idea—that automatically makes it primary or secondary in importance. The writer decides what to emphasize, and he or she may choose to emphasize the less profound or noteworthy of two ideas. Consider, for example, the following sentence: "Jane was reading a novel the day that Mount St. Helens erupted." Everyone, including the author of the sentence, knows that the Mount St. Helens eruption is a more noteworthy event than Jane's reading a novel. But the sentence concerns Jane, not the volcano, and so her reading is stated in the main clause, while the eruption is subordinated in a dependent clause.

Generally, writers place the ideas they consider important in main clauses, and other ideas go into dependent clauses. For example:

> When she was thirty years old, she made her first solo flight across the Atlantic.
>
> When she made her first solo flight across the Atlantic, she was thirty years old.

The first sentence emphasizes the solo flight; in the second, the emphasis is on the pilot's age.

Another way to achieve emphasis is to place the most important words, phrases, and clauses at the beginning or end of a sentence. The ending is the most emphatic part of a sentence; the beginning is less emphatic; and the middle is the least emphatic of all. The two sentences about the pilot put the main clause at the end, achieving special emphasis. The same thing occurs in a much longer kind of sentence, called a *periodic sentence*. Here is an example from John Updike:

> On the afternoon of the first day of spring, when the gutters were still heaped high with Monday's snow but the sky itself had been swept clean, we put on our galoshes and walked up the sunny side of Fifth Avenue to Central Park.

By holding the main clause back, Updike keeps his readers in suspense and so puts the most emphasis possible on his main idea.

A *loose sentence*, on the other hand, states its main idea at the beginning and then adds details in subsequent phrases and clauses. Rewritten as a loose sentence, Updike's sentence might read like this:

> We put on our galoshes and walked up the sunny side of Fifth Avenue to Central Park on the afternoon of the first day of spring, when the gutters were still heaped high with Monday's snow but the sky itself had been swept clean.

The main idea still gets plenty of emphasis, since it is contained in a main clause at the beginning of the sentence. Yet a loose sentence resembles the way people talk: it flows naturally and is easy to understand.

Another way to create emphasis is to use a *dramatically short sentence*. Especially following a long and involved sentence, a short declarative sentence helps drive a point home. Here are two examples, the first from Edwin Newman and the second from David Wise:

> Meaning no disrespect, I suppose there is, if not general rejoicing, at least some sense of relief when the football season ends. It's a long season.

The executive suite on the thirty-fifth floor of the Columbia Broadcasting System skyscraper in Manhattan is a tasteful blend of dark wood paneling, expensive abstract paintings, thick carpets, and pleasing colors. It has the quiet look of power.

Finally, since the subject of a sentence is automatically emphasized, writers may choose to use the *active voice* when they want to emphasize the doer of an action and the *passive voice* when they want to downplay or omit the doer completely. Here are two examples:

High winds pushed our sailboat onto the rocks, where the force of the waves tore it to pieces.

Our sailboat was pushed by high winds onto the rocks, where it was torn to pieces by the force of the waves.

The first sentence emphasizes the natural forces that destroyed the boat, while the second sentence focuses attention on the boat itself. The passive voice may be useful in placing emphasis, but it has important disadvantages. As the examples show, and as the terms suggest, active-voice verbs are more vigorous and vivid than the same verbs in the passive voice. Then, too, some writers use the passive voice to hide or evade responsibility. "It has been decided" conceals who did the deciding, whereas "I have decided" makes all clear. So the passive voice should be used only when necessary—as it is in this sentence.

Often, a writer wants to place equal emphasis on several facts or ideas. One way to do this is to give each its own sentence. For example:

Nancy Lopez selected her club. She lined up her shot. She chipped the ball to within a foot of the pin.

But a long series of short, simple sentences quickly becomes tedious. Many writers would combine these three sentences by using *coordination*. The coordinating conjunctions *and, but, or, nor, for, so,* and *yet* connect words, phrases, and clauses of equal importance:

Nancy Lopez selected her club, lined up her shot, *and* chipped the ball to within a foot of the pin.

By coordinating three sentences into one, the writer not only makes the same words easier to read, but also shows that Lopez's three actions are equally important parts of a single process.

When parts of a sentence are not only coordinated but also grammatically the same, they are *parallel*. Parallelism in a sentence is created by balancing a word with a word, a phrase with a phrase, or a clause with a clause. Parallelism is often used in speeches—for example, in the last sentence of Lincoln's *Gettysburg Address* ("government of the people, by the people, for the people, shall not perish from the . . ."). Here is another example, from the beginning of Mark Twain's *The Adventures of Huckleberry Finn:*

> Persons attempting to find a motive in this narrative will be prosecuted; persons attempting to find a moral in it will be banished; persons attempting to find a plot in it will be shot.

AN EYE-WITNESS ACCOUNT OF THE SAN FRANCISCO EARTHQUAKE

Jack London

Jack London (1876–1916) was born in San Francisco and attended school only until the age of fourteen. A prolific and popular fiction writer, he is perhaps best remembered for his novels The Call of the Wild *(1903),* The Sea Wolf *(1904), and* White Fang *(1906). London was working near San Francisco when the great earthquake hit that city in the early morning of April 16, 1906. In the aftermath of the 1989 earthquake in San Francisco, many people recalled London's account of the earlier disaster. Notice how, in this account of the quake's aftermath, London uses a variety of sentence structures to capture the feelings that this disaster evoked in him.*

The earthquake shook down in San Francisco hundreds of thousands of dollars' worth of walls and chimneys. But the conflagration that followed burned up hundreds of millions of dollars' worth of property. There is no estimating within hundreds of millions the actual damage wrought. Not in history has a modern imperial city been so completely destroyed. San Francisco is gone! Nothing remains of it but memories and a fringe of dwelling houses on its outskirts. Its industrial section is wiped out. Its social and residential section is wiped out. The factories and warehouses, the great stores and newspaper buildings, the hotels and the palaces of the nabobs, are all gone. Remains only the fringe of dwelling houses on the outskirts of what was once San Francisco.

Within an hour after the earthquake shock the smoke of San Francisco's burning was a lurid tower visible a hundred miles away. And for three days and nights this lurid tower swayed in the sky, reddening the sun, darkening the day, and filling the land with smoke.

On Wednesday morning at a quarter past five came the earth- 3
quake. A minute later the flames were leaping upward. In a dozen
different quarters south of Market Street, in the working-class
ghetto, and in the factories, fires started. There was no opposing the flames. There was no organization, no communication.
All the cunning adjustments of a twentieth-century city had been
smashed by the earthquake. The streets were humped into ridges
and depressions and piled with debris of fallen walls. The steel
rails were twisted into perpendicular and horizontal angles. The
telephone and telegraph systems were disrupted. And the great
water mains had burst. All the shrewd contrivances and safe-
guards of man had been thrown out of gear by thirty seconds'
twitching of the earth's crust.

By Wednesday afternoon, inside of twelve hours, half the heart 4
of the city was gone. At that time I watched the vast conflagration from out on the bay. It was dead calm. Not a flicker of wind
stirred. Yet from every side wind was pouring in upon the city.
East, west, north, and south, strong winds were blowing upon the
doomed city. The heated air rising made an enormous suck. Thus
did the fire of itself build its own colossal chimney through the
atmosphere. Day and night, this dead calm continued, and yet,
near to the flames, the wind was often half a gale, so mighty was
the suck. . . .

Wednesday night saw the destruction of the very heart of the 5
city. Dynamite was lavishly used, and many of San Francisco's
proudest structures were crumbled by man himself into ruins,
but there was no withstanding the onrush of the flames. Time and
again successful stands were made by the fire fighters, and every
time the flames flanked around on either side, or came up from
the rear, and turned to defeat the hard-won victory.

An enumeration of the buildings destroyed would be a direc- 6
tory of San Francisco. An enumeration of the buildings unde-
stroyed would be a line and several addresses. An enumeration of
the deeds of heroism would stock a library and bankrupt the
Carnegie medal fund.* An enumeration of the dead—will never
be made. All vestiges of them were destroyed by the flames. The
number of the victims of the earthquake will never be known.

---

*Fund established by the philanthropist Andrew Carnegie in 1905 for the rec-
ognition of heroic deeds.

Questions for Study and Discussion

1. In this short passage London draws contrasts between the forces of nature and those of humans. Why do you think London draws these contrasts? What is their effect?
2. In paragraph 4 London says that "the fire of itself [built] its own colossal chimney through the atmosphere." What does he mean?
3. From what vantage point does London describe the destruction of the city? Where does he tell us where he is?
4. What is the effect of the short sentences "San Francisco is gone!" and "It was dead calm" in paragraphs 1 and 4?
5. Why do you suppose London uses the passive voice instead of the active voice in paragraph 3? (Glossary: *Voice*)
6. Point out examples of parallelism in paragraphs 1, 2, and 6. How does London add emphasis through the use of this rhetorical device? (Glossary: *Parallelism*)

Vocabulary

Refer to your dictionary to define the following words as they are used in this selection. Then use each word in a sentence of your own.

conflagration (1)   contrivances (3)
nabobs (1)   vestiges (6)
lurid (2)

Suggested Writing Assignments

1. If you have ever been an eyewitness to a disaster, either natural or man-made, write an account similar to London's of its consequences. Give special attention to the variety of your sentences according to the advice provided in the introduction to "Effective Sentences."
2. Write a brief essay using one of the following sentences to focus and control the descriptive details you select. Place the sentence in the essay wherever it will have the greatest emphasis.

It was a strange party.
He was nervous.
I was shocked.
Music filled the air.
Dirt was everywhere.

PLAYING TO WIN

Margaret A. Whitney

Margaret A. Whitney is a writer by profession. In the following article, first published in 1988 in the New York Times Magazine, Whitney describes how her daughter overcame sexual stereotypes in the face of social resistance towards women in sports. As you read Whitney's account of her daughter Ann's love for sports, notice how the varied structures of Whitney's sentences enhance her descriptions of those experiences.

My daughter is an athlete. Nowadays, this statement won't strike many parents as unusual, but it does me. Until her freshman year in high school, Ann was only marginally interested in sport of any kind. When she played, she didn't swing hard, often dropped the ball, and had an annoying habit of tittering on field or court.

Indifference combined with another factor that did not bode well for a sports career. Ann was growing up to be beautiful. By the eighth grade, nature and orthodontics had produced a 5-foot-8-inch, 125-pound, brown-eyed beauty with a wonderful smile. People told her, too. And, as many young women know, it is considered a satisfactory accomplishment to be pretty and stay pretty. Then you can simply sit still and enjoy the unconditional positive regard. Ann loved the attention too, and didn't consider it demeaning when she was awarded "Best Hair," female category, in the eighth-grade yearbook.

So it came as a surprise when she became a jock. The first indication that athletic indifference had ended came when she joined the high-school cross-country team. She signed up in early September and ran third for the team within three days. Not only that. After one of those 3.1-mile races up hill and down dale on a rainy November afternoon, Ann came home muddy and bedraggled. Her hair was plastered to her head, and the mascara she had applied so carefully that morning ran in dark circles under her eyes. This is it, I thought. Wait until Lady Astor sees herself. But the kid with the best eighth-grade hair went on to finish the season and subsequently letter in cross-country, soccer, basketball and softball.

I love sports, she tells anyone who will listen. So do I, though 4 my midlife quest for a doctorate leaves me little time for either playing or watching. My love of sports is bound up with the goals in my life and my hopes for my three daughters. I have begun to hear the message of sports. It is very different from many messages that women receive about living, and I think it is good.

My husband, for example, talked to Ann differently when he 5 realized that she was a serious competitor and not just someone who wanted to get in shape so she'd look good in a prom dress. Be aggressive, he'd advise. Go for the ball. Be intense.

Be intense. She came in for some of the most scathing criticism 6 from her dad, when, during basketball season, her intensity waned. You're pretending to play hard, he said. You like it on the bench? Do you like to watch while your teammates play?

I would think, how is this kid reacting to such advice? For 7 years, she'd been told at home, at school, by countless advertisements, "Be quiet, Be good, Be still." When teachers reported that Ann was too talkative, not obedient enough, too flighty. When I dressed her up in frilly dresses and admonished her not to get dirty. When ideals of femininity are still, quiet, cool females in ads whose vacantness passes for sophistication. How can any adolescent girl know what she's up against? Have you ever really noticed intensity? It is neither quiet nor good. And it's definitely not pretty.

In the end, her intensity revived. At half time, she'd look for her 8 father, and he would come out of the bleachers to discuss tough defense, finding the open player, squaring up on her jump shot. I'd watch them at the edge of the court, a tall man and a tall girl, talking about how to play.

Of course I'm particularly sensitive at this point in my life to 9 messages about trying hard, being active, getting better through individual and team effort. Ann, you could barely handle a basketball two years ago. Now you're bringing the ball up against the press. Two defenders are after you. You must dribble, stop, pass. We're depending on you. We need you to help us. I wonder if my own paroxysms of uncertainty would be eased had more people urged me—be active, go for it!

Not that dangers don't lurk for the females of her generation. I occasionally run this horror show in my own mental movie theater: an unctuous but handsome lawyer-like drone of a young man spies my Ann. Hmmm, he says unconsciously to himself, good gene pool, and wouldn't she go well with my BMW and the condo? Then I see Ann with a great new hairdo kissing the drone goodbyehoney and setting off to the nearest mall with splendid-looking children to spend money.

10

But the other night she came home from softball tryouts at 6 in the evening. The dark circles under her eyes were from exhaustion, not makeup. I tried too hard today, she says. I feel like I'm going to puke.

11

After she has revived, she explains. She wants to play a particular position. There is competition for it. I can't let anybody else get my spot, she says, I've got to prove that I can do it. Later we find out that she has not gotten the much-wanted third-base position, but she will start with the varsity team. My husband talks about the machinations of coaches and tells her to keep trying. You're doing fine, he says. She gets that I-am-going-to-keep-trying look on her face. The horror-show vision of Ann-as-Stepford-Wife fades.

12

Of course, Ann doesn't realize the changes she has wrought, the power of her self-definition. I'm an athlete, Ma, she tells me when I suggest participation in the school play or the yearbook. But she has really caused us all to rethink our views of existence: her younger sisters who consider sports a natural activity for females, her father whose advocacy of women has increased, and me. Because when I doubt my own abilities, I say to myself, Get intense, Margaret. Do you like to sit on the bench?

13

And my intensity revives.

14

I am not suggesting that participation in sports is the answer for all young women. It is not easy—the losing, jealousy, raw competition and intense personal criticism of performance.

15

And I don't wish to imply that the sports scene is a morality play either. Girls' sports can be funny. You can't forget that out on that field are a bunch of people who know the meaning of the word cute. During one game, I noticed that Ann had a blue ribbon tied on her ponytail, and it dawned on me that every girl on the

16

team had an identical bow. Somehow I can't picture the Celtics gathered in the locker room of the Boston Garden agreeing to wear the same color sweatbands.

No, what has struck me, amazed me and made me hold my breath in wonder and in hope is both the ideal of sport and the reality of a young girl not afraid to do her best.

I watch her bringing the ball up the court. We yell encouragement from the stands, though I know she doesn't hear us. Her face is red with exertion, and her body is concentrated on the task. She dribbles, draws the defense to her, passes, runs. A teammate passes the ball back to her. They've beaten the press. She heads toward the hoop. Her father watches her, her sisters watch her, I watch her. And I think, drive, Ann, drive.

Questions for Study and Discussion

1. Why was Whitney surprised that Ann became interested in sports? What social attitudes worked against Ann's becoming a good athlete? How does the author feel about these attitudes? How do you feel about these attitudes?

2. In paragraph 7 Whitney says, "ideals of femininity are still, quiet, cool females in ads whose vacantness passes for sophistication." Do you agree? Find some ads to support your answer.

3. Why does the author wish she had been told to "go for it" when she was younger? How does Whitney believe this would have changed her life? Do you agree with her reasoning?

4. Would you describe Whitney's tone (Glossary: *Tone*) as angry, frustrated, resigned or something else? Is her tone different at different points in the essay or does it remain consistent? Cite examples of her diction (Glossary: *Diction*) to support your answer.

5. Whitney mixes short, dramatic sentences with longer, more detailed ones. Choose several instances of this and comment on the possible reasons for this strategy. (Glossary: *Emphasis*)

Vocabulary

Refer to your dictionary to define the following words as they are used in this selection. Then use each word in a sentence of your own.

marginally (1)   admonish (7)
titter (1)   paroxysm (9)
bode (2)   unctuous (10)
bedraggled (3)   machinations (12)
scathing (6)   wrought (13)
wane (6)

Suggested Writing Assignments

1. Read or reread Langston Hughes essay, "Salvation" (pp. 155–57). Write an essay in which you compare and contrast Whitney's variety of sentence structures with that of Hughes.

2. Without changing the meaning, rewrite the following paragraph using a variety of sentence structures to add interest and emphasis. When you have finished, add another paragraph to finish the idea, again paying attention to sentence structure.

> The score was 8 to 10. Allied was down. Allied was at bat. It was the bottom of the seventh inning. The bases were loaded. There were two strikes. There were two outs. Ronson's pitcher was throwing all strikes. Sweat was pouring from the batter's forehead. It was hot. The batter was nervous. This game determined the state champs. The state champs would go to the national tournament. The national tournament was in Washington, D.C. The batter took some practice swings. The batter pivoted the ball of her foot into the ground. The dirt was dusty. Dust flew into the umpire's face. The batter was ready. The batter nodded to the pitcher.

A BROTHER'S MURDER

Brent Staples

*Brent Staples was born in 1951 in Chester, Penn-
sylvania, an industrial city southwest of Philadelphia. He studied at Widener University in Chester
and at the University of Chicago. Formerly a teacher,
Staples began his newspaper career as a reporter for
the* Chicago Sun-Times. *He later became an editor
of the* New York Times Book Review *and now
serves as a member of the editorial board of the*
New York Times. *He is the author of* Parallel Time:
Growing Up in Black and White *(1994). The following essay first appeared in the* New York Times
Magazine. *In it Staples mourns the tragic death of
his younger brother, a victim of the male machismo
that stalks its prey in the African American ghettos
of large cities. Listen to Staples's sentences as you
read this essay. Notice how they add interest, readability, and drama to the story he is telling.*

It has been more than two years since my telephone rang with 1
the news that my younger brother Blake—just twenty-two
years old—had been murdered. The young man who killed him
was only twenty-four. Wearing a ski mask, he emerged from a car,
fired six times at close range with a massive .44 Magnum, then
fled. The two had once been inseparable friends. A senseless
rivalry—beginning, I think, with an argument over a girlfriend—
escalated from posturing, to threats, to violence, to murder. The
way the two were living, death could have come to either of them
from anywhere. In fact, the assailant had already survived multiple gunshot wounds from an accident much like the one in
which my brother lost his life.

As I wept for Blake I felt wrenched backward into events and 2
circumstances that had seemed light-years gone. Though a decade apart, we both were raised in Chester, Pennsylvania, an
angry, heavily black, heavily poor, industrial city southwest of

150

Philadelphia. There, in the 1960s, I was introduced to mortality, not by the old and failing, but by beautiful young men who lay wrecked after sudden explosions of violence. The first, I remembered from my fourteenth year—Johnny, brash lover of fast cars, stabbed to death two doors from my house in a fight over a pool game. The next year, my teenage cousin, Wesley, whom I loved very much, was shot dead. The summers blur. Milton, an angry young neighbor, shot a crosstown rival, wounding him badly. William, another teenage neighbor, took a shotgun blast to the shoulder in some urban drama and displayed his bandages proudly. His brother, Leonard, severely beaten, lost an eye and donned a black patch. It went on.

I recall not long before I left for college, two local Vietnam veterans—one from the Marines, one from the Army—arguing fiercely, nearly at blows about which outfit had done the most in the war. The most killing, they meant. Not much later, I read a magazine article that set that dispute in a context. In the story, a noncommissioned officer—a sergeant, I believe—said he would pass up any number of affluent, suburban-born recruits to get hard-core soldiers from the inner city. They jumped into the rice paddies with "their manhood on their sleeves," I believe he said. These two items—the veterans arguing and the sergeant's words—still characterize for me the circumstances under which black men in their teens and twenties kill one another with such frequency. With a touchy paranoia born of living battered lives, they are desperate to be *real* men. Killing is only machismo taken to the extreme. Incursions to be punished by death were many and minor, and they remain so: they include stepping on the wrong toe, literally; cheating in a drug deal; simply saying "I dare you" to someone holding a gun; crossing territorial lines in a gang dispute. My brother grew up to wear his manhood on his sleeve. And when he died, he was in that group—black, male and in its teens and early twenties—that is far and away the most likely to murder or be murdered.

I left the East Coast after college, spent the mid- and late 1970s in Chicago as a graduate student, taught for a time, then became a journalist. Within ten years of leaving my hometown, I was over-educated and "upwardly mobile," ensconced on a quiet, tree-lined street where voices raised in anger were scarcely ever heard. The telephone, like some grim umbilical, kept me connected to the old world with news of deaths, imprisonings and misfortune. I felt emotionally beaten up. Perhaps to protect myself, I added a psychological dimension to the physical distance I had already achieved. I rarely visited my hometown. I shut it out.

As I fled the past, so Blake embraced it. On Christmas of 1983, 5 I traveled from Chicago to a black section of Roanoke, Virginia, where he then lived. The desolate public housing projects, the hopeless, idle young men crashing against one another—these reminded me of the embittered town we'd grown up in. It was a place where once I would have been comfortable, or at least sure of myself. Now, hearing of my brother's forays into crime, his scrapes with police and street thugs, I was scared, unsteady on foreign terrain.

I saw that Blake's romance with the street life and the hustler 6 image had flowered dangerously. One evening that late December, standing in some Roanoke dive among drug dealers and grim, hair-trigger losers, I told him I feared for his life. He had affected the image of the tough he wanted to be. But behind the dark glasses and the swagger, I glimpsed the baby-faced toddler I'd once watched over. I nearly wept. I wanted desperately for him to live. The young think themselves immortal, and a dangerous light shone in his eyes as he spoke laughingly of making fools of the policemen who had raided his apartment looking for drugs. He cried out as I took his right hand. A line of stitches lay between the thumb and index finger. Kickback from a shotgun, he explained, nothing serious. Gunplay had become part of his life.

I lacked the language simply to say: Thousands have lived this 7 for you and died. I fought the urge to lift him bodily and shake him. This place and the way you are living smells of death to me, I said. Take some time away, I said. Let's go downtown tomorrow and buy a plane ticket anywhere, take a bus trip, anything to get away and cool things off. He took my alarm casually. We arranged to meet the following night—an appointment he would not keep. We embraced as though through glass. I drove away.

As I stood in my apartment in Chicago holding the receiver that 8 evening in February 1984, I felt as though part of my soul had been cut away. I questioned myself then, and I still do. Did I not reach back soon enough or earnestly enough for him? For weeks I awoke crying from a recurrent dream in which I chased him, urgently trying to get him to read a document I had, as though reading it would protect him from what had happened in waking life. His eyes shining like black diamonds, he smiled and danced just beyond my grasp. When I reached for him, I caught only the space where he had been.

Questions for Study and Discussion

1. Staples opens with a jarring account of his brother's death. How effective is this opening? (Glossary: *Beginnings and Endings*) How well does it set the tone of the essay? (Glossary: *Tone*)

2. When and where does Staples first encounter "mortality"? What is unusual about his encounter?

3. In paragraph 3, Staples relates the story of the Vietnam veterans and the sergeant. Why does he use these incidents to illustrate his point? How helpful are they to an understanding of his point? What does Staples mean when he writes that "killing is only machismo taken to the extreme"?

4. Staples is almost poetic in his use of language to capture feelings. Cite examples of his diction (Glossary: *Diction*), and discuss how his choice of words heightens the emotionalism and drama of his essay.

5. Staples alternates sentences of great length and detail with short sentences of five words or less. What is the effect of each kind of sentence? What is the effect of juxtaposing them?

6. Staples goes to great pains to contrast his life and that of his brother. What are some of the points of contrast? (Glossary: *Comparison and Contrast*) What does it reveal about his attitude toward his brother's fate?

7. What is the meaning of Staples's last line? Who or what does Staples "blame" for his brother's death?

Vocabulary

Refer to your dictionary to define the following words as they are used in this selection. Then use each word in a sentence of your own.

escalated (1)   umbilical (4)
affluent (3)   forays (5)
machismo (3)   hustler (6)
incursions (3)   swagger (6)
ensconced (4)

Suggested Writing Assignments

1. Staples suggests that his getting out of the ghetto was his salvation. However, for many poor African Americans living in the inner city, the solution is not so simple. Taking your cues from circumstances Staples mentions in his essay and your own knowledge of the problems facing the inner cities, write an essay in which you discuss what society and the law can do to help young men like Blake.

2. Just what is "machismo" and how much do you think it contributed to Blake's death? Was it only harmful when added to the other conditions of life in the ghetto? Is it less harmful and perhaps even desirable in any other situation you can think of? Write an essay in which you define "machismo" and discuss its positive and/or negative effects within American society today.

SALVATION

Langston Hughes

Born in Joplin, Missouri, Langston Hughes (1902–1967), an important figure in the black cultural movement of the 1920s known as the Harlem Renaissance, wrote poetry, fiction, and plays, and contributed a column to the New York Post. *He is best known for* The Weary Blues *(1926) and other books of poetry that express his racial pride, his familiarity with African American traditions, and his understanding of jazz rhythms. As you read the following selection from his autobiography* The Big Sea *(1940), notice how Hughes varies the types of sentences he uses as well as their length for the sake of emphasis.*

I was saved from sin when I was going on thirteen. But not really saved. It happened like this. There was a big revival at my Auntie Reed's church. Every night for weeks there had been much preaching, singing, praying, and shouting, and some very hardened sinners had been brought to Christ, and the membership of the church had grown by leaps and bounds. Then just before the revival ended, they held a special meeting for children, "to bring the young lambs to the fold." My aunt spoke of it for days ahead. That night I was escorted to the front row and placed on the mourners' bench with all the other young sinners, who had not yet been brought to Jesus.

My aunt told me that when you were saved you saw a light, and something happened to you inside! And Jesus came into your life! And God was with you from then on! She said you could see and hear and feel Jesus in your soul. I believed her. I have heard a great many old people say the same thing and it seemed to me they ought to know. So I sat there calmly in the hot, crowded church, waiting for Jesus to come to me.

The preacher preached a wonderful rhythmical sermon, all moans and shouts and lonely cries and dire pictures of hell, and then he sang a song about the ninety and nine safe in the fold, but one little lamb was left out in the cold. Then he said: "Won't you come? Won't you come to Jesus? Young lambs, won't you come?" And he held out his arms to all us young sinners there on the mourners' bench. And the little girls cried. And some of them jumped up and went to Jesus right away. But most of us just sat there.

A great many old people came and knelt around us and prayed,   4
old women with jet-black faces and braided hair, old men with work-gnarled hands. And the church sang a song about the lower lights are burning, some poor sinners to be saved. And the whole building rocked with prayer and song.

Still I kept waiting to *see* Jesus.   5

Finally all the young people had gone to the altar and were   6
saved, but one boy and me. He was a rounder's son named Westley. Westley and I were surrounded by sisters and deacons praying. It was very hot in the church, and getting late now. Finally Westley said to me in a whisper: "God damn! I'm tired o' sitting here. Let's get up and be saved." So he got up and was saved.

Then I was left all alone on the mourners' bench. My aunt came   7
and knelt at my knees and cried, while prayers and songs swirled all around me in the little church. The whole congregation prayed for me alone, in a mighty wail of moans and voices. And I kept waiting serenely for Jesus, waiting, waiting—but he didn't come. I wanted to see him, but nothing happened to me. Nothing! I wanted something to happen to me, but nothing happened.

I heard the songs and the minister saying: "Why don't you   8
come? My dear child, why don't you come to Jesus? Jesus is waiting for you. He wants you. Why don't you come? Sister Reed, what is this child's name?"

"Langston," my aunt sobbed.   9

"Langston, why don't you come? Why don't you come and be   10
saved? Oh, Lamb of God! Why don't you come?"

Now it was really getting late. I began to be ashamed of myself,   11
holding everything up so long. I began to wonder what God thought about Westley, who certainly hadn't seen Jesus either, but who was now sitting proudly on the platform, swinging his knick-erbockered legs and grinning down at me, surrounded by deacons and old women on their knees praying. God had not struck Westley dead for taking his name in vain or for lying in the

temple. So I decided that maybe to save further trouble, I'd better lie, too, and say that Jesus had come, and get up and be saved.

So I got up. 12

Suddenly the whole room broke into a sea of shouting, as they 13 saw me rise. Waves of rejoicing swept the place. Women leaped in the air. My aunt threw her arms around me. The minister took me by the hand and led me to the platform.

When things quieted down, in a hushed silence, punctuated by 14 a few ecstatic "Amens," all the new young lambs were blessed in the name of God. Then joyous singing filled the room.

That night, for the last time in my life but one—for I was a big 15 boy twelve years old—I cried. I cried, in bed alone, and couldn't stop. I buried my head under the quilts, but my aunt heard me. She woke up and told my uncle I was crying because the Holy Ghost had come into my life, and because I had seen Jesus. But I was really crying because I couldn't bear to tell her that I had lied, that I had deceived everybody in the church, that I hadn't seen Jesus, and that now I didn't believe there was a Jesus any more, since he didn't come to help me.

Questions for Study and Discussion

1. What is salvation? Is it important to young Langston Hughes that he be saved? Why is it important to Langston's aunt that he be saved?

2. Why does young Langston expect to be saved at the revival meeting? Once the children are in church, what appeals are made to them to encourage them to seek salvation?

3. Why does young Langston cry on the night of his being "saved"? Why is the story of his being saved so ironic? (Glossary: *Irony*)

4. What would be gained or lost if the essay began with the first two sentences combined as follows: "I was saved from sin when I was going on thirteen, but I was not really saved"?

5. Identify the coordinating conjunctions in paragraph 3. Rewrite the paragraph without them. Compare your para-

graph with the original, and explain what Hughes gains by using coordinating conjunctions. (Glossary: *Coordination*)

6. Identify the subordinating conjunctions in paragraph 15. What is it about the ideas in this last paragraph that makes it necessary for Hughes to use these subordinating conjunctions?

7. How does Hughes's choice of words, or diction, help to establish a realistic atmosphere for a religious revival meeting? (Glossary: *Diction*)

Vocabulary

Refer to your dictionary to define the following words as they are used in this selection. Then use each word in a sentence of your own.

dire (3)   punctuated (14)
gnarled (4)   ecstatic (14)
vain (11)

Suggested Writing Assignments

1. Like the young Langston Hughes, we sometimes find ourselves in situations in which, for the sake of conformity, we do things we do not believe in. Consider one such experience you have had, and write an essay about it. What is it about human nature that makes us occasionally act in ways that contradict our inner feelings? As you write, pay particular attention to your sentence variety.

2. Reread the introduction to this chapter. Then review one of the essays that you have written, paying particular attention to sentence structure. Recast sentences as necessary in order to make your writing more interesting and effective.

II

THE
LANGUAGE
OF THE
ESSAY

8

DICTION AND TONE

Diction

Diction refers to a writer's choice and use of words. Good diction is precise and appropriate—the words mean exactly what the writer intends, and the words are well suited to the writer's subject, purpose, and intended audience.

For careful writers it is not enough merely to come close to saying what they want to say; they select words that convey their exact meaning. Perhaps Mark Twain put this best when he said, "The difference between the right word and the almost right word is the difference between lightning and the lightning bug." Inaccurate, imprecise, or inappropriate diction not only fails to convey the writer's intended meaning but also may cause confusion and misunderstanding for the reader.

Connotation and Denotation

Both connotation and denotation refer to the meanings of words. Denotation is the dictionary meaning of a word, the literal meaning. Connotative meanings are the associations or emotional overtones that words have acquired gradually. For example, the word *home* denotes a place where someone lives, but it connotes warmth, security, family, comfort, affection, and other more private thoughts and images. The word *residence* also denotes a place where someone lives, but its connotations are colder and more formal.

Many words in English have synonyms, words with very similar denotations—for example, *mob, crowd, multitude,* and *bunch.* Deciding which to use depends largely on the connotations that each synonym has and the context in which the word is to be used. For example, you might say, "There was a crowd at the lecture," but not "There was a mob at the lecture." Good writers are sensitive to both the denotations and the connotations of words.

Abstract and Concrete Words

Abstract words name ideas, conditions, emotions—things nobody can touch, see, or hear. Some abstract words are *love, wisdom, cowardice, beauty, fear,* and *liberty.* People often disagree about abstract things. You may find a forest beautiful, while someone else might find it frightening, and neither of you would be wrong. Beauty and fear are abstract ideas; they exist in your mind, not in the forest along with the trees and the owls. Concrete words refer to things we can touch, see, hear, smell, and taste, such as *sandpaper, soda, birch trees, smog, cow, sailboat, rocking chair,* and *pancake.* If you disagree with someone on a concrete issue—say, you claim that the forest is mostly birch trees, while the other person says it is mostly pine—only one of you can be right, and both of you can be wrong; what kinds of trees grow in the forest is a concrete fact, not an abstract idea.

Good writing balances ideas and facts, and it also balances abstract and concrete diction. If the writing is too abstract, with too few concrete facts and details, it will be unconvincing and tiresome. If the writing is too concrete, devoid of ideas and emotions, it can seem pointless and dry.

General and Specific Words

General and *specific* do not necessarily refer to opposites. The same word can often be either general or specific, depending on the context: *Dessert* is more specific than *food,* but more general than *chocolate cream pie.* Being very specific is like being concrete: *chocolate cream pie* is something you can see and taste. Being general, on the other hand, is like being abstract. *Food, dessert,* and even *pie* are general classes of things that bring no particular taste or image to mind.

Good writing moves back and forth from the general to the specific. Without specific words, generalities can be unconvincing and even confusing: the writer's idea of "good food" may be very different from the reader's. But writing that does not relate specifics to each other by generalization often lacks focus and direction.

Clichés

Some words, phrases, and expressions have become trite through overuse. Let's assume your roommate has just returned from an evening out. You ask her "How was the concert?" She responds, "The concert was okay, but they had us *packed in* there *like sardines*. How was your evening?" And you reply, "Well, I finished my term paper, but the noise here is enough to *drive me crazy*. The dorm is a real *zoo*." At one time the italicized expressions were vivid and colorful, but through constant use they have grown stale and ineffective. The experienced writer always tries to avoid such clichés as *believe it or not, doomed to failure, hit the spot, let's face it, sneaking suspicion, step in the right direction,* and *went to great lengths.*

Jargon

Jargon, or technical language, is the special vocabulary of a trade or profession. Writers who use jargon do so with an awareness of their audience. If their audience is a group of coworkers or professionals, jargon may be used freely. If the audience is a more general one, jargon should be used sparingly and carefully so that readers can understand it. Jargon becomes inappropriate when it is overused, used out of context, or used pretentiously. For example, computer terms such as *input, output,* and *feedback* are sometimes used in place of *contribution, result,* and *response* in other fields, especially in business. If you think about it, the terms suggest that people are machines, receiving and processing information according to a program imposed by someone else.

Formal and Informal Diction

Diction is appropriate when it suits the occasion for which it is intended. If the situation is informal—a friendly letter, for example—the writing may be colloquial; that is, its words may be chosen to suggest the way people talk with each other. If, on the other hand, the situation is formal—a term paper or a research report, for example—then the words should reflect this formality. Informal writing tends to be characterized by slang, contractions, references to the reader, and concrete nouns. Formal writing tends to be impersonal, abstract, and free of contractions and references to the reader. Formal writing and informal writing are, of course, the extremes. Most writing falls between these two extremes and is a blend of those formal and informal elements that best fit the context.

Tone

Tone is the attitude a writer takes toward the subject and the audience. The tone may be friendly or hostile, serious or humorous, intimate or distant, enthusiastic or skeptical.

As you read the following paragraphs, notice how each writer has created a different tone and how that tone is supported by the diction—the writer's particular choice and use of words.

Nostalgic

> My generation is special because of what we missed rather than what we got, because in a certain sense we are the first and the last. The first to take technology for granted. (What was a space shot to us, except an hour cut from Social Studies to gather before a TV in the gym as Cape Canaveral counted down?) The first to grow up with TV. My sister was 8 when we got our set, so to her it seemed magic and always somewhat foreign. She had known books already and would never really replace them. But for me, the TV set was, like the kitchen sink and the telephone, a fact of life.
>
> Joyce Maynard, "An 18-Year-Old Looks Back on Life"

Angry

> Cans. Beer cans. Glinting on the verges of a million miles of roadways, lying in scrub, grass, dirt, leaves, sand, mud, but never hidden. Piels, Rheingold, Ballantine, Schaefer, Schlitz, shining in the sun or picked by moon or the beams of headlights at night; washed by rain or flattened by wheels, but never dulled, never buried, never destroyed. Here is the mark of savages, the testament of wasters, the stain of prosperity.
>
> Marya Mannes, "Wasteland"

Humorous

> In perpetrating a revolution, there are two requirements: someone or something to revolt against and someone to

actually show up and do the revolting. Dress is usually casual and both parties may be flexible about time and place but if either faction fails to attend the whole enterprise is likely to come off badly. In the Chinese Revolution of 1650 neither party showed up and the deposit on the hall was forfeited.

Woody Allen, "A Brief, Yet Helpful Guide to Civil Disobedience"

Resigned

I make my living humping cargo for Seaboard World Airlines, one of the big international airlines at Kennedy Airport. They handle strictly all cargo. I was once told that one of the Rockefellers is the major stockholder for the airline, but I don't really think about that too much. I don't get paid to think. The big thing is to beat that race with the time clock every morning of your life so the airline will be happy. The worst thing a man could ever do is to make suggestions about building a better airline. They pay people $40,000 a year to come up with better ideas. It doesn't matter that these ideas never work; it's just that they get nervous when a guy from South Brooklyn or Ozone Park acts like he has a brain.

Patrick Fenton, "Confessions of a Working Stiff"

Ironic

Once upon a time there was a small, beautiful, green and graceful country called Vietnam. It needed to be saved. (In later years no one could remember exactly what it needed to be saved from, but that is another story.) For many years Vietnam was in the process of being saved by France, but the French eventually tired of their labors and left. Then America took on the job. America was well equipped for country-saving. It was the richest and most powerful nation on earth. It had, for example, nuclear explosives on hand and ready to use equal to six tons of TNT for every man, woman, and child in the world. It had huge and very efficient factories, brilliant and dedicated scientists, and most (but not everybody) would agree, it had good intentions. Sadly, America had one fatal flaw—its inhabitants were in love with technology and thought it could do no wrong. A visitor to America during the time of this story would probably have guessed its outcome after seeing how its inhabitants were treating their own country. The air was mostly foul, the water putrid, and most of the land was either covered with concrete or garbage. But

Americans were never much on introspection, and they didn't foresee the result of their loving embrace on the small country. They set out to save Vietnam with the same enthusiasm and determination their forefathers had displayed in conquering the frontier.

The Sierra Club, "A Fable for Our Times"

The diction and tone of an essay are subtle forces, but they exert a tremendous influence on readers. They are instrumental in determining how we will feel while reading the essay and what attitude we will have toward its argument or the points that it makes. Of course, readers react in a variety of ways. An essay written informally but with a largely angry tone may make one reader defensive and unsympathetic; another may feel the author is being unusually honest and courageous, and may admire this and feel moved by it. Either way, the diction and tone of the piece have made a strong emotional impression. As you read the essays in this chapter and throughout this book, see if you can analyze how the word choice (diction) and tone are shaping your reactions.

On Being 17, Bright, and Unable to Read

David Raymond

When the following article appeared in the New York Times *in 1976, David Raymond was a high-school student in Connecticut. In his essay he poignantly discusses his great difficulty in reading because of dyslexia and the many problems he experienced in school as a result. As you read, pay attention to the naturalness of the author's diction.*

One day a substitute teacher picked me to read aloud from the textbook. When I told her "No, thank you," she came unhinged. She thought I was acting smart, and told me so. I kept calm, and that got her madder and madder. We must have spent 10 minutes trying to solve the problem, and finally she got so red in the face I thought she'd blow up. She told me she'd see me after class.

Maybe someone like me was a new thing for that teacher. But she wasn't new to me. I've been through scenes like that all my life. You see, even though I'm 17 and a junior in high school, I can't read because I have dyslexia. I'm told I read "at a fourth-grade level," but from where I sit, that's not reading. You can't know what that means unless you've been there. It's not easy to tell how it feels when you can't read your homework assignments or the newspaper or a menu in a restaurant or even notes from your own friends.

My family began to suspect I was having problems almost from the first day I started school. My father says my early years in school were the worst years of his life. They weren't so good for me, either. As I look back on it now, I can't find the words to express how bad it really was. I wanted to die. I'd come home from school screaming, "I'm dumb. I'm dumb—I wish I were dead!"

I guess I couldn't read anything at all then—not even my own name—and they tell me I didn't talk as good as other kids. But what I remember about those days is that I couldn't throw a ball where it was supposed to go, I couldn't learn to swim, and I wouldn't learn to ride a bike, because no matter what anyone told me, I knew I'd fail.

Sometimes my teachers would try to be encouraging. When I couldn't read the words on the board they'd say, "Come on, David, you know that word." Only I didn't. And it was embarrassing. I just felt dumb. And dumb was how the kids treated me. They'd make fun of me every chance they got, asking me to spell "cat" or something like that. Even if I knew how to spell it, I wouldn't; they'd only give me another word. Anyway, it was awful, because more than anything I wanted friends. On my birthday when I blew out the candles I didn't wish I could learn to read; what I wished for was that the kids would like me.

With the bad reports coming from school, and with me moaning about wanting to die and how everybody hated me, my parents began looking for help. That's when the testing started. The school tested me, the child-guidance center tested me, private psychiatrists tested me. Everybody knew something was wrong—especially me.

It didn't help much when they stuck a fancy name onto it. I couldn't pronounce it then—I was only in second grade—and I was ashamed to talk about it. Now it rolls off my tongue, because I've been living with it for a lot of years—dyslexia.

All through elementary school it wasn't easy. I was always having to do things that were "different," things the other kids didn't have to do. I had to go to a child psychiatrist, for instance.

One summer my family forced me to go to a camp for children with reading problems. I hated the idea, but the camp turned out pretty good, and I had a good time. I met a lot of kids who couldn't read and somehow that helped. The director of the camp said I had a higher I.Q. than 90 percent of the population. I didn't believe him.

About the worst thing I had to do in fifth and sixth grade was go to a special education class in another school in our town. A bus picked me up, and I didn't like that at all. The bus also picked up emotionally disturbed kids and retarded kids. It was like going to a school for the retarded. I always worried that someone I knew would see me on that bus. It was a relief to go to the regular junior high school.

Life began to change a little for me then, because I began to feel 11
better about myself. I found the teachers cared; they had meetings about me and I worked harder for them for a while. I began
to work on the potter's wheel, making vases and pots that the
teachers said were pretty good. Also, I got a letter for being on the
track team. I could always run pretty fast.

At high school the teachers are good and everyone is trying to 12
help me. I've gotten honors some marking periods and I've won a
letter on the cross-country team. Next quarter I think the school
might hold a show of my pottery. I've got some friends. But there
are still some embarrassing times. For instance, every time there
is writing in the class, I get up and go to the special education
room. Kids ask me where I go all the time. Sometimes I say, "to
Mars."

Homework is a real problem. During free periods in school I go 13
into the special ed room and staff members read assignments to
me. When I get home my mother reads to me. Sometimes she
reads an assignment into a tape recorder, and then I go into my
room and listen to it. If we have a novel or something like that to
read, she reads it out loud to me. Then I sit down with her and we
do the assignment. She'll write, while I talk my answers to her.
Lately I've taken to dictating into a tape recorder, and then someone—my father, a private tutor or my mother—types up what I've
dictated. Whatever homework I do takes someone else's time, too.
That makes me feel bad.

We had a big meeting in school the other day—eight of us, four 14
from the guidance department, my private tutor, my parents and
me. The subject was me. I said I wanted to go to college, and they
told me about colleges that have facilities and staff to handle
people like me. That's nice to hear.

As for what happens after college, I don't know and I'm worried 15
about that. How can I make a living if I can't read? Who will hire
me? How will I fill out the application form? The only thing that
gives me any courage is the fact that I've learned about well-
known people who couldn't read or had other problems and still
made it. Like Albert Einstein, who didn't talk until he was 4 and
flunked math. Like Leonardo da Vinci, who everyone seems to
think had dyslexia.

I've told this story because maybe some teacher will read it 16
and go easy on a kid in the classroom who has what I've got. Or,

maybe some parent will stop nagging his kid, and stop calling him lazy. Maybe he's not lazy or dumb. Maybe he just can't read and doesn't know what's wrong. Maybe he's scared, like I was.

Questions for Study and Discussion

1. What is dyslexia? Is it essential for an understanding of the essay that we know more about dyslexia than Raymond tells us? Explain.
2. What does Raymond say his purpose is in telling his story?
3. What does Raymond's story tell us about the importance of our early childhood experiences, especially within our educational system?
4. Raymond uses many colloquial and idiomatic expressions, such as "she got so red in the face I thought she'd blow up" and "she came unhinged" (1). Identify other examples of such diction and tell how they affect the essay.
5. In the context of the essay, comment on the appropriateness of each of the following possible choices of diction. Which word is better in each case? Why?
   a. *selected* for *picked* (1)
   b. *experience* for *thing* (2)
   c. *speak as well* for *talk as good* (4)
   d. *negative* for *bad* (6)
   e. *important* for *big* (14)
   f. *failed* for *flunked* (15)
   g. *frightened* for *scared* (16)
6. How would you describe Raymond's tone in this essay?

Vocabulary

Refer to your dictionary to define the following words as they are used in this selection. Then use each word in a sentence of your own.

dyslexia (2)   psychiatrists (6)

Suggested Writing Assignments

1. Imagine that you are away at school. Recently you were caught in a radar speed trap—you were going 70 miles per hour in a 55-mile-per-hour zone—and have just lost your license; you will not be able to go home this coming weekend, as you had planned. Write two letters in which you explain why you will not be able to go home, one to your parents and the other to your best friend. Your audience is different in each case, so be sure to choose your diction accordingly.

2. Select an essay you have already completed in this course, and rewrite it in a different tone. If the essay was originally formal or serious, lighten it so that it is now informal and humorous. Pay special attention to diction. Actually think in terms of a different reader as your audience—not your instructor but perhaps your classmates, your clergyman, your sister, or the state environmental protection board. Reshape your essay as necessary.

THE FLIGHT OF THE EAGLES

N. Scott Momaday

Celebrated writer and educator N. Scott Momaday is a Kiowa Indian. He has based much of his writing on his Indian ancestry and has written several books including The Way to Rainy Mountain *(1976),* The Ancient Child: A Novel *(1989),* In the Presence of the Sun: Stories and Poems, 1961–1991 *(1992), and* House Made of Dawn *(1969) for which he won the Pulitzer Prize. In the following selection, taken from* House Made of Dawn, *Momaday closely observes the mating flight of golden eagles.*

They were golden eagles, a male and a female, in their mating flight. They were cavorting, spinning and spiraling on the cold, clear columns of air, and they were beautiful. They swooped and hovered, leaning on the air, and swung close together, feinting and screaming with delight. The female was full-grown, and the span of her broad wings was greater than any man's height. There was a fine flourish to her motion; she was deceptively, incredibly fast, and her pivots and wheels were wide and full-blown. But her great weight was streamlined and perfectly controlled. She carried a rattlesnake; it hung shining from her feet, limp and curving out in the trail of her flight. Suddenly her wings and tail fanned, catching full on the wind, and for an instant she was still, widespread and spectral in the blue, while her mate flared past and away, turning around in the distance to look for her. Then she began to beat upward at an angle from the rim until she was small in the sky, and she let go of the snake. It fell slowly, writhing and rolling, floating out like a bit of silver thread against the wide backdrop of the land. She held still above, buoyed up on the cold current, her crop and hackles gleaming like copper in the sun. The male swerved and sailed. He was younger than she and a little more than half as large. He was quicker, tighter in his moves. He let the carrion drift by; then suddenly he gathered himself and stooped, sliding down in a blur of motion to the strike. He hit the snake in the head, with not the slightest deflection of his course or speed, cracking its long body like a whip. Then he rolled and swung upward in a great pendulum arc, riding out his momentum. At the top of his glide he let go of the snake in turn, but the female did not go for it. Instead she soared out over the plain, nearly out of sight, like a mote receding into the haze of the far mountain. The male followed.

Questions for Study and Discussion

1. What are the differences between the two eagles as Momaday describes them?
2. What role does the rattlesnake play in this description?
3. In describing the mating flight of the golden eagles, Momaday has tried to capture their actions accurately. Identify the strong verbs that he uses, and discuss how these verbs enhance his description. (Glossary: *Verb*)
4. Identify several examples of Momaday's use of concrete and specific diction. What effect does his language have on you?
5. Identify the figures of speech that Momaday uses in this selection and tell how you think each one functions in the essay. (Glossary: *Figures of Speech*)

Vocabulary

Refer to your dictionary to define the following words as they are used in this selection. Then use each word in a sentence of your own.

cavorting	carrion
feinting	mote
spectral	

Suggested Writing Assignments

1. Select one of the following activities as the subject for a brief descriptive essay. Be sure to use strong verbs, as Momaday has done, in order to describe the action accurately and vividly.

   the movements of a dancer
   the actions of a kite
   the antics of a pet
   a traffic jam
   a violent storm

2. Accounts of natural events often rely on scientific data and are frequently presented in the third person. Carefully observe some natural event (fire, hurricane, birth of an animal, bird migration, etc.), and note significant details and facts about that occurrence. Then, using very carefully chosen diction, write an account of the event.

LA VIDA LOCA (THE CRAZY LIFE): TWO GENERATIONS OF GANG MEMBERS

Luis J. Rodriguez

Luis Rodriguez managed to walk away from his
vida loca in the gangs. He now has three books in
print: Poems Across the Pavement *(1991),* The
Concrete River *(1991), and the autobiographical*
Always Running: Gang Days in L.A. *(1993). In the*
following selection, he uses vivid language to de-
scribe his gang experiences and the anguish he feels
when his son repeats some of his own mistakes.

L ate winter Chicago, 1991: The once-white snow that fell in   1
December has turned into a dark scum, an admixture of salt,
car oil and decay; icicles hang from rooftops and window sills like
the whiskers of old men. The bone-chilling temperatures force
my family to stay inside a one-and-a-half bedroom apartment in
a three-flat building in Humboldt Park. My third wife, Trini, our
child Ruben and my 15-year-old son Ramiro from a previous marriage huddle around the television set. Tensions build up like a
fever.

One evening, words of anger bounce back and forth between   2
the walls of our gray-stone flat. Two-year-old Ruben, confused and
afraid, crawls up to my leg and hugs it. Trini and I had jumped
on Ramiro's case for coming in late following weeks of trouble:
Ramiro had joined the Insane Campbell Boys, a group of Puerto
Rican and Mexican youth allied with the Spanish Cobras and
Dragons.

Within moments, Ramiro runs out of the house, entering the   3
freezing Chicago night. I go after him, sprinting down the gang-
way leading to a debris-strewn alley. I see Ramiro's fleeing figure,
his breath rising in quickly dissipating clouds.

I follow him toward Division Street, the neighborhood's main   4
drag. People yell out of windows and doorways: "Que pasa,

hombre?"* This is not an unfamiliar sight—a father or mother chasing some child down the street.

Watching my son's escape, it is as though he enters the waters of a distant time, back to my youth, back to when I ran, to when I jumped over fences, fleeing *vato locos*,** the police or my own shadow, in some drug-induced hysteria.

As Ramiro speeds off, I see my body enter the mouth of darkness, my breath cut the frigid flesh of night—my voice crack open the night sky.

We are a second-generation gang family. I was involved in gangs in Los Angeles in the late 1960s and early 1970s. When I was 2 years old, in 1956, my family emigrated from Mexico to Watts. I spent my teen years in a barrio called Las Lomas, east of Los Angeles.

I was arrested on charges ranging from theft, assaulting an officer to attempted murder. As a teenager, I did some time. I began using drugs at age 12—including pills, weed and heroin. I had a near-death experience at 16 from sniffing toxic spray. After being kicked out of three high schools, I dropped out at 15.

By the time I turned 18, some 25 friends had been killed by rival gangs, the police, overdoses, car crashes and suicides.

Three years ago, I brought Ramiro to Chicago to escape the violence. If I barely survived all this, it appeared unlikely my son would make it. But in Chicago, we found kindred conditions.

I had to cut Ramiro's bloodline to the street before it became too late. I had to begin the long, intense struggle to save his life from the gathering storm of street violence—some 20 years after I had sneaked out of the 'hood in the dark of night and removed myself from the death fires of *La Vida Loca*.

What to do with those whom society cannot accommodate? Criminalize them. Outlaw their actions and creations. Declare them the enemy, then wage war. Emphasize the differences—the shade of skin, the accent or manner of clothes. Like the scapegoat of the Bible, place society's ills on them, then "stone them" in absolution. It's convenient, it's logical.

It doesn't work.

---

*"What's happening, man?"

**Crazy guys

Gangs are not alien powers. They begin as unstructured group- 14
ings, our children who desire the same as any young person. Respect. A sense of belonging. Protection. This is no different than
the YMCA, Little League or the Boy Scouts. It wasn't any more
than what I wanted.

When I entered 109th Street School in Watts, I spoke perfect 15
Spanish. But teachers punished me for speaking it on the play-
ground. I peed in my pants a few times because I was unable to
say in English that I had to go. One teacher banished me to a
corner, to build blocks for a year. I learned to be silent within the
walls of my body.

The older boys who lived on 103rd Street would take my money 16
or food. They chased me through alleys and side streets. Fear
compelled my actions.

The police, I learned years later, had a strategy: They picked up 17
as many 7-year-old boys as they could—for loitering, throwing
dirt clods, curfew—whatever. By the time a boy turned 13, and
had been popped for something like stealing, he had accumulated
a detention record, and was bound for "juvey."

One felt besieged, under intense scrutiny. If you spoke out, 18
dared to resist, you were given a "jacket" of troublemaker; I'd
tried many times to take it off, but somebody always put it back on.

Soon after my family moved to South San Gabriel, a local group, 19
Thee Mystics, rampaged through the school. They carried bats,
chains, pipes and homemade zip guns. They terrorized teachers
and students alike. I was 12.

I froze as the head stomping came dangerously my way. But I 20
was intrigued. I wanted this power. I wanted to be able to bring a
whole school to its knees. All my school life until then had been
poised against me. I was broken and shy. I wanted what Thee
Mystics had. I wanted to hurt somebody.

Police sirens broke the spell. Thee Mystics scattered in all direc- 21
tions. But they had done their damage. They had left their mark
on the school—and on me.

Gangs flourish when there's a lack of social recreation, decent 22
education or employment. Today, many young people will never
know what it is to work. They can only satisfy their needs through
collective strength—against the police, who hold the power of life
and death, against poverty, against idleness, against their impotence in society.

Without definitive solutions, it's easy to throw blame. George   23
Bush and Dan Quayle, for example, say the lack of family values
is behind our problems.

But "family" is a farce among the propertyless and disenfran-   24
chised. Too many families are wrenched apart, as even children
are forced to supplement meager incomes. At age 9, my mother
walked me to the door and, in effect, told me: Now go forth and
work.

People can't just consume; they have to sell something, includ-   25
ing their ability to work. If so-called legitimate work is unavail-
able, people will do the next best thing—sell sex or dope.

You'll find people who don't care about whom they hurt, but   26
nobody I know *wants* to sell death to their children, their neighbors, friends. If there was a viable, productive alternative, they
would stop.

At 18, I had grown tired. I felt like a war veteran with a kind of   27
post-traumatic syndrome. I had seen too many dead across the
pavement; I'd walk the aisles in the church wakes as if in a daze;
I'd often watched my mother's weary face in hospital corridors,
outside of courtrooms and cells, refusing, finally, to have anything to do with me.

In addition, I had fallen through the cracks of two languages;   28
unable to communicate well in any.

I wanted the pain to end, the self-consuming hate to wither in   29
the sunlight. With the help of those who saw potential in me, perhaps for some poetry, I got out: No more heroin, spray or pills; no
more jails; no more trying to hurt somebody until I stopped
hurting—which never seemed to pass.

There is an aspect of suicide in gang involvement for those   30
whose options have been cut off. They stand on street corners,
flash hand signs and invite the bullets. It's life as stance, as bravado. They say "You can't touch this," but "Come kill me," is the
inner cry. It's either *la torcida** or death, a warrior's path, where
even self-preservation doesn't make a play. If they murder, the
targets are the ones who look like them, walk like them, those
closest to who they are—the mirror reflection. They murder and
they are killing themselves, over and over.

---

*Deceit

Ramiro stayed away for two weeks the day he ran off. When he   31
returned, we entered him into a psychotherapy hospital. After
three months, he was back home. Since then, I've had to pull
everyone into the battle for my son. I've spent hours with teachers. I've involved therapists, social workers, the police.

We all have some responsibility: Schools, the law, parents. But   32
at the same time, there are factors beyond our control. It's not a
simple matter of "good" or "bad" values, or even of choices. If we
all had a choice, I'm convinced nobody would choose *la vida loca,*
the "insane nation"—to gangbang. But it's going to take collective
action and a plan.

Recently, Ramiro got up at a Chicago poetry event and read a   33
piece about being physically abused by a stepfather. It stopped
everyone cold. He later read the poem at Chicago's Poetry Festival. Its title: "Running Away."

The best way to deal with your children is to help construct the   34
conditions for free and healthy development of all, but it's also
true you can't be for all children if you can't be for your own.

There's a small but intense fire burning in my son. Ramiro has   35
just turned 17; he's made it thus far, but it's day by day. Now I tell
him: You have an innate value outside of your job, outside the
"jacket" imposed on you since birth. Draw on your expressive
powers.

Stop running.   36

Questions for Study and Discussion

1. Identify several words in the first paragraph that Rodriguez
   uses to describe the conditions that led to Ramiro running
   away. What do they add to the selection? Why didn't Rodriguez simply say that it was cold and his family was getting cabin fever?

2. Why had Rodriguez brought Ramiro to Chicago? How did
   the move relate to his own gang experiences?

3. What do gangs offer their members? How did Rodriguez's
   experiences make him susceptible to the lure of gang life?

4. Reread paragraphs 27–29. What is the tone of the paragraphs? (Glossary: *Tone*) How does Rodriguez's choice of
words contribute to his tone?

5. What does "You can't touch this" often mean for gang members? Why are gang murders often a reflection of gang
members' suicidal tendencies?

6. What does Rodriguez suggest as ways to solve the problem
of gang violence? Is his ending optimistic? (Glossary: *Beginnings and Endings*) Why or why not?

Vocabulary

Refer to your dictionary to define the following words as they
are used in this selection. Then use each word in a sentence of
your own.

admixture (1)	impotence (22)
dissipating (3)	disenfranchised (24)
kindred (10)	innate (35)
absolution (12)	

Suggested Writing Assignments

1. Write an essay about a group that you joined as a teenager.
It can be a sports team, a school club, scouts, a band, a
gang—any group that made you feel like a member. Why
did you first join the group? How did you feel being a
member of the group? Was it an ultimately positive or
negative experience? Why? Make sure your diction and tone
communicate the feelings you had toward the group.

2. What do your parents do for a living? Would you like to
follow one or the other in their career choice? Write an objective essay in which you consider the pros and cons of
one parent's career, and explain why you would or would
not wish to follow in his or her footsteps. Choose your
words carefully in order to maintain your objectivity.

THE FOURTH OF JULY

Audre Lorde

Audre Lorde (1934–1992) was a professor of English at Hunter College in New York City. Born in New York, she studied at Hunter College and Columbia University. Her published works include several volumes of poetry, such as Undersong: Chosen Poems Old and New *(1982); an autobiography,* Zami: A New Spelling of My Name *(1982); and essay collections such as* Sister Outsider. *The following selection is taken from her autobiography, and it eloquently communicates the tragedy of racism.*

The first time I went to Washington, D.C., was on the edge of the summer when I was supposed to stop being a child. At least that's what they said to us all at graduation from the eighth grade. My sister Phyllis graduated at the same time from high school. I don't know what she was supposed to stop being. But as graduation presents for us both, the whole family took a Fourth of July trip to Washington, D.C., the fabled and famous capital of our country.

It was the first time I'd ever been on a railroad train during the day. When I was little, and we used to go to the Connecticut shore, we always went at night on the milk train, because it was cheaper.

Preparations were in the air around our house before school was even over. We packed for a week. There were two very large suitcases that my father carried, and a box filled with food. In fact, my first trip to Washington was a mobile feast; I started eating as soon as we were comfortably ensconced in our seats, and did not stop until somewhere after Philadelphia. I remember it was Philadelphia because I was disappointed not to have passed by the Liberty Bell.

My mother had roasted two chickens and cut them up into dainty bite-size pieces. She packed slices of brown bread and butter and green pepper and carrot sticks. There were little violently

yellow iced cakes with scalloped edges called "marigolds," that
came from Cushman's Bakery. There was a spice bun and rock-
cakes from Newton's, the West Indian bakery across Lenox
Avenue from St. Mark's School, and iced tea in a wrapped may-
onnaise jar. There were sweet pickles for us and dill pickles for
my father, and peaches with the fuzz still on them, individually
wrapped to keep them from bruising. And, for neatness, there
were piles of napkins and a little tin box with a washcloth damp-
ened with rosewater and glycerine for wiping sticky mouths.

I wanted to eat in the dining car because I had read all about   5
them, but my mother reminded me for the umpteenth time that
dining car food always cost too much money and besides, you
never could tell whose hands had been playing all over that food,
nor where those same hands had been just before. My mother
never mentioned that Black people were not allowed into railroad
dining cars headed south in 1947. As usual, whatever my mother
did not like and could not change, she ignored. Perhaps it would
go away, deprived of her attention.

I learned later that Phyllis's high school senior class trip had   6
been to Washington, but the nuns had given her back her deposit
in private, explaining to her that the class, all of whom were
white, except Phyllis, would be staying in a hotel where Phyllis
"would not be happy," meaning, Daddy explained to her, also in
private, that they did not rent rooms to Negroes. "We will take
among-you to Washington, ourselves," my father had avowed,
"and not just for an overnight in some measly fleabag hotel."

American racism was a new and crushing reality that my par-   7
ents had to deal with every day of their lives once they came to
this country. They handled it as a private woe. My mother and
father believed that they could best protect their children from
the realities of race in america and the fact of american racism by
never giving them name, much less discussing their nature. We
were told we must never trust white people, but *why* was never
explained, nor the nature of their ill will. Like so many other vital
pieces of information in my childhood, I was supposed to know
without being told. It always seemed like a very strange injunction coming from my mother, who looked so much like one of
those people we were never supposed to trust. But something
always warned me not to ask my mother why she wasn't white,
and why Auntie Lillah and Auntie Etta weren't, even though they

were all that same problematic color so different from my father and me, even from my sisters, who were somewhere in-between.

In Washington, D.C., we had one large room with two double   8
beds and an extra cot for me. It was a back-street hotel that belonged to a friend of my father's who was in real estate, and I spent the whole next day after Mass squinting up at the Lincoln Memorial where Marian Anderson had sung after the D.A.R. refused to allow her to sing in their auditorium because she was Black. Or because she was "Colored," my father said as he told us the story. Except that what he probably said was "Negro," because for his times, my father was quite progressive.

I was squinting because I was in that silent agony that charac-   9
terized all of my childhood summers, from the time school let out in June to the end of July, brought about by my dilated and vulnerable eyes exposed to the summer brightness.

I viewed Julys through an agonizing corolla of dazzling white-   10
ness and I always hated the Fourth of July, even before I came to realize the travesty such a celebration was for Black people in this country.

My parents did not approve of sunglasses, nor of their expense.   11

I spent the afternoon squinting up at monuments to freedom   12
and past presidencies and democracy, and wondering why the light and heat were both so much stronger in Washington, D.C., than back home in New York City. Even the pavement on the streets was a shade lighter in color than back home.

Late that Washington afternoon my family and I walked back   13
down Pennsylvania Avenue. We were a proper caravan, mother bright and father brown, the three of us girls step-standards in-between. Moved by our historical surroundings and the heat of early evening, my father decreed yet another treat. He had a great sense of history, a flair for the quietly dramatic and the sense of specialness of an occasion and a trip.

"Shall we stop and have a little something to cool off, Lin?"   14

Two blocks away from our hotel, the family stopped for a dish   15
of vanilla ice cream at a Breyer's ice cream and soda fountain. Indoors, the soda fountain was dim and fan-cooled, deliciously relieving to my scorched eyes.

Corded and crisp and pinafored, the five of us seated ourselves   16
one by one at the counter. There was I between my mother and father, and my two sisters on the other side of my mother. We

settled ourselves along the white mottled marble counter, and
when the waitress spoke at first no one understood what she was
saying, and so the five of us just sat there.

The waitress moved along the line of us closer to my father and   17
spoke again. "I said I kin give you to take out, but you can't eat
here. Sorry." Then she dropped her eyes looking very embarrassed, and suddenly we heard what it was she was saying all at
the same time, loud and clear.

Straight-backed and indignant, one by one, my family and I got   18
down from the counter stools and turned around and marched
out of the store, quiet and outraged, as if we had never been Black
before. No one would answer my emphatic questions with anything other than a guilty silence. "But we hadn't done anything!"
This wasn't right or fair! Hadn't I written poems about Bataan
and freedom and democracy for all?

My parents wouldn't speak of this injustice, not because they   19
had contributed to it, but because they felt they should have an-
ticipated it and avoided it. This made me even angrier. My fury
was not going to be acknowledged by a like fury. Even my two
sisters copied my parents' pretense that nothing unusual and
anti-american had occurred. I was left to write my angry letter
to the president of the united states all by myself, although my
father did promise I could type it out on the office typewriter next
week, after I showed it to him in my copybook diary.

The waitress was white, and the counter was white, and the ice   20
cream I never ate in Washington, D.C., that summer I left childhood was white, and the white heat and the white pavement and
the white stone monuments of my first Washington summer
made me sick to my stomach for the whole rest of that trip and it
wasn't much of a graduation present after all.

Questions for Study and Discussion

1. Lorde takes great care in describing the food her family
   took on the train with them to Washington. What is Lorde's
   purpose in describing the food? (Glossary: *Purpose*)
2. Why did Lorde dislike the Fourth of July as a child? Why
   does she dislike it as an adult?

3. Do you see any irony in Lorde's title? (Glossary: *Irony*) In what way? Do you think it is an appropriate title for her essay?

4. Lorde's essay is not long or hyperbolic, but her essay is a very effective indictment of racism. Identify some of the words Lorde uses to communicate her outrage when she writes of the racism that she and her family faced. How does her choice of words contribute to her message?

5. What is the tone of Lorde's essay? (Glossary: *Tone*) Identify passages to support your answer.

6. Why do you think Lorde's family deals with racism by ignoring it? In what way is Lorde different?

Vocabulary

Refer to your dictionary to define the following words as they are used in this selection. Then use each word in a sentence of your own.

ensconced (3)	travesty 910)
measly (6)	pinafored (16)
injunction (7)	emphatic (18)
corolla (10)	

Suggested Writing Assignments

1. When read with the ideals of the American Revolution and the Constitution in mind, Lorde's essay is strongly ironic. What does the Fourth of July mean to you? Why? How do your feelings relate to the stated ideals of our forebears? Choose your words carefully, and use specific personal experiences to support your general statements.

2. Imagine that you are Audre Lorde in 1947. Write a letter to Harry Truman in which you protest the reception you received in the nation's capital on the Fourth of July. Do not overstate your case. Show the president how you and your family were treated unfairly rather than merely stating that you were discriminated against, and carefully choose words that will help President Truman see the irony of your experience.

9

FIGURATIVE LANGUAGE

Figurative language is language used in an imaginative rather than a literal sense. Although it is most often associated with poetry, figurative language is used widely in our daily speech and in our writing. Prose writers have long known that figurative language not only brings freshness and color to writing, but also helps to clarify ideas.

Two of the most commonly used figures of speech are the simile and the metaphor. A *simile* is an explicit comparison between two essentially different ideas or things that uses the words *like* or *as* to link them.

> Canada geese sweep across the hills and valleys like a formation of strategic bombers.
>
> Benjamin B. Bachman

> I walked toward her and hailed her as a visitor to the moon might salute a survivor of a previous expedition.
>
> John Updike

A *metaphor,* on the other hand, makes an implicit comparison between dissimilar ideas or things without using *like* or *as.*

> She was very old and small and she walked slowly in the dark pine shadows, moving a little from side to side in her steps, with the balanced heaviness and lightness of a pendulum in a grandfather clock.
>
> Eudora Welty

> Charm is the ultimate weapon, the supreme seduction, against which there are few defenses.
>
> Laurie Lee

In order to take full advantage of the richness of a particular comparison, writers sometimes use several sentences or even a whole paragraph to develop a metaphor. Such a comparison is called an *extended metaphor.*

The point is that you have to strip down your writing before you can build it back up. You must know what the essential tools are and what job they were designed to do. If I may belabor the metaphor on carpentry, it is first necessary to be able to saw wood neatly and to drive nails. Later you can bevel the edges or add elegant finials, if that is your taste. But you can never forget that you are practicing a craft that is based on certain principles. If the nails are weak, your house will collapse. If your verbs are weak and your syntax is rickety, your sentences will fall apart.

William Zinsser

Another frequently used figure of speech is *personification*. In personification the writer attributes human qualities to animals or inanimate objects.

Blond October comes striding over the hills wearing a crimson shirt and faded green trousers.

Hal Borland

Indeed, haste can be the assassin of elegance.

T. H. White

In the preceding examples, the writers have, through the use of figurative language, both livened up their prose and given emphasis to their ideas. Keep in mind that figurative language should never be used merely to "dress up" writing; above all, it should help you to develop your ideas and to clarify your meaning for the reader.

THE BARRIO

Robert Ramirez

*Robert Ramirez has worked as a cameraman, re-
porter, anchorman, and producer for the news team
at KGBT-TV in Edinburg, Texas. Presently, he works
in the Latin American division of the Northern
Trust Bank in Chicago. In the following essay,
notice how Ramirez uses figurative language to
awaken the reader's senses to the sights, smells, and
sounds that are the essence of the barrio.*

The train, its metal wheels squealing as they spin along the   1
silvery tracks, rolls slower now. Through the gaps between
the cars blinks a streetlamp, and this pulsing light on a barrio
streetcorner beats slower, like a weary heartbeat, until the train
shudders to a halt, the light goes out, and the barrio is deep asleep.

Throughout Aztlán (the Nahuatl term meaning "land to the   2
north"), trains grumble along the edges of a sleeping people. From
Lower California, through the blistering Southwest, down the Rio
Grande to the muddy Gulf, the darkness and mystery of dreams
engulf communities fenced off by railroads, canals, and express-
ways. Paradoxical communities, isolated from the rest of the town
by concrete columned monuments of progress, and yet stranded
in the past. They are surrounded by change. It eludes their reach,
in their own backyards, and the people, unable and unwilling to
see the future, or even touch the present, perpetuate the past.

Leaning from the expressway or jolting across the tracks, one   3
enters a different physical world permeated by a different attitude.
The physical dimensions are impressive. It is a large section of
town which extends for fifteen blocks north and south along the
tracks, and then advances eastward, thinning into nothingness
beyond the city limits. Within the invisible (yet sensible) walls of
the barrio, are many, many people living in too few houses. The
homes, however, are much more numerous than on the outside.

Members of the barrio describe the entire area as their home.   4
It is a home, but it is more than this. The barrio is a refuge from

the harshness and the coldness of the Anglo world. It is a forced refuge. The leprous people are isolated from the rest of the community and contained in their section of town. The stoical pariahs of the barrio accept their fate, and from the angry seeds of rejection grow the flowers of closeness between outcasts, not the thorns of bitterness and the mad desire to flee. There is no want to escape, for the feeling of the barrio is known only to its inhabitants, and the material needs of life can also be found here.

The *tortillería* [tortilla factory] fires up its machinery three   5
times a day, producing steaming, round, flat slices of barrio bread. In the winter, the warmth of the tortilla factory is a wool *sarape* [blanket] in the chilly morning hours, but in the summer, it unbearably toasts every noontime customer.

The *panadería* [bakery] sends its sweet messenger aroma down   6
the dimly lit street, announcing the arrival of fresh, hot sugary *pan dulce* [sweet rolls].

The small corner grocery serves the meal-to-meal needs of cus-   7
tomers, and the owner, a part of the neighborhood, willingly gives credit to people unable to pay cash for foodstuffs.

The barbershop is a living room with hydraulic chairs, radio,   8
and television, where old friends meet and speak of life as their salted hair falls aimlessly about them.

The pool hall is a junior level country club where *'chucos*,   9
[young men] strangers in their own land, get together to shoot pool and rap, while veterans, unaware of the cracking, popping balls on the green felt, complacently play dominoes beneath rudely hung *Playboy* foldouts.

The *cantina* [canteen or snackbar] is the night spot of the bar-   10
rio. It is the country club and the den where the rites of puberty are enacted. Here the young become men. It is in the taverns that a young dude shows his *machismo* through the quantity of beer he can hold, the stories of *rucas* [women] he has had, and his willingness and ability to defend his image against hardened and scarred old lions.

No, there is no frantic wish to flee. It would be absurd to leave   11
the familiar and nervously step into the strange and cold Anglo community when the needs of the Chicano can be met in the barrio.

The barrio is closeness. From the family living unit, familial re-   12
lationships stretch out to immediate neighbors, down the block,

around the corner, and to all parts of the barrio. The feeling of family, a rare and treasurable sentiment, pervades and accounts for the inability of the people to leave. The barrio is this attitude manifested on the countenances of the people, on the faces of their homes, and in the gaiety of their gardens.

The color-splashed homes arrest your eyes, arouse your curios- 13
ity, and make you wonder what life scenes are being played out in them. The flimsy, brightly colored, wood-frame houses ignore no neon-brilliant color. Houses trimmed in orange, chartreuse, lime-green, yellow, and mixtures of these and other hues beckon the beholder to reflect on the peculiarity of each home. Passing through this land is refreshing like Brubeck,* not narcoticizing like revolting rows of similar houses, which neither offend nor please.

In the evenings, the porches and front yards are occupied with 14
men calmly talking over the noise of children playing baseball in the unpaved extension of the living room, while the women cook supper or gossip with female neighbors as they water the *jardines* [gardens]. The gardens mutely echo the expressive verses of the colorful houses. The denseness of multicolored plants and trees gives the house the appearance of an oasis or a tropical island hideaway, sheltered from the rest of the world.

Fences are common in the barrio, but they are fences and not 15
the walls of the Anglo community. On the western side of town, the high wooden fences between houses are thick, impenetrable walls, built to keep the neighbors at bay. In the barrio, the fences may be rusty, wire contraptions or thick green shrubs. In either case you can see through them and feel no sense of intrusion when you cross them.

Many lower-income families of the barrio manage to maintain 16
a comfortable standard of living through the communal action of family members who contribute their wages to the head of the family. Economic need creates interdependence and closeness. Small barefooted boys sell papers on cool, dark Sunday mornings, deny themselves pleasantries, and give their earnings to *mamá*. The older the child, the greater the responsibility to help the head of the household provide for the rest of the family.

There are those, too, who for a number of reasons have not 17
achieved a relative sense of financial security. Perhaps it results

---

*Dave Brubeck, pianist, composer, and conductor of "cool" modern jazz.

from too many children too soon, but it is the homes of these people and their situation that numbs rather than charms. Their houses, aged and bent, oozing children, are fissures in the horn of plenty. Their wooden homes may have brick-pattern asbestos tile on the outer walls, but the tile is not convincing.

Unable to pay city taxes or incapable of influencing the city to live up to its duty to serve all the citizens, the poorer barrio families remain trapped in the nineteenth century and survive as best they can. The backyards have well-worn paths to the outhouses, which sit near the alley. Running water is considered a luxury in some parts of the barrio. Decent drainage is usually unknown, and when it rains, the water stands for days, an incubator of health hazards and an avoidable nuisance. Streets, costly to pave, remain rough, rocky trails. Tires do not last long, and the constant rattling and shaking grind away a car's life and spread dust through screen windows.   18

The houses and their *jardines*, the jollity of the people in an adverse world, the brightly feathered alarm clock pecking away at supper and cautiously eyeing the children playing nearby, produce a mystifying sensation at finding the noble savage alive in the twentieth century. It is easy to look at the positive qualities of life in the barrio, and look at them with a distantly envious feeling. One wishes to experience the feelings of the barrio and not the hardships. Remembering the illness, the hunger, the feeling of time running out on you, the walls, both real and imagined, reflecting on living in the past, one finds his envy becoming more elusive, until it has vanished altogether.   19

Back now beyond the tracks, the train creaks and groans, the cars jostle each other down the track, and as the light begins its pulsing, the barrio, with all its meanings, greets a new dawn with yawns and restless stretchings.   20

Questions for Study and Discussion

1. What is the barrio? Where is it? What does Ramirez mean that "There is no want to escape, for the feeling of the barrio is known only to its inhabitants, and the material needs of life can also be found there"?

2. Ramirez uses Spanish phrases throughout his essay. Why do you suppose he uses them? What is their effect on the reader? He also uses the words "home," "refuge," "family," and "closeness." What do they connote in the context of this essay? (Glossary: *Connotation/Denotation*) In what ways, if any, are they essential to his purpose? (Glossary: *Purpose*)

3. Identify several of the metaphors Ramirez uses in his essay and explain why they are particularly appropriate for this essay?

4. Explain Ramirez's use of the imagery of walls and fences to describe a sense of cultural isolation. What might this imagery be symbolic of? (Glossary: *Symbol*)

5. Ramirez goes into some detail about the many groups in the barrio. Identify those groups. In what ways do they participate in the unity of life in the barrio?

6. Ramirez begins his essay with a relatively positive picture of the barrio, but ends on a more disheartening note. Why has he organized his essay this way? What might the effect have been if he had reversed these images? (Glossary: *Beginnings and Endings*)

Vocabulary

Refer to your dictionary to define the following words as they are used in this selection. Then use each word in a sentence of your own.

paradoxical (2)	Chicano (11)
eludes (2)	countenances (12)
permeated (3)	fissures (17)
stoical (4)	elusive (19)
pariahs (4)	adverse (19)
complacently (9)	

Suggested Writing Assignments

1. Write a brief essay in which you describe your own neighborhood.

2. In paragraph 19 of his essay Ramirez says, "One wishes to experience the feelings of the barrio and not the hardships." Explore his meaning in light of what you have just read and other experience or knowledge you may have of "ghetto" living. In what way can it be said that the hardships of such living are a necessary part of its "feelings"? How might barrio life change, for the good or the bad, if the city were to "live up to its duty to serve all the citizens"?

THE DEATH OF BENNY PARET

Norman Mailer

Norman Mailer, born in Long Branch, New Jersey, in 1923, graduated from Harvard University in 1943 with a degree in engineering. While at Harvard, he made the decision to become a writer and, with the publication of his first novel, The Naked and the Dead *(1948), based on his war experiences in the Pacific during World War II, Mailer established himself as a writer of note. Mailer's literary interests have ranged widely over the years, from novels to nonfiction and journalism; from politics, sports, feminism, and lunar exploration to popular culture, ancient Egyptian culture, and criminality. In this account of the welterweight championship fight between Benny Paret and Emile Griffith, we can experience what Mailer himself felt as he sat at ringside the fateful night of March 25, 1962, the night of Paret's last fight. As you read, notice the way Mailer uses figures of speech to evoke the scene for the reader.*

Paret was a Cuban, a proud club fighter who had become 1
welterweight champion because of his unusual ability to take a punch. His style of fighting was to take three punches to the head in order to give back two. At the end of ten rounds, he would still be bouncing, his opponent would have a headache. But in the last two years, over the fifteen-round fights, he had started to take some bad maulings.

This fight had its turns. Griffith won most of the early rounds, 2
but Paret knocked Griffith down in the sixth. Griffith had trouble getting up, but made it, came alive and was dominating Paret again before the round was over. Then Paret began to wilt. In the middle of the eighth round, after a clubbing punch had turned his back to Griffith, Paret walked three disgusted steps away, show-

ing his hindquarters. For a champion, he took much too long to turn back around. It was the first hint of weakness Paret had ever shown, and it must have inspired a particular shame, because he fought the rest of the fight as if he were seeking to demonstrate that he could take more punishment than any man alive. In the twelfth, Griffith caught him. Paret got trapped in a corner. Trying to duck away, his left arm and his head became tangled on the wrong side of the top rope. Griffith was in like a cat ready to rip the life out of a huge boxed rat. He hit him eighteen right hands in a row, an act which took perhaps three or four seconds, Griffith making a pent-up whimpering sound all the while he attacked, the right hand whipping like a piston rod which has broken through the crankcase, or like a baseball bat demolishing a pumpkin. I was sitting in the second row of that corner—they were not ten feet away from me, and like everybody else, I was hypnotized. I had never seen one man hit another so hard and so many times. Over the referee's face came a look of woe as if some spasm had passed its way through him, and then he leaped on Griffith to pull him away. It was the act of a brave man. Griffith was uncontrollable. His trainer leaped into the ring, his manager, his cut man, there were four people holding Griffith, but he was off on an orgy, he had left the Garden, he was back on a hoodlum's street. If he had been able to break loose from his handlers and the referee, he would have jumped Paret to the floor and whaled on him there.

And Paret? Paret died on his feet. As he took those eighteen punches something happened to everyone who was in psychic range of the event. Some part of his death reached out to us. One felt it hover in the air. He was still standing in the ropes, trapped as he had been before, he gave some little half-smile of regret, as if he were saying, "I didn't know I was going to die just yet," and then, his head leaning back but still erect, his death came to breathe about him. He began to pass away. As he passed, so his limbs descended beneath him, and he sank slowly to the floor. He went down more slowly than any fighter had ever gone down, he went down like a large ship which turns on end and slides second by second into its grave. As he went down, the sound of Griffith's punches echoed in the mind like a heavy ax in the distance chopping into a wet log. 3

Questions for Study and Discussion

1. What differentiated Paret and Griffith for Mailer? Who was the welterweight champion?
2. What are the implications of Griffith's actions in the twelfth round of the fight for the sport of boxing in general?
3. Identify at least three similes in this essay. Why do you think Mailer felt the need to use figures of speech in describing Paret's death?
4. Mailer starts paragraph 3 with a question. What effect does this question have on you as a reader? (Glossary: *Rhetorical Question*)
5. Does Mailer place the blame for Paret's death on anyone? Explain.
6. Explain how Mailer personifies death in paragraph 3.

Vocabulary

Refer to your dictionary to define the following words as they are used in this selection. Then use each word in a sentence of your own.

wilt (2)	psychic (3)
spasm (2)	hover (3)

Suggested Writing Assignments

1. The death of Benny Paret was neither the first nor the last death to occur in professional boxing. Should boxing, therefore, be banned? Write an essay arguing for or against the continuation of professional boxing. As you write, use several figures of speech to enliven your essay.
2. Sports commentators and critics have pointed to the role fans have played in the promotion of violence in sports. If you feel that fans promote violent behavior, what do you suggest can be done, if anything, to alleviate the negative effect fans have? Using examples from your own experience in attending sporting events, write an essay explaining your position on this subject. Enrich your descriptions with figures of speech.

THE THIRSTY ANIMAL

Brian Manning

In a very moving essay, first published in the New
York Times *in 1985, Brian Manning uses the powerful metaphor of a "thirsty animal" to define the
irresistible urge he has to consume alcohol, even
though he no longer drinks. He wistfully returns to
his first contacts with wine, his experiences with
alcohol in college, and the parties and the drinking
companions, and the desire he still harbors: "From
time to time, I daydream about summer afternoons
and cold beer. I know such dreams will never go
away." His is a personal essay but one that tran-
scends and sheds light on a desire, an addiction
really, that many in our society struggle with every
minute of every day.*

I was very young, but I still vividly remember how my father 1
fascinated my brothers and me at the dinner table by running
his finger around the rim of his wineglass. He sent a wonderful,
crystal tone wafting through the room, and we loved it. When we
laughed too raucously, he would stop, swirl the red liquid in his
glass and take a sip.

There was a wine cellar in the basement of the house we moved 2
into when I was eleven. My father put a few cases of Bordeaux
down there in the dark. We played there with other boys in the
neighborhood, hid there, made a secret place. It was musty and
cool and private. We wrote things and stuck them in among the
bottles and imagined someone way in the future baffled by our
messages from the past.

Many years later, the very first time I drank, I had far too much. 3
But I found I was suddenly able to tell a girl at my high school
that I was mad about her.

When I drank in college with the men in my class, I was trying 4
to define a self-image I could feel comfortable with. I wanted to

be "an Irishman," I decided, a man who could drink a lot of liquor and hold it. My favorite play was Eugene O'Neill's *Long Day's Journey into Night,* my model the drunken Jamie Tyrone.

I got out of college, into the real world, and the drunk on week- 5
ends started to slip into the weekdays. Often I didn't know when one drunk ended and another began. The years were measured in hangovers. It took a long time to accept, and then to let the idea sink in, that I was an alcoholic.

It took even longer to do anything about it. I didn't want to be- 6
lieve it, and I didn't want to deny myself the exciting, brotherly feeling I had whenever I went boozing with my friends. For a long time, in my relationships with women, I could only feel comfort-able with a woman who drank as much as I did. So I didn't meet many women and spent my time with men in dark barrooms, try-ing to be like them and hoping I'd be accepted.

It is now two years since I quit drinking, and that, as all al- 7
coholics know who have come to grips with their problem, is not long ago at all. The urge to have "just one" includes a genuine longing for all the accouterments of drink: the popping of a cork, the color of Scotch through a glass, the warmth creeping over my shoulders with the third glass of stout. Those were joys. Ever since I gave them up I remember them as delicious.

I go to parties now and start off fine, but I have difficulty deal- 8
ing with the changing rhythms as the night wears on. Everyone around me seems to be having a better time the more they drink, and I, not they, become awkward. I feel like a kid with a broken chain when everyone else has bicycled around the corner out of sight. I fight against feeling sorry for myself.

What were the things I was looking for and needed when I 9
drank? I often find that what I am looking for when I want a drink is not really the alcohol, but the memories and laughter that seemed possible only with a glass in my hand. In a restaurant, I see the bottle of vintage port on the shelf, and imagine lolling in my chair, swirling the liquid around in the glass, inhaling those marvelous fumes. I think of my neighbor, Eileen, the funniest woman I ever got smashed with, and I want to get up on a bar stool next to her to hear again the wonderful stories she told. She could drink any man under the table, she claimed, and I wanted to be one of those men who tried. She always won, but it made me

feel I belonged when I staggered out of the bar, her delighted laughter following me.

I had found a world to cling to, a way of belonging, and it still attracts me. I pass by the gin mills and pubs now and glance in at the men lined up inside, and I don't see them as suckers or fools. I remember how I felt sitting there after work, or watching a Sunday afternoon ball game, and I long for the smell of the barroom and that ease—toasts and songs, jokes and equality. I have to keep reminding myself of the wasting hangovers, the lost money, the days down the drain.   10

I imagine my problem as an animal living inside me, demanding a drink before it dies of thirst. That's what it says, but it will never die of thirst. The fact an alcoholic faces is that this animal breathes and waits. It is incapable of death and will spring back to lustful, consuming life with even one drop of sustenance.   11

When I was eighteen and my drinking began in earnest, I didn't play in the wine cellar at home anymore; I stole there. I sneaked bottles to my room, sat in the window and drank alone while my parents were away. I hated the taste of it, but I kept drinking it, without the kids from the neighborhood, without any thought that I was feeding the animal. And one day, I found one of those old notes we had hidden down there years before. It fell to the ground when I pulled a bottle from its cubbyhole. I read it with bleary eyes, then put the paper back into the rack. "Beware," it said, above a childish skull and crossbones, "all ye who enter here." A child, wiser than I was that day, had written that note.   12

I did a lot of stupid, disastrous, sometimes mean things in the years that followed, and remembering them is enough to snap me out of the memories and back to the reality that I quit just in time. I've done something I had to do, something difficult and necessary, and that gives me satisfaction and the strength to stay on the wagon. I'm very lucky so far. I don't get mad that I can't drink anymore; I can handle the self-pity that overwhelmed me in my early days of sobriety. From time to time, I daydream about summer afternoons and cold beer. I know such dreams will never go away. The thirsty animal is there, getting a little fainter every day. It will never die. A lot of my life now is all about keeping it in a very lonely cage.   13

Questions for Study and Discussion

1. Why did Manning drink in college? Why did it take him a long time to do something about his alcoholism?
2. How does Manning organize paragraphs 1–8? (Glossary: *Organization*) Why does he begin his essay in this way?
3. What is Manning's purpose in his essay? (Glossary: *Purpose*) What positive things does he associate with drinking alcohol? What are the negative things?
4. What metaphor does Manning use to describe his craving for alcohol? (Glossary: *Metaphor*) Why does he use a metaphor?
5. In what way was Manning the child more intelligent than Manning the young adult?
6. Manning ends by returning to his metaphor for his craving for alcohol. Is his ending effective in your opinion? (Glossary: *Beginnings and Endings*) Explain your answer.

Vocabulary

Refer to your dictionary to define the following words as they are used in this selection. Then use each word in a sentence of your own.

wafting (1)   vintage (9)
raucously (1)   sustenance (11)
accouterments (7)

Suggested Writing Assignments

1. Write an essay explaining why you like or do not like to drink alcohol. If you drink use language that will help someone who does not drink understand your motivations and experiences. If you do not drink, write an essay explaining why you do not. Also describe the ways that you think alcohol affects your peers when they drink and, if appropriate, how they feel about your drinking.

2. Have you ever given something up? It can be a bad habit, a harmful substance, a sport that you can't afford any more, or anything else that you miss. What about it do you miss the most? What activities, sensations, or emotions are associated with it in your mind? Use language that will make your experiences and emotions understandable to your audience.

III

TYPES
OF
ESSAYS

10

ILLUSTRATION

Illustration is the use of examples to make ideas more concrete and to make generalizations more specific and detailed. Examples enable writers not just to tell but to show what they mean. For example, an essay about recently developed alternative sources of energy becomes clear and interesting with the use of some examples—say, solar energy or the heat from the earth's core. The more specific the example, the more effective it is. Along with general statements about solar energy, the writer might offer several examples of how the home building industry is installing solar collectors instead of conventional hot water systems, or building solar greenhouses to replace conventional central heating.

In an essay a writer uses examples to clarify or support the thesis; in a paragraph, to clarify or support the main idea. Sometimes a single striking example suffices; sometimes a whole series of related examples is necessary. The following paragraph presents a single extended example—an anecdote, or story—that illustrates the author's point about cultural differences:

> Whenever there is a great cultural distance between two people, there are bound to be problems arising from differences in behavior and expectations. An example is the American couple who consulted a psychiatrist about their marital problems. The husband was from New England and had been brought up by reserved parents who taught him to control his emotions and to respect the need for privacy. His wife was from an Italian family and had been brought up in close contact with all the members of her large family, who were extremely warm, volatile and demonstrative. When the husband came home after a hard day at the office, dragging his feet and longing for peace and quiet, his wife would rush to him and smother him. Clasping his hands, rubbing his brow, crooning over his weary head, she never left him alone. But when the wife was upset or anxious about her day, the husband's response was to withdraw completely and leave her alone. No comforting, no affectionate embrace, no atten-

tion—just solitude. The woman became convinced her husband didn't love her and, in desperation, she consulted a psychiatrist. Their problem wasn't basically psychological but cultural.

Edward T. Hall

This single example is effective because it is *representative*—that is, essentially similar to other such problems he might have described and familiar to many readers. Hall tells the story with enough detail that readers can understand the couple's feelings and so better understand the point he is trying to make.

In contrast, Edwin Way Teale supports his topic sentence about country superstitions with eleven examples:

In the folklore of the country, numerous superstitions relate to winter weather. Back-country farmers examine their corn husks—the thicker the husk, the colder the winter. They watch the acorn crop—the more acorns, the more severe the season. They observe where white-faced hornets place their paper nests—the higher they are, the deeper will be the snow. They examine the size and shape and color of the spleens of butchered hogs for clues to the severity of the season. They keep track of the blooming of dogwood in the spring—the more abundant the blooms, the more bitter the cold in January. When chipmunks carry their tails high and squirrels have heavier fur and mice come into country houses early in the fall, the superstitious gird themselves for a long, hard winter. Without any scientific basis, a wider-than-usual black band on a woolly-bear caterpillar is accepted as a sign that winter will arrive early and stay late. Even the way a cat sits beside the stove carries its message to the credulous. According to a belief once widely held in the Ozarks, a cat sitting with its tail to the fire indicates very cold weather is on the way.

Edwin Way Teale

Teale uses numerous examples because he is writing about various superstitions. Also, putting all those strange beliefs side by side in a kind of catalogue makes the paragraph fun to read as well as informative.

Illustration is often found in effective writing; nearly every essay in this book contains one or more examples. Likewise this introduction has used examples to clarify its points about illustration.

A CRIME OF COMPASSION

Barbara Huttmann

Barbara Huttmann is a nurse, a teacher, and a writer. Her interest in the patients' rights issue is clearly evident in her two books, The Patient's Advocate *and* Code Blue. *In the following essay, which first appeared in* Newsweek *in 1983, Huttmann narrates the final months of the life of Mac, one of her favorite patients. By using emotional and graphic detail, Huttmann hopes her example of Mac will convince her audience of the need for new legislation which would permit terminally-ill patients to choose to die rather than suffer great pain and indignity.*

"Murderer," a man shouted. "God help patients who get *you* for a nurse." 1

"What gives you the right to play God?" another one asked. 2

It was the Phil Donahue show where the guest is a fatted calf 3
and the audience a 200-strong flock of vultures hungering to pick at the bones. I had told them about Mac, one of my favorite cancer patients. "We resuscitated him 52 times in just one month. I refused to resuscitate him again. I simply sat there and held his hand while he died."

There wasn't time to explain that Mac was a young, witty, 4
macho cop who walked into the hospital with 32 pounds of attack equipment, looking as if he could single-handedly protect the whole city, if not the entire state. "Can't get rid of this cough," he said. Otherwise, he felt great.

Before the day was over, tests confirmed that he had lung can- 5
cer. And before the year was over, I loved him, his wife, Maura, and their three kids as if they were my own. All the nurses loved him. And we all battled his disease for six months without ever giving death a thought. Six months isn't such a long time in the whole scheme of things, but it was long enough to see him lose his youth, his wit, his macho, his hair, his bowel and bladder

control, his sense of taste and smell, and his ability to do the slightest thing for himself. It was also long enough to watch Maura's transformation from a young woman into a haggard, beaten old lady.

When Mac had wasted away to a 60-pound skeleton kept alive   6
by liquid food we poured down a tube, i.v. solutions we dripped into his veins, and oxygen we piped to a mask on his face, he begged us: "Mercy . . . for God's sake, please just let me go."

The first time he stopped breathing, the nurse pushed the but-   7
ton that calls a "code blue" throughout the hospital and sends a team rushing to resuscitate the patient. Each time he stopped breathing, sometimes two or three times in one day, the code team came again. The doctors and technicians worked their miracles and walked away. The nurses stayed to wipe the saliva that drooled from his mouth, irrigate the big craters of bedsores that covered his hips, suction the lung fluids that threatened to drown him, clean the feces that burned his skin like lye, pour the liquid food down the tube attached to his stomach, put pillows between his knees to ease the bone-on-bone pain, turn him every hour to keep the bedsores from getting worse, and change his gown and linen every two hours to keep him from being soaked in perspiration.

At night I went home and tried to scrub away the smell of de-   8
caying flesh that seemed woven into the fabric of my uniform. It was in my hair, the upholstery of my car—there was no washing it away. And every night I prayed that Mac would die, that his agonized eyes would never again plead with me to let him die.

Every morning I asked his doctor for a "no-code" order. With-   9
out that order, we had to resuscitate every patient who stopped breathing. His doctor was one of several who believe we must extend life as long as we have the means and knowledge to do it. To not do it is to be liable for negligence, at least in the eyes of many people, including some nurses. I thought about what it would be like to stand before a judge, accused of murder, if Mac stopped breathing and I didn't call a code.

And after the fifty-second code, when Mac was still lucid enough   10
to beg for death again, and Maura was crumbled in my arms again, and when no amount of pain medication stilled his moaning and agony, I wondered about a spiritual judge. Was all this misery and suffering supposed to be building character or infusing us all with the sense of humility that comes from impotence?

Had we, the whole medical community, become so arrogant 11
that we believed in the illusion of salvation through science? Had
we become so self-righteous that we thought meddling in God's
work was our duty, our moral imperative and our legal obligation? Did we really believe that we had the right to force "life" on
a suffering man who had begged for the right to die?

Such questions haunted me more than ever early one morning 12
when Maura went home to change her clothes and I was bathing
Mac. He had been still for so long, I thought he at last had the
blessed relief of coma. Then he opened his eyes and moaned,
"Pain . . . no more . . . Barbara . . . do something . . . God, let me
go."

The desperation in his eyes and voice riddled me with guilt. "I'll 13
stop," I told him as I injected the pain medication.

I sat on the bed and held Mac's hands in mine. He pressed his 14
bony fingers against my hand and muttered, "Thanks." Then
there was one soft sigh and I felt his hands go cold in mine.
"Mac?" I whispered, as I waited for his chest to rise and fall again.

A clutch of panic banded my chest, drew my finger to the code 15
button, urged me to do something, anything . . . but sit there
alone with death. I kept one finger on the button, without pressing it, as a waxen pallor slowly transformed his face from person
to empty shell. Nothing I've ever done in my 47 years has taken so
much effort as it took *not* to press that code button.

Eventually, when I was as sure as I could be that the code team 16
would fail to bring him back, I entered the legal twilight zone and
pushed the button. The team tried. And while they were trying,
Maura walked into the room and shrieked, "No . . . don't let them
do this to him . . . for God's sake . . . please, no more."

Cradling her in my arms was like cradling myself, Mac, and all 17
those patients and nurses who had been in this place before, who
do the best they can in a death-denying society.

So a TV audience accused me of murder. Perhaps I am guilty. If 18
a doctor had written a no-code order, which is the only *legal*
alternative, would he have felt any less guilty? Until there is
legislation making it a criminal act to code a patient who has
requested the right to die, we will all of us risk the same fate as
Mac. For whatever reason, we developed the means to prolong
life, and now we are forced to use it. We do not have the right
to die.

Questions for Study and Discussion

1. Why did people in the audience of the Phil Donahue Show call Huttmann a "murderer"? Is there any sense in which their accusation is justified? In what ways do you think Huttmann might agree with them?

2. In paragraph 15, Huttmann says, "Nothing I've ever done in my 47 years has taken so much effort as it took *not* to press that code button." How effectively does she illustrate her struggle against pressing the button? What steps led to her ultimate decision not to press the code button?

3. What, according to Huttmann, is the "only legal alternative" to her action? What does she find hypocritical about that choice?

4. Huttmann makes a powerfully emotional appeal for a patient's right to die. Some readers might even find some of her story shocking or offensive. Cite examples of some of the graphic scenes Huttmann describes and discuss their impact on you as a reader. Did they help persuade you to Huttmann's point of view or did you find them overly unnerving? What would have been gained or lost had she left them out?

5. The story in Huttmann's example covers a period of six months. In paragraphs 4–6, she describes the first five months of Mac's illness; in paragraphs 7–10, the sixth month; and in paragraphs 11–17, the final morning. In what ways does her use of time illustrate her point that a patient must be permitted to choose to die? Explain.

6. Huttmann concludes her essay with the statement, "We do not have the right to die." What does she mean by this? In your opinion, is she exaggerating, or simply stating the facts? Does her example of Mac adequately illustrate Huttmann's concluding point?

Vocabulary

Refer to your dictionary to define the following words as they are used in this selection. Then use each word in a sentence of your own.

resuscitate (3)   imperative (11)
irrigate (7)   waxen (15)
lucid (10)   pallor (15)

Suggested Writing Assignments

1. Write a letter to the editor of *Newsweek* in which you respond to Huttmann's essay. Would you be for or against legislation that would give terminally ill patients the right to die? Give examples from your personal experience or from your reading to support your opinion.

2. Using one of the following sentences as your thesis statement, write an essay giving examples from personal experience or from reading to support your opinion.

   Consumers have more power than they realize.

   Most products do/do not measure up to the claims of their advertisements.

   Religion is/is not alive and well.

   Government works far better than its critics claim.

   Being able to write well is more than a basic skill.

   The seasons for professional sports are too long.

   Today's college students are serious minded when it comes to academics.

WINTER BIRDS

Gale Lawrence

While living in Vermont, Gale Lawrence became interested in the natural world and wrote about her expanding knowledge in a weekly column in The Rutland Herald. *The following selection is from* The Beginning Naturalist, *a collection of nature essays published in 1979. Lawrence is also the author of* A Field Guide to the Familiar *(1985) and* The Indoor Naturalist *(1987). Watch how she presents her information in such a way that you can see and hear the world she describes.*

If you've been leading an indoor life but have been wanting to spend more time outdoors, don't wait until spring. Bundle up and take advantage of the cold winter months to start learning about nature. Winter, in fact, is an excellent time to begin. Many birds have migrated south. Many mammals are sleeping. Reptiles and amphibians are hibernating, and therefore can be ignored until spring. Insects are in a condition similar to hibernation, called diapause.

The plant kingdom is also simplified. Many plants have either died or withdrawn into their roots, where they will remain dormant for the winter. Leaves are gone from most trees, so you can examine their basic shapes and look closely at their twigs and buds. In short, nature is almost manageable for a beginner during the long, inactive weeks of December, January, and February.

If you'd like to begin learning about nature this winter, the first thing you might do is put up a bird feeder near a window. Invite winter birds close to your house in order to see them better. If you offer sunflower seeds, you will probably be visited very shortly by black-capped chickadees, blue jays, and evening grosbeaks.

Chickadees are the most numerous visitors to my bird feeder. I must have over a dozen of them who are regulars. I call them "one-at-a-timers" because each flies in, grabs a seed, and flies to a perch nearby to eat it. They remind me of a busy airport with planes landing and taking off as fast as the control tower will let them.

My second most numerous visitors are blue jays. I had always thought of blue jays as somewhat ugly—perhaps because they are noisy and aggressive. When I saw them up close I was surprised to discover what a beautiful shade of blue they are. Their stark black, white, and blue markings are actually very handsome.

Blue jays come to the feeder to eat or to stock up on seeds. If a blue jay is on a supply mission it will gobble up fourteen or fifteen seeds. When it has as many seeds as it can cram into its mouth and throat, it will fly off to hide its treasures. This hoarding accounts for the disappearance of many of my sunflower seeds.

Evening grosbeaks are large, mustard-yellow birds with black markings. They have strong seed-cracking beaks. They travel in flocks, and when they visit a feeder they drive the chickadees, blue jays, and other birds away. An evening grosbeak is a gluttonous eater—it perches on the feeder and eats seed after seed, strewing the shells every which way in its haste.

Evening grosbeaks are an interesting species. In response to the food available in bird feeders they have altered their natural feeding and nesting habits. Winter feeding has invited them into areas where they never lived before. Some people don't like evening grosbeaks because they are domineering and seem to eat more than their fair share of seeds. I have even heard them referred to as "feeder bums."

If in addition to sunflower seeds you offer mixed seeds, you will be inviting other birds to your feeders. I offer only sunflower seeds at one window and mixed seeds at another. I also throw some mixed seeds on top of a low wooden storage box that's just outside my front door. The mixed seeds bring redpolls, juncos, tree sparrows, and pine siskins.

I also hang an onion bag of suet in a shrub that's close to my sunflower feeder. The suet is appealing to some of the seedeaters, but it also attracts woodpeckers. Making the distinction between the downy and the hairy woodpecker can be your first exercise in close observation. The hairy woodpecker is bigger than the downy and has a longer bill. Otherwise they are almost identical.

If you are serious about learning to identify your bird visitors by name, especially the small look-alikes that come for mixed seed, you should buy yourself a field guide. Most field guides include both pictures and descriptive information to help you determine the name of the bird you're looking at. You will have to pay close attention to size, color, shape, and distinctive markings. You might find binoculars helpful when it comes to small details like eye rings, wing bars, and patches of color.

Once you've had some practice identifying the woodpeckers and seedeaters right outside your windows, you'll be ready for the new birds returning in the spring. It will take you much longer than a year to master all the warblers, sparrows, and thrushes you'll see, but once you start paying attention to birds you'll be hooked. Learning about them won't seem like work anymore.   12

One note of caution: if you decide to feed wild birds during the winter, consider yourself committed. The birds will come to depend on the food you offer them, and it isn't fair to stop feeding them during the lean winter months when wild food is scarce. If you had never fed them they would have spread out in search of food. The seeds in your feeder are now part of the food supply that supports the local population. If your seeds disappear, there's not enough food to go around, and that means some birds will starve.   13

Other birds stay in the North through the winter, but you won't see them at your feeders. You'll have to go out looking for them, and even then you may never see them. Walking in the woods you may scare up a ruffed grouse, and it will probably scare you as much as you scare it—the sudden rush of wings is always a surprise. Ruffed grouse survive the winter by eating wild seeds, nuts, and buds they find in the woods.   14

Owls are around too, but they're hard to see because they're nocturnal. Another difference between owls and the feeder birds is that owls are predators: they prefer mice and rabbits to seeds and suet. Listen for owls at about the time the sun goes down or after dark, and watch for one if you hear crows or blue jays making a racket around a tree.   15

While you're beginning to watch and listen outdoors, learn the sounds a chickadee makes. If you hear one nearby, frequently you can call it in close to where you're standing by talking to it and making pshhh-wshhh-wshhh sounds. When it comes to look you over it may bring friends and may even introduce you to a nuthatch.   16

Other familiar birds you may notice during the winter are the   17
resourceful scavengers—gulls and crows—and the imported species—pigeons and house sparrows.

If you become interested enough in watching birds to want to   18
keep track of what you're seeing, a state agency, an Audubon Society, or a local nature center may have a checklist of all the birds
in your area. While the checklists don't describe the birds or tell
you where to find them, they do indicate relative abundance and
seasonal status. You'll find that these local checklists nicely complement your more comprehensive field guide.

Watching winter birds is only one way to acquaint yourself   19
with the natural world. But the nice thing about birds is that they
will invite you to notice many other things—such as the trees they
perch in and the plant and animal food they eat. Finally, an interest in birds will help you begin to understand how everything
interacts in the natural world.

Questions for Study and Discussion

1. According to Lawrence, why is winter a good time to begin
   to study nature? What is a good first step for someone who
   wants to start?
2. Reread paragraphs 4–8. Discuss how Lawrence communicates the personalities of the birds through the use of illustration. Why does Lawrence use illustration in what is, to
   some degree, a "how-to" essay?
3. If someone installed three feeders and wanted to attract
   three different groups of birds, what food could they put
   in each? Which birds would be attracted to which food?
   What is a good way to identify the birds that have similar
   appearances?
4. Who is Lawrence's intended audience? (Glossary: *Audience*)
   Is her writing style suitable for her audience? (Glossary:
   Style) Explain your answer.
5. What are some birds that stay North in winter but don't
   come to feeders? How can they be observed? Why does
   Lawrence discuss them in her essay?

6. What is the purpose of Lawrence's essay? (Glossary: *Purpose*) How does her last sentence contribute to the effectiveness of the essay?

Vocabulary

Refer to your dictionary to define the following words as they are used in this selection. Then use each word in a sentence of your own.

diapause (1)   gluttonous (7)
cram (6)   nocturnal (15)
hoarding (6)

Suggested Writing Assignments

1. Lawrence writes that observing winter birds is a good starting point for studying nature. Write an essay about a good way to begin a hobby or activity that you know and like. For instance, assume your audience would like to take up downhill skiing, woodworking, pottery, or skydiving—how should they begin? Why? What is rewarding about the activity? Be sure to illustrate your essay with examples and anecdotes based on your personal experience.

2. Write an essay about a type of animal that is common and has many different breeds such as dogs, cats, or horses. Choose three or four breeds. What, in your experience, is each breed like? Which ones do you enjoy interacting with? Which ones do you have trouble getting along with? Why? Try providing a powerful anecdote, such as jogging past a mean Rottweiler, for emphasis. Model your essay on Lawrence's discussion of birds.

DUMPSTER DIVING

Lars Eighner

Born in Texas in 1948, Lars Eighner attended the University of Texas at Austin. After graduation, he wrote essays and fiction, and several of his articles have been published in such magazines as Three-penny Review, The Guide, *and* Inches. *His volume of short stories, entitled* Bayou Boys and Other Stories, *was published in 1985. He became home-less in 1988 when he left his job as an attendant at a mental hospital. The following piece appeared in the* Utne Reader *in 1992, abridged from a piece that appeared in* Threepenny Review.

I began Dumpster diving about a year before I became homeless.

I prefer the term *scavenging*. I have heard people, evidently meaning to be polite, use the word *foraging*, but I prefer to reserve that word for gathering nuts and berries and such, which I also do, according to the season and opportunity.

I like the frankness of the word *scavenging*. I live from the refuse of others. I am a scavenger. I think it a sound and honorable niche, although if I could I would naturally prefer to live the comfortable consumer life, perhaps—and only perhaps—as a slightly less wasteful consumer owing to what I have learned as a scavenger.

Except for jeans, all my clothes come from Dumpsters. Boom boxes, candles, bedding, toilet paper, medicine, books, a type-writer, a virgin male love doll, coins sometimes amounting to many dollars: all came from Dumpsters. And, yes, I eat from Dumpsters, too.

There is a predictable series of stages that a person goes through in learning to scavenge. At first the new scavenger is filled with disgust and self-loathing. He is ashamed of being seen.

This stage passes with experience. The scavenger finds a pair of running shoes that fit and look and smell brand-new. He finds a pocket calculator in perfect working order. He finds pristine ice cream, still frozen, more than he can eat or keep. He begins to understand: people do throw away perfectly good stuff, a lot of perfectly good stuff.

At this stage he may become lost and never recover. All the   7
Dumpster divers I have known come to the point of trying to acquire everything they touch. Why not take it, they reason, it is all free. This is, of course, hopeless, and most divers come to realize that they must restrict themselves to items of relatively immediate utility.

The finding of objects is becoming something of an urban art.   8
Even respectable, employed people will sometimes find something tempting sticking out of a Dumpster or standing beside one. Quite a number of people, not all of them of the bohemian type, are willing to brag that they found this or that piece in the trash.

But eating from Dumpsters is the thing that separates the dil-   9
ettanti from the professionals. Eating safely involves three principles: using the senses and common sense to evaluate the condition of the found materials; knowing the Dumpsters of a given area and checking them regularly; and seeking always to answer the question "Why was this discarded?"

Yet perfectly good food can be found in Dumpsters. Canned   10
goods, for example, turn up fairly often in the Dumpsters I frequent. I also have few qualms about dry foods such as crackers, cookies, cereal, chips, and pasta if they are free of visible contaminants and still dry and crisp. Raw fruits and vegetables with intact skins seem perfectly safe to me, excluding, of course, the obviously rotten. Many are discarded for minor imperfections that can be pared away.

A typical discard is a half jar of peanut butter—though nonor-   11
ganic peanut butter does not require refrigeration and is unlikely to spoil in any reasonable time. One of my favorite finds is yogurt—often discarded, still sealed, when the expiration date has passed—because it will keep for several days, even in warm weather.

No matter how careful I am I still get dysentery at least once a   12
month, oftener in warm weather. I do not want to paint too romantic a picture. Dumpster diving has serious drawbacks as a way of life.

I find from the experience of scavenging two rather deep   13
lessons. The first is to take what I can use and let the rest go. I

have come to think that there is no value in the abstract. A thing I cannot use or make useful, perhaps by trading, has no value, however fine or rare it may be.

The second lesson is the transience of material being. I do not   14
suppose that ideas are immortal, but certainly they are longer-lived than material objects.

The things I find in Dumpsters, the love letters and rag dolls of   15
so many lives, remind me of this lesson. Now I hardly pick up a thing without envisioning the time I will cast it away. This, I think, is a healthy state of mind. Almost everything I have now has already been cast out at least once, proving that what I own is valueless to someone.

I find that my desire to grab for the gaudy bauble has been   16
largely sated. I think this is an attitude I share with the very wealthy—we both know there is plenty more where whatever we have came from. Between us are the rat-race millions who have confounded their selves with the objects they grasp and who nightly scavenge the cable channels for they know not what.

I am sorry for them.   17

Questions for Study and Discussion

1. Why does Eighner prefer the word scavenging to foraging or Dumpster diving? What does this exploration of scavenging diction tell the reader about Eighner at the beginning of the essay? (Glossary: *Diction*)

2. How does Eighner use illustration to depict the evolution of a person from a new to an experienced scavenger? What does it contribute to the essay?

3. What words does Eighner use to describe the actual items he finds while scavenging?

4. What "separates the dilettanti from the professionals" of Dumpster divers?

5. What are the two lessons Eighner learns from scavenging? Why are they important to him?

6. Eighner says "Dumpster diving has serious drawbacks as a way of life." (paragraph 12) But he concludes his essay by

saying "I am sorry for [the rat-race millions]." In what way has scavenging benefited him? In what way has it harmed him?

7. Eighner refers to elements of Dumpster diving that are concrete (e.g., "He finds pristine ice cream, still frozen, more than he can eat or keep."), as well as abstract (e.g., "The second lesson is the transience of material being."). Discuss the difference between these elements. (Glossary: *Concrete/ Abstract*) What does Eighner achieve by using both types of elements?

Vocabulary

Refer to your dictionary to define the following words as they are used in this selection. Then use each word in a sentence of your own.

refuse (3)	transience (14)
niche (3)	sated (16)
dilettanti (9)	rat-race (16)
qualms (10)	

Suggested Writing Assignments

1. Eighner emphasizes the transience of material objects in his essay. How important are material objects to you? Why? Which ones give you the most pleasure? Can you envision disposing of them? When and why? Be sure to illustrate your essay with examples and anecdotes.

2. Write an essay about a time when you experienced a transition in your way of life. It can involve moving from one place to another, starting a job or going to school, or any situation in which you had to become comfortable with your new situation. Illustrate your essay with examples of how your situation changed and what you did to adapt.

CONTROLLING THE ELECTRONIC HOME

Ellen Cobb Wade

*Ellen Cobb Wade, of Houston, Texas, wrote the fol-
lowing essay in 1984. It appeared in* Newsweek's
*"My Turn," a weekly public opinion column written
by readers of the magazine. Although not a professional writer, Wade eloquently communicates her
frustrations with some of the modern "conveniences" that sometimes seem to make life more
difficult not less.*

I was watching "Wall Street Week" in my parents' living room   1
when their new telephone rang: it was a delightful little jingle
quite unlike the standard ring I've always known. Reaching for
the remote-control unit so I could lower the television sound before I answered the phone, I confronted a baffling array of tiny
buttons. The "vol" button that I pushed only raised the noise level
higher. I could neither hush the electronic voices nor turn off the
set. And by the time I learned how, the caller had decided no one
was home.

After that I started to notice the newly hostile appliances I en-   2
counter every day. Mother's trilling cordless phone has an antenna
and a variety of bewildering switches never seen—nor needed—
before. Every phone in her house is different, and I need a training session before I can use them. When my parents visit me, they
are baffled by the VCR and made helpless by the microwave oven.
It's not that they don't have these amenities in their own home—
they do—but the gadget controls are so different.

When I was growing up in the 1960s and 1970s, learning how to   3
run a home, technology was standard and friendly. Refrigerators,
ovens, washing machines, radios, televisions, record players—a
10-year-old could run them all. Once you learned one model, all
the other brands were easily mastered. Not so the appliances of
the 1980s, particularly now that new gadgets have proliferated
and old ones have been transmogrified.

The digital revolution caused a lot of this confusion. A clock   4
radio, for example, used to have a face and a slender hand that
you'd set pointing to the time you wanted to get up. Nowadays, a
clock radio is a formidable machine: programmable to the minute, it can wake you and your mate at different times, let one or
both of you "snooze," even activate the coffee maker. But just
unplug the thing for a 10th of a second, and you'll be back studying the owner's manual as the display automatically blinks out
12:00—as though time were standing still.

There is nothing inherently hostile or confusing, of course, in   5
individual digital clocks or video recorders. Rather, it is the almost infinite variety of available options and control mechanisms
that is so distressing. The root of the problem is not in the products themselves, but in the marketplace. Why do there seem to be
200 different kinds of microwave ovens to choose from?

Competition is supposed to eliminate all but the few, best ver-   6
sions of a given product, but that market mechanism has evidently gone haywire. Perhaps it is malfunctioning because "the
marketplace" as a simple constant no longer exists: no one store,
not even one megamall, can begin to stock all the available brands.
Even our currency is no longer standard. I can buy a modular
telephone from Sears or from any one of a score of specialty catalogs; I can get one free with a new television or "earn" one by
saving diaper boxtops, by sitting through a sales pitch for a time-
sharing condominium or by making enough purchases with my
bank card.

As a consumer, I am not delighted by the cornucopia of goods   7
available to me. Instead, I am angry that I can't begin to make a
systematic comparison and thus a rational choice. And so I buy
haphazardly, as other consumers must do as well, and the marketplace continues to be an overstocked bazaar.

AT&T once gave us telephones that anyone—even a frightened   8
child faced with an emergency—could use. The federal government, long ago, did a nice job of standardizing the controls of
automobiles so that driving an unfamiliar car is relatively easy. I
am not advocating a return to the "good old days" of monopoly,
and I do not like the idea of Congress spending time arguing
about clock radio controls. But the time has come for some standards or regulations. Someone, perhaps the manufacturers themselves or their associations, should set standards for the design

and the description of how all these gadgets and gimcracks work.

I don't really know what the answer is; I just see a problem that 9 is growing worse each year. Because the list of instructions for running our household began to take the form of a small book, my husband and I have given up our old habit of inviting single friends or college students to house-sit when we're out of town. Because we discontinued this house-sitting practice, we installed a burglar-alarm system, which, ironically, no one can operate but us. I fumble in friends' kitchens these days, unable to use their food processors or microwaves; I feel dumb making a call on their modular telephones because I need to ask for help every time.

Instead of universalizing and improving communication, ad- 10 vanced technology is turning middle-class households into electronic fortresses. It is even reinforcing sex-role specialization: my husband is in charge of the VCR, while I am the only one in the family who understands the mysteries of our microwave.

And we haven't even begun to shop for a home computer. 11

Questions for Study and Discussion

1. What is Wade's thesis? (Glossary: *Thesis*) Where is it most clearly stated?

2. Why does Wade begin with the story about her parents' telephone? How does this story help illustrate her argument?

3. What is the difference between appliances in the 1980s and appliances in the 1960s? What is the problem with the new appliances?

4. What does Wade mean by "market mechanism"? How has the market mechanism gone haywire with electronic goods? Do you agree with Wade's assessment? Why or why not?

5. Examine Wade's diction. (Glossary: *Diction*) What words does she use to effectively illustrate the problems she presents?

6. Do you find the last sentence effective? (Glossary: *Beginnings and Endings*) Why or why not?

Vocabulary

Refer to your dictionary to define the following words as they are used in this selection. Then use each word in a sentence of your own.

hostile (2)   inherently (5)
trilling (2)   cornucopia (7)
proliferated (3)   haphazardly (7)
transmogrified (3)

Suggested Writing Assignments

1. Write about an electronic appliance that has changed your life for the better. How has it changed your life? What has it done to make your life better? Illustrate your essay with anecdotes about the appliance.

2. Have you ever had a term paper "eaten" by your computer? Write about an experience with an electronic device that didn't work the way it should have. What happened? What would have prevented it? What would you suggest to the manufacturer to make the "marvelous" electronic device work better?

11

NARRATION

To *narrate* is to tell a story or to tell what happened. Whenever you relate an incident or use an anecdote to make a point, you use narration. In its broadest sense, narration is any account of an event or series of events. Although most often associated with fiction, narration is effective and useful in all kinds of writing.

Good narration has four essential features: a clear context; well-chosen details; a logical, often chronological organization; and an appropriate and consistent point of view. Consider, for example, the following paragraph from Willie Morris's "On a Commuter Train":

> One afternoon in late August, as the summer's sun streamed into the [railroad] car and made little jumping shadows on the windows, I sat gazing out at the tenement-dwellers, who were themselves looking out of their windows from the gray crumbling buildings along the tracks of upper Manhattan. As we crossed into the Bronx, the train unexpectedly slowed down for a few miles. Suddenly from out of my window I saw a large crowd near the tracks, held back by two policemen. Then, on the other side from my window, I saw a sight I would never be able to forget: a little boy almost severed in halves, lying at an incredible angle near the track. The ground was covered with blood, and the boy's eyes were opened wide, strained and disbelieving in his sudden oblivion. A policeman stood next to him, his arms folded, staring straight ahead at the windows of our train. In the orange glow of late afternoon the policemen, the crowd, the corpse of the boy were for a brief moment immobile, motionless, a small tableau to violence and death in the city. Behind me, in the next row of seats, there was a game of bridge. I heard one of the four men say as he looked out at the sight, "God, that's horrible." Another said, in a whisper, "Terrible, terrible." There was a momentary silence, punctuated only by the clicking of the wheels on the track. Then, after the pause, I heard the first man say: "Two hearts."
>
> Willie Morris

This paragraph contains all the elements of good narration. At the beginning Morris establishes a clear context for his narrative, telling when, where, and to whom the action happened. He has chosen details well, including enough detail so that we know what is happening but not so much that we become overwhelmed, confused, or bored. Morris organizes his narration logically, with a beginning that sets the scene, a middle that paints the picture, and an end that makes his point, all arranged chronologically. Finally, he tells the story from the first-person point of view: We experience the event directly through the writer's eyes and ears, as if we too had been on the scene of the action.

Morris could have told his story from the third-person point of view. In this point of view, the narrator is not a participant in the action, and does not use the pronoun *I*. In the following example, William Allen White narrates his daughter's fatal accident:

> The last hour of her life was typical of its happiness. She came home from a day's work at school, topped off by a hard grind with the copy on the High School Annual, and felt that a ride would refresh her. She climbed into her khakis, chattering to her mother about the work she was doing, and hurried to get her horse and be out on the dirt roads for the country air and the radiant green fields of the spring. As she rode through the town on an easy gallop she kept waving at passers-by. She knew everyone in town. For a decade the little figure with the long pig-tail and the red hair ribbon has been familiar on the streets of Emporia, and she got in the way of speaking to those who nodded at her. She passed the Kerrs, walking the horse, in front of the Normal Library, and waved at them; passed another friend a few hundred feet further on, and waved at her. The horse was walking and, as she turned into North Merchant street she took off her cowboy hat, and the horse swung into a lope. She passed the Tripletts and waved her cowboy hat at them, still moving gaily north on Merchant street. A Gazette carrier passed—a High School boy friend—and she waved at him, but with her bridle hand: the horse veered quickly, plunged into the parking area where the low-hanging limb faced her, and, while she still looked back waving the blow came. But she did not fall from the horse; she slipped off, dazed a bit, staggered and fell in a faint. She never quite recovered consciousness.
>
> William Allen White

SHAME

Dick Gregory

*Dick Gregory, the well-known comedian, has long
been active in the civil rights movement. During
the 1960s Gregory was also an outspoken critic of
America's involvement in Vietnam. In the following
episode from his autobiography* Nigger *(1964), he
narrates the story of a childhood experience that
taught him the meaning of shame. Through his use
of realistic dialogue and vivid details, he dramatically re-creates this experience for his readers.*

I never learned hate at home, or shame. I had to go to school for
that. I was about seven years old when I got my first big lesson.
I was in love with a little girl named Helene Tucker, a light-
complexioned little girl with pigtails and nice manners. She was
always clean and she was smart in school. I think I went to school
then mostly to look at her. I brushed my hair and even got me a
little old handkerchief. It was a lady's handkerchief, but I didn't
want Helene to see me wipe my nose on my hand. The pipes were
frozen again, there was no water in the house, but I washed my
socks and shirt every night. I'd get a pot, and go over to Mister
Ben's grocery store, and stick my pot down into his soda machine.
Scoop out some chopped ice. By evening the ice melted to water
for washing. I got sick a lot that winter because the fire would go
out at night before the clothes were dry. In the morning I'd put
them on, wet or dry, because they were the only clothes I had.

Everybody's got a Helene Tucker, a symbol of everything you
want. I loved her for her goodness, her cleanness, her popularity.
She'd walk down my street and my brothers and sisters would
yell, "Here comes Helene," and I'd rub my tennis sneakers on the
back of my pants and wish my hair wasn't so nappy and the white
folks' shirt fit me better. I'd run out on the street. If I knew my
place and didn't come too close, she'd wink at me and say hello.
That was a good feeling. Sometimes I'd follow her all the way
home, and shovel the snow off her walk and try to make friends

227

with her Momma and her aunts. I'd drop money on her stoop late at night on my way back from shining shoes in the taverns. And she had a Daddy, and he had a good job. He was a paper hanger.

I guess I would have gotten over Helene by summertime, but something happened in that classroom that made her face hang in front of me for the next twenty-two years. When I played the drums in high school it was for Helene and when I broke track records in college it was for Helene and when I started standing behind microphones and heard applause I wished Helene could hear it, too. It wasn't until I was twenty-nine years old and married and making money that I finally got her out of my system. Helene was sitting in that classroom when I learned to be ashamed of myself.

It was on a Thursday. I was sitting in the back of the room, in a seat with a chalk circle drawn around it. The idiot's seat, the troublemaker's seat.

The teacher thought I was stupid. Couldn't spell, couldn't read, couldn't do arithmetic. Just stupid. Teachers were never interested in finding out that you couldn't concentrate because you were so hungry, because you hadn't had any breakfast. All you could think about was noontime, would it ever come? Maybe you could sneak into the cloakroom and steal a bite of some kid's lunch out of a coat pocket. A bite of something. Paste. You can't really make a meal of paste, or put it on bread for a sandwich, but sometimes I'd scoop a few spoonfuls out of the paste jar in the back of the room. Pregnant people get strange tastes. I was pregnant with poverty. Pregnant with dirt and pregnant with smells that made people turn away, pregnant with cold and pregnant with shoes that were never bought for me, pregnant with five other people in my bed and no Daddy in the next room, and pregnant with hunger. Paste doesn't taste too bad when you're hungry.

The teacher thought I was a troublemaker. All she saw from the front of the room was a little black boy who squirmed in his idiot's seat and made noises and poked the kids around him. I guess she couldn't see a kid who made noises because he wanted someone to know he was there.

It was on a Thursday, the day before the Negro payday. The eagle always flew on Friday. The teacher was asking each student how much his father would give to the Community Chest. On Friday night, each kid would get the money from his father, and on Monday he would bring it to the school. I decided I was going to buy me a Daddy right then. I had money in my pocket from shining shoes and selling papers, and whatever Helene Tucker pledged for her Daddy I was going to top it. And I'd hand the money right in. I wasn't going to wait until Monday to buy me a Daddy.

I was shaking, scared to death. The teacher opened her book 8 and started calling out names alphabetically.

"Helene Tucker?" 9

"My daddy said he'd give two dollars and fifty cents." 10

"That's very nice, Helene. Very, very nice indeed." 11

That made me feel pretty good. It wouldn't take too much to top 12 that. I had almost three dollars in dimes and quarters in my pocket. I stuck my hand in my pocket and held onto the money, waiting for her to call my name. But the teacher closed her book after she called everybody else in the class.

I stood up and raised my hand. 13

"What is it now?" 14

"You forgot me." 15

She turned toward the blackboard. "I don't have time to be 16 playing with you, Richard."

"My Daddy said he'd . . ." 17

"Sit down, Richard, you're disturbing the class." 18

"My Daddy said he'd give . . . fifteen dollars." 19

She turned around and looked mad. "We are collecting this 20 money for you and your kind, Richard Gregory. If your Daddy can give fifteen dollars you have no business being on relief."

"I got it right now, I got it right now, my Daddy gave it to me to 21 turn in today, my Daddy said . . ."

"And furthermore," she said, looking right at me, her nostrils 22 getting big and her lips getting thin and her eyes opening wide, "we know you don't have a Daddy."

Helene Tucker turned around, her eyes full of tears. She felt 23 sorry for me. Then I couldn't see her too well because I was crying, too.

"Sit down, Richard." 24

And I always thought the teacher kind of liked me. She always 25 picked me to wash the blackboard on Friday, after school. That was a big thrill, it made me feel important. If I didn't wash it, come Monday the school might not function right.

"Where are you going, Richard?"

I walked out of school that day, and for a long time I didn't go back very often. There was shame there.

Now there was shame everywhere. It seemed like the whole world had been inside that classroom, everyone had heard what the teacher had said, everyone had turned around and felt sorry for me. There was shame in going to the Worthy Boys Annual Christmas Dinner for you and your kind, because everybody knew what a worthy boy was. Why couldn't they just call it the Boys Annual Dinner; why'd they have to give it a name? There was shame in wearing the brown and orange and white plaid mackinaw the welfare gave to three thousand boys. Why'd it have to be the same for everybody so when you walked down the street the people could see you were on relief? It was a nice warm mackinaw and it had a hood, and my Momma beat me and called me a little rat when she found out I stuffed it in the bottom of a pail full of garbage way over on Cottage Street. There was shame in running over to Mister Ben's at the end of the day and asking for his rotten peaches, there was shame in asking Mrs. Simmons for a spoonful of sugar, there was shame in running out to meet the relief truck. I hated that truck, full of food for you and your kind. I ran into the house and hid when it came. And then I started to sneak through alleys, to take the long way home so the people going into White's Eat Shop wouldn't see me. Yeah, the whole world heard the teacher that day, we all know you don't have a Daddy.

Questions for Study and Discussion

1. What does Gregory mean by "shame"? What precisely was he ashamed of, and what in particular did he learn from the incident?

2. How do the first three paragraphs of the essay help to establish a context for the narrative that follows?

3. Why do you think Gregory narrates this episode in the first-person point of view? What would be gained or lost if he instead wrote it in the third-person point of view?

4. What is the teacher's attitude toward Gregory? Consider her own words and actions as well as Gregory's opinion in arriving at your answer.

5. What role does money play in Gregory's narrative? How does money relate to his sense of shame?

6. Specific details can enhance the reader's understanding and appreciation of a narrative. Gregory's description of Helene Tucker's manners or the plaid of his mackinaw, for example, makes his account vivid and interesting. Cite several other specific details he gives, and consider how the narrative would be different without them.

7. Consider the diction of this essay. What effect does Gregory's repetition of the word *shame* have on you? Why do you think Gregory uses simple vocabulary to narrate this particular experience? (Glossary: *Diction*)

Vocabulary

Refer to your dictionary to define the following words as they are used in this selection. Then use each word in a sentence of your own.

   nappy (2)   mackinaw (28)

Suggested Writing Assignments

1. Using Dick Gregory's essay as a model, write an essay narrating an experience that made you especially afraid, angry, surprised, embarrassed, or proud. Include sufficient detail so that your readers will know exactly what happened.

2. Most of us have had frustrating experiences with mechanical objects that seem to have perverse minds of their own. Write a brief narrative recounting one such experience with a vending machine, typewriter, television set, pay toilet, computer, pay telephone, or any other such machine. Be sure to establish a clear context for your narrative.

38 WHO SAW MURDER DIDN'T CALL POLICE

Martin Gansberg

Martin Gansberg was born in 1920 in Brooklyn, New York, and graduated from St. John's University. A long-time reporter, Gansberg wrote the following article for the New York Times *two weeks after the early morning events he so poignantly narrates. Once you've finished reading the essay, you will understand why it has been so often reprinted and why the name Kitty Genovese is still invoked whenever questions of public apathy arise.*

For more than half an hour 38 respectable, law-abiding citizens in Queens watched a killer stalk and stab a woman in three separate attacks in Kew Gardens.

Twice their chatter and the sudden glow of their bedroom lights interrupted him and frightened him off. Each time he returned, sought her out, and stabbed her again. Not one person telephoned the police during the assault; one witness called after the woman was dead.

That was two weeks ago today.

Still shocked is Assistant Chief Inspector Frederick M. Lussen, in charge of the borough's detectives and a veteran of 25 years of homicide investigations. He can give a matter-of-fact recitation on many murders. But the Kew Gardens slaying baffles him—not because it is a murder, but because the "good people" failed to call the police.

"As we have reconstructed the crime," he said, "the assailant had three chances to kill this woman during a 35-minute period. He returned twice to complete the job. If we had been called when he first attacked, the woman might not be dead now."

This is what the police say happened beginning at 3:20 A.M. in the staid, middle-class, tree-lined Austin Street area:

Twenty-eight-year-old Catherine Genovese, who was called 7
Kitty by almost everyone in the neighborhood, was returning
home from her job as manager of a bar in Hollis. She parked her
red Fiat in a lot adjacent to the Kew Gardens Long Island Rail
Road Station, facing Mowbray Place. Like many residents of the
neighborhood, she had parked there day after day since her arrival from Connecticut a year ago, although the railroad frowns on
the practice.

She turned off the lights of her car, locked the door, and started 8
to walk the 100 feet to the entrance of her apartment at 82–70
Austin Street, which is in a Tudor building, with stores in the first
floor and apartments on the second.

The entrance to the apartment is in the rear of the building be- 9
cause the front is rented to retail stores. At night the quiet neighborhood is shrouded in the slumbering darkness that marks most
residential areas.

Miss Genovese noticed a man at the far end of the lot, near a 10
seven-story apartment house at 82–40 Austin Street. She halted.
Then, nervously, she headed up Austin Street toward Lefferts
Boulevard, where there is a call box to the 102nd Police Precinct
in nearby Richmond Hill.

She got as far as a street light in front of a bookstore before the 11
man grabbed her. She screamed. Lights went on in the 10-story
apartment house at 82–67 Austin Street, which faces the bookstore. Windows slid open and voices punctuated the early-morning
stillness.

Miss Genovese screamed: "Oh, my God, he stabbed me! Please 12
help me! Please help me!"

From one of the upper windows in the apartment house, a man 13
called down: "Let that girl alone!"

The assailant looked up at him, shrugged, and walked down 14
Austin Street toward a white sedan parked a short distance away.
Miss Genovese struggled to her feet.

Lights went out. The killer returned to Miss Genovese, now try- 15
ing to make her way around the side of the building by the park-
ing lot to get to her apartment. The assailant stabbed her again.

"I'm dying!" she shrieked. "I'm dying!" 16

Windows were opened again, and lights went on in many apart- 17
ments. The assailant got into his car and drove away. Miss Geno-

vese staggered to her feet. A city bus, O–10, the Lefferts Boulevard line to Kennedy International Airport, passed. It was 3:35 A.M.

The assailant returned. By then, Miss Genovese had crawled to 18 the back of the building, where the freshly painted brown doors to the apartment house held out hope for safety. The killer tried the first door; she wasn't there. At the second door, 82–62 Austin Street, he saw her slumped on the floor at the foot of the stairs. He stabbed her a third time—fatally.

It was 3:50 by the time the police received their first call, from 19 a man who was a neighbor of Miss Genovese. In two minutes they were at the scene. The neighbor, a 70-year-old woman, and another woman were the only persons on the street. Nobody else came forward.

The man explained that he had called the police after much de- 20 liberation. He had phoned a friend in Nassau County for advice and then he had crossed the roof of the building to the apartment of the elderly woman to get her to make the call.

"I didn't want to get involved," he sheepishly told the police. 21

Six days later, the police arrested Winston Moseley, a 29-year- 22 old business-machine operator, and charged him with homicide. Moseley had no previous record. He is married, has two children and owns a home at 133–19 Sutter Avenue, South Ozone Park, Queens. On Wednesday, a court committed him to Kings County Hospital for psychiatric observation.

When questioned by the police, Moseley also said that he had 23 slain Mrs. Annie May Johnson, 24, of 146–12 133d Avenue, Jamaica, on Feb. 29 and Barbara Kralik, 15, of 174–17 140th Avenue, Springfield Gardens, last July. In the Kralik case, the police are holding Alvin L. Mitchell, who is said to have confessed that slaying.

The police stressed how simple it would have been to have got- 24 ten in touch with them. "A phone call," said one of the detectives, "would have done it." The police may be reached by dialing "O" for operator or SPring 7–3100.

Today witnesses from the neighborhood, which is made up of 25 one-family homes in the $35,000 to $60,000 range with the exception of the two apartment houses near the railroad station, find it difficult to explain why they didn't call the police.

A housewife, knowingly if quite casually, said, "We thought it 26 was a lovers' quarrel." A husband and wife both said, "Frankly, we were afraid." They seemed aware of the fact that events might have been different. A distraught woman, wiping her hands in her apron, said, "I didn't want my husband to get involved."

One couple, now willing to talk about that night, said they heard the first screams. The husband looked thoughtfully at the bookstore where the killer first grabbed Miss Genovese. 27

"We went to the window to see what was happening," he said, "but the light from our bedroom made it difficult to see the street." The wife, still apprehensive, added: "I put out the light and we were able to see better." 28

Asked why they hadn't called the police, she shrugged and replied: "I don't know." 29

A man peeked out from a slight opening in the doorway to his apartment and rattled off an account of the killer's second attack. Why hadn't he called the police at the time? "I was tired," he said without emotion. "I went back to bed." 30

It was 4:25 A.M. when the ambulance arrived to take the body of Miss Genovese. It drove off. "Then," a solemn police detective said, "the people came out." 31

Questions for Study and Discussion

1. What is the author's purpose in this selection? What are the advantages or disadvantages in using narration to accomplish this purpose? Explain. (Glossary: *Purpose*)

2. Where does the narrative actually begin? What is the function of the material that precedes the beginning of the narrative proper?

3. What reasons did Kitty Genovese's neighbors give for not calling the police when they first heard her calls for help? What, in your opinion, do their reasons say about contemporary American society? Explain.

4. How would you describe Gansberg's tone? Is the tone appropriate for the story Gansberg narrates? Explain. (Glossary: *Tone*)

5. Gansberg uses dialogue throughout his essay. How many people does he quote? What does he accomplish by using dialogue? (Glossary: *Dialogue*)

6. What do you think Gansberg achieves by giving the addresses of the victims in paragraph 23?
7. Reflect on Gansberg's ending. What would be lost or gained by adding a paragraph that analyzed the meaning of the narrative for the reader? (Glossary: *Beginnings and Endings*)

Vocabulary

Refer to your dictionary to define the following words as they are used in this selection. Then use each word in a sentence of your own.

stalk (1)	shrouded (9)
recitation (4)	sheepishly (21)
assailant (5)	apprehensive (28)
staid (6)	

Suggested Writing Assignments

1. Gansberg's essay is about public apathy and fear. What is your own experience with the public? Modeling an essay after Gansberg's, narrate yet another event or series of events that you personally know about. Or, write a narration about public involvement, one that contradicts Gansberg's essay.

2. It is common when using narration to tell about firsthand experience and to tell the story in the first person. It is good practice, however, to try writing a narration about something you don't know about firsthand but must learn about, much the same as a newspaper reporter must do. For several days, be attentive to events occurring around you—in your neighborhood, school, community, region—events that would be an appropriate basis for a narrative essay. Interview the principal characters involved in your story, take detailed notes, and then write your narration.

THE DARE

Roger Hoffmann

*Born in 1948, Roger Hoffmann is a free-lance
writer and the author of* The Complete Software
Marketplace *(1984). In "The Dare," first published
in the* New York Times Magazine *in 1986, Hoffmann recounts how in his youth he accepted a
friend's challenge to dive under a moving freight
train and to roll out the other side. As an adult,
Hoffmann appreciates the act for what it was—a
crazy, dangerous childhood stunt. But he also remembers what the episode meant to him as a seventh grader trying to prove himself to his peers.*

The secret to diving under a moving freight train and rolling   1
out the other side with all your parts attached lies in picking
the right spot between the tracks to hit with your back. Ideally,
you want soft dirt or pea gravel, clear of glass shards and railroad
spikes that could cause you instinctively, and fatally, to sit up.
Today, at thirty-eight, I couldn't be threatened or baited enough to
attempt that dive. But as a seventh grader struggling to make the
cut in a tough Atlanta grammar school, all it took was a dare.

I coasted through my first years of school as a fussed-over   2
smart kid, the teacher's pet who finished his work first and then
strutted around the room tutoring other students. By the seventh
grade, I had more A's than friends. Even my old cronies, Dwayne
and O.T., made it clear I'd never be one of the guys in junior high
if I didn't dirty up my act. They challenged me to break the rules,
and I did. The I-dare-you's escalated: shoplifting, sugaring teachers' gas tanks, dropping lighted matches into public mailboxes.
Each guerrilla act won me the approval I never got for just being
smart.

Walking home by the railroad tracks after school, we started   3
playing chicken with oncoming trains. O.T., who was failing that
year, always won. One afternoon he charged a boxcar from the

side, stopping just short of throwing himself between the wheels. I was stunned. After the train disappeared, we debated whether someone could dive under a moving car, stay put for a 10-count, then scramble out the other side. I thought it could be done and said so. O.T. immediately stepped in front of me and smiled. Not by me, I added quickly, I certainly didn't mean that I could do it. "A smart guy like you," he said, his smile evaporating, "you could figure it out easy." And then, squeezing each word for effect, "I . . . DARE . . . you." I'd just turned twelve. The monkey clawing my back was Teacher's Pet. And I'd been dared.

As an adult, I've been on both ends of life's implicit business   4
and social I-dare-you's, although adults don't use those words. We provoke with body language, tone of voice, ambiguous phrases. I dare you to: argue with the boss, tell Fred what you think of him, send the wine back. Only rarely are the risks physical. How we respond to dares when we are young may have something to do with which of the truly hazardous male inner dares—attacking mountains, tempting bulls at Pamplona—we embrace or ignore as men.

For two weeks, I scouted trains and tracks. I studied moving   5
boxcars close up, memorizing how they squatted on their axles, never getting used to the squeal or the way the air fell hot from the sides. I created an imaginary, friendly train and ran next to it. I mastered a shallow, head-first dive with a simple half-twist. I'd land on my back, count to ten, imagine wheels and, locking both hands on the rail to my left, heave myself over and out. Even under pure sky, though, I had to fight to keep my eyes open and my shoulders between the rails.

The next Saturday, O.T., Dwayne and three eighth graders met   6
me below the hill that backed up to the lumberyard. The track followed a slow bend there and opened to a straight, slightly up-hill climb for a solid third of a mile. My run started two hundred yards after the bend. The train would have its tongue hanging out.

The other boys huddled off to one side, a circle on another   7
planet, and watched quietly as I double-knotted my shoelaces. My hands trembled. O.T. broke the circle and came over to me. He kept his hands hidden in the pockets of his jacket. We looked at each other. BB's of sweat appeared beneath his nose. I stuffed my

wallet in one of his pockets, rubbing it against his knuckles on the way in, and slid my house key, wired to a red-and-white fishing bobber, into the other. We backed away from each other, and he turned and ran to join the four already climbing up the hill.

I watched them all the way to the top. They clustered together 8 as if I were taking their picture. Their silhouette resembled a round-shouldered tombstone. They waved down to me, and I dropped them from my mind and sat down on the rail. Immediately, I jumped back. The steel was vibrating.

The train sounded like a cow going short of breath. I pulled my 9 shirttail out and looked down at my spot, then up the incline of track ahead of me. Suddenly the air went hot, and the engine was by me. I hadn't pictured it moving that fast. A man's bare head leaned out and stared at me. I waved to him with my left hand and turned into the train, burying my face in the incredible noise. When I looked up, the head was gone.

I started running alongside the boxcars. Quickly, I found their 10 pace, held it, and then eased off, concentrating on each thick wheel that cut past me. I slowed another notch. Over my shoulder, I picked my car as it came off the bend, locking in the image of the white mountain goat painted on its side. I waited, leaning forward like the anchor in a 440-relay, wishing the baton up the track behind me. Then the big goat fired by me, and I was flying and then tucking my shoulder as I dipped under the train.

A heavy blanket of red dust settled over me. I felt bolted to the 11 earth. Sheet-metal bellies thundered and shook above my face. Count to ten, a voice said, watch the axles and look to your left for daylight. But I couldn't count, and I couldn't find left if my life depended on it, which it did. The colors overhead went from brown to red to black to red again. Finally, I ripped my hands free, forced them to the rail, and, in one convulsive jerk, threw myself into the blue light.

I lay there face down until there was no more noise, and I could 12 feel the sun against the back of my neck. I sat up. The last ribbon of train was slipping away in the distance. Across the tracks, O.T. was leading a cavalry charge down the hill, five very small, galloping boys, their fists whirling above them. I pulled my knees to my chest. My corduroy pants puckered wet across my thighs. I didn't care.

Questions for Study and Discussion

1. Why did Hoffmann accept O.T.'s dare when he was twelve years old? Would he accept the same dare today? Why or why not?

2. How does paragraph 4 function in the context of Hoffmann's narrative?

3. How has Hoffmann organized his essay? (Glossary: *Organization*) What period of time is covered in paragraphs 2–5? In paragraphs 6–12? What conclusions about narrative time can you draw from what Hoffmann has done?

4. What were Hoffmann's feelings on the day of his dive under the moving freight train? Do you think he was afraid? How do you know?

5. Identify four figures of speech that Hoffmann uses in his essay. (Glossary: *Figures of Speech*) What does each figure add to his narrative?

6. Hoffmann tells his story in the first person: the narrator is the principal actor. What would have been gained or lost had Hoffmann used the third person, with O.T. or Dwayne telling the story? Explain.

Vocabulary

Refer to your dictionary to define the following words as they are used in this selection. Then use each word in a sentence of your own.

shards (1)	evaporating (3)
baited (1)	implicit (4)
cronies (2)	ambiguous (4)
escalated (2)	convulsive (11)
guerrilla (2)	

Suggested Writing Assignments

1. Can you remember any dares that you made or accepted while growing up? What were the consequences of these dares? Did you and your peers find dares a way to test or

prove yourselves? Write a narrative essay about a dare that you made, accepted, or simply witnessed.

2. Each of us can tell of an experience that has been unusually significant for us. Think about your past, identify one experience that has been especially important for you, and write an essay about it. In preparing to write your narrative, you may find it helpful to ask such questions as: Why is the experience important for me? What details are necessary for me to re-create the experience in an interesting and engaging way? How can my narrative of the experience be most effectively organized? Over what period of time did the experience occur? What point of view will work best?

MOMMA, THE DENTIST, AND ME

Maya Angelou

Maya Angelou is best known as the author of
I Know Why the Caged Bird Sings *(1970), the first
of four books in the series which constitutes her
autobiography and for "On the Pulse of Morning,"
a characteristically optimistic poem on the need for
personal and national renewal she read at President
Clinton's inauguration on January 20, 1993. Starting with her beginnings in St. Louis in 1928, Angelou presents a life story of joyful triumph over
hardships that tested her courage and threatened
her spirit. Trained as a dancer, Angelou has also
published books of poetry, acted in the television
series "Roots," and, at the request of Martin Luther
King, Jr., served as a coordinator of the Southern
Christian Leadership Conference. In the following excerpt from* I Know Why the Caged Bird
Sings, *Angelou narrates what happened, and what
might have happened, when her grandmother, the
"Momma" of the story, takes her to the local dentist.*

The angel of the candy counter had found me out at last, and   1
was exacting excruciating penance for all the stolen Milky
Ways, Mounds, Mr. Goodbars and Hersheys with Almonds. I had
two cavities that were rotten to the gums. The pain was beyond
the bailiwick of crushed aspirins or oil of cloves. Only one thing
could help me, so I prayed earnestly that I'd be allowed to sit
under the house and have the building collapse on my left jaw.
Since there was no Negro dentist in Stamps, nor doctor either, for
that matter, Momma had dealt with previous toothaches by pulling them out (a string tied to the tooth with the other end looped
over her fist), pain killers and prayer. In this particular instance
the medicine had proved ineffective; there wasn't enough enamel

left to hook a string on, and the prayers were being ignored because the Balancing Angel was blocking their passage.

I lived a few days and nights in blinding pain, not so much toying with as seriously considering the idea of jumping in the well, and Momma decided I had to be taken to a dentist. The nearest Negro dentist was in Texarkana, twenty-five miles away, and I was certain that I'd be dead long before we reached half the distance. Momma said we'd go to Dr. Lincoln, right in Stamps, and he'd take care of me. She said he owed her a favor.

I knew there were a number of whitefolks in town that owed her favors. Bailey and I had seen the books which showed how she had lent money to Blacks and whites alike during the Depression, and most still owed her. But I couldn't aptly remember seeing Dr. Lincoln's name, nor had I ever heard of a Negro's going to him as a patient. However, Momma said we were going, and put water on the stove for our baths. I had never been to a doctor, so she told me that after the bath (which would make my mouth feel better) I had to put on freshly starched and ironed underclothes from inside out. The ache failed to respond to the bath, and I knew then that the pain was more serious than that which anyone had ever suffered.

Before we left the Store, she ordered me to brush my teeth and then wash my mouth with Listerine. The idea of even opening my clamped jaws increased the pain, but upon her explanation that when you go to a doctor you have to clean yourself all over, but most especially the part that's to be examined, I screwed up my courage and unlocked my teeth. The cool air in my mouth and the jarring of my molars dislodged what little remained of my reason. I had frozen to the pain, my family nearly had to tie me down to take the toothbrush away. It was no small effort to get me started on the road to the dentist. Momma spoke to all the passers-by, but didn't stop to chat. She explained over her shoulder that we were going to the doctor and she'd "pass the time of day" on our way home.

Until we reached the pond the pain was my world, an aura that haloed me for three feet around. Crossing the bridge into whitefolks' county, pieces of sanity pushed themselves forward. I had to stop moaning and start walking straight. The white towel, which was drawn under my chin and tied over my head, had to be arranged. If one was dying, it had to be done in style if the dying took place in whitefolks' part of town.

On the other side of the bridge the ache seemed to lessen as if a whitebreeze blew off the whitefolks and cushioned everything in their neighborhood—including my jaw. The gravel road was smoother, the stones smaller and the tree branches hung down around the path and nearly covered us. If the pain didn't diminish then, the familiar yet strange sights hypnotized me into believing that it had. 6

But my head continued to throb with the measured insistence of a bass drum, and how could a toothache pass the calaboose, hear the songs of the prisoners, their blues and laughter, and not be changed? How could one or two or even a mouthful of angry tooth roots meet a wagonload of powhitetrash children, endure their idiotic snobbery and not feel less important? 7

Behind the building which housed the dentist's office ran a small path used by servants and those tradespeople who catered to the butcher and Stamps' one restaurant. Momma and I followed that lane to the backstairs of Dentist Lincoln's office. The sun was bright and gave the day a hard reality as we climbed up the steps to the second floor. 8

Momma knocked on the back door and a young white girl opened it to show surprise at seeing us there. Momma said she wanted to see Dentist Lincoln and to tell him Annie was there. The girl closed the door firmly. Now the humiliation of hearing Momma describe herself as if she had no last name to the young white girl was equal to the physical pain. It seemed terribly unfair to have a toothache and a headache and have to bear at the same time the heavy burden of Blackness. 9

It was always possible that the teeth would quiet down and maybe drop out of their own accord. Momma said we would wait. We leaned in the harsh sunlight on the shaky railings of the dentist's back porch for over an hour. 10

He opened the door and looked at Momma. "Well, Annie, what can I do for you?" 11

He didn't see the towel around my jaw or notice my swollen face. 12

Momma said, "Dentist Lincoln. It's my grandbaby here. She got two rotten teeth that's giving her a fit." 13

She waited for him to acknowledge the truth of her statement. He made no comment, orally or facially. 14

"She had this toothache purt' near four days now, and today I 15
said, 'Young lady, you going to the Dentist.'"

"Annie?" 16

"Yes, sir, Dentist Lincoln." 17

He was choosing words the way people hunt for shells. "Annie, 18
you know I don't treat nigra, colored people."

"I know, Dentist Lincoln. But this here is just my little grand- 19
baby, and she ain't gone be no trouble to you . . ."

"Annie, everybody has a policy. In this world you have to have 20
a policy. Now, my policy is I don't treat colored people."

The sun had baked the oil out of Momma's skin and melted the 21
Vaseline in her hair. She shone greasily as she leaned out of the
dentist's shadow.

"Seem like to me, Dentist Lincoln, you might look after her, she 22
ain't nothing but a little mite. And seems like maybe you owe me
a favor or two."

He reddened slightly. "Favor or no favor. The money has all 23
been repaid to you and that's the end of it. Sorry, Annie." He had
his hand on the doorknob. "Sorry." His voice was a bit kinder on
the second "Sorry," as if he really was.

Momma said, "I wouldn't press on you like this for myself but 24
I can't take No. Not for my grandbaby. When you come to borrow
my money you didn't have to beg. You asked me, and I lent it.
Now, it wasn't my policy. I ain't no moneylender, but you stood to
lose this building and I tried to help you out."

"It's been paid, and raising your voice won't make me change 25
my mind. My policy . . ." He let go of the door and stepped nearer
Momma. The three of us were crowded on the small landing.
"Annie, my policy is I'd rather stick my hand in a dog's mouth
than in a nigger's."

He had never once looked at me. He turned his back and went 26
through the door into the cool beyond. Momma backed up inside herself for a few minutes. I forgot everything except her face
which was almost a new one to me. She leaned over and took the
doorknob, and in her everyday soft voice she said, "Sister, go on
downstairs. Wait for me. I'll be there directly."

Under the most common of circumstances I knew it did no 27
good to argue with Momma. So I walked down the steep stairs,
afraid to look back and afraid not to do so. I turned as the door
slammed, and she was gone.

Momma walked in that room as if she owned it. She shoved that   28
silly nurse aside with one hand and strode into the dentist's office.
He was sitting in his chair, sharpening his mean instruments and
putting extra sting into his medicines. Her eyes were blazing like live
coals and her arms had doubled themselves in length. He looked up
at her just before she caught him by the collar of his white jacket.

"Stand up when you see a lady, you contemptuous scoundrel."   29
Her tongue had thinned and the words rolled off well enunciated.
Enunciated and sharp like little claps of thunder.

The dentist had no choice but to stand at R.O.T.C. attention. His   30
head dropped after a minute and his voice was humble. "Yes,
ma'am, Mrs. Henderson."

"You knave, do you think you acted like a gentleman, speaking to   31
me like that in front of my granddaughter?" She didn't shake him,
although she had the power. She simply held him upright.

"No, ma'am, Mrs. Henderson."   32

"No, ma'am, Mrs. Henderson, what?" Then she did give him the   33
tiniest of shakes, but because of her strength the action set his head
and arms to shaking loose on the ends of his body. He stuttered
much worse than Uncle Willie. "No, ma'am, Mrs. Henderson, I'm
sorry."

With just an edge of her disgust showing, Momma slung him   34
back in his dentist's chair. "Sorry is as sorry does, and you're about
the sorriest dentist I ever laid my eyes on." (She could afford to slip
into the vernacular because she had such eloquent command of
English.)

"I didn't ask you to apologize in front of Marguerite, because I   35
don't want her to know my power, but I order you, now and here-
with. Leave Stamps by sundown."

"Mrs. Henderson, I can't get my equipment . . ." He was shaking   36
terribly now.

"Now, that brings me to my second order. You will never again   37
practice dentistry. Never! When you get settled in your next place,
you will be a vegetarian caring for dogs with the mange, cats with
the cholera and cows with the epizootic. Is that clear?"

The saliva ran down his chin and his eyes filled with tears. "Yes,   38
ma'am. Thank you for not killing me. Thank you, Mrs. Henderson."

Momma pulled herself back from being ten feet tall with eight-foot   39
arms and said, "You're welcome for nothing, you varlet, I wouldn't
waste a killing on the likes of you."

On her way out she waved her handkerchief at the nurse and   40
turned her into a crocus sack of chicken feed.

Momma looked tired when she came down the stairs, but who   41
wouldn't be tired if they had gone through what she had. She
came close to me and adjusted the towel under my jaw (I had forgotten the toothache; I only knew that she made her hands gentle
in order not to awaken the pain). She took my hand. Her voice
never changed. "Come on, Sister."

I reckoned we were going home where she would concoct a   42
brew to eliminate the pain and maybe give me new teeth too. New
teeth that would grow overnight out of my gums. She led me
toward the drugstore, which was in the opposite direction from
the Store. "I'm taking you to Dentist Baker in Texarkana."

I was glad after all that I had bathed and put on Mum and   43
Cashmere Bouquet talcum powder. It was a wonderful surprise.
My toothache had quieted to solemn pain, Momma had obliter-
ated the evil white man, and we were going on a trip to Texarkana, just the two of us.

On the Greyhound she took an inside seat in the back, and I   44
sat beside her. I was so proud of being her granddaughter and
sure that some of her magic must have come down to me. She
asked if I was scared. I only shook my head and leaned over on
her cool brown upper arm. There was no chance that a dentist,
especially a Negro dentist, would dare hurt me then. Not with
Momma there. The trip was uneventful, except that she put her
arm around me, which was very unusual for Momma to do.

The dentist showed me the medicine and the needle before he   45
deadened my gums, but if he hadn't I wouldn't have worried.
Momma stood right behind him. Her arms were folded and she
checked on everything he did. The teeth were extracted and she
bought me an ice cream cone from the side window of a drug
counter. The trip back to Stamps was quiet, except that I had to
spit into a very small empty snuff can which she had gotten for
me and it was difficult with the bus humping and jerking on our
country roads.

At home, I was given a warm salt solution, and when I washed   46
out my mouth I showed Bailey the empty holes, where the clotted
blood sat like filling in a pie crust. He said I was quite brave, and
that was my cue to reveal our confrontation with the peckerwood
dentist and Momma's incredible powers.

I had to admit that I didn't hear the conversation, but what else   47
could she have said than what I said she said? What else done?
He agreed with my analysis in a lukewarm way, and I happily
(after all, I'd been sick) flounced into the Store. Momma was preparing our evening meal and Uncle Willie leaned on the door sill.
She gave her version.

"Dentist Lincoln got right uppity. Said he'd rather put his hand   48
in a dog's mouth. And when I reminded him of the favor, he
brushed it off like a piece of lint. Well, I sent Sister downstairs
and went inside. I hadn't never been in his office before, but I
found the door to where he takes out teeth, and him and the
nurse was in there thick as thieves. I just stood there till he caught
sight of me." Crash bang the pots on the stove. "He jumped just
like he was sitting on a pin. He said, 'Annie, I done tole you, I ain't
gonna mess around in no niggah's mouth.' I said, 'Somebody's got
to do it then,' and he said, 'Take her to Texarkana to the colored
dentist' and that's when I said, 'If you paid me my money I could
afford to take her.' He said, 'It's all been paid.' I tole him everything but the interest been paid. He said ''Twasn't no interest.' I
said, ''Tis now. I'll take ten dollars as payment in full.' You know,
Willie, it wasn't no right thing to do, 'cause I lent that money without thinking about it.

"He tole that little snippety nurse of his'n to give me ten dollars   49
and make me sign a 'paid in full' receipt. She gave it to me and I
signed the papers. Even though by rights he was paid up before, I
figger, he gonna be that kind of nasty, he gonna have to pay for it."

Momma and her son laughed and laughed over the white man's   50
evilness and her retributive sin.

I preferred, much preferred, my version.   51

Questions for Study and Discussion

1. What is Angelou's purpose in narrating the story she tells?
   (Glossary: *Purpose*)
2. Compare and contrast the content and style of the interaction between Momma and the dentist that is given in italics
   with the one given at the end of the narrative. (Glossary:
   Comparison and Contrast)

3. Angelou tells her story chronologically and in the first person. What are the advantages of the first-person narrative?

4. Identify three similes that Angelou uses in her narrative. Explain how each simile serves her purposes. (Glossary: *Figures of Speech*)

5. Why do you suppose Angelou says she prefers her own version of the episode to that of her grandmother?

6. This story is a story of pain and not just the pain of a toothache. How does Angelou describe the pain of the toothache? What other pain does Angelou tell of in this autobiographical narrative?

Vocabulary

Refer to your dictionary to define the following words as they are used in this selection. Then use each word in a sentence of your own.

bailiwick (1)	varlet (39)
calaboose (7)	concoct (42)
mite (22)	snippety (49)
vernacular (34)	retributive (50)

Suggested Writing Assignments

1. One of Angelou's themes in "Momma, the Dentist, and Me" is that cruelty, whether racial, social, professional, or personal, is very difficult to endure and leaves a lasting impression on a person. Think of a situation where an unthinking or insensitive person made you feel inferior for reasons beyond your control. List the sequence of events in your narrative before you draft it. You may find it helpful to reread the introduction to this section before you begin working.

2. Write a narrative in which, like Angelou, you give two versions of an actual event—one the way you thought or wished it happened and the other the way events actually took place.

12

DESCRIPTION

To describe is to create a verbal picture. A person, a place, a thing—even an idea or a state of mind—can be made vividly concrete through description. Here, for example, is Thomas Mann's brief description of a delicatessen:

> It was a narrow room, with a rather high ceiling, and crowded from floor to ceiling with goodies. There were rows and rows of hams and sausages of all shapes and colors— white, yellow, red, and black; fat and lean and round and long—rows of canned preserves, cocoa and tea, bright translucent glass bottles of honey, marmalade, and jam; round bottles and slender bottles, filled with liqueurs and punch— all these things crowded every inch of the shelves from top to bottom.

Writing any description requires, first of all, that the writer gather many details about a subject, relying not only on what the eyes see but on the other sense impressions—touch, taste, smell, hearing—as well. From this catalogue of details the writer selects those that will most effectively create a *dominant impression*—the single quality, mood, or atmosphere that the writer wishes to emphasize. Consider, for example, the details that Mary McCarthy uses to evoke the dominant impression in the following passage from *Memories of a Catholic Girlhood:*

> Whenever we children came to stay at my grandmother's house, we were put to sleep in the sewing room, a bleak, shabby, utilitarian rectangle, more office than bedroom, more attic than office, that played to the hierarchy of chambers the role of poor relation. It was a room without pride: the old sewing machine, some cast-off chairs, a shadeless lamp, rolls of wrapping paper, piles of cardboard boxes that might someday come in handy, papers of pins, and remnants of a material united with the iron folding cots put out for our use and the bare floor boards to give an impression of intense and ruthless temporality. Thin white spreads, of the kind

used in hospitals and charity institutions, and naked blinds at the windows reminded us of our orphaned condition and of the ephemeral character of our visit; there was nothing here to encourage us to consider this our home.

The dominant impression that McCarthy creates is one of clutter, bleakness, and shabbiness. There is nothing in the sewing room that suggests permanence or warmth.

Writers must also carefully plan the order in which to present their descriptive details. The pattern of organization must fit the subject of the description logically and naturally, and must also be easy to follow. For example, visual details can be arranged spatially—from left to right, top to bottom, near to far, or in any other logical order. Other patterns include smallest to largest, softest to loudest, least significant to most significant, most unusual to least unusual. McCarthy suggests a jumble of junk not only by her choice of details but by the apparently random order in which she presents them.

How much detail is enough? There is no fixed answer. A good description includes enough vivid details to create a dominant impression and to bring a scene to life, but not so many that readers are distracted, confused, or bored. In an essay that is purely descriptive, there is room for much detail. Usually, however, writers use description to create the setting for a story, to illustrate ideas, to help clarify a definition or a comparison, or to make the complexities of a process more understandable. Such descriptions should be kept short, and should include just enough detail to make them clear and helpful.

THE SOUNDS OF THE CITY

James Tuite

James Tuite has had a long career at the New York Times, *where he once served as sports editor. As a free-lance writer he has contributed to all of the major sports magazines and has written* Snowmobiles and Snowmobiling *(1973) and* How to Enjoy Sports on TV *(1976). The following selection is a model of how a place can be described by using a sense other than sight. Tuite describes New York City by its sounds, which for him comprise the very life of the city.*

N ew York is a city of sounds: muted sounds and shrill 1
sounds; shattering sounds and soothing sounds; urgent
sounds and aimless sounds. The cliff dwellers of Manhattan—
who would be racked by the silence of the lonely woods—do not
hear these sounds because they are constant and eternally urban.

The visitor to the city can hear them, though, just as some ani- 2
mals can hear a high-pitched whistle inaudible to humans. To the
casual caller to Manhattan, lying restive and sleepless in a hotel
twenty or thirty floors above the street, they tell a story as fascinating as life itself. And back of the sounds broods the silence.

Night in midtown is the noise of tinseled honky-tonk and vio- 3
lence. Thin strains of music, usually the firm beat of rock 'n' roll
or the frenzied outbursts of the discotheque, rise from ground
level. This is the cacophony, the discordance of youth, and it
comes on strongest when nights are hot and young blood restless.

Somewhere in the canyons below there is shrill laughter or 4
raucous shouting. A bottle shatters against concrete. The whine
of a police siren slices through the night, moving ever closer, until
an eerie Doppler effect* brings it to a guttural halt.

---

*The drop in pitch that occurs as a source of sound quickly passes by a
listener.

There are few sounds so exciting in Manhattan as those of fire apparatus dashing through the night. At the outset there is the tentative hint of the first-due company bullying his way through midtown traffic. Now a fire whistle from the opposite direction affirms that trouble is, indeed, afoot. In seconds, other sirens converging from other streets help the skytop listener focus on the scene of excitement.

But he can only hear and not see, and imagination takes flight. Are the flames and smoke gushing from windows not far away? Are victims trapped there, crying out for help? Is it a conflagration, or only a trash-basket fire? Or, perhaps, it is merely a false alarm.

The questions go unanswered and the urgency of the moment dissolves. Now the mind and the ear detect the snarling, arrogant bickering of automobile horns. People in a hurry. Taxicabs blaring, insisting on their checkered priority.

Even the taxi horns dwindle down to a precocious few in the gray and pink moments of dawn. Suddenly there is another sound, a morning sound that taunts the memory for recognition. The growl of a predatory monster? No, just garbage trucks that have begun a day of scavenging.

Trash cans rattle outside restaurants. Metallic jaws on sanitation trucks gulp and masticate the residue of daily living, then digest it with a satisfied groan of gears. The sounds of the new day are businesslike. The growl of buses, so scattered and distant at night, becomes a demanding part of the traffic bedlam. An occasional jet or helicopter injects an exclamation point from an unexpected quarter. When the wind is right, the vibrant bellow of an ocean liner can be heard.

The sounds of the day are as jarring as the glare of a sun that outlines the canyons of midtown in drab relief. A pneumatic drill frays countless nerves with its rat-a-tat-tat, for dig they must to perpetuate the city's dizzy motion. After each screech of brakes there is a moment of suspension, of waiting for the thud or crash that never seems to follow.

The whistles of traffic policemen and hotel doormen chirp from all sides, like birds calling for their mates across a frenzied aviary. And all of these sounds are adult sounds, for childish laughter has no place in these canyons.

Night falls again, the cycle is complete, but there is no surcease   12
from sound. For the beautiful dreamers, perhaps, the "sounds of
the rude world heard in the day, lulled by the moonlight have all
passed away," but this is not so in the city.

Too many New Yorkers accept the sounds about them as bland   13
parts of everyday existence. They seldom stop to listen to the
sounds, to think about them, to be appalled or enchanted by
them. In the big city, sounds are life.

Questions for Study and Discussion

1. What is Tuite's purpose in describing the sounds of New
   York City? (Glossary: *Purpose*)
2. How does Tuite organize his essay? Do you think that the
   organization is effective? (Glossary: *Organization*)
3. Tuite describes "raucous shouting" and the "screech of
   brakes." Make a list of the various other sounds that he describes in his essay. How do the varied adjectives and verbs
   Tuite uses to capture the essence of each sound enhance his
   description? (Glossary: *Diction*)
4. According to Tuite, why are visitors to New York City more
   sensitive to or aware of the multitude of sounds than the
   "cliff dwellers of Manhattan" (1)? What does he believe New
   Yorkers have missed when they fail to take notice of these
   sounds?
5. Locate several metaphors and similes in the essay. What
   picture of the city does each one give you? (Glossary: *Figures of Speech*)
6. What dominant impression of New York City does Tuite
   create in this essay? (Glossary: *Dominant Impression*)

Vocabulary

Refer to your dictionary to define the following words as they
are used in this selection. Then use each word in a sentence of
your own.

muted (1)   precocious (8)
inaudible (2)   taunts (8)
restive (2)   vibrant (9)
raucous (4)   perpetuate (10)
tentative (5)

Suggested Writing Assignments

1. In a short composition describe a city or another place that you know well. Try to capture as many sights, sounds, and smells as you can to depict the place you describe. Your goal should be to create a single dominant impression of the place, as Tuite does in his essay.

2. Describe an inanimate object familiar to you so as to bring out its character and make it interesting to a reader. First determine your purpose for describing the object. For example, suppose your family has had a dining table ever since you can remember. Think of what that table has been a part of over the years—the birthday parties, the fights, the holiday meals, the sad times, the intimate times, the long hours of studying and doing homework. Probably such a table would be worth describing for the way it has figured prominently in the history of your family. Next make an exhaustive list of the object's physical features; then write your descriptive essay.

Unforgettable Miss Bessie

Carl T. Rowan

*Carl T. Rowan is a former ambassador to Finland
and was director of the United States Information
Agency. Born in 1925 in Ravenscroft, Tennessee,
he received degrees from Oberlin College and the
University of Minnesota. Once a columnist for the*
Minneapolis Tribune *and the* Chicago Sun-Times,
*Rowan is now a syndicated columnist. In the fol-
lowing essay, Rowan describes his former high-
school teacher whose lessons went far beyond the
subjects she taught.*

She was only about five feet fall and probably never weighed 1
more than 110 pounds, but Miss Bessie was a towering presence in the classroom. She was the only woman tough enough to
make me read *Beowulf* and think for a few foolish days that I
liked it. From 1938 to 1942, when I attended Bernard High School
in McMinnville, Tenn., she taught me English, history, civics—
and a lot more than I realized.

I shall never forget the day she scolded me into reading 2
Beowulf.

"But Miss Bessie," I complained, "I ain't much interested in it." 3

Her large brown eyes became daggerish slits. "Boy," she said, 4
"how dare you say 'ain't' to me! I've taught you better than that."

"Miss Bessie," I pleaded, "I'm trying to make first-string end on 5
the football team, and if I go around saying 'it isn't' and 'they
aren't,' the guys are gonna laugh me off the squad."

"Boy," she responded, "you'll play football because you have 6
guts. But do you know what *really* takes guts? Refusing to lower
your standards to those of the crowd. It takes guts to say you've
got to live and be somebody fifty years after all the football games
are over."

I started saying "it isn't" and "they aren't," and I still made 7
first-string end—and class valedictorian—without losing my buddies' respect.

During her remarkable 44-year career, Mrs. Bessie Taylor 8
Gwynn taught hundreds of economically deprived black youngsters—including my mother, my brother, my sisters and me. I remember her now with gratitude and affection—especially in this
era when Americans are so wrought-up about a "rising tide of
mediocrity" in public education and the problems of finding com-
petent, caring teachers. Miss Bessie was an example of an informed, dedicated teacher, a blessing to children and an asset to
the nation.

Born in 1895, in poverty, she grew up in Athens, Ala., where 9
there was no public school for blacks. She attended Trinity
School, a private institution for blacks run by the American Missionary Association, and in 1911 graduated from the Normal
School (a "super" high school) at Fisk University in Nashville.
Mrs. Gwynn, the essence of pride and privacy, never talked about
her years in Athens; only in the months before her death did she
reveal that she had never attended Fisk University itself because
she could not afford the four-year course.

At Normal School she learned a lot about Shakespeare, but 10
most of all about the profound importance of education—especially, for a people trying to move up from slavery. "What you put
in your head, boy," she once said, "can never be pulled out by the
Ku Klux Klan, the Congress or anybody."

Miss Bessie's bearing of dignity told anyone who met her that 11
she was "educated" in the best sense of the word. There was never
a discipline problem in her classes. We didn't dare mess with a
woman who knew about the Battle of Hastings, the Magna Carta
and the Bill of Rights—and who could also play the piano.

This frail-looking woman could make sense of Shakespeare, 12
Milton, Voltaire, and bring to life Booker T. Washington and
W. E. B. DuBois. Believing that it was important to know who the
officials were that spent taxpayers' money and made public
policy, she made us memorize the names of everyone on the Supreme Court and in the President's Cabinet. It could be embarrassing to be unprepared when Miss Bessie said, "Get up and tell
the class who Frances Perkins is and what you think about her."

Miss Bessie knew that my family, like so many others during 13
the Depression, couldn't afford to subscribe to a newspaper. She
knew we didn't even own a radio. Still, she prodded me to "look
out for your future and find some way to keep up with what's

going on in the world." So I became a delivery boy for the Chattanooga *Times*. I rarely made a dollar a week, but I got to read a newspaper every day.

Miss Bessie noticed things that had nothing to do with school-work, but were vital to a youngster's development. Once a few classmates made fun of my frayed, hand-me-down overcoat, calling me "Strings." As I was leaving school, Miss Bessie patted me on the back of that old overcoat and said, "Carl, never fret about what you *don't* have. Just make the most of what you *do* have—a brain." 14

Among the things that I did not have was electricity in the little frame house that my father had built for $400 with his World War I bonus. But because of her inspiration, I spent many hours squinting beside a kerosene lamp reading Shakespeare and Thoreau, Samuel Pepys and William Cullen Bryant. 15

No one in my family had ever graduated from high school, so there was no tradition of commitment to learning for me to lean on. Like millions of youngsters in today's ghettos and barrios, I needed the push and stimulation of a teacher who truly cared. Miss Bessie gave plenty of both, as she immersed me in a wonderful world of similes, metaphors and even onomatopoeia. She led me to believe that I could write sonnets as well as Shakespeare, or iambic-pentameter verse to put Alexander Pope to shame. 16

In those days the McMinnville school system was rigidly "Jim Crow," and poor black children had to struggle to put anything in their heads. Our high school was only slightly larger than the once-typical little red schoolhouse, and its library was outrageously inadequate—so small, I like to say, that if two students were in it and one wanted to turn a page, the other one had to step outside. 17

Negroes, as we were called then, were not allowed in the town library, except to mop floors or dust tables. But through one of those secret Old South arrangements between whites of conscience and blacks of stature, Miss Bessie kept getting books smuggled out of the white library. That is how she introduced me to the Brontës, Byron, Coleridge, Keats and Tennyson. "If you don't read, you can't write, and if you can't write, you might as well stop dreaming," Miss Bessie once told me. 18

So I read whatever Miss Bessie told me to, and tried to remember the things she insisted that I store away. Forty-five years 19 later, I can still recite her "truths to live by," such as Henry Wadsworth Longfellow's lines from "The Ladder of St. Augustine":

> The heights by great men reached and kept
> Were not attained by sudden flight.
> But they, while their companions slept,
> Were toiling upward in the night.

Years later, her inspiration, prodding, anger, cajoling and 20 almost osmotic infusion of learning finally led to that lovely day when Miss Bessie dropped me a note saying, "I'm so proud to read your column in the Nashville *Tennessean*."

Miss Bessie was a spry 80 when I went back to McMinnville 21 and visited her in a senior citizens' apartment building. Pointing out proudly that her building was racially integrated, she reached for two glasses and a pint of bourbon. I was momentarily shocked, because it would have been scandalous in the 1930s and '40s for word to get out that a teacher drank, and nobody had ever raised a rumor that Miss Bessie did.

I felt a new sense of equality as she lifted her glass to mine. 22 Then she revealed a softness and compassion that I had never known as a student.

"I've never forgotten that examination day," she said, "when 23 Buster Martin held up seven fingers, obviously asking you for help with question number seven, 'Name a common carrier.' I can still picture you looking at your exam paper and humming a few bars of 'Chattanooga Choo Choo.' I was so tickled, I couldn't punish either of you."

Miss Bessie was telling me, with bourbon-laced grace, that I 24 never fooled her for a moment.

When Miss Bessie died in 1980, at age 85, hundreds of her for- 25 mer students mourned. They knew the measure of a great teacher: love and motivation. Her wisdom and influence had rippled out across generations.

Some of her students who might normally have been doomed 26 to poverty went on to become doctors, dentists and college professors. Many, guided by Miss Bessie's example, became public-school teachers.

"The memory of Miss Bessie and how she conducted her class- 27 room did more for me than anything I learned in college," recalls Gladys Wood of Knoxville, Tenn., a highly respected English teacher who spent 43 years in the state's school system. "So many times, when I faced a difficult classroom problem, I asked myself, *How would Miss Bessie deal with this?* And I'd remember that she would handle it with laughter and love."

No child can get all the necessary support at home, and mil- 28
lions of poor children get *no* support at all. This is what makes a wise, educated, warm-hearted teacher like Miss Bessie so vital to the minds, hearts and souls of this country's children.

Questions for Study and Discussion

1. Throughout the essay Rowan offers details of Miss Bessie's physical appearance. What specific details does he give, and in what context does he give them? Did Miss Bessie's physical characteristics match the quality of her character? Explain.

2. How would you sum up the character of Miss Bessie? Make a list of the key words that Rowan uses that you feel best describe her.

3. At what point in the essay does Rowan give us the details of Miss Bessie's background? Why do you suppose he delays giving us this important information? (Glossary: *Beginnings and Endings*)

4. How does dialogue serve Rowan's purposes? (Glossary: *Dialogue*)

5. Does Miss Bessie's drinking influence your opinion of her? Explain. Why do you think Rowan included this part of her behavior in his essay?

6. In his opening paragraph Rowan states that Miss Bessie "taught me English, history, civics—and a lot more than I realized." What did she teach her students beyond the traditional public school curriculum?

Vocabulary

Refer to your dictionary to define the following words as they are used in this selection. Then use each word in a sentence of your own.

civics (1)   cajoling (20)
barrios (16)   osmotic (20)
conscience (18)   measure (25)

Suggested Writing Assignments

1. Think of all the teachers you have had, and write a description of the one that has had the greatest influence on you. Remember to give some consideration to the balance you want to achieve between physical attributes and personality traits.

2. In paragraph 18 Rowan writes the following: "'If you don't read, you can't write, and if you can't write, you might as well stop dreaming,' Miss Bessie once told me." Write an essay in which you explore this theme that, in essence, is also the theme of *Models for Writers*.

GROCER'S DAUGHTER

Marianne Wiggins

Marianne Wiggins was born in 1948. She has published four novels and two collections of short stories during her writing career, most of which depict women who challenge traditional roles that society has given them. "Grocer's Daughter," which appeared in her book Bet They'll Miss Us When We're Gone *(1991), is both a tribute and a description of her father, and it also reveals important aspects of her own childhood.*

I am shameless in the way I love my father. 1

Like little girls who ride big horses, big girls who hold their 2
fathers in devotion are talked about in overtones of sexual pathology. Love is always judged. No one's love is like another's. What
I feel is mine, alone. If my heart is in my mouth, and if I speak it,
judgment comes. Surviving judgment, like admitting love, takes
courage. Here is what John Wiggins taught me:

The moon at crescent is God's fingernail. 3

When your shelves look empty, stack your canned goods to- 4
ward the front.

Keep your feet off other people's furniture. 5

Don't lean your belly on the scale weighing out the produce, or 6
the Devil will tip it his way when your time comes.

Take anybody's check. 7

Go nowhere in a hurry. 8

Sing. 9

Take your hat off inside churches and in the rain, when the 10
spirit moves you.

Don't wax cucumbers. 11

Don't sleep late on Sundays. 12

Start each week with gratitude and six clean aprons. 13

He was born in Pennsylvania, died in the woods and never, to 14
my knowledge, saw an island. He sunburned easily. He wore a

yellow pencil stub behind his ear for jotting orders. He was so accustomed to jotting grocery orders on a pad for a clerk to read, he lost his longhand. The supermarkets in the suburbs squeezed him out. We moved a lot. Each time we moved, the house got smaller, things we didn't need got sold. We didn't need his army helmet or the cardboard notebooks, black and white, in which he'd learned to write. One can't save everything. One trims the fat, one trims the lettuce: produce, when it comes in crates from Florida, needs trimming. For years I saved the only letter he'd written in his lifetime to me. He'd printed it, of course, so there'd be no misunderstanding in the way a pen can curve a word. I lost that letter in my latest move. It's said three moves are like a single fire in their power to destroy one's camp. We moved nine times before I was eighteen. I search in vain, sometimes, for anything my father might have touched.

He always liked a good laugh; his jokes weren't always funny. He concocted odd pranks. He scared my mother half to death one year, when they were first married, by burglarizing their apartment. He rigged a water bucket on his sister's bedroom door the night of her first date: that was 1939, when cotton dresses took half an hour's pressing and a girl might spend an afternoon wrapping dark hair on a curling iron. To my mother, who gets dizzy looking in round mirrors, he wrote love letters that germinated from the center of the page and spiraled out. Those days, he still wrote in script. I think I could identify his longhand, if need be. Handwriting speaks. I think I could remember his.

15

I remember what his footsteps sounded like: heavier on one leg than the other, made the change rattle in his pocket. He always carried change, most grocers did, because the kids would come in to buy cookies from the bin with pennies and their pennies crowded up the cash drawer. Year in, year out, he wore pleated pants in dark colors. He had three good suits—one gray, one black, one brown. I see him in them in the photographs. The gray one took a lot of coaxing from my mother and wasn't often worn. Every year for Christmas he received:

16

six new pairs of black socks
six new undershirts
six pairs of boxer shorts
two new sweater vests

six white shirts
six aprons
one subdued pastel shirt from me
one knit tie from my sister

The year I knew there was no Santa Claus was the year he fell   17
asleep beneath the Christmas tree assembling my sister's tricycle.

His favorite pie was something only Grandma Wiggins made: 18
butterscotch custard. Even when my sister and I were kids and
loved sweet things, its sweetness made our teeth hurt. I never
knew his favorite color. I think he must have had a favorite song,
I never knew it, he was always singing, had a song for each occasion, favored "Someone's in the Kitchen with Dinah" while he was
washing dishes and "Oh Promise Me" while he was driving in the
car. Sometimes, early in the mornings, he'd sing "Buckle Down,
Winsocki." I used to think Winsocki was as funny-sounding a
name as that of his favorite politician, Wendell Wilkie. He liked
FDR, hated Truman, voted for Dwight Eisenhower. By 1960, I was
old enough to reason through my parents' pig Latin and moder-
ately schooled in spelling, so everything they had to say in front
of me, they couldn't code. My father was Republican, my mother
fell for Kennedy's charisma. "Who did you vote for, John?" my
mother asked him that November.

"Mary," my father answered, needing to be secret. "What do you   19
think that curtain in the voting booth is for—?"

"What the hell," he told me later. "If I'd voted like I wanted to,   20
your mother and me, we would have canceled one another out.
What's the point of voting like you want to when you know that
you'll be canceled out?"

I wonder if he ever dreamed that he could change things. He   21
taught me how to pitch softball. We played croquet in the front
yard. He taught me how to spot a plant called preacher-in-the-
pulpit along the country roads. He taught me harmony to "Jingle
Bells." He taught me how to drive a car. He unscrewed the training wheels and taught me how to ride a bike. He told me strange,
portenting things: if I ate too much bread, I'd get dandruff. He
read *Reader's Digest*, *Coronet* and *Pageant* and didn't believe in
evolution. There were times I didn't like him. He left abruptly. He
left me much unfinished business.

He visited New York City four times in his lifetime. He was in   22
Times Square, a tourist, on V-J Day. Somehow, I'm glad for him,
as a believer is for a novitiate, that he was there: celebration
needs a crowd. He thought not badly of large cities, after that: but
he never lived in one.

He never sailed, his life was landlocked. I think he clammed   23
once, with my uncle, at Virginia Beach. I cannot say for certain
that he knew his body's way in water. Water was not an element
he knew, except as rain on crops. He was a farmer's son. Without
the farmer's land, his legacy was vending farmer's goods. I
planted a garden last week, north of where he lived and died, on
an island where all roads lead to water. "Now, when you plant a
small plot," he once said, "plant what you and yours can eat, or
plant what makes you happy, like a sunflower, and offer your
surplus to the ones who want. Don't waste. For God's sake, don't
waste."

I wish that he could see the things I've sown. Diluted in me is   24
John Wiggins, as today's rain will be in summer's harvest. I wish
that I could see him once again, hear his footfalls on the gravel
driveway, heavy on one foot: These dried leavings aren't complete
in their remembrance, like the trimmings swept from green
growth on the grocer's floor, they crumble on my fingertips and
fly piecemeal to the wind. I do not do my father justice, that was
his charge. I've borne his name, in and out of marriage, a name
that is my own, sometimes I wish his strain would leave me,
sometimes I'd like to choke it to full bloom. I'd like to turn to him
today and say, "I love you: too late: I'm sorry: you did the best you
could: you were my father: I learned from you: you were an
honest man."

I cultivate a tiny garden, "plot" reminds me of a cemetery. I   25
plant only what my family guarantees to eat. The rest I give to
those who want. Had you known him, I'd like to think you would
have bought your groceries from John Wiggins. He always had a
pleasant word. He could tell you how to plan a meal for twenty
people, give you produce wholesale, trim your cut of meat before
he weighed it, profit wasn't Daddy's motive, life was. Life defeated
him. He taught me how to pack a grocery bag, I worked there
weekends, canned goods on the bottom, perishables on top.
Someone puts tomatoes on the bottom of my bag these days, I

repack it. I was taught respect of certain order. One sees one's father's face, as one grows older, in the most peculiar places. I see Daddy in each bud. I see his stance on corners. I, myself, wear grocer's aprons, when I cook. My mother always said there was no cleaning that damned blood from those white aprons. My father left a stain: I miss him. I write longhand, and in ink.

Martha's Vineyard
May 1979

Questions for Study and Discussion

1. How does Wiggins's first sentence influence the rest of the essay? (Glossary: *Beginnings and Endings*)
2. What does the list of things that John Wiggins taught his daughter tell the reader about him?
3. Discuss Wiggins's writing style in "Grocer's Daughter." (Glossary: *Style*) Is it effective for you? Why or why not?
4. Why did the Wiggins family move so often?
5. Wiggins says "I wonder if he ever dreamed that he could change things." How did he change things for his daughter?
6. Wiggins never states how or when her father died. Why do you think she explores the impact of his death, rather than describing its occurrence? How and when do you think John Wiggins died? Defend your answer with excerpts from the essay.

Vocabulary

Refer to your dictionary to define the following words as they are used in this selection. Then use each word in a sentence of your own.

pathology (2)
concocted (15)
germinated (15)
charisma (18)

portenting (21)
novitiate (22)
piecemeal (24)

Suggested Writing Assignments

1. Describe a close relative of yours, such as a parent or sibling. Be sure to establish a purpose for your description. Your audience will not know your subject—what are the little things that make up his or her character and make him or her special?

2. In her essay Wiggins reveals something of herself—her tastes, her values, her intelligence. Write an essay in which you argue that every writer, to a lesser or greater degree, reveals something of himself or herself in writing about any subject. Choose whatever examples you wish to make your point. You might, however, decide to use Carl Rowan and his essay on Miss Bessie as your primary example. Finally, you might wish to emphasize the significance of the self-revealing qualities of writing.

BORDERS

Barry Lopez

*Barry Lopez was born in New York state in 1945,
grew up in the San Fernando Valley, and received a
B.A. from Notre Dame. Lopez is a contributing
editor to the* North American Review *and* Harper's
*and writes about the American West, especially its
natural history and environment. His book* Of
Wolves and Men *(1978) was a best-seller, and the
following selection is taken from* Crossing Open
Ground, *published in 1988. Lopez enjoys an out-
standing reputation as a wordsmith. Notice his
choice of words as he ponders the meaning of
borders and describes the vast open territory of
Alaska and the Yukon Territory.*

In early September, the eastern Arctic coast of Alaska shows   1
several faces, most of them harsh. But there are days when the
wind drops and the sky is clear, and for reasons too fragile to
explain—the overflight of thousands of migrating ducks, the
bright, silent austerity of the Romanzof Mountains under fresh
snow, the glassy stillness of the ocean—these days have an edge
like no others. The dawn of such a clear and windless day is cher-
ished against memories of late August snow squalls and days of
work in rough water under leaden skies.

One such morning, a few of us on a biological survey in the   2
Beaufort Sea set that work aside with hardly a word and headed
east over the water for the international border, where the state of
Alaska abuts the Yukon Territory. The fine weather encouraged
this bit of adventure.

There are no settlements along this part of the arctic coast. We   3
did not in fact know if the border we were headed to was even
marked. A northeast wind that had been driving loose pack ice
close to shore for several days forced us to run near the beach in

a narrow band of open water. In the lee of larger pieces of sea ice, the ocean had begun to freeze, in spite of the strong sunlight and a benign feeling in the air. Signs of winter.

As we drove toward Canada, banking the open, twenty-foot 4 boat in graceful arcs to avoid pieces of drift ice, we hung our heads far back to watch migrating Canada geese and black brant pass over. Rifling past us and headed west at fifty miles an hour a foot off the water were flocks of oldsquaw, twenty and thirty ducks at a time. Occasionally, at the edge of the seaward ice, the charcoal-gray snout of a ringed seal would break the calm surface of the ocean for breath.

We drew nearer the border, wondering aloud how we would 5 know it. I remembered a conversation of years before, with a man who had escaped from Czechoslovakia to come to America and had later paddled a canoe the length of the Yukon. He described the border where the river crossed into Alaska as marked by a great swath cut through the spruce forest. In the middle of nowhere, I said ruefully; what a waste of trees, how ugly it must have seemed. He looked silently across the restaurant table at me and said it was the easiest border crossing of his life.

I thought, as we drove on east, the ice closing in more now, 6 forcing us to run yet closer to the beach, of the geographer Carl Sauer and his concept of biologically distinct regions. The idea of bioregionalism, as it has been developed by his followers, is a political concept that would reshape human life. It would decentralize residents of an area into smaller, more self-sufficient, environmentally responsible units, occupying lands the borders of which would be identical with the borders of natural regions— watersheds, for example. I thought of Sauer because we were headed that day for a great, invisible political dividing line: 141 degrees western longitude. Like the border between Utah and Colorado, this one is arbitrary. If it were not actually marked— staked—it would not be discernible. Sauer's borders are noticeable. Even the birds find them.

On the shore to our right, as we neared the mouth of Demar- 7 cation Bay, we saw the fallen remains of an Eskimo sod house, its meat-drying racks, made of driftwood, leaning askew. Someone who had once come this far to hunt had built the house. The house eventually became a dot on U.S. Coast and Geodetic Survey maps. Now its location is vital to the Inuit, for it establishes a politically important right of prior use, predating the establishment of the Arctic National Wildlife Refuge, within whose borders it has been included. I recall all this as we pass, from poring over our detailed maps the night before. Now, with the warmth of sunlight on the side of my face, with boyhood thoughts of the Yukon Territory welling up inside, the nearness of friends, with whom work has been such keen satisfaction these past few weeks, I have no desire to see maps.

Ahead, it is becoming clear that the closing ice is going to force   8
us right up on the beach before long. The wedge of open water is narrowing. What there is is very still, skimmed with fresh slush ice. I think suddenly of my brother, who lives in a house on Block Island, off the coast of Rhode Island. When I visit we walk and drive around the island. Each time I mean to ask him, does he feel any more ordered in his life for being able to see so clearly the boundary between the ocean and the land in every direction? But I am never able to phrase the question right. And the old and dour faces of the resident islanders discourage it.

Far ahead, through a pair of ten-power binoculars, I finally see   9
what appears to be a rampart of logs weathered gray-white and standing on a bluff where the tundra falls off fifteen or twenty feet to the beach. Is this the border?

We are breaking ice now with the boat. At five miles an hour,   10
the bow wave skitters across the frozen surface of the ocean to either side in a hundred broken fragments. The rumbling that accompanies this shattering of solid ice is like the low-throttled voice of the outboard engines. Three or four hundred yards of this and we stop. The pack ice is within twenty feet of the beach. We cannot go any farther. That we are only a hundred feet from our destination seems a part of the day, divinely fortuitous.

We climb up the bluff. Arctic-fox tracks in the patchy snow are   11
fresh. Here and there on the tundra are bird feathers, the remnants of the summer molt of hundreds of thousands of birds that have come this far north to nest, whose feathers blow inland and out to sea for weeks. Although we see no animals but a flock of snow geese in the distance, evidence of their residence and passage is everywhere. Within a few hundred feet I find caribou droppings. On a mossy tundra mound, like one a jaeger might use, I find two small bones that I know to be a ptarmigan's.

We examine the upright, weathered logs and decide on the 12 basis of these and several pieces of carved wood that this is, indeed, the border. No one, we reason, would erect something like this on a coast so unfrequented by humans if it were not. (This coast is ice-free only eight or ten weeks in the year.) Yet we are not sure. The bluff has a certain natural prominence, though the marker's placement seems arbitrary. But the romance of it— this foot in Canada, that one in Alaska—is fetching. The delightful weather and the presence of undisturbed animals has made us almost euphoric. It is, after days of bottom trawls in thirty-one-degree water, of cold hours of patient searching for seals, so clearly a holiday for us.

I will fly over this same spot a week later, under a heavy over- 13 cast, forced down to two hundred feet above the water in a search for migrating bowhead whales. That trip, from the small settlement of Inuvik on the East Channel of the Mackenzie River in the Northwest Territories to Deadhorse, Alaska, will make this border both more real and more peculiar than it now appears. We will delay our arrival by circling over Inuvik until a Canadian customs officer can get there from the village of Tuktoyaktuk on the coast, though all we intend to do is to drop off an American scientist and buy gas. On our return trip we are required by law to land at the tiny village of Kaktovik to check through U.S. Customs. The entry through Kaktovik is so tenuous as to not exist at all. One might land, walk the mile to town, and find or not find the customs officer around. Should he not be there, the law requires we fly 250 miles south to Fort Yukon. If no one is there we are to fly on to Fairbanks before returning to Deadhorse on the coast, in order to reenter the country legally. These distances are immense. We could hardly carry the fuel for such a trip. And to fly inland would mean not flying the coast to look for whales, the very purpose of being airborne. We fly straight to Deadhorse, looking for whales. When we land we fill out forms to explain our actions and file them with the government.

Here, standing on the ground, the border seems nearly whim- 14 sical. The view over tens of square miles of white, frozen ocean and a vast expanse of tundra which rolls to the foot of snow-covered mountains is unimpeded. Such open space, on such a calm and innocent day as this, gives extraordinary release to the imagination. At such a remove—from horrible images of human death on borders ten thousand miles away, from the press of human anxiety one feels in a crowded city—at such a remove one is lulled nearly to foundering by the simple peace engendered, even at the border between two nations, by a single day of good weather.

As we turn to leave the monument, we see two swans coming toward us. They are immature tundra swans, in steel-gray plumage. Something odd is in their shape. Primary feathers. They have no primary feathers yet. Too young. And their parents, who should be with them, are nowhere to be seen. They are coming from the east, from Canada, paddling in a strip of water a few inches deep right at the edge of the beach. They show no fear of us, although they slow and are cautious. They extend their necks and open their pink bills to make gentle, rattling sounds. As they near the boat they stand up in the water and step ashore. They walk past us and on up the beach. Against the gritty coarseness of beach sand and the tundra-stained ice, their smooth gray feathers and the deep lucidity of their eyes vibrate with beauty. I watch them until they disappear from view. The chance they will be alive in two weeks is very slim. Perhaps it doesn't exist at all. 15

In two weeks I am thousands of miles south. In among the letters and magazines in six weeks of mail sitting on the table is a thick voter-registration pamphlet. One afternoon I sit down and read it. I try to read it with the conscientiousness of one who wishes to vote wisely. I think of Carl Sauer, whose ideas I admire. And of Wendell Berry, whose integrity and sense of land come to mind when I ponder any vote and the effect it might have. I think of the invisible borders of rural landscapes, of Frost pondering the value of fences. I read in the pamphlet of referendums on statewide zoning and of the annexation of rural lands, on which I am expected to vote. I read of federal legislative reapportionment and the realignment of my county's border with that of an Indian reservation, though these will not require my vote. I must review, again, how the districts of my state representative and state senator overlap and determine if I am included now within the bounds of a newly created county commissioner's territory. 16

These lines blur and I feel a choking coming up in my neck and my face flushing. I set the pamphlet on the arm of the chair and get up and walk outside. It is going to take weeks, again, to get home. 17

Questions for Study and Discussion

1. Why do you think Lopez titled his essay "Borders"? (Glossary: *Title*) What borders does he discuss other than the border between Alaska and the Yukon Territory?
2. Lopez doesn't dwell on the cold, but he communicates the image of a very cold, harsh environment. Identify some of the words and phrases he uses to describe the cold environment. (Glossary: *Description*)
3. What is the importance of the Eskimo sod house?
4. Why are Lopez and his companions euphoric when they reach what they guess to be the border?
5. What is Lopez's purpose in paragraph 13? (Glossary: *Purpose*) Why does he digress or move away from his discussion of the day trip to the border?
6. What animals does Lopez see? What does their plight say about life in the Arctic?
7. Why does Lopez have difficulty readjusting to life at home?

Vocabulary

Refer to your dictionary to define the following words as they are used in this selection. Then use each word in a sentence of your own.

austerity (1)	fortuitous (10)
lee (3)	arbitrary (12)
bioregionalism (6)	whimsical (14)
decentralize (6)	engendered (14)
askew (7)	conscientiousness (16)

Suggested Writing Assignments

1. Describe a trip that you have taken that you remember well and that had some kind of impact on you. Using Lopez's essay as an example, describe not only your surroundings and activities, but also describe the issues, events, ideas, etc. that had an impact on you and why they affected you.

2. When people return from a trip abroad, they sometimes face what is called "culture shock." It could be said that Lopez faced culture shock when he returned from northern Alaska (you don't have do go overseas or to an exotic location). Describe a time when you had to readjust to your normal routine upon returning from a trip. What about the trip made it difficult to readjust?

13

PROCESS ANALYSIS

When you give directions for getting to your house, tell how to make ice cream, or explain how a president is elected, you are using *process analysis.*

Process analysis usually arranges a series of events in order and relates them to one another, as narration and cause and effect do, but it has different emphases. Whereas narration tells mainly *what* happens and cause and effect focuses on *why* it happens, process analysis tries to explain—in detail—*how* it happens.

There are two types of process analysis: directional and informational. The *directional* type provides instructions on how to do something. These instructions can be as brief as the directions printed on a label for making instant coffee or as complex as the directions in a manual for building a home computer. The purpose of directional process analysis is simple: to give the reader directions to follow that lead to the desired results.

Consider the directions for constructing an Astro Tube, a cylindrical airfoil made out of a sheet of heavy writing paper, on p. 276.

The *informational* type of process analysis, on the other hand, tells how something works, how something is made, or how something occurred. You would use informational process analysis if you wanted to explain how the human heart functions, how an atomic bomb works, how hailstones are formed, how you selected the college you are attending, or how the polio vaccine was developed. Rather than giving specific directions, informational process analysis explains and informs.

Clarity is crucial for successful process analysis. The most effective way to explain a process is to divide it into steps and to present those steps in a clear (usually chronological) sequence. Transitional words and phrases such as *first, next, after* and *before* help to connect steps to one another. Naturally, you must be sure that no step is omitted or out of order. Also, you may sometimes have to explain *why* a certain step is necessary, especially if it is not obvious. With intricate, abstract, or particularly difficult steps, you might use analogy or comparison to clarify the steps for your reader.

Making an Astro Tube

Start with an 8.5-inch by 11-inch sheet of heavy writing paper. (Never use newspaper in making paper models because it isn't strongly bonded and can't hold a crease.) Follow these numbered steps, corresponding to the illustrations.

1. With the long side of the sheet toward you, fold up one third of the paper.

2. Fold the doubled section in half.

3. Fold the section in half once more and crease well.

4. Unfold preceding crease.

5. Curve the ends together to form a tube, as shown in the illustration.

6. Insert the right end inside the left end between the single outer layer and the doubled layers. Overlap the ends about an inch and a half. (This makes a tube for right-handers, to be used with an underhand throw. For an overhand tube, or an underhand version to be thrown by a lefty, reverse the directions, and insert the left end inside the right end at this step.)

7. Hold the tube at the seam with one hand, where shown by the dot in the illustration, and turn the rim inward along the crease made in step 3. Start turning in at the seam and roll the rim under, moving around the circumference in a circular manner. Then round out the rim.

8. Fold the fin to the left, as shown, then raise it so that it's perpendicular to the tube. Be careful not to tear the paper at the front.

9. Hold the tube from above, near the rim. Hold it between the thumb and fingers.

The rim end should be forward, with the fin on the bottom. Throw the tube underhanded, with a motion like throwing a bowling ball, letting it spin off the fingers as it is released. The tube will float through the air, spinning as it goes. Indoor flights of 30 feet or more are easy. With practice you can achieve remarkable accuracy.

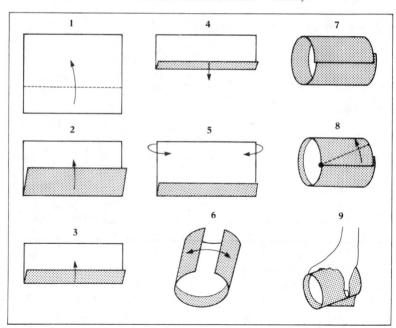

How to Build a Fire in a Fireplace

Bernard Gladstone

Bernard Gladstone frequently writes on do-it-yourself building and home maintenance. As home improvement editor of the New York Times *for over ten years, he has written useful articles about common household problems, new home products, and how to use new and old tools. In the following selection from his book* The New York Times Complete Manual of Home Repair *(1972), Gladstone gives directions for building a fire in a fireplace.*

Though "experts" differ as to the best technique to follow when building a fire, one generally accepted method consists of first laying a generous amount of crumpled newspaper on the hearth between the andirons. Kindling wood is then spread generously over this layer of newspaper and one of the thickest logs is placed across the back of the andirons. This should be as close to the back of the fireplace as possible, but not quite touching it. A second log is then placed an inch or so in front of this, and a few additional sticks of kindling are laid across these two. A third log is then placed on top to form a sort of pyramid with air space between all logs so that flames can lick freely up between them. 1

A mistake frequently made is in building the fire too far forward so that the rear wall of the fireplace does not get properly heated. A heated back wall helps increase the draft and tends to suck smoke and flames rearward with less chance of sparks or smoke spurting out into the room. 2

Another common mistake often made by the inexperienced fire-tender is to try to build a fire with only one or two logs, instead of using at least three. A single log is difficult to ignite properly, and even two logs do not provide an efficient bed with adequate fuel-burning capacity. 3

Use of too many logs, on the other hand, is also a common fault and can prove hazardous. Building too big a fire can create more 4 smoke and draft than the chimney can safely handle, increasing the possibility of sparks or smoke being thrown out into the room. For best results, the homeowner should start with three medium-size logs as described above, then add additional logs as needed if the fire is to be kept burning.

Questions for Study and Discussion

1. What type of process analysis has been used in this essay, directional or informational? Why is this type of process analysis especially appropriate to the author's purpose? (Glossary: *Purpose*)
2. Make a list of the steps Gladstone describes for building a fire in a fireplace.
3. What is the purpose of paragraphs 2, 3, and 4 in this process analysis?
4. Identify the transitional words that Gladstone uses in paragraph 1 to indicate the sequence of steps involved in making a fire. (Glossary: *Transitions*)
5. Why is making too big a fire potentially hazardous?

Vocabulary

Refer to your dictionary to define the following words as they are used in this selection. Then use each word in a sentence of your own.

hearth (1)   kindling (1)
andirons (1)

Suggested Writing Assignments

1. Write a directional process analysis for one of the following operations, or any other suitable process:

   how to paddle a canoe
   how to study for an exam

how to determine miles per gallon for a car
how to make your favorite sandwich
how to hem a dress
how to make great popcorn
how to tie a necktie

2. Write a process analysis for a potentially dangerous process, such as slicing vegetables or splitting wood. Using Gladstone's essay as a model, include an analysis of what to do, plus common mistakes that one should avoid making.

HOW TO PUT OFF DOING A JOB

Andy Rooney

Andy Rooney was born in Albany, New York, in 1920. He began his writing career as a reporter for Stars and Stripes *in Europe during World War II. After the war, Rooney enjoyed a successful career as a writer/producer for CBS and other television networks. He has earned three Emmy awards and six Best Script of the Year awards from the Writers Guild, but he is best known now for his humorous commentary on the popular television show* 60 Minutes. *In addition to his television work, Rooney is the author of seven books, a widely read syndicated column, and articles in magazines such as* Esquire *and* Saturday Review.

February is one of the most difficult times of the year to put off doing some of the things you've been meaning to do. There's no vacation coming up, there are no long weekends scheduled in the immediate future; it's just this long, grim February. Don't tell me it's a short month. February is the longest by a week.

Because I have so many jobs that I don't like to do, I've been reviewing the notebook I keep with notes in it for how to put off doing a job. Let's see now, what could I use today?

—Go to the store to get something. This is one of my most dependable putter-offers. If I start a job and find I need some simple tool or a piece of hardware, I stop right there. I put on some better clothes, get in the car and drive to the store. If that store doesn't have what I'm looking for, I go to another. Often I'm attracted to some item that has nothing whatsoever to do with the job I was about to start and I buy that instead. For instance, if I go to the hardware store to buy a new snow shovel so I can clean out the driveway, but then I see a can of adhesive spray that will keep rugs in place on the floor, I'm apt to buy the adhesive spray. That ends the idea I had to shovel out the driveway.

—Tidy up the work area before starting a job. This has been   4
useful to me over the years as a way of not getting started. Things are such a mess in my workshop, on my desk, in the kitchen and in the trunk of the car that I decide I've got to go through some of the junk before starting to work.

—Make those phone calls. There's no sense trying to do a job if   5
you have other things on your mind, so get them out of the way first. This is a very effective way of not getting down to work. Call friends you've been meaning to call, or the distant relative you've been out of touch with. Even if someone is in California, Texas or Chicago and you're in Florida, call. Paying for a long-distance call is still easier and less unpleasant than actually getting down to work.

—Study the problem. It's foolish to jump right into a job before   6
you've thought it through. You might be doing the wrong thing. There might be an easier way to accomplish what you want to do, so think it over carefully from every angle. Perhaps someone has written a how-to book about the job you have in front of you. Buy the book and then sit down and read it. Ask friends who have had the same job for advice about the best way to do it.

Once you've studied the problem from every angle, don't make   7
a quick decision. Sleep on it.

—Take a coffee break. Although the term "coffee break" as-   8
sumes that you are drinking coffee in an interim period between stretches of solid work, this is not necessarily so. Don't be bound by old ideas about when it's proper to take a coffee break. If taking it before you get started is going to help keep you from doing the work, by all means take your coffee break first.

—As a last resort before going to work, think this thing over. Is   9
this really what you want to do with your life? Philosophize. Nothing is better for putting off doing something than philosophizing. Are you a machine, trapped in the same dull, day-after-day routine that everyone else is in? Or are you a person who makes up his or her own mind about things? Are you going to do these jobs because that's what's expected of you, or are you going to break the mold and live the way you feel like living?

Try these as ways for not getting down to work.   10

Questions for Study and Discussion

1. Explain the irony in Rooney's "how-to" article. (Glossary: *Irony*)

2. Why does February seem like the longest month of the year to Rooney? How does his discussion of February tie in with the rest of the article?

3. Why is going to the store one of Rooney's most dependable "putter-offers?"

4. What's the last resort Rooney uses to put off doing a job? What consequences can using this technique have?

5. What is the tone of the article? (Glossary: *Tone*) In what way does it differ from most "how-to" articles?

Vocabulary

Refer to your dictionary to define the following words as they are used in this selection. Then use each word in a sentence of your own.

adhesive (3)	interim (8)
accomplish (6)	philosophize (9)
how-to (6)	mold (9)

Suggested Writing Assignments

1. What are your three favorite methods of putting off a job? Write a process analysis in which you explain your methods so that others might recognize them.

2. Write a how-to article in which you explain how to complete a job quickly and efficiently. Just as Rooney has provided techniques for avoiding work, describe four or five ways to prepare for working without delay. Provide explanations about how these methods will help people get to work.

How to Organize Your Thoughts for Better Communication

Sherry Sweetnam

Sherry Sweetnam is a communications consultant for major corporations who specializes in written communication skills. She has conducted workshops on business communications all over the world. Her book, The Executive Memo: A Guide to Persuasive Business Communications, *was published in 1986. As you read the following article, which appeared in* Personnel *in 1986, note how Sweetnam herself uses the writing techniques she describes to catch your attention.*

D o you want to analyze the way you communicate and the way you think and organize your thoughts? Study your writing. It will tell you whether you are reader-sensitive or whether you are communicating strictly from your own point of view. 1

This example shows communication strictly from the writer's point of view: 2

The Personnel Department
is pleased to announce that
MARY R. NAKOVEY
formerly special assistant to the director
executive director of human resources
and associate executive director
Department of Manpower Planning
has joined the firm
as manager of personnel.

What's the problem with this business announcement? *It wastes time.* The big news is the new personnel manager; so why not say it up front? Instead, the writer forces you to wade through 30 words to get to the main point. Stalling the main point causes frustration, annoyance, and tension in the reader and creates negative feelings toward the writer and the information. 3

Many of us fail to get to the point when we communicate—both   4
orally and in writing. There are logical explanations as to why we
organize our thoughts like this. They are:

1. *We're trying to impress.* Often, we're so concerned about
   building our credibility and establishing our importance
   that we show off when we write. But showing off turns
   most people off. Readers don't care how great a person, department, or unit is. The readers' business concerns are:
   What's new? How is this going to affect me?

2. *We're trying to figure out what we think.* Writing helps us
   clarify thought. It is an excellent tool for moving through
   the thinking process itself. However, writers need to edit
   their work so that their key information is not buried in the
   maze of the process itself.

3. *We're not clear about what is important to our readers.* In
   writing sheerly from our own point of view, we lose sight of
   the reader's concerns and interests. It's fine to write this
   way in the initial drafts, but the final draft should be reshaped with the reader's interests in mind.

4. *We tend to organize information chronologically rather than
   psychologically.* Most of us are natural storytellers. ("Guess
   what happened on the subway today!" "Let me tell you
   what happened in yesterday's marketing meeting.") As storytellers, we naturally slip into a system of ordering information chronologically. There's nothing wrong with using
   the story format in the appropriate environment. The
   "right" organization to use always depends on who is reading the report and what their needs are.

5. *We were trained to write that way in school.* We learned to
   put the summary, conclusion, the last word, the bottom
   line, at the end of our school compositions and reports. We
   memorized and religiously followed the academic formula:
   (1) introduction, (2) body, (3) conclusion. And we continue
   to use it.

There's nothing wrong with organizing our communications   5
that way *if* we have a captive audience, *if* we are so interesting no
one can put our writing down, and *if* people have a lot of time.
But that is rarely true in business. Most people are very busy with

their own agendas and don't have time to wade through a lot of words to get to the point. When we bury our key points we lose credibility because we are not being sensitive to our reader's interests and time constraints.

Positioning Your Thoughts

Effective business communication organizes thought in the opposite way. The rule is to get to your point up front; then give the background and details. That is why executive summaries are so popular. After getting the nuggets up front, the reader can decide whether he or she wants to continue reading. 6

The most critical ideas should be in the most powerful of the three positions on the page—the beginning, middle, or end. 7

The beginning. The most powerful position is the first 50 words of a memo, letter, report, or proposal. Since the opening paragraph is key, that's where you want to load your most important ideas. 8

The middle. This is no-man's land—the weakest position on a page. It may or may not get read, depending on whether you've been able to hold your reader's interest up front. 9

The end. This is the second strongest position (assuming the reader gets to it). Why? Because it is the last thing that the reader will read. Therefore, it has greater impact than what was in no-man's land. 10

How to Frontload Writing

Frontloading means placing your key idea first. To do this, first go through your writing with a pencil and underline the key ideas in sentences and paragraphs. Then rearrange those key phrases and ideas so that they appear at the beginning of the memo, paragraph, or sentence. 11

Consider, for example, the difference in impact between these titles: 12

> *Subject: Statistical Data Due Dates*
> *vs.*
> *Subject: Due Dates for Statistical Data*

The phrase *statistical data* is not the critical information in the title. It doesn't hook the reader because it doesn't answer such 13 critical questions as: What do I have to do? Why is it important that I read this? The phrase *due date* is urgent; therefore, it needs to be frontloaded.

Frontloading Letters

Here is an example of how writers backload key information in   14
a letter. The key information is italicized and appears at the end of the letter.

> Due to a processing error, your June payroll deduction, cred-
> ited to your account on January 24, 1986, was inadvertently
> priced at $33.15145. The correct price for this transaction
> should have been $36.4214. *We have corrected this problem
> and adjusted your account accordingly.*

The last sentence should be repositioned so that it becomes the   15
first sentence. The result could possibly read, "We have adjusted your account because we made an error in our calculations."

Why does this work? Because it is written from the reader's   16
point of view. When it comes to problems and solutions, what most readers and customers want to know is: Have you solved the problem? If the news is good, then don't bury it! As a rule, give your reader the good news first instead of striking a negative note at the outset.

Frontloading Action Requests

The following is an example of a request for action. Notice that   17
the request is buried in the second paragraph:

> *Steve, I have been searching the lower Minneapolis area for
> over three months for qualified candidates with a strong knowl-
> edge of AVS to support the chemical data system. I have been
> unsuccessful. As a result, the project is in jeopardy.*
>
> *Therefore,* I have been requesting your support to obtain the neces-
> sary approvals *required to begin reviewing candidates from
> outside the lower Minneapolis area.*

By repositioning the request at the beginning of the piece, it would become a far more powerful communication.

Why don't we state requests up front? Because we don't want to   18
appear too bold or too aggressive. In fact, however, stating your

request up front is considered by many to be direct, forthright, and nonmanipulative. It is also good business because it gets to the point quickly. Again, there's no waste of time.

Frontloading to Persuade

Writing to persuade someone about an idea, service, or product 19 is trickier than writing to inform or request action. You must decide how interested your reader is in what you're trying to persuade him of. If your reader is interested, then state your idea up front. For example, you might start out by writing: "I recommend that we buy XYZ computer."

However, if your reader isn't so interested, backload your 20 recommendation and frontload the benefits of your idea or product so the reader will be sold.

Tough Messages: The Three Exceptions to Frontloading

There are three situations in which frontloading your key idea 21 doesn't work:

1. *When you have to say "no."* When you have to tell someone "no," it makes much more sense to begin with a positive tone or a kiss. Then you can ease into the bad news or the kick in the second paragraph. In this way, the *no* isn't such a blow.

2. *When your reader is not interested in buying your new idea, service, or product.* When you have to convince someone of your ideas, then it makes sense to frontload the benefits and advantages and conclude with your recommendations.

3. *When you know your reader doesn't want to comply with your request.* The best thing to do in this instance is to ease into your request or suggestions.

Why Rethink?

One of the best ways to achieve force and interest in your 22 writing is to frontload ideas. This means frontloading in all your writing—your titles; all types of memos, letters and reports; and at the sentence and paragraph level. Frontloading will grab your reader's interest and get your memos read. The inner voice of your reader will be saying, "Here's a writer who knows what's important and doesn't waste my time."

A fringe benefit of reorganizing your written communications is that you will find yourself getting to the point more often when you're speaking to people. Frontloading is a mental exercise that trains you to get to the point in all of your communications.

Questions for Study and Discussion

1. Analyze Sweetnam's first paragraph. (Glossary: *Beginnings and Endings*) Is it effective? What does she accomplish in these three sentences?
2. What does "frontloading" mean? Why is it important for business communications?
3. Why do people tend to avoid frontloading in their written communication? When *should* they avoid it?
4. Sweetnam's use of subheads makes it easy to see how she organizes her essay. (Glossary: *Organization*) Briefly summarize each section. Why is her organization effective?
5. Why does Sweetnam describe the middle of the page as "no-man's land?"
6. What techniques does Sweetnam use to make her article easy to read and to hold the reader's attention?
7. Who is Sweetnam's intended audience? (Glossary: *Audience*) Based on the techniques she describes in the article, do you think that the audience is receptive or skeptical of Sweetnam's advice?

Vocabulary

Refer to your dictionary to define the following words as they are used in this selection. Then use each word in a sentence of your own.

personnel (2)	chronologically (4)
credibility (4)	captive (5)
clarify (4)	inadvertently (14)
sheerly (4)	nonmanipulative (18)

Suggested Writing Assignments

1. Write a business memo based on the techniques Sweetnam describes in her article. Include a directional process analysis in the memo. Choose an office topic, such as how to load paper into a new copier, how to make good coffee in the office machine without making a mess, or how to use a new word processor.

2. Write a process essay in which you explain how to write a good college essay. How will it differ from the techniques Sweetnam describes for writing a good business memo?

THE SPIDER AND THE WASP

Alexander Petrunkevitch

Alexander Petrunkevitch (1875–1964), a Russian-born zoologist, was a leading authority on spiders. He published his first important work, The Index Catalogue of Spiders of North, Central, and South America, *in 1911. In addition to his scientific research, Petrunkevitch was also widely recognized for his translations of Russian and English poetry. In this essay, first published in* Scientific American *(1952), Petrunkevitch describes the process involved in one of nature's annual happenings, the way in which the "intelligence" of digger wasps is pitted against the "instincts" of tarantula spiders.*

In the feeding and safeguarding of their progeny insects and spiders exhibit some interesting analogies to reasoning and some crass examples of blind instinct. The case I propose to describe here is that of the tarantula spiders and their archenemy, the digger wasps of the genus *Pepsis*. It is a classic example of what looks like intelligence pitted against instinct—a strange situation in which the victim, though fully able to defend itself, submits unwittingly to its destruction.

Most tarantulas live in the tropics, but several species occur in the temperate zone and a few are common in the southern U.S. Some varieties are large and have powerful fangs with which they can inflict a deep wound. These formidable-looking spiders do not, however, attack man; you can hold one in your hand, if you are gentle, without being bitten. Their bite is dangerous only to insects and small mammals such as mice; for man it is no worse than a hornet's sting.

Tarantulas customarily live in deep cylindrical burrows, from which they emerge at dusk and into which they retire at dawn. Mature males wander about after dark in search of females and occasionally stray into houses. After mating, the male dies in a few weeks, but a female lives much longer and can mate several years in succession. In a Paris museum is a tropical specimen which is said to have been living in captivity for 25 years.

A fertilized female tarantula lays from 200 to 400 eggs at a time; thus it is possible for a single tarantula to produce several thousand young. She takes no care of them beyond weaving a cocoon of silk to enclose the eggs. After they hatch, the young walk away, find convenient places in which to dig their burrows and spend the rest of their lives in solitude. The eyesight of tarantulas is poor, being limited to a sensing of change in the intensity of light and to the perception of moving objects. They apparently have little or no sense of hearing, for a hungry tarantula will pay no attention to a loudly chirping cricket placed in its cage unless the insect happens to touch one of its legs.

But all spiders, and especially hairy ones, have an extremely delicate sense of touch. Laboratory experiments prove that tarantulas can distinguish three types of touch: pressure against the body wall, stroking of the body hair, and riffling of certain very fine hairs on the legs called trichobothria. Pressure against the body, by the finger or the end of a pencil, causes the tarantula to move off slowly for a short distance. The touch excites no defensive response unless the approach is from above where the spider can see the motion, in which case it rises on its hind legs, lifts its front legs, opens its fangs and holds this threatening posture as long as the object continues to move.

The entire body of a tarantula, especially its legs, is thickly clothed with hair. Some of it is short and wooly, some long and stiff. Touching this body hair produces one of two distinct reactions. When the spider is hungry, it responds with an immediate and swift attack. At the touch of a cricket's antennae the tarantula seizes the insect so swiftly that a motion picture taken at the rate of 64 frames per second shows only the result and not the process of capture. But when the spider is not hungry, the stimulation of its hairs merely causes it to shake the touched limb. An insect can walk under its hairy belly unharmed.

The trichobothria, very fine hairs growing from disklike membranes on the legs, are sensitive only to air movement. A light breeze makes them vibrate slowly, without disturbing the common hair. When one blows gently on the trichobothria, the tarantula reacts with a quick jerk of its four front legs. If the front and hind legs are stimulated at the same time, the spider makes a sudden jump. This reaction is quite independent of the state of its appetite.

These three tactile responses—to pressure on the body wall, to moving of the common hair, and to flexing of the trichobothria— are so different from one another that there is no possibility of confusing them. They serve the tarantula adequately for most of its needs and enable it to avoid most annoyances and dangers. But they fail the spider completely when it meets its deadly enemy, the digger wasp *Pepsis*. 8

These solitary wasps are beautiful and formidable creatures. Most species are either a deep shiny blue all over, or deep blue with rusty wings. The largest have a wing span of about four inches. They live on nectar. When excited, they give off a pungent odor—a warning that they are ready to attack. The sting is much worse than that of a bee or common wasp, and the pain and swelling last longer. In the adult stage the wasp lives only a few months. The female produces but a few eggs, one at a time at intervals of two or three days. For each egg the mother must provide one adult tarantula, alive but paralyzed. The mother wasp attaches the egg to the paralyzed spider's abdomen. Upon hatching from the egg, the larva is many hundreds of times smaller than its living but helpless victim. It eats no other food and drinks no water. By the time it has finished its single Gargantuan meal and become ready for wasphood, nothing remains of the tarantula but its indigestible chitinous skeleton. 9

The mother wasp goes tarantula-hunting when the egg in her ovary is almost ready to be laid. Flying low over the ground late on a sunny afternoon, the wasp looks for its victim or for the mouth of a tarantula burrow, a round hole edged by a bit of silk. The sex of the spider makes no difference, but the mother is highly discriminating as to species. Each species of *Pepsis* requires a certain species of tarantula, and the wasp will not attack the wrong species. In a cage with a tarantula which is not its normal prey, the wasp avoids the spider and is usually killed by it in the night. 10

Yet when a wasp finds the correct species, it is the other way about. To identify the species the wasp apparently must explore the spider with her antennae. The tarantula shows an amazing tolerance to this exploration. The wasp crawls under it and walks 11 over it without evoking any hostile response. The molestation is so great and so persistent that the tarantula often rises on all eight legs, as if it were on stilts. It may stand this way for several minutes. Meanwhile the wasp, having satisfied itself that the victim is of the right species, moves off a few inches to dig the spider's grave. Working vigorously with legs and jaws, it excavates a hole 8 to 10 inches deep with a diameter slightly larger than the spider's girth. Now and again the wasp pops out of the hole to make sure that the spider is still there.

When the grave is finished, the wasp returns to the tarantula to 12 complete her ghastly enterprise. First she feels it all over once more with her antennae. Then her behavior becomes more aggressive. She bends her abdomen, protruding her sting, and searches for the soft membrane at the point where the spider's legs join its body—the only spot where she can penetrate the horny skeleton. From time to time, as the exasperated spider slowly shifts ground, the wasp turns on her back and slides along with the aid of her wings, trying to get under the tarantula for a shot at the vital spot. During all this maneuvering, which can last for several minutes, the tarantula makes no move to save itself. Finally the wasp corners it against some obstruction and grasps one of its legs in her powerful jaws. Now at last the harassed spider tries a desperate but vain defense. The two contestants roll over and over on the ground. It is a terrifying sight and the outcome is always the same. The wasp finally manages to thrust her sting into the soft spot and holds it there for a few seconds while she pumps in the poison. Almost immediately the tarantula falls paralyzed on its back. Its legs stop twitching; its heart stops beating. Yet it is not dead, as is shown by the fact that if taken from the wasp it can be restored to some sensitivity by being kept in a moist chamber for several months.

After paralyzing the tarantula, the wasp cleans herself by 13 dragging her body along the ground and rubbing her feet, sucks a drop of blood oozing from the wound in the spider's abdomen, then grabs a leg of the flabby, helpless animal in her jaws and drags it down to the bottom of the grave. She stays there for many minutes, sometimes for several hours, and what she does all that time in the dark we do not know. Eventually she lays her egg and attaches it to the side of the spider's abdomen with a sticky secretion. Then she emerges, fills the grave with soil carried bit by bit in her jaws, and finally tramples the ground all around to hide any trace of the grave from prowlers. Then she flies away, leaving her descendant safely started in life.

In all this the behavior of the wasp evidently is qualitatively different from that of the spider. The wasp acts like an intelligent animal. This is not to say that instinct plays no part or that she reasons as man does. But her actions are to the point; they are not automatic and can be modified to fit the situation. We do not know for certain how she identifies the tarantula—probably it is by some olfactory or chemo-tactile sense—but she does it purposefully and does not blindly tackle a wrong species.

On the other hand, the tarantula's behavior shows only confusion. Evidently the wasp's pawing gives it no pleasure, for it tries to move away. That the wasp is not simulating sexual stimulation is certain because male and female tarantulas react in the same way to its advances. That the spider is not anesthetized by some odorless secretion is easily shown by blowing lightly at the tarantula and making it jump suddenly. What, then, makes the tarantula behave as stupidly as it does?

No clear, simple answer is available. Possibly the stimulation by the wasp's antennae is masked by a heavier pressure on the spider's body, so that it reacts as when prodded by a pencil. But the explanation may be much more complex. Initiative in attack is not in the nature of tarantulas; most species fight only when cornered so that escape is impossible. Their inherited patterns of behavior apparently prompt them to avoid problems rather than attack them. For example, spiders always weave their webs in three dimensions, and when a spider finds that there is insufficient space to attach certain threads in the third dimension, it leaves the place and seeks another, instead of finishing the web in a single plane. This urge to escape seems to arise under all circumstances, in all phases of life, and to take the place of reasoning. For a spider to change the pattern of its web is as impossible as for an inexperienced man to build a bridge across a chasm obstructing his way.

In a way the instinctive urge to escape is not only easier but often more efficient than reasoning. The tarantula does exactly what is most efficient in all cases except in an encounter with a ruthless and determined attacker dependent for the existence of her own species on killing as many tarantulas as she can lay eggs.

Perhaps in this case the spider follows its usual pattern of trying to escape, instead of seizing and killing the wasp, because it is not aware of its danger. In any case, the survival of the tarantula species as a whole is protected by the fact that the spider is much more fertile than the wasp.

Questions for Study and Discussion

1. In what way is the *Pepsis* wasp's destruction of tarantulas a "classic example of what looks like intelligence pitted against instinct"?
2. How has Petrunkevitch organized his essay? (Glossary: *Organization*) You may find it helpful to outline the essay in answering this question.
3. What are the three tactile responses of the tarantula? What is Petrunkevitch's purpose in discussing them? (Glossary: *Purpose*)
4. In what part of his essay does Petrunkevitch actually write a process analysis? What transitional or linking devices has he used to give coherence to his description of the process? (Glossary: *Transitions*)
5. What are some of the possible reasons why the tarantula does not try to escape from the wasp until it is too late?
6. How is the tarantula able to survive as a species despite its helplessness against the wasp?

Vocabulary

Refer to your dictionary to define the following words as they are used in this selection. Then use each word in a sentence of your own.

progeny (1)	molestation (11)
tactile (8)	qualitatively (14)
Gargantuan (9)	olfactory (14)
chitinous (9)	initiative (16)

Suggested Writing Assignments

1. Our world is filled with hundreds of predator/prey relationships. In this piece, Petrunkevitch has written a process analysis of an unusual relationship, but there are many more straightforward ones, such as cat and mouse, lion and antelope, wolf and moose, and so on. Write an informational process analysis of a predator/prey relationship, using Petrunkevitch's essay as a model.

2. Use a directional process analysis for a "simple" task that could prove unfortunate or even harmful if not explained correctly. For example, changing a tire, driving a standard shift, packing for a camping trip, or loading a camera.

14

DEFINITION

To communicate precisely what you want to say, you will frequently need to *define* key words. Your reader needs to know just what you mean when you use unfamiliar words, such as *accouterment*, or words that are open to various interpretations, such as *liberal*, or words that, while generally familiar, are used in a particular sense. Failure to define important terms, or to define them accurately, confuses readers and hampers communication.

There are three basic ways to define a word; each is useful in its own way. The first method is to give a *synonym*, a word that has nearly the same meaning as the word you wish to define: *face* for *countenance, nervousness* for *anxiety.* No two words ever have *exactly* the same meaning, but you can, nevertheless, pair an unfamiliar word with a familiar one and thereby clarify your meaning.

Another way to define a word quickly, often within a single sentence, is to give a *formal definition;* that is, to place the term to be defined in a general class and then to distinguish it from other members of that class by describing its particular characteristics. For example:

WORD	CLASS	CHARACTERISTICS
A *watch*	is a *mechanical device*	*for telling time* and is usually *carried* or *worn.*
Semantics	is an *area of linguistics*	*concerned with the study of the meaning of words.*

The third method is known as *extended definition*. While some extended definitions require only a single paragraph, more often than not you will need several paragraphs or even an entire essay to define a new or difficult term or to rescue a controversial word from misconceptions and associations that may obscure its meaning.

One controversial term that illustrates the need for extended definition is *obscene*. What is obscene? Books that are banned in one school system are considered perfectly acceptable in another. Movies that are shown in one town cannot be shown in a neighboring town. Clearly, the meaning of *obscene* has been clouded by contrasting personal opinions as well as by conflicting social norms. Therefore, if you use the term *obscene* (and especially if you tackle the issue of obscenity itself), you must be careful to define clearly and thoroughly what you mean by that term—that is, you have to give an extended definition. There are a number of methods you might use to develop such a definition. You could define *obscene* by explaining what it does not mean. You could also make your meaning clear by narrating an experience, by comparing and contrasting it to related terms such as *pornographic* or *exotic*, by citing specific examples, or by classifying the various types of obscenity.

A JERK

Sydney J. Harris

For over forty years Sydney J. Harris wrote a syndicated column for the Chicago Daily News *entitled "Strictly Personal," in which he considered virtually every aspect of contemporary American life. In the following essay from his book* Last Things First *(1961), Harris defines the term* jerk *by differentiating it from other similar slang terms.*

I don't know whether history repeats itself, but biography certainly does. The other day, Michael came in and asked me what a "jerk" was—the same question Carolyn put to me a dozen years ago.

At that time, I fluffed her off with some inane answer, such as "A jerk isn't a very nice person," but both of us knew it was an unsatisfactory reply. When she went to bed, I began trying to work up a suitable definition.

It is a marvelously apt word, of course. Until it was coined, not more than 25 years ago, there was really no single word in English to describe the kind of person who is a jerk—"boob" and "simp" were too old hat, and besides they really didn't fit, for they could be lovable, and a jerk never is.

Thinking it over, I decided that a jerk is basically a person without insight. He is not necessarily a fool or a dope, because some extremely clever persons can be jerks. In fact, it has little to do with intelligence as we commonly think of it; it is, rather, a kind of subtle but persuasive aroma emanating from the inner part of the personality.

I know a college president who can be described only as a jerk. He is not an unintelligent man, nor unlearned, nor even unschooled in the social amenities. Yet he is a jerk *cum laude*, because of a fatal flaw in his nature—he is totally incapable of looking into the mirror of his soul and shuddering at what he sees there.

A jerk, then, is a man (or woman) who is utterly unable to   6
see himself as he appears to others. He has no grace, he is tactless without meaning to be, he is a bore even to his best friends,
he is an egotist without charm. All of us are egotists to some extent, but most of us—unlike the jerk—are perfectly and horribly
aware of it when we make asses of ourselves. The jerk never
knows.

Questions for Study and Discussion

1. What, according to Harris, is a jerk?
2. Jerks, boobs, simps, fools, and dopes are all in the same
   class. How does Harris differentiate a jerk from a boob or a
   simp on the one hand, and a fool or a dope on the other?
3. What does Harris see as the relationship between intelligence and/or cleverness and the idea of a jerk?
4. In paragraph 5 Harris presents the example of the college
   president. How does this example support his definition?
5. In the first two paragraphs Harris tells how both his son
   and daughter asked him what *jerk* was. How does this brief
   anecdote serve to introduce Harris's essay? (Glossary: *Beginnings and Endings*) Do you think it works well? Explain.

Vocabulary

Refer to your dictionary to define the following words as they
are used in this selection. Then use each word in a sentence of
your own.

inane (2)	emanating (4)
apt (3)	amenities (5)
coined (3)	tactless (6)

Suggested Writing Assignments

1. Write one or two paragraphs in which you give your own
   definition of *jerk* or another slang term of your choice.

2. Every generation develops its own slang, which generally enlivens the speech and writing of those who use it. Ironically, however, no generation can arrive at a consensus definition of even its most popular slang terms—for example, *nimrod, air-head, flag.* Select a slang term that you use frequently, and write an essay in which you define the term. Read your definition aloud in class. Do the other members of your class agree with your definition?

INFLATION

Marilu Hurt McCarty

*Marilu Hurt McCarty writes about economic topics
for students and popular audiences. Among her
publications are the books* Money and Banking:
Financial Institutions and Economic Policy
(1982) and Dollars and Sense *(1979), from which
the following is excerpted. Notice how she makes
this complex topic more easily understood by explaining the basic economic concepts involved.*

I t has been said that if you ask five economists for their opinion   1
on a subject, you will get six opinions—one can't make up his
(or her) mind.

This is particularly true of the subject of inflation. Because the   2
sources of inflation are difficult to pinpoint, it is often hard to
choose the proper policy for correcting the problem. Before policy alternatives can be evaluated, the problem must be carefully
analyzed and the process by which it travels through the system
understood. If the problem is approached haphazardly, any action may bring about results opposite from those intended.

Inflation can be defined as a general rise in the price level of   3
goods and services. Prices are rising and falling all the time. As
long as the *average* price level remains the same, inflation is not
a problem. When the average price level for all goods and services
increases, we have inflation.

Primitive Production

Early humans had to struggle just to stay alive. Because groups   4
were isolated, they had to be self-sufficient. A group produced its
entire reserve of game, grain, shelter, and cloth or skins. Later,
some groups began to specialize and trade with neighboring tribes.
Specialization made possible greater production so that the en-

tire community could enjoy rising standards of living. Material gains were accomplished at the expense of self-sufficiency, but that was a small price to pay.

Specialization and trade required the use of money to overcome the difficulties of barter. Primitive tribes used as money whatever tokens they found at hand—special beads and stones and rare shells. As long as the supply of money remained in balance with the supply of goods, there was no problem of rising prices. There was just enough money to exchange for goods at their customary prices.

Economic Development

As knowledge expanded, however, output grew. More money was needed to symbolize the greater values. A paradox arose: Money had to be of a scarce material to prevent misuse, but it also had to be expansible if it was to be exchanged for a growing supply of goods. Gold fulfilled both requirements for many centuries. But eventually, fewer new sources of gold (as well as the difficulty of hauling it around in one's pockets) made it necessary to find a substitute. Paper money "tied" to gold was the result.*

Balancing the supply of money and goods grew more difficult as economic life became more complex. This might be seen as a problem of *form* versus *substance*. On the one hand, the supply of goods (substance) might grow faster than the supply of money (form). Or, what is more common, the supply of money might grow faster than the real substance of goods.

When the supply of money increases faster than the supply of goods, holders of money will bid for the smaller quantity of goods. Prices will tend to rise; the economy will experience *inflation*. When the supply of money increases more slowly than the supply of goods, sellers will compete for the smaller quantity of money. Prices will tend to fall; the economy will experience *deflation*.

---

*Our money is no longer tied to gold except in a very limited sense. When the U.S. Treasury buys newly mined gold, it may issue currency in payment. However, most of our currency is issued by the Federal Reserve banks which are not limited by the supply of gold.

Why All the Fuss about Inflation?

Why should inflation concern us? A one-dollar bill and a ten   9
look pretty much the same. Why should it matter whether a day's
welding, a truckload of soybeans, a college course, or a suit of
clothes is counted as ten or one?

It matters if a day's welding *today* at forty dollars is to be ex-   10
changed in ten years for a suit of clothes. By that time the value
of forty dollars may have evaporated and a suit might cost as
much as *five* days' welding. Inflation is especially hard on those
people who depend on *stored* money value: savers, the elderly,
pensioners. (We'll all be there one day!)

It matters, too, if the price of a college course, for example,   11
rises more slowly than the price of a truckload of soybeans. Those
groups who depend on income from the sale of college courses
may be unfairly penalized by uneven price changes. Inflation
means a lower standard of living for people whose occupations or
incomes are relatively *fixed:* teachers, civil servants, low-skilled or
technically obsolete workers, and those who depend on government transfer payments.

Inflation interferes with our ability to plan for the future. We   12
have been taught to save part of our income to provide security
for our retirement years. Our savings may earn interest of up to,
say, 7 percent a year. But suppose the value of our money is declining at the rate of 10 percent a year because of inflation. The
thrifty saver will actually *lose* 3 percent in purchasing power. The
saver will be worse off than the scoundrel who squanders money
on frivolous living!

What may be even more disturbing is the fact that the saver's   13
interest earnings of 7 percent are taxed as part of personal income. In effect, he or she is being taxed twice for being virtuous—
once through inflation and once by the Internal Revenue Service!

Those who make loans and borrow money (creditors and debt-   14
ors) are also affected by inflation. In fact, inflation may benefit
the debtor, who pays back less in actual purchasing power than
originally borrowed. Lenders are understandably reluctant to
lock themselves into long-term loans when interest rates may not
compensate for inflation.

Rampant inflation is often followed by recession or depression.   15
During expansion, there is feverish spending for capital invest-

ment and production of goods and services. The result may be overproduction and stockpiling inventories. Investment and production will eventually fall off, and unemployment and economic distress follow.

Questions for Study and Discussion

1. Reread the first sentence. Why do you think McCarty begins her article in this way? (Glossary: *Beginnings and Endings*) Do you think it is an effective beginning?
2. Why does McCarty provide a general definition of inflation before going on to a more detailed discussion of the forces behind it?
3. McCarty makes her language as easy to understand as possible. For instance, she explains that inflation is a problem of form (money) over substance (goods), a very familiar concept outside of economics. Why does she avoid jargon? (Glossary: *Jargon*)
4. Why, according to McCarty, should inflation be of concern to her readers?
5. What usually follows a period of inflation? Why?

Vocabulary

Refer to your dictionary to define the following words as they are used in this selection. Then use each word in a sentence of your own.

haphazardly (2) frivolous (12)
self-sufficiency (4) virtuous (13)
barter (5) rampant (15)
obsolete (11)

Suggested Writing Assignments

1. Most people know what inflation is, but few know what causes it. Write a short definition of one of the following choices. Use McCarty's essay as a model, and be sure to

define both the word itself and the forces that cause it. Research the topic if necessary.

hurricane
traffic jam
blackout
runner's high
stock market collapse
acid rain

2. Write a short essay in which you define a word that has more than one meaning depending on one's point of view. For example, macho, liberal, success, superstar, improvement, creativity, friend, or a term of your own choosing.

THE UNDERCLASS

Herbert J. Gans

Herbert J. Gans is a professor of sociology at Columbia University in New York City. He is the author of many articles and books, including Sociology in America *(1990) and* People, Plans, and Policies: Essays on Poverty *(1991). In the following selection, written for the* Washington Post *in September 1990, he considers the possible effects on society at large of stereotyping a group of people in moralistic terms because of their economic situation.*

S ticks and stones may break my bones, but names can never   1
hurt me goes the old proverb. But like many old proverbs,
this one is patent nonsense, as anyone knows who has ever been
hurt by ethnic, racist or sexist insults and stereotypes.

The most frequent victims of insults and stereotypes have been   2
the poor, especially those thought to be undeserving of help because someone decided—justifiably or not—that they had not
acted properly. America has a long history of insults for the
"undeserving" poor. In the past they were bums, hoboes, vagrants
and paupers; more recently they have been culturally deprived
and the hard-core poor. Now they are "the underclass."

Underclass was originally a 19th-century Swedish term for the   3
poor. In the early 1960s, the Swedish economist Gunnar Myrdal
revived it to describe the unemployed and unemployables being
created by the modern economy, people who, he predicted, would
soon be driven out of that economy unless it was reformed.
Twenty years later, in Ronald Reagan's America, the word sprang
to life again, this time not only to describe but also to condemn.
Those normally consigned to the underclass include: women who
start their families before marriage and before the end of adolescence, youngsters who fail to finish high school or find work, and
welfare "dependents"—whether or not the behavior of any of

these people is their own fault. The term is also applied to low-income delinquents and criminals—but not to affluent ones.

"Underclass" has become popular because it seems to grab   4
people's attention. What grabs is the image of a growing horde of beggars, muggers, robbers and lazy people who do not carry their part of the economic load, all of them threatening nonpoor Americans and the stability of American society. The image may be inaccurate, but then insults and pejoratives don't have to be accurate. Moreover, underclass sounds technical, academic, and not overtly pejorative, so it can be used without anyone's biases showing. Since it is now increasingly applied to blacks and Hispanics, it is also a respectable substitute word with which to condemn them.

There are other things wrong with the word underclass. For   5
one, it lumps together in a single term very diverse poor people with diverse problems. Imagine all children's illnesses being described with the same word, and the difficulties doctors would have in curing them.

For example, a welfare recipient often requires little more than   6
a decent paying job—and a male breadwinner who also has such a job—to make a normal go of it, while a high school dropout usually needs both a better-equipped school, better teachers and fellow students—and a rationale for going to school when he or she has no assurance that a decent job will follow upon graduation. Neither the welfare recipient nor the high school dropout deserves to be grouped with, or described by, the same word as muggers or drug dealers.

Labeling poor people as underclass is to blame them for their   7
poverty, which enables the blamers to blow off the steam of self-righteousness. That steam does not, however, reduce their poverty. Unfortunately, underclass, like other buzzwords for calling the poor undeserving, is being used to avoid starting up needed antipoverty programs and other economic reforms.

Still, the greatest danger of all lies not in the label itself but in   8
the possibility that the underclass is a symptom of a possible, and dark, American future: that we are moving toward a "post-post-industrial" economy in which there may not be enough decent jobs for all. Either too many more jobs will move to Third World countries where wages are far lower or they will be performed by ever more efficient computers and other machines.

If this happens, the underclass label may turn out to be a signal 9
that the American economy, and our language, are preparing to
get ready for a future in which some people are going to be more
or less permanently jobless—and will be blamed for their jobless-
ness to boot.

Needless to say, an American economy with a permanently job- 10
less population would be socially dangerous, for all of the country's current social problems, from crime and addiction to mental
illness would be sure to increase considerably. America would
then also become politically more dangerous, for various kinds of
new protests have to be expected, not to mention the rise of quasi-
facist movements. Such movements can already be found in
France and other European countries.

Presumably, Americans—the citizenry and elected officials 11
both—will not let any of this happen here and will find new
sources of decent jobs, as they have done in past generations,
even if today this requires a new kind of New Deal. Perhaps there
will be another instance of what always saved America in the
past: new sources of economic growth that cannot even be imagined now.

The only problem is that in the past, America ruled the world 12
economically, and now it does not—and it shows in our lack of economic growth. Consequently, the term underclass could become
a permanent entry in the dictionary of American pejoratives.

Questions for Study and Discussion

1. How does America treat its poor citizens? What are some of
   the terms that have been used for them in the past?
2. What is Gunnar Myrdal's precise definition of "underclass"?
   How has it been changed in the United States?
3. Why is underclass an acceptable term to use for the poor?
4. Examine Gans's choice of words in paragraph 4. In your
   opinion, is his diction effective? (Glossary: *Diction*) Why?
5. In what way does Gans think the underclass is a symptom
   of a dark American future?
6. What is the tone of Gans's article? (Glossary: *Tone*)

Vocabulary

Refer to your dictionary to define the following words as they are used in this selection. Then use each word in a sentence of your own.

paupers (2)   biases (4)
condemn (3)   rationale (6)
pejorative (4)

Suggested Writing Assignments

1. Write an essay in which you define middle class, upper class, and/or the jet set. How might lumping any group of people along economic classifications create problems?
2. Using Gans essay as a model, write a short essay in which you define one of the following abstract terms, or another similar term of your own choosing. You may find it useful to begin your essay with a concrete example that illustrates your point.

   friendship

   freedom

   trust

   commitment

   love

   hatred

   charm

   peace

They've Gotta Keep It:
People Who Save Everything

Lynda W. Warren and Jonnae C. Ostrom

Lynda Warren is a counseling psychologist and pro-
fessor of psychology at California State University,
San Bernardino. Jonnae Ostrom is a clinical social
worker working at Hoag Memorial Hospital in
Newport Beach, California. In the following article,
originally published in Psychology Today *in 1988,*
Warren and Ostrom discuss "pack rats" and how
they differ from "collectors." Notice how the article
is full of details, both general and specific, on the
life of a "pack rat."

Most of us have more things than we need and use. At times   1
they pile up in corners and closets or accumulate in the
recesses of attics, basements or garages. But we sort through our
clutter periodically and clean it up, saving only what we really
need and giving away or throwing out the excess. This isn't the
case, unfortunately, with people we call "pack rats"—those who
collect, save or hoard insatiably, often with only the vague rationale that the items may someday be useful. And because they
rarely winnow what they save, it grows and grows.

While some pack rats specialize in what they collect, others   2
seem to save indiscriminately. And what they keep, such as junk
mail, supermarket receipts, newspapers, business memos, empty
cans, clothes or old Christmas and birthday cards, often seem to
be worthless. Even when items have some value, such as lumber
scraps, fabric remnants, auto parts, shoes and plastic meat trays,
they tend to be kept in huge quantities that no one could use in
a lifetime.

Although pack rats collect, they are different from collectors,   3
who save in a systematic way. Collectors usually specialize in one
of a few classes of objects, which they organize, display and even
catalogue. But pack rats tend to stockpile their possessions haphazardly and seldom use them.

Our interest in pack rats was sparked by a combination of personal experience with some older relatives and recognition of similar saving patterns in some younger clients one of us saw in therapy sessions. Until then, we, like most people, assumed that pack rats were all older people who had lived through the Great Depression of the 1930s—eccentrics who were stockpiling stuff just in case another Depression came along. We were surprised to discover a younger generation of pack rats, born long after the 1930s.   4

None of these clients identified themselves during therapy as pack rats or indicated that their hoarding tendencies were causing problems in any way. Only after their partners told us how annoyed and angry they were about the pack rats' unwillingness to clean up the growing mess at home did they acknowledge their behavior. Even then, they defended it and had little interest in changing. The real problem, they implied, was their partner's intolerance rather than their own hoarding.   5

Like most people, we had viewed excessive saving as a rare and harmless eccentricity. But when we discussed our initial observations with others, we gradually came to realize that almost everyone we met either admitted to some strong pack-rat tendencies or seemed to know someone who had them. Perhaps the greatest surprise, however, was how eager people were to discuss their own pack-rat experiences. Although our observations are admittedly based on a small sample, we now believe that such behavior is common and that, particularly when it is extreme, it may create problems for the pack rats or those close to them.   6

When we turned to the psychological literature, we found surprisingly little about human collecting or hoarding in general and almost nothing about pack-rat behavior. Psychoanalysts view hoarding as one characteristic of the "anal" character type, first described by Freud. Erich Fromm later identified the "hoarding orientation" as one of the four basic ways in which people may adjust unproductively to life.   7

While some pack rats do have typically anal-retentive* characteristics such as miserliness, orderliness and stubbornness, we   8

---

*A psychoanalytic term describing a type of personality who shows traits such as meticulousness (being overly precise), greed, and stubbornness; its origin is associated with infantile pleasure in retaining one's feces.

suspect that they vary as much in personality characteristics as they do in education, socioeconomic status and occupation. But they do share certain ways of thinking and feeling about their possessions that shed some light on the possible causes and consequences of their behavior.

Why do some people continue to save when there is no more 9 space for what they have and they own more of something than could ever be used? We have now asked that question of numerous students, friends and colleagues who have admitted their pack-rat inclinations. They readily answer the question with seemingly good reasons, such as possible future need ("I might need this sometime"), sentimental attachment ("Aunt Edith gave this to me"), potential value ("This might be worth something someday") and lack of wear or damage ("This is too good to throw away"). Such reasons are difficult to challenge; they are grounded in some truth and logic and suggest that pack-rat saving reflects good sense, thrift and even foresight. Indeed, many pack rats proudly announce, "I've never thrown anything away!" or "You would not believe what I keep!"

But on further questioning, other, less logical reasons become 10 apparent. Trying to get rid of things may upset pack rats emotionally and may even bring on physical distress. As one woman said, "I get a headache or sick to my stomach if I have to throw something away."

They find it hard to decide what to keep and what to throw 11 away. Sometimes they fear they will get rid of something that they or someone else might value, now or later. Having made such a "mistake" in the past seems to increase such distress. "I've always regretted throwing away the letters Mother sent me in college. I will never make that mistake again," one client said. Saving the object eliminates the distress and is buttressed by the reassuring thought, "Better to save this than be sorry later."

Many pack rats resemble compulsive personalities in their ten- 12 dency to avoid or postpone decisions, perhaps because of an inordinate fear of making a mistake. Indeed, in the latest edition of the psychiatric diagnostic bible (DSM-III-R), the kind of irrational hoarding seen in pack rats ("inability to discard worn-out or worthless objects even when they have no sentimental value") is described as a characteristic of people with obsessive compulsive personality disorder.

Some pack rats seem to have a depressive side, too. Discarding 13
things seems to reawaken old memories and feelings of loss or
abandonment, akin to grief or the pain of rejection. "I feel incredibly sad—it's really very painful," one client said of the process.
Another client, a mental-health counselor, said, "I don't understand why, but when I have to throw something away, even something like dead flowers, I feel my old abandonment fears and I
also feel lonely."

Some pack rats report that their parents discarded certain trea- 14
sured possessions, apparently insensitive to their attachment to
the objects. "My Dad went through my room one time and threw
out my old shell collection that I had in a closet. It devastated
me," said one woman we interviewed. Such early experiences
continue to color their feelings as adults, particularly toward possessions they especially cherish.

It's not uncommon for pack rats to "personalize" their posses- 15
sions or identify with them, seeing them as extensions of themselves. One pack rat defiantly said about her things, "This is me—
this is my individuality and you are not going to throw it out!"

At times the possessions are viewed akin to beloved people. For 16
example, one woman said, "I can't let my Christmas tree be destroyed! I love my Christmas ornaments—I adore them!" Another
woman echoed her emotional involvement: "My jewelry is such a
comfort to me. I just love my rings and chains." Discarding such
personalized possessions could easily trigger fears, sadness or
guilt because it would be psychologically equivalent to a part of
oneself dying or abandoning a loved one.

In saving everything, the pack rat seems to have found the per- 17
fect way to avoid indecision and the discomfort of getting rid of
things. It works—but only for a while. The stuff keeps mounting,
and so do the problems it produces.

Attempts to clean up and organize may be upsetting because 18
there is too much stuff to manage without spending enormous
amounts of time and effort. One pack rat sighed, "Just thinking
about cleaning it up makes me tired before I begin." And since
even heroic efforts at cleaning bring barely visible results, such
unrewarding efforts are unlikely to continue.

At this point, faced with ever-growing goods and ineffective 19
ways of getting rid of the excess, pack rats may begin to feel controlled by their possessions. As one put it, "I'm at the point where
I feel impotent about getting my bedroom cleaned."

Even if the clutter doesn't get the pack rats down, it often irks 20
others in the household who do not share the same penchant for
saving. Since hoarding frequently begins in the bedroom, the
pack rat's partner is usually the first to be affected. He or she begins to feel squeezed out by accumulated possessions, which may
seem to take precedence over the couple's relationship.

At first, the partner may simply feel bewildered about the 21
growing mess and uncertain about what to do, since requests to
remove the "junk" tend to be ignored or met with indignation or
even anger. One exasperated husband of a pack-rat client said:
"She keeps her stuff in paper bags all over the bedroom. You can
now hardly get to the bed. I tried talking to her about it but nothing seems to work. When she says she has cleaned it out, I can
never see any change. I'm ready to hire a truck to cart it all away."

As the junk piles accumulate, the partner may try to clean up 22
the mess. But that generally infuriates the pack rat and does nothing to break the savings habit. As the partner begins to feel increasingly impotent, feelings of frustration and irritation escalate
and the stockpiled possessions may become an emotional barrier
between the two. This situation is even worse if the pack rat is
also a compulsive shopper whose spending sprees are creating financial problems and excessive family debt.

Children are also affected by a parent's pack-rat behavior. They 23
may resent having the family's living space taken over by piles of
possessions and may hesitate to ask their friends over because
they are embarrassed by the excessive clutter and disarray. One
child of a pack rat said, "As long as I can remember, I've always
warned people what to expect the first time they come to our
house. I told them it was OK to move something so they would
have a place to sit down." Even the adults may rarely invite non-
family members to visit because the house is never presentable.

Children may also be caught in the middle of the escalating ten- 24
sion between their parents over what to do about all the stuff in
the house. But whatever their feelings, it is clear that the children are being raised in an environment in which possessions are
especially important and laden with complex emotions.

Our clients and other people we have consulted have helped 25
make us aware of the problems pack rats can pose for themselves
and those around them. Now we hope that a new study of excessive savers will provide some preliminary answers to a number of
deeper questions: What predisposes people to become pack rats,

and when does hoarding typically start? Can the behavior be averted or changed? Is excessive saving associated with earlier emotional or economic deprivation? Does such saving cause emotional distress directly or are pack rats only bothered when others disapprove of their behavior? Do pack rats run into problems at work the same way they often do at home?

Whatever additional information we come up with, we're already sure of at least one thing: This article will be saved forever by all the pack rats of the world.   26

Questions for Study and Discussion

1. According to Warren and Ostrom, what is a "pack rat"? How are pack rats different from collectors?

2. Why did the authors become interested in studying the behavior of pack rats? What work had been done in this area before?

3. Why do the authors use so many quotes from pack rats and their family members?

4. What are some of the "symptoms" displayed by pack rats that are similar to other psychological conditions?

5. For what audience do Warren and Ostrom write about pack rats? (Glossary: *Audience*) What is the purpose of the article? (Glossary: *Purpose*)

6. What attitude do the authors have toward pack rats? (Glossary: *Attitude*) Explain your answer.

7. What do the last two paragraphs accomplish? Do you think that the last paragraph is an effective end to the article? (Glossary: *Beginnings and Endings*)

Vocabulary

Refer to your dictionary to define the following words as they are used in this selection. Then use each word in a sentence of your own.

winnow (1)
haphazardly (3)
hoarding (5)
miserliness (8)
buttressed (11)
compulsive (12)

inordinate (12)
akin (13)
irks (20)
impotent (22)
deprivation (25)

Suggested Writing Assignments

1. Identify and define a personality type. Are you, or do you know, a neat freak, a procrastinator, a couch potato? What are this person's recognizable characteristics? What behavior is associated with the personality type? What may cause this behavior? If it's positive behavior, what can be done to encourage it? If negative, how can it be improved?

2. Paragraph 25 contains several questions that need to be studied in order to understand the behavior of pack rats. Choose one of the questions and design a research project that would study the behavior and try to answer the question. Assume that you have fifty pack-rats and their families who are willing to cooperate in your study. What questions would you ask the pack rats? What conditions would you impose on them? Explain your reasoning and support with examples the conclusions you reach.

15

DIVISION AND CLASSIFICATION

To divide is to separate a class of things or ideas into categories, whereas to classify is to group separate things or ideas into those categories. The two processes can operate separately but often go together. Division and classification can be a useful organizational strategy in writing. Here, for example, is a passage about levers in which the writer first discusses generally how levers work and then, in the second paragraph, uses division to establish three categories of levers and classification to group individual levers into those categories:

> Every lever has one fixed point called the "fulcrum" and is acted upon by two forces—the "effort" (exertion of hand muscles) and the "weight" (object's resistance). Levers work according to a simple formula: the effort (how hard you push or pull) multiplied by its distance from the fulcrum (effort arm) equals the weight multiplied by its distance from the fulcrum (weight arm). Thus two pounds of effort exerted at a distance of four feet from the fulcrum will raise eight pounds located one foot from the fulcrum.
>
> There are three types of levers, conventionally called "first kind," "second kind," and "third kind." Levers of the first kind have the fulcrum located between the effort and the weight. Examples are a pump handle, an oar, a crowbar, a weighing balance, a pair of scissors, and a pair of pliers. Levers of the second kind have the weight in the middle and magnify the effort. Examples are the handcar crank and doors. Levers of the third kind, such as a power shovel or a baseball batter's forearm, have the effort in the middle and always magnify the distance.

In writing, division and classification are affected directly by the writer's practical purpose. That purpose—what the writer wants to explain or prove—determines the class of things or ideas being divided and classified. For instance, a writer might divide television programs according to their audiences—adults, families, or children—and then classify individual programs into each of these categories in order to show how much emphasis the television stations place on reaching each audience. A different purpose would require different categories. A writer concerned about the prevalence of violence in television programming would first divide television programs into those which include fights and murders, and those which do not, and would then classify a large sample of programs into those categories. Other writers with different purposes might divide television programs differently—by the day and time of broadcast, for example, or by the number of women featured in prominent roles—and then classify individual programs accordingly.

The following guidelines can help you in using division and classification in your writing:

1. *Identify a clear purpose, and be sure that your principle of division is appropriate to that purpose.* To determine the makeup of a student body, for example, you might consider the following principles of division: college or program, major, class level, sex. It would not be helpful to divide students on the basis of their toothpaste unless you had a purpose and thus a reason for doing so.

2. *Divide your subject into categories that are mutually exclusive.* An item can belong to only one category. For example, it would be unsatisfactory to divide students as men, women, and athletes.

3. *Make your division and classification complete.* Your categories should account for all items in a subject class. In dividing students on the basis of geographic origin, for example, it would be inappropriate to consider only home states, for such a division would not account for foreign students. Then, for your classification to be complete, every student must be placed in one of the established categories.

4. *Be sure to state clearly the conclusion that your division and classification lead you to draw.* For example, a study of the student body might lead to the conclusion that 45 percent of the male athletes with athletic scholarships come from west of the Mississippi.

THE WAYS OF MEETING OPPRESSION

Martin Luther King, Jr.

*Martin Luther King, Jr. (1929–1968) was the lead-
ing spokesman for the rights of African Americans
during the 1950s and 1960s before he was assassinated in 1968. He established the Southern Christian Leadership Conference, organized many civil
rights demonstrations, and opposed the Vietnam
War and the draft. In 1964 he was awarded the
Nobel Prize for Peace. In the following essay, taken
from his book* Stride Toward Freedom *(1958), King
classifies the three ways oppressed people throughout history have reacted to their oppressors.*

Oppressed people deal with their oppression in three char-   1
acteristic ways. One way is acquiescence: the oppressed
resign themselves to their doom. They tacitly adjust themselves to
oppression, and thereby become conditioned to it. In every movement toward freedom some of the oppressed prefer to remain oppressed. Almost 2800 years ago Moses set out to lead the children
of Israel from the slavery of Egypt to the freedom of the promised
land. He soon discovered that slaves do not always welcome their
deliverers. They become accustomed to being slaves. They would
rather bear those ills they have, as Shakespeare pointed out, than
flee to others that they know not of. They prefer the "fleshpots of
Egypt" to the ordeals of emancipation.

There is such a thing as the freedom of exhaustion. Some peo-   2
ple are so worn down by the yoke of oppression that they give up.
A few years ago in the slum areas of Atlanta, a Negro guitarist
used to sing almost daily: "Been down so long that down don't
bother me." This is the type of negative freedom and resignation
that often engulfs the life of the oppressed.

But this is not the way out. To accept passively an unjust system   3
is to cooperate with that system; thereby the oppressed become

as evil as the oppressor. Noncooperation with evil is as much a moral obligation as is cooperation with good. The oppressed must never allow the conscience of the oppressor to slumber. Religion reminds every man that he is his brother's keeper. To accept injustice or segregation passively is to say to the oppressor that his actions are morally right. It is a way of allowing his conscience to fall asleep. At this moment the oppressed fails to be his brother's keeper. So acquiescence—while often the easier way—is not the moral way. It is the way of the coward. The Negro cannot win the respect of his oppressor by acquiescing; he merely increases the oppressor's arrogance and contempt. Acquiescence is interpreted as proof of the Negro's inferiority. The Negro cannot win the respect of the white people of the South or the peoples of the world if he is willing to sell the future of his children for his personal and immediate comfort and safety.

A second way that oppressed people sometimes deal with oppression is to resort to physical violence and corroding hatred. Violence often brings about momentary results. Nations have frequently won their independence in battle. But in spite of temporary victories, violence never brings permanent peace. It solves no social problem; it merely creates new and more complicated ones.

Violence as a way of achieving racial justice is both impractical and immoral. It is impractical because it is a descending spiral ending in destruction for all. The old law of an eye for an eye leaves everybody blind. It is immoral because it seeks to humiliate the opponent rather than win his understanding; it seeks to annihilate rather than to convert. Violence is immoral because it thrives on hatred rather than love. It destroys community and makes brotherhood impossible. It leaves society in monologue rather than dialogue. Violence ends by defeating itself. It creates bitterness in the survivors and brutality in the destroyers. A voice echoes through time saying to every potential Peter, "Put up your sword."* History is cluttered with the wreckage of nations that failed to follow this command.

If the American Negro and other victims of oppression succumb to the temptation of using violence in the struggle for free-

---

*The apostle Peter had drawn his sword to defend Christ from arrest. The voice was Christ's, who surrendered himself for trial and crucifixion (John 18:11).

dom, future generations will be the recipients of a desolate night of bitterness, and our chief legacy to them will be an endless reign of meaningless chaos. Violence is not the way.

The third way open to oppressed people in their quest for free-   7
dom is the way of nonviolent resistance. Like the synthesis in Hegelian philosophy, the principle of nonviolent resistance seeks to reconcile the truths of two opposites—the acquiescence and violence—while avoiding the extremes and immoralities of both. The nonviolent resister agrees with the person who acquiesces that one should not be physically aggressive toward his opponent; but he balances the equation by agreeing with the person of violence that evil must be resisted. He avoids the nonresistance of the former and the violent resistance of the latter. With nonviolent resistance, no individual or group need submit to any wrong, nor need anyone resort to violence in order to right a wrong.

It seems to me that this is the method that must guide the ac-   8
tions of the Negro in the present crisis in race relations. Through nonviolent resistance the Negro will be able to rise to the noble height of opposing the unjust system while loving the perpetrators of the system. The Negro must work passionately and unrelentingly for full stature as a citizen, but he must not use inferior methods to gain it. He must never come to terms with falsehood, malice, hate, or destruction.

Nonviolent resistance makes it possible for the Negro to re-   9
main in the South and struggle for his rights. The Negro's problem will not be solved by running away. He cannot listen to the glib suggestion of those who would urge him to migrate en masse to other sections of the country. By grasping his great opportunity in the South he can make a lasting contribution to the moral strength of the nation and set a sublime example of courage for generations yet unborn.

By nonviolent resistance, the Negro can also enlist all men of   10
good will in his struggle for equality. The problem is not a purely racial one, with Negroes set against whites. In the end, it is not a struggle between people at all, but a tension between justice and injustice. Nonviolent resistance is not aimed against oppressors but against oppression. Under its banner consciences, not racial groups, are enlisted.

Questions for Study and Discussion

1. What are the disadvantages that King sees in meeting oppression with acquiescence or with violence?
2. Why, according to King, do slaves not always welcome their deliverers?
3. What does King mean by the "freedom of exhaustion" (2)?
4. What is King's purpose in writing this essay? How does classifying the three types of resistance to oppression serve this purpose? (Glossary: *Purpose*)
5. What principle of division does King use in this essay?
6. Why do you suppose that King discusses acquiescence, violence, and nonviolent resistance in that order? (Glossary: *Organization*)
7. King states that he favors nonviolent resistance over the other two ways of meeting oppression. Look closely at the words he uses to describe nonviolent resistance and those he uses to describe acquiescence and violence. How does his choice of words contribute to his argument? Show examples. (Glossary: *Connotation/Denotation*)

Vocabulary

Refer to your dictionary to define the following words as they are used in this selection. Then use each word in a sentence of your own.

acquiescence (1)   desolate (6)
tacitly (1)   synthesis (7)
corroding (4)   sublime (9)
annihilate (5)

Suggested Writing Assignments

1. Write an essay about a problem of some sort in which you use division and classification to discuss various possible solutions. You might discuss something personal such as

the problems of giving up smoking or something that concerns everyone such as the difficulties of coping with the
homeless. Whatever your topic, use an appropriate principle of division to establish categories that suit the purpose
of your discussion.

2. Consider any one of the following topics for an essay of
classification:

   movies
   college courses
   spectators
   life styles
   country music
   newspapers
   pets
   grandparents

Friends, Good Friends —and Such Good Friends

Judith Viorst

Judith Viorst has written several volumes of light verse as well as many articles that have appeared in popular magazines. The following essay appeared in her regular column in Redbook. *In it she analyzes and classifies the various types of friends that a person can have. As you read the essay, assess its validity by trying to place your friends in Viorst's categories.*

Women are friends, I once would have said, when they totally love and support and trust each other, and bare to each other the secrets of their souls, and run—no questions asked—to help each other, and tell harsh truths to each other (no, you can't wear that dress unless you lose ten pounds first) when harsh truths must be told.

Women are friends, I once would have said, when they share the same affection for Ingmar Bergman, plus train rides, cats, warm rain, charades, Camus, and hate with equal ardor Newark and Brussels sprouts and Lawrence Welk and camping.

In other words, I once would have said that a friend is a friend all the way, but now I believe that's a narrow point of view. For the friendships I have and the friendships I see are conducted at many levels of intensity, serve many different functions, meet different needs and range from those as all-the-way as the friendship of the soul sisters mentioned above to that of the most nonchalant and casual playmates.

Consider these varieties of friendship:

1. Convenience friends. These are women with whom, if our paths weren't crossing all the time, we'd have no particular reason to be friends: a next-door neighbor, a woman in our car pool, the mother of one of our children's closest friends or maybe some mommy with whom we serve juice and cookies each week at the Glenwood Co-op Nursery.

Convenience friends are convenient indeed. They'll lend us their cups and silverware for a party. They'll drive our kids to soccer when we're sick. They'll take us to pick up our car when we need a lift to the garage. They'll even take our cats when we go on vacation. As we will for them.

But we don't, with convenience friends, ever come too close or tell too much; we maintain our public face and emotional distance. "Which means," says Elaine, "that I'll talk about being overweight but not about being depressed. Which means I'll admit being mad but not blind with rage. Which means that I might say that we're pinched this month but never that I'm worried sick over money."

But which doesn't mean that there isn't sufficient value to be found in these friendships of mutual aid, in convenience friends.

2. Special-interest friends. These friendships aren't intimate, and they needn't involve kids or silverware or cats. Their value lies in some interest jointly shared. And so we may have an office friend or a yoga friend or a tennis friend or a friend from the Women's Democratic Club.

"I've got one woman friend," says Joyce, "who likes, as I do, to take psychology courses. Which makes it nice for me—and nice for her. It's fun to go with someone you know and it's fun to discuss what you've learned, driving back from the classes." And for the most part, she says, that's all they discuss.

"I'd say that what we're doing is *doing* together, not being together," Suzanne says of her Tuesday-doubles friends. "It's mainly a tennis relationship, but we play together well. And I guess we all need to have a couple of playmates."

I agree.

My playmate is a shopping friend, a woman of marvelous taste, a woman who knows exactly *where* to buy *what*, and furthermore is a woman who always knows beyond a doubt what one ought to be buying. I don't have the time to keep up with what's new in eyeshadow, hemlines and shoes and whether the smock look is in or finished already. But since (oh, shame!) I care a lot about eyeshadow, hemlines and shoes, and since I don't *want* to wear smocks if the smock look is finished, I'm very glad to have a shopping friend.

3. Historical friends. We all have a friend who knew us when ... maybe way back in Miss Meltzer's second grade, when our family lived in that three-room flat in Brooklyn, when our dad

was out of work for seven months, when our brother Allie got in that fight where they had to call the police, when our sister married the endodontist from Yonkers and when, the morning after we lost our virginity, she was the first, the only, friend we told.

The years have gone by and we've gone separate ways and we've little in common now, but we're still an intimate part of each other's past. And so whenever we go to Detroit we always go to visit this friend of our girlhood. Who knows how we looked before our teeth were straightened. Who knows how we talked before our voice got un-Brooklyned. Who knows what we ate before we learned about artichokes. And who, by her presence, puts us in touch with an earlier part of ourself, a part of ourself it's important never to lose.

"What this friend means to me and what I mean to her," says Grace, "is having a sister without sibling rivalry. We know the texture of each other's lives. She remembers my grandmother's cabbage soup. I remember the way her uncle played the piano. There's simply no other friend who remembers those things."

4. Crossroads friends. Like historical friends, our crossroads friends are important for *what was*—for the friendship we shared at a crucial, now past, time of life. A time, perhaps, when we roomed in college together; or worked as eager young singles in the Big City together; or went together, as my friend Elizabeth and I did, through pregnancy, birth and that scary first year of new motherhood.

Crossroads friends forge powerful links, links strong enough to endure with not much more contact than once-a-year letters at Christmas. And out of respect for those crossroad years, for those dramas and dreams we once shared, we will always be friends.

5. Cross-generational friends. Historical friends and crossroads friends seem to maintain a special kind of intimacy—dormant but always ready to be revived—and though we may rarely meet, whenever we do connect, it's personal and intense. Another kind of intimacy exists in the friendships that form across generations in what one woman calls her daughter-mother and her mother-daughter relationships.

Evelyn's friend is her mother's age—"but I share so much more than I ever could with my mother"—a woman she talks to of music, of books and of life. "What I get from her is the benefit of her experience. What she gets—and enjoys—from me is a youthful perspective. It's a pleasure for both of us."

I have in my own life a precious friend, a woman of 65 who has   21
lived very hard, who is wise, who listens well; who has been
where I am and can help me understand it; and who represents
not only an ultimate ideal mother to me but also the person I'd
like to be when I grow up.

In our daughter role we tend to do more than our share of self-   22
revelation; in our mother role we tend to receive what's revealed.
It's another kind of pleasure—playing wise mother to a questing
younger person. It's another very lovely kind of friendship.

6. Part-of-a-couple friends. Some of the women we call our   23
friends we never see alone—we see them as part of a couple at
couples' parties. And though we share interests in many things
and respect each other's views, we aren't moved to deepen the
relationship. Whatever the reason, a lack of time or—and this is
more likely—a lack of chemistry, our friendship remains in the
context of a group. But the fact that our feeling on seeing each
other is always, "I'm *so* glad she's here" and the fact that we spend
half the evening talking together says that this too, in its own way,
counts as a friendship.

(Other part-of-a-couple friends are the friends that came with   24
the marriage, and some of these are friends we could live without.
But sometimes, alas, she married our husband's best friend; and
sometimes, alas, she *is* our husband's best friend. And so we find
ourself dealing with her, somewhat against our will, in a spirit of
what I'll call *reluctant* friendship.)

7. Men who are friends. I wanted to write just of women   25
friends, but the women I've talked to won't let me—they say I
must mention man-woman friendships too. For these friendships
can be just as close and as dear as those that we form with
women. Listen to Lucy's description of one such friendship:

"We've found we have things to talk about that are different   26
from what he talks about with my husband and different from
what I talk about with his wife. So sometimes we call on the
phone or meet for lunch. There are similar intellectual interests—
we always pass on to each other the books that we love—but
there's also something tender and caring too."

In a couple of crises, Lucy says, "he offered himself for talking   27
and for helping. And when someone died in his family he wanted
me there. The sexual, flirty part of our friendship is very small,
but *some*—just enough to make it fun and different." She thinks—

and I agree—that the sexual part, though small, is always *some*, is always there when a man and a woman are friends.

It's only in the past few years that I've made friends with men, in the sense of a friendship that's *mine*, not just part of two couples. And achieving with them the ease and the trust I've found with women friends has value indeed. Under the dryer at home last week, putting on mascara and rouge, I comfortably sat and talked with a fellow named Peter. Peter, I finally decided, could handle the shock of me minus mascara under the dryer. Because we care for each other. Because we're friends. 28

8. There are medium friends, and pretty good friends, and very good friends indeed, and these friendships are defined by their level of intimacy. And what we'll reveal at each of these levels of intimacy is calibrated with care. We might tell a medium friend, for example, that yesterday we had a fight with our husband. And we might tell a pretty good friend that this fight with our husband made us so mad that we slept on the couch. And we might tell a very good friend that the reason we got so mad in that fight that we slept on the couch had something to do with that girl that works in his office. But it's only to our very best friends that we're willing to tell all, to tell what's going on with that girl in his office. 29

The best of friends, I still believe, totally love and support and trust each other, and bare to each other the secrets of their souls, and run—no questions asked—to help each other, and tell harsh truths to each other when they must be told. 30

But we needn't agree about everything (only 12-year-old girl friends agree about *everything*) to tolerate each other's point of view. To accept without judgment. To give and to take without ever keeping score. And to *be* there, as I am for them and as they are for me, to comfort our sorrows, to celebrate our joys. 31

Questions for Study and Discussion

1. In her opening paragraph Viorst explains how she once would have defined friendship. Why does she now think differently?
2. What is Viorst's purpose in this essay? Why is division and classification an appropriate strategy for her to use? (Glossary: *Purpose*)

3. Into what categories does Viorst divide her friends?
4. What principles of division does Viorst use to establish her categories of friends? Where does she state these principles?
5. Discuss the ways in which Viorst makes her categories distinct and memorable.
6. Viorst wrote this essay for *Redbook*, and so her audience was women between the ages of twenty-five and thirty-five. If she had been writing on the same topic for an audience of men of the same age, how might her categories have been different? How might her examples have been different? (Glossary: *Audience*)

Vocabulary

Refer to your dictionary to define the following words as they are used in this selection. Then use each word in a sentence of your own.

ardor (2)	forge (18)
nonchalant (3)	dormant (19)
sibling (16)	perspective (20)

Suggested Writing Assignments

1. If for any reason you dislike or disagree with Viorst's classification of friends, write a classification essay of your own on the same topic. In preparation for writing, you may wish to interview your classmates and dorm members for their ideas on the various types of friends a person can have.
2. The following (p. 331) is a basic exercise in classification. By determining the features that the figures have in common, establish the general class to which they all belong. Next, establish subclasses by determining the distinctive features that distinguish one subclass from another. Finally, place each figure in an appropriate subclass within your classification system. You may wish to compare your classification system with those developed by other members of your class and to discuss any differences that exist.

WHAT YOU DO IS WHAT YOU ARE

Nickie McWhirter

Nickie McWhirter was born in Peoria, Illinois in 1929. She graduated from the University of Michigan in 1951 and began her writing career soon thereafter. She joined the staff of the Detroit Free Press *in 1963 as a features writer, then started her own four-times weekly column for the paper in 1977. She has received numerous local awards for her writing. Note how she uses mild sarcasm to make her point in the following selection.*

Americans, unlike people almost everywhere else in the   1
world, tend to define and judge everybody in terms of the
work they do, especially work performed for pay. Charlie is a doctor; Sam is a carpenter; Mary Ellen is a copywriter at a small ad
agency. It is as if by defining how a person earns his or her rent
money, we validate or reject that person's existence. Through the
work and job title, we evaluate the worth of the life attached.
Larry is a laid-off auto worker; Tony is a retired teacher; Sally is
a former showgirl and blackjack dealer from Vegas. It is as if by
learning that a person currently earns no money at a job—and
maybe hasn't earned any money at a job for years—we assign that
person to limbo, at least for the present. We define such non-
employed persons in terms of their past job history.

This seems peculiar to me. People aren't cast in bronze because   2
of the jobs they hold or once held. A retired teacher, for example,
may spend a lot of volunteer time working with handicapped
children or raising money for the Loyal Order of Hibernating
Hibiscus. That apparently doesn't count. Who's Tony? A retired
teacher. A laid-off auto worker may pump gas at his cousin's gas
station or sell encyclopedias on weekends. But who's Larry? Until
and unless he begins to work steadily again, he's a laid-off auto
worker. This is the same as saying he's nothing now, but he used
to be something: an auto worker.

There is a whole category of other people who are "just" some- 3
thing. To be "just" anything is the worst. It is not to be recognized
by society as having much value at all, not now and probably not
in the past either. To be "just" anything is to be totally discounted,
at least for the present. There are lots of people who are "just"
something. "Just" a housewife immediately and painfully comes
to mind. We still hear it all the time. Sometimes women who have
kept a house and reared six children refer to themselves as "'just'
a housewife." "Just" a bum, "just" a kid, "just" a drunk, bag lady,
old man, student, punk are some others. You can probably add to
the list. The "just" category contains present non-earners, people
who have no past job history highly valued by society and people
whose present jobs are on the low-end of pay and prestige scales.
A person can be "just" a cab driver, for example, or "just" a janitor.
No one is ever "just" a vice-president, however.

We're supposed to be a classless society, but we are not. We 4
don't recognize a titled nobility. We refuse to acknowledge dynastic privilege. But we certainly separate the valued from the valueless, and it has a lot to do with jobs and the importance or prestige we attach to them.

It is no use arguing whether any of this is correct or proper. 5
Rationally it is silly. That's our system, however, and we should
not only keep it in mind, we should teach our children how it
works. It is perfectly swell to want to grow up to be a cowboy or
a nurse. Kids should know, however, that quite apart from earnings potential, the cattle breeder is much more respected than the
hired hand. The doctor gets a lot more respect and privilege than
the nurse.

I think some anthropologist ought to study our uncataloged 6
system of awarding respect and deference to each other based
on jobs we hold. Where does a vice-president–product planning
fit in? Is that better than vice-president–sales in the public consciousness, or unconsciousness? Writers earn diddly dot, but I
suspect they are held in higher esteem than wealthy rock musicians—that is, if everybody older than 40 gets to vote.

How do we decide which jobs have great value and, therefore, 7
the job-holders are wonderful people? Why is someone who
builds shopping centers called an entrepreneur while someone
who builds freeways is called a contractor? I have no answers to
any of this, but we might think about the phenomenon the next

time we are tempted to fawn over some stranger because we find out he happens to be a judge, or the next time we catch ourselves discounting the personal worth of the garbage collector.

Questions for Study and Discussion

1. What is McWhirter's thesis? (Glossary: *Thesis*) Does she state it outright or is it implied?
2. Add several more people to McWhirter's list of people who are "just" housewives, old men, and so on.
3. According to McWhirter, why should we teach our children how the system works? Do you think her recommendation is serious or tongue-in-cheek? Why?
4. What is McWhirter's tone? (Glossary: *Tone*) Support your answer with examples from the essay.
5. Does income necessarily dictate how others view each job? What are the most important factors?
6. According to McWhirter, how are unemployed people viewed in America's "job classification"?

Vocabulary

Refer to your dictionary to define the following words as they are used in this selection. Then use each word in a sentence of your own.

validate (1)	dynastic (4)
limbo (1)	deference (6)
prestige (3)	fawn (7)

Suggested Writing Assignments

1. Within each classification that we make, there are subclassifications. For instance, Michael Jordan and Dan Jansen are both great athletes, but there are obvious differences between them: summer vs. winter sport, amateur vs. professional, etc. The same holds true for Steven King and

Jacques Cousteau—they are both writers, but their works are nonetheless very different in content and style. Choose one of the following jobs (or another of your own choosing) and write a short essay in which you establish three or four subclassifications, with examples of each:

  athletes
  teachers
  writers
  lawyers
  politicians

2. Do you agree with McWhirter's contention that we are classified in society by what job we do? Write an essay stating why you agree or do not agree with McWhirter. Provide some evidence to support your reasons, for instance, how has job classification influenced your current choice of careers?

THE TEN MOST MEMORABLE BORES

Margot Mifflin

Margot Mifflin spent her early years in Swarth-more, Pennsylvania, before entering Occidental College and earning her B.A. in 1982. She received a M.A. in journalism from New York University in 1986 and traveled to Europe, Africa, and Japan on a Watson fellowship. Since her return, she has writ-ten articles for such publications as Vogue, Enter-tainment Weekly, *and* Elle. *The following selection appeared in* Cosmopolitan *in April 1990.*

E xactly what *is* a bore? According to comic Henny Young-man, he's "a guy with a cocktail glass in one hand and your lapel in the other."

Boring people can't be diverted by polite interjections or gap-ing yawns—they just go on happily torturing anyone who's unwit-tingly jumped onto their tedium treadmill. And although *Winnie the Pooh* author A. A. Milne divided bores into two classes—"those who have their own particular subject, and those who do not need a subject"—they actually come in many flavors. Here are the ten most irritating types.

1. Gasbag Bores

Gasbags can't abide a second of silence, so they fill the air with their own observations, relevant or not. Agonizingly thorough in their descriptions, which include recaps of entire film plots and blow-by-blows of recent jaunts to Disneyland or the Amish coun-try, their attention to detail borders on the pathological. Brand names, proper names, prices embellish their every tale. The gas-bag bore is a species that takes its name from the *Honeymooners* episode in which Ralph makes his long-winded "king of the castle" speech, proclaiming his superiority in the Kramden home, to which Alice responds, "Now that your gasbag has been filled, why don't you float away?"

2. Vain Bores

You may be wondering why that blond dinner guest is sitting across the table from you, blowing smoke rings at some unseen camera lens and delivering one-line responses to everything you ask her. Are you boring her? Get it straight—*you're* doing all the work; *she's* the bore, and for all her self-importance she's about as personable as the preop Bride of Frankenstein. At parties, such dreary sorts are inevitably a few inches taller than you are—just enough to graze the top of your head with their vacant gazes and make you feel, well, short. But then they'll drop a comment like "Cyndi Lauper didn't get famous until she was thirty; that's probably what'll happen to me," revealing their mental midgetry.

3. Shy Bores

These social paralytics honestly can't help it. Too reserved to inquire about your life, too modest to satisfy inquiries about their own, shy bores are a difficult and pitiable brood. They were born without a love of anecdotes or a command of adjectives, and they'll greet your own stories with a blank stare or polite smile that asks, "Is that the punch line?"

Capable of boring the dead, the bashful bores reduce you to conversational idiocy by forcing you to keep things moving. You find yourself frantically scraping the bottom of your salad bowl, saying, "I myself have always loved arugula. Do you love arugula?" If you have to spend any length of time with a shy bore, for God's sake, go to the movies.

4. Pontificating Bores

This category includes the righteous (they have an ax to grind), and the academic (they insist on using ridiculously self-conscious words like *copacetic*). Pontificating bores have a point to make, whether you want to hear it or not, and often work their theories out in public. *Your* opinion, however, has no value in the development of their theses. For academic bores, all the world's a classroom, the bore is the professor, and you're the unlucky student. Similarly, righteous bores occupy an invisible podium, and their index fingers wag perpetually.

Righteous bores often have a religious mission, but increas-   8
ingly they tend to manifest themselves as self-help advocates
intent on convincing you that you're hopelessly messed up and in
need of Adult Children of Alcoholics or Jack LaLanne. It never
occurs to them before embarking on, say, an animal-rights diatribe that you may be president of the Humane Society. *You*,
sucker, are gonna get educated.

5. Monotone Bores

When author Laurence Peter said, "a bore is a fellow talker who   9
can change the subject to his topic of conversation faster than
you can change it back to your own," he was describing a monotone bore. They've elevated the construction of run-on sentences
to an art form, which lets them ramble without interruption for
hours. Because of this expertise in tedium, they're immune to a
victim's desperate escape maneuvers, which makes them especially trying on the telephone. "My husband has just been thrown
from his exercise bike and is lying unconscious on the piano—
gotta go!" you exclaim, calmly filling in the last blank of a crossword puzzle. And they drone on, unfazed.

Monotone bores are unique in that they appear to bore even   10
themselves. Yet they persist, bridging topics from underarm razor
burn to turmoil in the Middle East, and *nothing* can stop them.

6. Hyperbolic Bores

Let's call this person Harry. First he's describing a woman   11
whose nose is the size of Mount Rushmore, next he's discussing
his teenage son, who hasn't bathed since his fifth birthday. The
hyperbolic bore is like the boy who cried wolf—no one believes a
word of it, even when he's *not* exaggerating.

7. Chemically Altered Bores

These weekend Dionysians assume that whatever they've been   12
smoking or drinking, you have smoked and drunk too. Drunken
bores usually just drool, mumble, and repeat themselves, while
people reacting to more-exotic intoxicants will march right up to
you and say, "I've been trance-channeling with a light being
named Ariel who lives on the outer ring of Mars." When you come

back with "But Mars doesn't *have* rings," the response is invariably (snort, giggle) "Gosh, don't be so literal!"

The worst chemically altered bores are couples in a mutual daze. At any given moment, one of them will point at some stationary object and the pair will dissolve into helpless laughter (you may even discover that you are the source of their amusement). When you retreat, they *will* be offended . . . but they *won't* remember a thing in the morning.

13

8. Techno-Bores

Techno-bores are like chemically altered bores in that their condition (infatuation with technology—often computers) blinds them to the possibility that *your* reality simply isn't theirs. Details about the latest software or synthesizer are lost on you.

14

The curious thing about computer-obsessed bores is that their behavior appears to have been directly influenced by the machines they love—you can see little floppy disks spinning in their eyes when they speak; their sentences roll out in a robotic cadence. Don't even consider launching a personal question in the direction of a techno-bore—you may cause a short circuit.

15

9. Slow-Talking Bores

In the time it takes them to finish one thought and start another, you've redecorated your living room, planned a trip around the world, married and raised a family. These are the people French author Jules Renard once described as "so boring that they make you waste an entire day in five minutes." On first meeting, slow talkers appear to be hard of hearing. They will return your questions with long silences, and stare stubbornly at the carpet, dredging a response from the depth of their souls—inevitably a strained "Yeah."

16

Like shy bores, slow talkers seem to be in some sort of pain, so initially, at least, have pity on them. Wait it out and you *may* find a little pot of gold at the end of their tongue-tied silences.

17

10. Boring Relatives

There's the great-aunt who's about to tell you for the tenth consecutive Christmas about her 1957 trip to Alaska, the uncle for whom World War II never ended, the cousin who's bent on giving

18

you annual reports on her kid's learning disability. Boring relatives have a little refrain they like to incant: *"Isn't* that wonderful!" . . . whether you've just described a recent subway mugging or been told you have lipstick on your teeth.

The peril of boring relatives is that, like it or not, you're just as 19 boring to *them* as they are to *you.* When you're pulling into the driveway thinking "God, how will I survive this?" be assured that the feeling is mutual. The only relief from this ennui is family scandal, and if none exists, it's *your* duty to create it . . . even if you have to get a little, well, *hyperbolic.*

Questions for Study and Discussion

1. What does the use of quotes from Henny Youngman and A. A. Milne accomplish at the beginning of Mifflin's essay? (Glossary: *Beginnings and Endings*)
2. What are some traits that all ten of Mifflin's bores share?
3. How does Mifflin keep her essay from turning into a boring list?
4. What does Mifflin accomplish by addressing her audience as "you," as in the sentence "You, sucker, are gonna get educated"? (8)
5. Mifflin maintains an informal tone by using colloquial expressions throughout her essay. (Glossary: *Colloquial Expressions*) Identify several colloquial expressions. Do you think they add or detract from the effectiveness of the essay. Why?
6. Why do you think Mifflin ends with boring relatives?

Vocabulary

Refer to your dictionary to define the following words as they are used in this selection. Then use each word in a sentence of your own.

lapel (1)
pathological (3)
paralytics (5)
copacetic (7)
pontificating (7)
manifest (8)

diatribe (8)
hyperbolic (11)
cadence (15)
incant (18)
ennui (19)

Suggested Writing Assignments

1. Write an essay in which you classify people the way Mifflin did, but according to the opposite of bores people whom others like to have around. Be sure to illustrate why they are desirable company and include examples and anecdotes to describe each classification.

2. Write an essay in which you describe an experience that you have had with someone Mifflin would call a bore. Which of her classifications did this person fit into and why? What about the person bored you in particular? How did you deal with him or her?

16

COMPARISON AND CONTRAST

A *comparison* points out the ways that two or more persons, places, or things are alike. A *contrast* points out how they differ. The subjects of a comparison or contrast should be in the same class or general category; if they have nothing in common, there is no good reason for setting them side by side.

The function of any comparison or contrast is to clarify and explain. The writer's purpose may be simply to inform, or to make readers aware of similarities or differences that are interesting and significant in themselves. Or, the writer may explain something unfamiliar by comparing it with something very familiar, perhaps explaining squash by comparing it with tennis. Finally, the writer can point out the superiority of one thing by contrasting it with another—for example, showing that one product is the best by contrasting it with all its competitors.

As a writer, you have two main options for organizing a comparison or contrast: the subject-by-subject pattern or the point-by-point pattern. For a short essay comparing and contrasting the Atlanta Braves and the Los Angeles Dodgers, you would probably follow the *subject-by-subject* pattern of organization. By this pattern you first discuss the points you wish to make about one team, and then go on to discuss the corresponding points for the other team. An outline of your essay might look like this:

    I. Atlanta Braves
       A. Pitching
       B. Fielding
       C. Hitting
   II. Los Angeles Dodgers
       A. Pitching
       B. Fielding
       C. Hitting

The subject-by-subject pattern presents a unified discussion of each team by placing the emphasis on the teams and not on the three points of comparison. Since these points are relatively few, readers should easily remember what was said about the Braves' pitching when you later discuss the Dodgers' pitching and should be able to make the appropriate connections between them.

For a somewhat longer essay comparing and contrasting solar energy and wind energy, however, you should consider the *point-by-point* pattern of organization. With this pattern, your essay is organized according to the various points of comparison. Discussion alternates between solar and wind energy for each point of comparison. An outline of your essay might look like this:

I. Installation Expenses	IV. Convenience
A. Solar	A. Solar
B. Wind	B. Wind
II. Efficiency	V. Maintenance
A. Solar	A. Solar
B. Wind	B. Wind
III. Operating Costs	VI. Safety
A. Solar	A. Solar
B. Wind	B. Wind

The point-by-point pattern allows the writer to make immediate comparisons between solar and wind energy, thus enabling readers to consider each of the similarities and differences separately.

Each organizational pattern has its advantages. In general, the subject-by-subject pattern is useful in short essays where there are few points to be considered, whereas the point-by-point pattern is preferable in long essays where there are numerous points under consideration.

A good essay of comparison and contrast tells readers something significant that they do not already know. That is, it must do more than merely point out the obvious. As a rule, therefore, writers tend to draw contrasts between things that are usually perceived as being similar or comparisons between things usually perceived as different. In fact, comparison and contrast often go together. For example, an essay about Minneapolis and St. Paul might begin by showing how much they are alike, but end with a series of contrasts revealing how much they differ. Or, a consumer magazine might report the contrasting claims made by six car manufacturers, and then go on to demonstrate that the cars all actually do much the same thing in the same way.

Analogy is a special form of comparison. When a subject is unobservable, complex, or abstract—when it is so generally unfamiliar that readers may have trouble understanding it—*analogy* can be most effective. By pointing out the certain similarities between a difficult subject and a more familiar or concrete subject, writers can help their readers achieve a firmer grasp of the difficult subject. Unlike a true comparison, though, which analyzes items that belong to the same class—breeds of dogs or types of engines— analogy pairs things from different classes, things that have nothing in common except through the imagination of the writer. In addition, whereas comparison seeks to illuminate specific features of both subjects, the primary purpose of analogy is to clarify the one subject that is complex or unfamiliar. For example, an exploration of the similarities (and differences) between short stories and novels—two forms of fiction—would constitute a logical comparison; short stories and novels belong to the same class (fiction), and your purpose is to reveal something about both. If, however, your purpose is to explain the craft of fiction writing, you might note its similarities to the craft of carpentry. Then, you would be drawing an analogy, because the two subjects clearly belong to different classes. Carpentry is the more concrete subject and the one more people will have direct experience with. If you use your imagination, you will easily see many ways the tangible work of the carpenter can be used to help readers understand the more abstract work of the novelist. Depending on its purpose, an analogy can be made in several paragraphs to clarify a particular aspect of the larger topic being discussed, as in the example below, or it can provide the organizational strategy for an entire essay.

> It has long struck me that the familiar metaphor of "climbing the ladder" for describing the ascent to success or fulfillment in any field is inappropriate and misleading. There are no ladders that lead to success, although there may be some escalators for those lucky enough to follow in a family's fortunes.
>
> A ladder proceeds vertically, rung by rung, with each rung evenly spaced, and with the whole apparatus leaning against

a relatively flat and even surface. A child can climb a ladder as easily as an adult, and perhaps with a surer footing.

Making the ascent in one's vocation or profession is far less like ladder climbing than mountain climbing, and here the analogy is a very real one. Going up a mountain requires a variety of skills, and includes a diversity of dangers, that are in no way involved in mounting a ladder.

Young people starting out should be told this, both to dampen their expectations and to allay their disappointments. A mountain is rough and precipitous, with uncertain footing and a predictable number of falls and scrapes, and sometimes one has to take the long way around to reach the shortest distance.

Sydney J. Harris

THAT LEAN AND HUNGRY LOOK

Suzanne Britt

Suzanne Britt makes her home in Raleigh, North Carolina, where she is a free-lance writer. In 1983 she published Show & Tell, *a collection of her characteristically informal essays. The following essay first appeared in* Newsweek *and became the basis for her book,* Skinny People Are Dull and Crunchy Like Carrots *(1982), titled after a line in the essay. As you read her essay, notice the way that Britt has organized the points of her contrast of fat and thin people.*

Caesar was right. Thin people need watching. I've been watching them for most of my adult life, and I don't like what I see. When these narrow fellows spring at me, I quiver to my toes. Thin people come in all personalities, most of them menacing. You've got your "together" thin person, your mechanical thin person, your condescending thin person, your tsk-tsk thin person, your efficiency-expert thin person. All of them are dangerous.

In the first place, thin people aren't fun. They don't know how to goof off, at least in the best, fat sense of the word. They've always got to be adoing. Give them a coffee break, and they'll jog around the block. Supply them with a quiet evening at home, and they'll fix the screen door and lick S&H green stamps. They say things like "there aren't enough hours in the day." Fat people never say that. Fat people think the day is too damn long already.

Thin people make me tired. They've got speedy little metabolisms that cause them to bustle briskly. They're forever rubbing their bony hands together and eyeing new problems to "tackle." I like to surround myself with sluggish, inert, easygoing fat people, the kind who believe that if you clean it up today, it'll just get dirty again tomorrow.

Some people say the business about the jolly fat person is a myth, that all of us chubbies are neurotic, sick, sad people. I disagree. Fat people may not be chortling all day long, but they're a hell of a lot *nicer* than the wizened and shriveled. Thin people turn surly, mean, and hard at a young age because they never learn the value of a hot-fudge sundae for easing tension. Thin people don't like gooey soft things because they themselves are neither gooey nor soft. They are crunchy and dull, like carrots. They go straight to the heart of the matter while fat people let things stay all blurry and hazy and vague, the way things actually are. Thin people want to face the truth. Fat people know there is no truth. One of my thin friends is always staring at complex, unsolvable problems and saying, "The key thing is . . ." Fat people never say that. They know there isn't any such thing as the key thing about anything.

Thin people believe in logic. Fat people see all sides. The sides 5 fat people see are rounded blobs, usually gray, always nebulous and truly not worth worrying about. But the thin person persists. "If you consume more calories than you burn," says one of my thin friends, "you will gain weight. It's that simple." Fat people always grin when they hear statements like that. They know better.

Fat people realize that life is illogical and unfair. They know 6 very well that God is not in his heaven and all is not right with the world. If God was up there, fat people could have two doughnuts and a big orange drink anytime they wanted it.

Thin people have a long list of logical things they are always 7 spouting off to me. They hold up one finger at a time as they reel off these things, so I won't lose track. They speak slowly as if to a young child. The list is long and full of holes. It contains tidbits like "get a grip on yourself," "cigarettes kill," "cholesterol clogs," "fit as a fiddle," "ducks in a row," "organize," and "sound fiscal management." Phrases like that.

They think these 2,000-point plans lead to happiness. Fat peo- 8 ple know happiness is elusive at best and even if they could get the kind thin people talk about, they wouldn't want it. Wisely, fat people see that such programs are too dull, too hard, too off the mark. They are never better than a whole cheesecake.

Fat people know all about the mystery of life. They are the ones 9 acquainted with the night, with luck, with fate, with playing it by ear. One thin person I know once suggested that we arrange all the parts of a jigsaw puzzle into groups according to size, shape, and color. He figured this would cut the time needed to complete the puzzle by at least 50 percent. I said I wouldn't do it. One, I like to muddle through. Two, what good would it do to finish early? Three, the jigsaw puzzle isn't the important thing. The important thing is the fun of four people (one thin person included) sitting around a card table, working a jigsaw puzzle. My thin friend had no use for my list. Instead of joining us, he went outside and mulched the boxwoods. The three remaining fat people finished the puzzle and made chocolate, double-fudged brownies to celebrate.

The main problem with thin people is they oppress. Their good intentions, bony torsos, tight ships, neat corners, cerebral machinations, and pat solutions loom like dark clouds over the loose, comfortable, spread-out, soft world of the fat. Long after fat people have removed their coats and shoes and put their feet up on the coffee table, thin people are still sitting on the edge of the sofa, looking neat as a pin, discussing rutabagas. Fat people are heavily into fits of laughter, slapping their thighs and whopping it up, while thin people are still politely waiting for the punch line. 10

Thin people are downers. They like math and morality and reasoned evaluation of the limitations of human beings. They have their skinny little acts together. They expound, prognose, probe, and prick. 11

Fat people are convivial. They will like you even if you're irregular and have acne. They will come up with a good reason why you never wrote the great American novel. They will cry in your beer with you. They will put your name in the pot. They will let you off the hook. Fat people will gab, giggle, guffaw, gallumph, gyrate, and gossip. They are generous, giving, and gallant. They are gluttonous and goodly and great. What you want when you're down is soft and jiggly, not muscled and stable. Fat people know this. Fat people have plenty of room. Fat people will take you in. 12

Questions for Study and Discussion

1. Does Britt use a subject-by-subject or a point-by-point pattern of organization to contrast fat and thin people? Explain. What points of contrast does Britt discuss?

2. How does Britt characterize thin people? Fat people?

3. What does Britt seem to have against thin people? Why does she consider thin "dangerous"? What do you think Britt looks like? How do you know?

4. What is Britt's purpose in this essay? (Glossary: *Purpose*) Is she serious, partially serious, mostly humorous? Are fat and thin people really her subject?

5. Britt makes effective use of the short sentence. Identify examples of sentences with three or fewer words and explain what function they serve.

6. Britt uses many clichés in her essay. Identify at least a dozen examples. What do you suppose is her purpose in using them? (Glossary: *Cliché*)

7. It is somewhat unusual for an essayist to use alliteration (the repetition of initial consonant sounds), a technique more commonly found in poetry. Where has Britt used alliteration and why do you suppose she has used this particular technique?

Vocabulary

Refer to your dictionary to define the following words as they are used in this selection. Then use each word in a sentence of your own.

menacing (1)	nebulous (5)
adoing (2)	rutabagas (10)
metabolism (3)	prognose (11)
inert (3)	convivial (12)
chortling (4)	gallant (12)

Suggested Writing Assignments

1. Write a counterargument in favor of thin people, using comparison and contrast and modeled on Britt's "That Lean and Hungry Look."

2. Reread paragraphs 3–6, and notice how these paragraphs are developed by contrasting the features of thin and fat people. Select two items from the following categories—

people, products, events, institutions, places—and make a list of their contrasting features. Then write an essay modeled on Britt's, using the entries on your list.

GRANT AND LEE: A STUDY IN CONTRASTS

Bruce Catton

Bruce Catton (1899–1978) was born in Petoskey, Michigan, and attended Oberlin College. Early in his career, Catton worked as a reporter for various newspapers, among them the Cleveland Plain Dealer. *Having an interest in history, Catton became a leading authority on the Civil War and published a number of books on this subject. These include* Mr. Lincoln's Army *(1951),* Glory Road *(1952),* A Stillness at Appomattox *(1953),* The Hallowed Ground *(1956),* The Coming Fury *(1961),* Never Call Retreat *(1966), and* Gettysburg: The Final Fury *(1974). Catton was awarded both the Pulitzer Prize and the National Book Award in 1954.*

The following selection was included in The American Story, *a collection of historical essays edited by Earl Schenk Miers. In it Catton considers "two great Americans, Grant and Lee—very different, yet under everything very much alike."*

When Ulysses S. Grant and Robert E. Lee met in the parlor of a modest house at Appomattox Court House, Virginia, on April 9, 1865, to work out the terms for the surrender of Lee's Army of Northern Virginia, a great chapter in American life came to a close, and a great new chapter began.

These men were bringing the Civil War to its virtual finish. To be sure, other armies had yet to surrender, and for a few days the fugitive Confederate government would struggle desperately and vainly, trying to find some way to go on living now that its chief support was gone. But in effect it was all over when Grant and

Lee signed the papers. And the little room where they wrote out the terms was the scene of one of the poignant, dramatic contrasts in American history.

They were two strong men, these oddly different generals, and they represented the strengths of two conflicing currents that, through them, had come into final collision.

Back of Robert E. Lee was the notion that the old aristocratic concept might somehow survive and be dominant in American life.

Lee was tidewater Virginia, and in his background were family, culture, and tradition . . . the age of chivalry transplanted to a New World which was making its own legends and its own myths. He embodied a way of life that had come down through the age of knighthood and the English country squire. America was a land that was beginning all over again, dedicated to nothing much more complicated than the rather hazy belief that all men had equal rights and should have an equal chance in the world. In such a land Lee stood for the feeling that it was somehow of advantage to human society to have a pronounced inequality in the social structure. There should be a leisure class, backed by ownerhsip of land; in turn, society itself should be keyed to the land as the chief source of wealth and influence. It would bring forth (according to this ideal) a class of men with a strong sense of obligation to the community; men who lived not to gain advantage for themselves, but to meet the solemn obligations which had been laid on them by the very fact that they were privileged. From them the country would get its leadership; to them it could look for the higher values—of thought, of conduct, of personal deportment—to give it strength and virtue.

Lee embodied the noblest elements of this aristocratic ideal. Through him, the landed nobility justified itself. For four years, the Southern states had fought a desperate war to uphold the ideals for which Lee stood. In the end, it almost seemed as if the Confederacy fought for Lee; as if he himself was the Confederacy . . . the best thing that the way of life for which the Confederacy stood could ever have to offer. He had passed into legend before Appomattox. Thousands of tired, underfed, poorly clothed Confederate soldiers, long since past the simple enthusiasm of the early days of the struggle, somehow considered Lee the symbol of everything for which they had been willing to die. But they could not quite put this feeling into words. If the Lost Cause, sanctified by so much heroism and so many deaths, had a living justification, its justification was General Lee.

Grant, the son of a tanner on the Western frontier, was every- 7 thing Lee was not. He had come up the hard way and embodied nothing in particular except the eternal toughness and sinewy fiber of the men who grew up beyond the mountains. He was one of a body of men who owed reverence and obeisance to no one, who were self-reliant to a fault, who cared hardly anything for the past but who had a sharp eye for the future.

These frontier men were the precise opposite of the tidewater 8 aristocrats. Back of them, in the great surge that had taken people over the Alleghenies and into the opening Western country, there was a deep, implicit dissatisfaction with a past that had settled into grooves. They stood for democracy, not from any reasoned conclusion about the proper ordering of human society, but simply because they had grown up in the middle of democracy and knew how it worked. Their society might have privileges, but they would be privileges each man had won for himself. Forms and patterns meant nothing. No man was born to anything, except perhaps to a chance to show how far he could rise. Life was competition.

Yet along with this feeling had come a deep sense of belonging 9 to a national community. The Westerner who developed a farm, opened a shop, or set up in business as a trader, could hope to prosper only as his own community prospered—and his community ran from the Atlantic to the Pacific and from Canada down to Mexico. If the land was settled, with towns and highways and accessible markets, he could better himself. He saw his fate in terms of the nation's own destiny. As its horizons expanded, so did his. He had, in other words, an acute dollars-and-cents stake in the continued growth and development of his country.

And that, perhaps, is where the contrast between Grant and Lee 10 becomes most striking. The Virginia aristocrat, inevitably, saw himself in relation to his own region. He lived in a static society which could endure almost anything except change. Instinctively, his first loyalty would go to the locality in which that society existed. He would fight to the limit of endurance to defend it, because in defending it he was defending everything that gave his own life its deepest meaning.

The Westerner, on the other hand, would fight with an equal   11
tenacity for the broader concept of society. He fought so because
everything he lived by was tied to growth, expansion, and a constantly widening horizon. What he lived by would survive or fall
with the nation itself. He could not possibly stand by unmoved in
the face of an attempt to destroy the Union. He would combat it
with everything he had, because he could only see it as an effort
to cut the ground out from under his feet.

So Grant and Lee were in complete contrast, representing two   12
diametrically opposed elements in American life. Grant was the
modern man emerging; beyond him, ready to come on the stage,
was the great age of steel and machinery, of crowded cities and a
restless burgeoning vitality. Lee might have ridden down from the
old age of chivalry, lance in hand, silken banner fluttering over his
head. Each man was the perfect champion of his cause, drawing
both his strengths and his weaknesses from the people he led.

Yet is was not all contrast, after all. Different as they were—in   13
background, in personality, in underlying aspiration—these two
great soldiers had much in common. Under everything else, they
were marvelous fighters. Furthermore, their fighting qualities
were really very much alike.

Each man had, to begin with, the great virtue of utter tenacity   14
and fidelity. Grant fought his way down the Mississippi Valley in
spite of acute personal discouragement and profound military
handicaps. Lee hung on in the trenches at Petersburg after hope
itself had died. In each man there was an indomitable quality . . .
the born fighter's refusal to give up as long as he can still remain
on his feet and lift his two fists.

Daring and resourcefulness they had, too; the ability to think   15
faster and move faster than the enemy. These were the qualities
which gave Lee the dazzling campaigns of Second Manassas and
Chancellorsville and won Vicksburg for Grant.

Lastly, and perhaps greatest of all, there was the ability, at the   16
end, to turn quickly from war to peace once the fighting was over.
Out of the way these two men behaved at Appomattox came the
possibility of a peace of reconciliation. It was a possibility not
wholly realized, in the years to come, but which did, in the end,
help the two sections to become one nation again . . . after a war
whose bitterness might have seemed to make such a reunion
wholly impossible. No part of either man's life became him more

than the part he played in their brief meeting in the McLean house at Appomattox. Their behavior there put all succeeding generations of Americans in their debt. Two great Americans, Grant and Lee—very different, yet under everything very much alike. Their encounter at Appomattox was one of the great moments of American history.

Questions for Study and Discussion

1. In paragraphs 10–12 Catton discusses what he considers to be the most striking contrast between Grant and Lee. What is that difference?

2. List the similarities that Catton sees between Grant and Lee. Which similarity does Catton believe is most important? Why?

3. What would have been lost had Catton compared Grant and Lee before contrasting them? Would anything have been gained?

4. How does Catton organize the body of his essay (3–16)? You may find it helpful in answering this question to summarize the point of comparison in each paragraph and label it as being concerned with Lee, Grant, or both.

5. What attitudes and ideas does Catton describe to support the view that tidewater Virginia was a throwback to the "age of chivalry" (5)?

6. Catton says that Grant was "the modern man emerging" (12). How does he support that statement? Do you agree?

7. Catton has carefully made clear transitions between paragraphs. For each paragraph identify the transitional devices he uses. How do they help your reading? (Glossary: *Transitions*)

Vocabulary

Refer to your dictionary to define the following words as they are used in this selection. Then use each word in a sentence of your own.

poignant (2)   obeisance (7)
chivalry (5)   tidewater (8)
sanctified (6)   tenacity (11)
sinewy (7)   aspiration (13)

Suggested Writing Assignments

1. Compare and contrast any two world leaders (or popular singers or singing groups). In selecting a topic, you should consider (1) what your purpose will be, (2) whether you will emphasize similarities or differences, (3) what specific points you will discuss, and (4) what organizational pattern will best suit your purpose.

2. Select one of the following topics for an essay of comparison and contrast:

   two cities
   two friends
   two ways to heat a home
   two restaurants
   two actors or actresses
   two mountains
   two books by the same author
   two sports heroes
   two cars
   two teachers
   two brands of pizza

MY SON,
MY TEACHER

Barney Cohen

*Few people stop to think of the beneficial influence
that children have over their parents, how they
expand them, sharpen them, polish them—making
their parents better people. In the following essay,
first published in the June/July (1990) issue of*
Parenting, *Barney Cohen reflects on his relationship with his son Ivan. Cohen uses a central analogy to both explain and describe the steady, unseen,
and beneficial influence that Ivan had not only on
his tennis game but also on his life.*

There was once this guy, this mythological guy, who was the 1
strongest guy there ever was—for his time. When he was a
little kid, his father gave him a baby calf and told him to take care
of it. The little fellow was instructed to feed and clean the calf
every day, and then to lift it up, once, over his head.

Well, you can figure out what happened. As the kid grew, so did 2
the calf. Every day, when the boy lifted the calf up over his head,
he was lifting another pound or so. And by the time the guy was
15 he was able to lift a kicking, bucking, full-grown bull over his
head.

But who was this guy? My friend Dennis, a movie director, says 3
it was Beowulf, but I suspect he just says that because he worked
on a film about that antique English hero and thinks he knows
his stuff. I looked for the reference in the Beowulf poem and I
couldn't find it. My Aunt Harriet, who graduated from a prestigious Eastern college, thinks it comes from the myth of Hercules.
But I haven't found it there either.

If you know the name of this guy, and of his fabulously epis- 4
temological father, please drop me a line. If not, don't worry; just
hold the thought for a minute because, as I relate this story about
my own son, Ivan, we'll be coming back to it.

You know me. I take my kids' athletic training fairly seriously. I'm no martinet with a whistle and a "personal best" chart, but I believe that stuff about a sound mind and a sound body, and I encourage the kids every chance I get. This includes, of course, playing sports with them whenever I can.

Now here's where I'd love to tell you that I, myself, figured out something akin to our obscure mythological hero's calf and that now my kids are superathletes. But I didn't. No, this is a story about something my kids did for me and that your kids are probably doing for you, whether you know it or not.

In my case, it begins on a municipal tennis court in Seattle. I am playing a couple of sets with my son. He's ten at the time, but I have been doing this with him since he was three. In fact, Ivan has been, since the age of five, my only tennis partner.

Anyway, there's this local tennis team, a bunch of kids, playing on the next court. The grown-up, probably the coach, comes over to me as I'm picking up some stray balls and says, "Your son really carries a gun."

Realizing immediately that Ivan not only is being complimented, but also being recruited, I let the guy down easy. "We're from New York City," I say.

"Shame," he says.

I'm flattered for Ivan, and happy for him. I tell him about the coach's comments on the drive back to his aunt and uncle's house. But I'm also curious about what, exactly, the guy saw in Ivan's game.

For the last few years, Ivan has been telling me about his rapid progress in school tennis. He's been telling me that he's moved ahead of this guy or that guy. That he beat some kid who's a country-club champ. And I sort of let all this go in one ear and out the other because, to tell you the truth, I really haven't seen much improvement.

Oh, he's grown more proficient at certain things. He's making far fewer unforced errors. He's certainly able to hit the ball harder than he used to. He's able to hit the ball harder than me! Still, I wonder, how could Ivan be getting so darn much better if he keeps getting his ears pinned by his old man?

One thing you need to know about me before we go any further: I've always believed that it's the ultimate insult to any human being to compete against him at anything less than your best. I mean, when Ivan was five, I didn't smash the ball at his feet, but I didn't throw games to him either. He had to measure himself against me by how well he played, not by whether he won or lost. The fact is, he always lost.

At the time of our Seattle match, Ivan had never beaten me in 15 tennis. He had not even won a set. And we'd played a thousand games. Then, after we returned to New York, a strange thing happened. An old friend came into town and was staying at a hotel that had court rights at a local tennis bubble. He invited me for a game. Now this guy used to beat me regularly. And when I asked if he'd kept up his game, he smiled at me his sparkly California grin and said, "Every day of the year."

I threw up my first serve with enormous foreboding. It sliced 16 past him and hit the green retainer. I won't bore you with the details of my spectacular demolition of this dude. Suffice it to say, it surprised us both.

Then, in the taxi home, I figured it out. It was Ivan! It had to 17 be. He was my only tennis partner. Remember the guy with the calf? Ivan was my calf! As Ivan's tennis had improved, so had my own. In my desire to always be out front as an example, to always give him a good match, I had lifted my game without knowing it. Each time Ivan improved, he forced a consequent gain in my own game. Like the calf that got heavier every morning, Ivan got better each time out. And like the guy who lifted the calf, I lifted my own increasing burden. As I urged and taught and challenged, Ivan was giving me something back. He was forcing me to push the envelope of my own abilities. To discover new strength and new resolve. He was teaching me that I could work harder, stretch farther, go longer than I ever thought I could. And he was doing it in increments so small, I never realized that I was growing.

You know, I think all kids must be doing this. In a thousand 18 ways that you never even thought about, they're making you pick yourself up a notch. They work on the quality of your caring and the coolness of your panic response. They teach you when to surrender and when to hold firm.

I saw it in sport. But it must be happening, unseen, in every 19 phase of your life. It's weird when you think about kids that way.

While you're training them, teaching them, growing them up, they're expanding you, sharpening you, polishing you, making you not just better parents, but better tennis players. In fact, better people all around.

Questions for Study and Discussion

1. Cohen opens his essay with the story of the small boy and the baby calf. How does this story function in the context of his essay? (Glossary: *Analogy*) Is the analogy of the boy and the calf an effective one for the point Cohen wishes to make? Explain.
2. Cohen failed to see his son's improvement. How does he explain his failure? What caused him to recognize his mistake?
3. In paragraph 14, Cohen says he never let his son win. Why not? Do you agree with his reasoning? Explain.
4. Cohen explains the way in which his son helped his tennis game and then goes on to make a larger point. What is it?
5. Cite examples of Cohen's use of slang, and describe the tone it sets for his essay. (Glossary: *Tone*) What does Cohen's choice of language suggest to you about his relationship with his son?

Vocabulary

Refer to your dictionary to define the following words as they are used in this selection. Then use each word in a sentence of your own.

mythological (1)	demolition (16)
epistemological (4)	suffice (16)
martinet (5)	resolve (17)
recruited (9)	notch (18)
proficient (13)	surrender (18)
throw (14)	

Suggested Writing Assignments

1. In an essay use comparison and contrast to explain the different ways a child and a parent might approach the same activity. For example, handling money, driving a car, conducting a relationship, relaxing, or performing household tasks.

2. Use an analogy to explain your relationship with one of your parents or another adult you are close to.

A CASE OF "SEVERE BIAS"

Patricia Raybon

*A resident of Denver, Colorado, Patricia Raybon
is a practicing journalist as well as an associate
professor of journalism at the University of Colorado School of Journalism and Mass Communication in Boulder. She was born in 1941 and
graduated from Ohio State University in 1971 and
earned her master's degree from the University of
Colorado in 1977. She has worked as a reporter and
editor, and her writing has appeared in such publications as the* New York Times, *the* Wall Street
Journal, USA Today, *and the* Washington Post.
The following essay first appeared in Newsweek *in
1989 and reflects two of Raybon's main interests—
race and the media. Here, Raybon highlights the
differences she sees between the portrayal of African
Americans by the media and the reality of their lives
as she knows it.*

This is who I am not. I am not a crack addict. I am not a wel- 1
fare mother. I am not illiterate. I am not a prostitute. I have
never been in jail. My children are not in gangs. My husband
doesn't beat me. My home is not a tenement. None of these things
defines who I am, nor do they describe the other black people I've
known and worked with and loved and befriended over these
forty years of my life.

Nor does it describe most of black America, period. 2

Yet in the eyes of the American news media, this is what black 3
America is: poor, criminal, addicted, and dysfunctional. Indeed,
media coverage of black America is so one-sided, so imbalanced
that the most victimized and hurting segment of the black community—a small segment, at best—is presented not as the exception but as the norm. It is an insidious practice, all the uglier for
its blatancy.

In recent months, I have observed a steady offering of media reports on crack babies, gang warfare, violent youth, poverty, and homelessness—and in most cases, the people featured in the photos and stories were black. At the same time, articles that discuss other aspects of American life—from home buying to medicine to technology to nutrition—rarely, if ever, show blacks playing a positive role, or for that matter, any role at all.

Day after day, week after week, this message—that black America is dysfunctional and unwhole—gets transmitted across the American landscape. Sadly, as a result, America never learns the truth about what is actually a wonderful, vibrant, creative community of people.

Most black Americans are *not* poor. Most black teenagers are *not* crack addicts. Most black mothers are *not* on welfare. Indeed, in sheer numbers, more *white* Americans are poor and on welfare than are black. Yet one never would deduce that by watching television or reading American newspapers and magazines.

Why do the American media insist on playing this myopic, inaccurate picture game? In this game, white America is always whole and lovely and healthy while black America is usually sick and pathetic and deficient. Rarely, indeed, is black America ever depicted in the media as functional and self-sufficient. The free press, indeed, as the main interpreter of American culture and American experience, holds the mirror on American reality—so much so that what the media say is *is*, even if it's not that way at all. The media are guilty of a severe bias and the problem screams out for correction. It is worse than simply lazy journalism, which is bad enough; it is inaccurate journalism.

For black Americans like myself, this isn't just an issue of vanity—of wanting to be seen in a good light. Nor is it a matter of closing one's eyes to the very real problems of the urban underclass—which undeniably is disproportionately black. To be sure, problems besetting the black underclass deserve the utmost attention of the media, as well as the understanding and concern of the rest of American society.

But if their problems consistently are presented as the *only* reality for blacks, any other experience known in the black community ceases to have validity, or to be real. In this scenario, millions of blacks are relegated to a sort of twilight zone, where who we are and what we are isn't based on fact but on image and perception. That's what it feels like to be a black American whose lifestyle is outside of the aberrant behavior that the media present as the norm.

For many of us, life is a curious series of encounters with white   10
people who want to know why we are "different" from other blacks—when, in fact, most of us are only "different" from the now common negative images of black life. So pervasive are these images that they aren't just perceived as the norm, they're *accepted* as the norm.

I am reminded, for example, of the controversial Spike Lee film   11
Do the Right Thing and the criticism by some movie reviewers that the film's ghetto neighborhood isn't populated by addicts and drug pushers—and thus is not a true depiction.

In fact, millions of black Americans live in neighborhoods where   12
the most common sights are children playing and couples walking their dogs. In my own inner-city neighborhood in Denver—an area that the local press consistently describes as "gang territory"—I have yet to see a recognizable "gang" member or any "gang" activity (drug dealing or drive-by shootings), nor have I been the victim of "gang violence."

Yet to students of American culture—in the case of Spike Lee's   13
film, the movie reviewers—a black, inner-city neighborhood can only be one thing to be real: drug-infested and dysfunctioning. Is this my ego talking? In part, yes. For the millions of black people like myself—ordinary, hard-working, law-abiding, tax-paying Americans—the media's blindness to the fact that we even exist, let alone to our contributions to American society, is a bitter cup to drink. And as self-reliant as most black Americans are—because we've had to be self-reliant—even the strongest among us still crave affirmation.

I want that. I want it for my children. I want it for all the   14
beautiful, healthy, funny, smart black Americans I have known and loved over the years.

And I want it for the rest of America, too.   15

I want America to know us—all of us—for who we really are.   16
To see us in all of our comlexity, our subtleness, our artfulness, our enterprise, our specialness, our loveliness, our Americanness. That is the real portrait of black America—that we're strong people, surviving people, capable people. That may be the best-kept secret in America. If so, it's time to let the truth be known.

Questions for Study and Discussion

1. What is the basic contrast that Raybon establishes in her first paragraph? What examples does she use to establish the contrast that she sees? Can you think of any other examples?

2. Why do you think Raybon feels it is necessary to define herself by contrast in her opening paragraph. Why doesn't she simply say who she is in a positive manner?

3. How are paragraphs 1 and 6 stylistically similar? Why do you think Raybon wrote them in the way she did?

4. What is Raybon's thesis in this essay? Where does she present it? Does she support her thesis accurately in your view? Why or why not?

5. What do you think is the purpose of Raybon's comparison and contrast technique? What does she want? What do you think she wants us to think and/or do as a result of reading her essay?

6. How would you describe Raybon's tone in this essay? (Glossary: *Tone*)

Vocabulary

Refer to your dictionary to define the following words as they are used in this selection. Then use each word in a sentence of your own.

tenement (1)	scenario (9)
dysfunctional (3)	aberrant (9)
insidious (3)	pervasive (10)
myopic (7)	subtleness (16)
besetting (8)	enterprise (16)

Suggested Writing Assignments

1. Write an essay in which you compare and/or contrast the issues and argumentative strategies used by Patricia Raybon with those of Joanmarie Kalter in "Exposing Media Myths: TV Doesn't Affect You as Much as You Think,"

found in the Argument section of *Models for Writers* on pp. 421–26.

2. Using one of the following "before and after" situations, write a short essay of comparison and/or contrast:

before and after a diet
before and after urban renewal
before and after a visit to the dentist
before and after a final exam

A BATTLE OF CULTURES

K. Connie Kang

Born in Korea, K. Connie Kang grew up in Japan and the United States. After graduating from the School of Journalism at the University of Missouri, Kang went on to earn a master of science in journalism from the Medill School of Journalism at Northwestern University. During her nearly three decades in journalism, this award-winning newspaperwoman has worked as a reporter, editor, foreign correspondent, columnist and editorial writer for the San Francisco Examiner, San Francisco Chronicle, *and* United Press International. *Currently, she is a reporter for the* Los Angeles Times. *Kang's career in journalism began in June 1964, when there were only a handful of Asians in the metropolitan newsrooms in the United States. Always mindful of her Asian heritage, she wrote about Asians and the issues affecting their community long before they were considered newsworthy. Her book about Korean Americans will be published next year. In the following article, which first appeared in* Asian Week *in May 1990, Kang reminds us that we need both "cultural insight" and understanding if we are to "make democracy work" in a multicultural society.*

A volatile inner-city drama is taking place in New York where 1 blacks have been boycotting Korean groceries for four months.

The recent attack on three Vietnamese men by a group of 2 blacks who mistook them for Koreans has brought this long-simmering tension between two minority groups to the world's attention. Korean newspapers from San Francisco to Seoul have been running front-page stories. Non-Asian commentators around the country, whose knowledge of Korea may not be much more than images from the Korean war and the ridiculous television series "M.A.S.H.," are making all sorts of comments.

As I see it, the problem in the Flatbush area of Brooklyn started 3 with cultural misunderstanding and was compounded by a lack of bilingual and bicultural community leaders to intervene quickly.

Frictions between Korean store owners in New York and blacks 4 had been building for years. Korean merchants have been complaining about thefts. On the other hand, their black customers have been accusing immigrant store owners of making money in their neighborhoods without putting anything back into the community. They have also complained about store owners being brusque. Over the past eight years, there have been sporadic boycotts but none has lasted as long as the current one, which stemmed from an accusation by a black customer in January that she had been attacked by a store employee. In defense, the store owner has said the employee caught the woman stealing.

The attack on the Vietnamese on May 13 wasn't the first time 5 one group of Asians has been mistaken for another in America. But the publicity surrounding the case has made this unfortunate situation a case study in inter-ethnic tension.

What's missing in this inner-city drama is cultural insight. 6

What struck me more than anything was a recent remark by a 7 black resident: "The Koreans are a very, very rude people. They don't understand you have to smile."

I wondered whether her reaction would have been the same, 8 had she known that Koreans don't smile at Koreans either without a reason. To a Korean, a smile is not a facial expression he can turn on and off mechanically. Koreans have a word for it—mu-ttuk-ttuk-hada" (stiff). In other words, the Korean demeanor is "myu-po-jung"—lack of expression.

It would be an easy thing for blacks who are naturally friendly 9 and gregarious to misunderstand Korean ways.

As a Korean American I've experienced this many times. When- 10 ever I'm in Korea, which is often, I'm chided for smiling too much. "Why do you smile so easily? You act like a Westerner," people tell me. My inclination is to retort: "Why do you always have to look like you've got indigestion?" But I restrain myself be-cause I know better.

In our culture, a smile is reserved for people we know and for 11 a proper occasion. Herein lies a big problem when newcomers from Korea begin doing business in America's poor inner-city neighborhoods.

Culturally and socially, many newcomers from Korea, like other   12
Asian immigrants, are ill-equipped to run businesses in America's inner-cities. But because they are denied entry into mainstream job markets, they pool resources and open mom-and-pop operations in the only places where they can afford it. They work 14 and 15 hours a day, seven days a week, dreaming of the day when their children will graduate from prestigious schools and make their sacrifices worthwhile.

From the other side, inner-city African Americans must wonder   13
how these new immigrants find the money to run their own businesses, when they themselves can't even get a small loan from a bank. Their hope of getting out of the poverty cycle is grim, yet they see newcomers living in better neighborhoods and driving new cars.

"They ask me, 'Where do you people get the money to buy a   14
business?'" Bong-jae Jang, owner of one of the grocery stores being boycotted, told me, "How can I explain to my neighbors in my poor English the concept of our family system, the idea of 'kye' (uniquely Korean private money-lending system), our way of life?"

I think a little learning is in order on both sides. Korean immi-   15
grants, like other newcomers, need orientation before they leave their country as well as when they arrive in the United States. It's also important for Korean immigrants, like other Asians who live in the United States, to realize that they are indebted to blacks for the social gains won by their civil rights struggle. They face less discrimination today because blacks have paved the way. Instead of looking down on their culture, it would be constructive to learn their history, literature, music and values and see our African American brothers and sisters in their full humanity.

I think it is also important to remind ourselves that while the   16
Confucian culture has taught us how to be good parents, sons and daughters and how to behave with people we know, it has not prepared us for living in a democracy. The Confucian ethos lacks the value of social conscience, which makes democracy work.

It isn't enough that we think of educating our children and send   17
them to the best schools. We need to think of other peoples' children, too. Most of all, we need to be more tolerant of other peo-

ples' cultures. We need to celebrate our similarities as well as our differences.

Jang, the grocer, told me this experience has been painful but   18
he has learned an important lesson. "We Koreans must learn to participate in this society," he said. "When this is over, I'm going to reach out. I want to give part-time work to black youths."

He also told me that he has been keeping a journal. "I'm not a   19
writer but I've been keeping a journal," he said. "I want to write about this experience someday. It may help someone."

By reaching out, we can make a difference. The Korean grocer's   20
lesson is a reminder to us all that making democracy work in a multicultural society is difficult but we have no choice but to strive for it.

Questions for Study and Discussion

1. What is the battle of cultures named in the title? (Glossary: *Title*)
2. Why are the Korean grocery stores being boycotted by African American customers?
3. What is causing the conflict, according to Kang? How does she use comparison and contrast to argue her thesis? (Glossary: *Thesis*)
4. Why are most Asian immigrants ill-equipped to run businesses in the United States? Why are they indebted to African Americans?
5. How does Kang's point of view contribute to the effectiveness of the essay? (Glossary: *Point of View*)
6. What is it about the Korean culture that makes it difficult for them to adapt to life in a multicultural society?

Vocabulary

Refer to your dictionary to define the following words as they are used in this selection. Then use each word in a sentence of your own.

volatile (1) sporadic (4)
boycotting (1) gregarious (9)
bilingual (3) inclination (10)
intervene (3) ethos (16)
brusque (4)

Suggested Writing Assignments

1. Choose another ethnic group that lives in the United States. Compare its culture with your own. What could you do to understand the other culture better?

2. Choose a country that you have studied, visited, or at least read about. Compare who you are now with who you think you would be if you were born in that country. How do you think you would be different? Why?

17

CAUSE AND EFFECT

Every time you try to answer a question that asks *why*, you engage in the process of *causal analysis*—you attempt to determine a *cause* or series of causes for a particular *effect*. When you try to answer a question that asks *what if*, you attempt to determine what *effect* will result from a particular *cause*. You will have frequent opportunity to use cause and effect analysis in writing that you will do in college. For example, in history you might be asked to determine the causes of the Seven-Day War between Egypt and Israel; in political science you might be asked to determine the reasons why Bill Clinton won the 1992 presidential election; in sociology you might be asked to analyze the effects that the AIDS epidemic has had on sexual behavior patterns among Americans; and in economics you might be asked to predict what would happen to our country if we do not address the problem of our national debt.

Determining causes and effects is usually thought-provoking and quite complex. One reason for this is that there are two types of causes: *immediate causes*, which are readily apparent because they are closest to the effect, and *ultimate causes*, which, being somewhat removed, are not so apparent and perhaps even hidden. Furthermore, ultimate causes may bring about effects which themselves become immediate causes, thus creating a *causal chain*. For example, consider the following causal chain: Sally, a computer salesperson, prepared extensively for a meeting with an important client (ultimate cause), impressed the client (immediate cause), and made a very large sale (effect). The chain did not stop there: the large sale caused her to be promoted by her employer (effect).

A second reason why causal analysis can be so complex is that an effect may have any number of possible or actual causes, and a cause may have any number of possible or actual effects. An upset stomach may be caused by eating spoiled food, but it may also be caused by overeating, flu, allergy, nervousness, pregnancy, or any combination of factors. Similarly, the high cost of electricity may have multiple effects: higher profits for utility companies, fewer sales of electrical appliances, higher prices for other products, and the development of alternative sources of energy.

Sound reasoning and logic, while present in all good writing, are central to any causal analysis. Writers of believable causal analysis examine their material objectively and develop their essays carefully. They examine methodically all causes and effects and evaluate them. They are convinced by their own examination of the material but are not afraid to admit other possible causes and effects. Above all, they do not let their own prejudices interfere with the logic of their analyses and presentations.

Because people are accustomed to thinking of causes with their effects, they sometimes commit an error in logic known as the "after this, therefore because of this" fallacy (in Latin, *post hoc, ergo propter hoc*). This fallacy leads people to believe that because one event occurred after another event the first event somehow caused the second; that is, they sometimes make causal connections that are not proven. For example, if students began to perform better after a free breakfast program was instituted at their school, one could not assume that the improvement was caused by the breakfast program. There could of course be any number of other causes for this effect, and a responsible writer on the subject would analyze and consider them all before suggesting the cause.

NEVER GET SICK IN JULY

Marilyn Machlowitz

Marilyn Machlowitz earned her doctorate in psychology at Yale and is now a management psychologist. She contributes a regular column to Working Woman *magazine, has written* Workaholics *(1980) and* Advanced Career Strategies: Corporate Smarts for Women on the Way Up *(1984), and is at work on a new book dealing with the consequences of succeeding at an early age. Notice in the following selection, first published in* Esquire *magazine in July 1978, how Machlowitz analyzes why it is a bad idea to get sick in July.*

One Harvard medical school professor warns his students to
stay home—as he does—on the Fourth of July. He fears he
will become one of the holiday's highway casualties and wind up
in an emergency room with an inexperienced intern "practicing"
medicine on *him*.

Just the mention of July makes medical students, nurses, interns, residents, and "real doctors" roll their eyes. While hospital
administrators maintain that nothing is amiss that month, members of the medical profession know what happens when the
house staff turns over and the interns take over each July 1.

This July 1, more than 13,000 new doctors will invade over 600
hospitals across the country. Within minutes they will be overwhelmed: last July 1, less than a month after finishing medical
school, Dr. John Baumann, then twenty-five, walked into Washington, D.C.'s, Walter Reed Army Medical Center, where he was
immediately faced with caring for "eighteen of the sickest people
I had ever seen."

Pity the patient who serves as guinea pig at ten A.M.—or three
A.M.—that first day. Indeed, according to Dr. Russell K. Laros, Jr.,
professor and vice-chairman of obstetrics, gynecology, and reproductive sciences at the University of California, San Francisco,

"There is no question that patients throughout the country are mismanaged during July. Without the most meticulous supervision," he adds, "serious errors can be made."

And they are. Internship provides the first chance to practice   5
one's illegible scrawl on prescription blanks, a golden opportunity to make lots of mistakes. Interns—who are still known to most people by that name, even though they are now officially called first-year residents—have ordered the wrong drug in the wrong dosage to be administered the wrong way at the wrong times to the wrong patient. While minor mistakes are most common, serious errors are the sources of hospital horror stories. One intern prescribed an anti-depressant without knowing that it would inactivate the patient's previously prescribed antihypertensive medication.* The patient then experienced a rapid increase in blood pressure and suffered a stroke.

When interns do not know what to do, when they cannot co-   6
vertly consult *The Washington Manual* (a handbook of medical therapeutics), they can always order tests. The first time one intern attempted to perform a pleural biopsy—a fairly difficult procedure—he punctured the patient's lung. When an acquaintance of mine entered an emergency room one Friday night in July with what was only an advanced case of the flu, she wound up having a spinal tap. While negative findings are often necessary to rule out alternative diagnoses, some of the tests are really unwarranted. Interns admit that the results are required only so they can cover themselves in case a resident or attending physician decides to give them the third degree.

Interns' hours only increase their inadequacy. Dr. Jay Dobkin,   7
president of the Physicians National Housestaff Association, a Washington-based organization representing 12,000 interns and residents, says that "working conditions . . . directly impact and influence the quality of patient care. After thirty-six hours 'on,' most interns find their abilities compromised." Indeed, their schedules (they average 110 hours a week) and their salaries (last year, they averaged $13,145) make interns the chief source of cheap labor. No other hospital personnel will do as much "scut" work—drawing blood, for instance—or dirty work, such as manually disimpacting severely constipated patients.

---

*A depressant medicine used to lower high blood pressure.

Even private patients fall prey to interns, because many physi- 8
cians prefer being affiliated with hospitals that have interns to
perform these routine duties around the clock. One way to reduce
the likelihood of falling into the hands of an intern is to rely upon
a physician in group practice whose partners can provide substitute coverage. Then, too, it probably pays to select a physician who
has hospital privileges at the best teaching institution in town.
There, at least, you are unlikely to encounter any interns who slept
through school, as some medical students admit they do: only the
most able students survive the computer-matching process to win
the prestigious positions at university hospitals.

It may be reassuring to remember that while veteran nurses 9
joke about scheduling their vacations to start July 1, they monitor
interns most carefully and manage to catch many mistakes. Residents bear much more responsibility for supervision and surveil-
lance, and Dr. Lawrence Boxt, president of the 5,000-member,
Manhattan-based Committee of Interns and Residents and a resident himself, emphasizes that residents are especially vigilant during July. One of the interns he represents agreed: "You're watched
like a hawk. You have so much support and backup. They're not
going to let you kill anybody." So no one who requires emergency
medical attention should hesitate to be hospitalized in July.

I asked Dr. Boxt whether he also had any advice for someone 10
about to enter a hospital for elective surgery.

"Yes," he said. "Stay away." 11

Questions for Study and Discussion

1. Machlowitz begins her essay with the anecdote of the Harvard medical school professor. Does this brief story effectively introduce her essay? (Glossary: *Beginnings and
   Endings*) Why, or why not?

2. What, according to Machlowitz, are the immediate causes
   of the problems many hospitals experience during the
   month of July?

3. What does she say are the causes of intern inadequacy? Explain how Machlowitz uses examples and quotations from
   authorities to substantiate the cause and effect relationship.

4. Why, according to Machlowitz, do interns sometimes order unwarranted tests?

5. What suggestions does Machlowitz give for minimizing patient risk during the month of July?

6. How would you interpret Dr. Boxt's answer to the final question Machlowitz asks him?

Vocabulary

Refer to your dictionary to define the following words as they are used in this selection. Then use each word in a sentence of your own.

meticulous (4)   affiliated (8)
diagnoses (6)   prestigious (8)
unwarranted (6)   vigilant (9)
compromised (7)

Suggested Writing Assignments

1. Write an essay in which you argue for changes in the ways hospitals handle the "July" problem. Make sure your proposals are realistic, clearly stated, and have some chance of producing the desired effects. You may wish to consider some possible objections to your proposals and how they might be overcome.

2. There is often more than one cause for an event. Make a list of at least six possible causes for one of the following:

   a quarrel with a friend

   an upset victory in a football game

   a well-done exam

   a broken leg

   a change of major

   Examine your list, and identify the causes that seem most probable. Which of these are immediate causes and which are ultimate causes? Using this material, write a short cause-and-effect essay.

THE BOUNTY OF THE SEA

Jacques Cousteau

*Jacques Cousteau, born in France in 1910, is per-
haps the most famous oceanographer in the world.
In his popular books and television shows, Cousteau has expressed wonder and admiration for the
world beneath the ocean's surface and a growing
concern for the future health of this world. The following essay, written in the mid-sixties, offers a
grim scenario for humanity if the marine environment is not protected.*

During the past thirty years, I have observed and studied the 1
oceans closely, and with my own two eyes I have seen them
sicken. Certain reefs that teemed with fish only ten years ago are
now almost lifeless. The ocean bottom has been raped by trawl-
ers. Priceless wetlands have been destroyed by landfill. And everywhere are sticky globs of oil, plastic refuse, and unseen clouds of
poisonous effluents. Often, when I describe the symptoms of the
oceans' sickness, I hear remarks like "they're only fish" or "they're
only whales" or "they're only birds." But I assure you that our des-
tinies are linked with theirs in the most profound and fundamental manner. For if the oceans should die—by which I mean that all
life in the sea would finally cease—this would signal the end not
only for marine life but for all other animals and plants of this
earth, including man.

With life departed, the ocean would become, in effect, one enor- 2
mous cesspool. Billions of decaying bodies, large and small, would
create such an insupportable stench that man would be forced to
leave all the coastal regions. But far worse would follow.

The ocean acts as the earth's buffer. It maintains a fine balance 3
between the many salts and gases which make life possible. But
dead seas would have no buffering effect. The carbon dioxide
content of the atmosphere would start on a steady and remorse-
less climb, and when it reached a certain level a "greenhouse

effect" would be created. The heat that normally radiates outward from the earth to space would be blocked by the CO_2, and sea level temperatures would dramatically increase.

One catastrophic effect of this heat would be melting of the icecaps at both the North and South Poles. As a result, the ocean would rise by 100 feet or more, enough to flood almost all the world's major cities. These rising waters would drive one-third of the earth's billions inland, creating famine, fighting, chaos, and disease on a scale almost impossible to imagine. 4

Meanwhile, the surface of the ocean would have scummed over with a thick film of decayed matter, and would no longer be able to give water freely to the skies through evaporation. Rain would become a rarity, creating global drought and even more famine. 5

But the final act is yet to come. The wretched remnant of the human race would now be packed cheek by jowl on the remaining highlands, bewildered, starving, struggling to survive from hour to hour. Then would be visited upon them the final plague, anoxia (lack of oxygen). This would be caused by the extinction of plankton algae and the reduction of land vegetation, the two sources that supply the oxygen you are now breathing. 6

And so man would finally die, slowly gasping out his life on some barren hill. He would have survived the oceans by perhaps thirty years. And his heirs would be bacteria and a few scavenger insects. 7

Questions for Study and Discussion

1. What is Cousteau's thesis in this essay? (Glossary: *Thesis*)
2. What evidence does Cousteau give to convince the reader that the oceans are indeed sick? (Glossary: *Evidence*)
3. How will the human race die if the oceans die? What will remain living on earth?
4. The term "greenhouse effect" is used here in an essay written twenty-five years before it became widely known. What is it? What would the consequences of the "greenhouse effect" be for humanity?

5. What descriptive words does Cousteau use to emphasize what the ocean will become if it remains polluted? (Glossary: *Description*) Why does Cousteau use these words?
6. Identify the cause-and-effect elements in the essay.

Vocabulary

Refer to your dictionary to define the following words as they are used in this selection. Then use each word in a sentence of your own.

teemed (1)	buffer (3)
effluents (1)	radiates (3)
fundamental (1)	famine (4)

Suggested Writing Assignments

1. Write an essay discussing the causes and effects of another form of pollution. It can be a general form of pollution, such as air pollution, or more specific, such as the discharge of phosphates into a freshwater lake or river. Research the subject you choose if necessary.
2. Many people are concerned about what they can do as individuals to stop pollution and save the environment. Write an essay in which you discuss what individuals can do to help in one area of concern. Explain the situation and outline the goals. What effects do you hope will occur because of the actions you propose?

HALFWAY TO DICK AND JANE

Jack Agueros

Jack Agueros was born in Harlem in 1934. As a Puerto Rican in the New York City area, he became very aware of the problems that he and people from other ethnic groups faced as they moved into American society. Some of the problems are examined in "Halfway to Dick and Jane," which comes from Agueros' book The Immigrant Experience: The Anguish of Becoming American, *published in 1971.*

I am an only child. My parents and I always talked about my becoming a doctor. The law and politics were not highly regarded in my house. Lawyers, my mother would explain, had to defend people whether they were guilty or not, while politicians, my father would say, were all crooks. A doctor helped everybody, rich and poor, white and black. If I became a doctor, I could study hay fever and find a cure for it, my godmother would say. Also, I could take care of my parents when they were old. I like the idea of helping, and for nineteen years my sole ambition was to study medicine.

My house had books, not many, but my parents encouraged me to read. As I became a good reader they bought books for me and never refused me money for their purchase. My father once built a bookcase for me. It was an important moment, for I had always believed that my father was not too happy about my being a bookworm. The atmosphere at home was always warm. We seemed to be a popular family. We entertained frequently, with two standing parties a year—at Christmas and for my birthday. Parties were always large. My father would dismantle the beds and move all the furniture so that the full two rooms could be used for dancing. My mother would cook up a storm, particularly at Christmas. *Pasteles, lechon asado, arroz con gandules,* and a lot of *coquito* to drink (meat-stuffed plantain, roast pork, rice with pigeon peas, and coconut nog). My father always brought in a band. They played without compensation and were guests at the party. They ate and drank and danced while a victrola covered the intermissions. One year my father brought home a whole pig and hung it in the foyer doorway. He and my mother prepared it by rubbing it down with oil, orègano, and garlic. After preparation, the pig was taken down and carried over to a local bakery where it was cooked and returned home. Parties always went on till daybreak, and in addition to the band, there were always volunteers to sing and declaim poetry.

My mother kept an immaculate household. Bedspreads (chenille seemed to be very in) and lace curtains, washed at home like everything else, were hung up on huge racks with rows of tight nails. The racks were assembled in the living room, and the moisture from the wet bedspreads would fill the apartment. In a sense, that seems to be the lasting image of that period of my life. The house was clean. The neighbors were clean. The streets, with few cars, were clean. The buildings were clean and uncluttered with people on the stoops. The park was clean. The visitors to my house were clean, and the relationships that my family had with other Puerto Rican families, and the Italian families that my father had met through baseball and my mother through the garment center, were clean. Second Avenue was clean and most of the apartment windows had awnings. There was always music, there seemed to be no rain, and snow did not become slush. School was fun, we wrote essays about how grand America was, we put up hunchbacked cats at Halloween, we believed Santa Claus visited everyone. I believed everyone was Catholic. I grew up with dogs, nightingales, my godmother's guitar, rocking chair, cat, guppies, my father's occasional roosters, kept in a cage on the fire escape. Laundry delivered and collected by horse and wagon, fruits and vegetables sold the same way, windowsill refrigeration in winter, iceman and box in summer. The police my friends, likewise the teachers. 3

In short, the first seven or so years of my life were not too great a variation on Dick and Jane, the schoolbook figures who, if my memory serves me correctly, were blond Anglo-Saxons, not immigrants, not migrants like the Puerto Ricans, and not the children of either immigrants or migrants. 4

My family moved in 1941 to Lexington Avenue into a larger apartment where I could have my own room. It was a light, sunny, 5 railroad flat on the top floor of a well-kept building. I transferred to a new school, and whereas before my classmates had been mostly black, the new school had few blacks. The classes were made up of Italians, Irish, Jews, and a sprinkling of Puerto Ricans. My block was populated by Jews, Italians, and Puerto Ricans.

And then a whole series of different events began. I went to junior high school. We played in the backyards, where we tore down fences to build fires to cook stolen potatoes. We tore up whole hedges, because the green tender limbs would not burn when they were peeled, and thus made perfect skewers for our stolen "mickies." We played tag in the abandoned buildings, tearing the plaster off the walls, tearing the wire lath off the wooden slats, tearing the wooden slats themselves, good for fires, for kites, for sword fighting. We ran up and down the fire escapes playing tag and over and across many rooftops. The war ended and the heavy Puerto Rican migration began. The Irish and the Jews disappeared from the neighborhood. The Italians tried to consolidate east of Third Avenue.

What caused the clean and open world to end? Many things. Into an ancient neighborhood came pouring four to five times more people than it had been designed to hold. Men who came running at the promise of jobs were jobless as the war ended. They were confused. They could not see the economic forces that ruled their lives as they drank beer on the corners, reassuring themselves of good times to come while they were hell-bent toward alcoholism. The sudden surge in numbers caused new resentments, and prejudice was intensified. Some were forced to live in cellars, and were then characterized as cave dwellers. Kids came who were confused by the new surroundings; their Puerto Rican-ness forced us against a mirror asking, "If they are Puerto Ricans, what are we?" and thus they confused us. In our confusion we were sometimes pathetically reaching out, sometimes pathologically striking out. Gangs. Drugs. Wine. Smoking. Girls. Dances and slow-drag music. Mambo. Spics, Spooks, and Wops. Territories, brother gangs, and war councils establishing rules for right of way on blocks and avenues and for seating in the local theater. Pegged pants and zip guns. Slang.

Dick and Jane were dead, man. Education collapsed. Every classroom had ten kids who spoke no English. Black, Italian, Puerto Rican relations in the classroom were good, but we all knew we couldn't visit one another's neighborhoods. Sometimes we could not move too freely within our own blocks. On 109th, from the lamp post west, the Latin Aces, and from the lamp post east, the Senecas, the "club" I belonged to. The kids who spoke no English became known as Marine Tigers, picked up from a popular Spanish song. (The Marine Tiger and the Marine Shark were two ships that sailed from San Juan to New York and brought over many, many migrants from the island.)

The neighborhood had its boundaries. Third Avenue and east, Italian. Fifth Avenue and west, black. South, there was a hill on 103rd Street known locally as Cooney's Hill. When you got to the top of the hill, something strange happened: America began, because from the hill south was where the "Americans" lived. Dick and Jane were not dead: they were alive and well in a better neighborhood.   9

When, as a group of Puerto Rican kids, we decided to go swimming to Jefferson Park Pool, we knew we risked a fight and a beating from the Italians. And when we went to La Milagrosa Church in Harlem, we knew we risked a fight and a beating from the blacks. But when we went over Cooney's Hill, we risked dirty looks, disapproving looks, and questions from the police like, "What are you doing in this neighborhood?" and "Why don't you kids go back where you belong?"   10

Where we belonged! Man I had written compositions about America. Didn't I belong on the Central Park tennis courts, even if I didn't know how to play? Couldn't I watch Dick play? Weren't these policemen working for me too? . . .   11

Questions for Study and Discussion

1. What does the title "Halfway to Dick and Jane" mean? (Glossary: *Title*) Why is it an effective title?

2. What was Agueros's early childhood like? Why does he describe it in such detail? (Glossary: *Description*)

3. Agueros says in the third paragraph "There was always music, there seemed to be no rain, and snow did not become slush." Why does he use exaggeration here?

4. What, besides his family's move to Lexington Avenue, caused Agueros's ideal world to change so drastically?

5. What does Agueros mean when he says "Dick and Jane were dead, man"?

6. What happens to the Puerto Ricans when they leave "their" neighborhood?

7. What is the cause and effect in Agueros's essay? (Glossary: *Cause and Effect*)

Vocabulary

Refer to your dictionary to define the following words as they are used in this selection. Then use each word in a sentence of your own.

compensation (2) consolidate (6)
declaim (2) pathologically (7)
immaculate (3)

Suggested Writing Assignments

1. Write a cause-and-effect essay in which you identify how prejudice develops, using Agueros's essay as a reference. For instance, how would overcrowding and high unemployment in a neighborhood contribute to general prejudice toward its inhabitants? Also identify ways in which prejudice can be stopped.

2. Write an essay about the neighborhood of your childhood. How has the neighborhood changed? What has caused the changes?

LEGALIZE DRUGS

Ethan A. Nadelmann

Writer, speaker, and teacher Ethan Nadelmann was born in 1957 in New York City. His many degrees include a B.A. from McGill University, an M.S. in international relations from the London School of Economics, and both a law degree and a Ph.D. from Harvard University. His extensive writings, which focus on international crime and law enforcement in general, and U.S. drug policy in particular, have appeared in journals such as Foreign Policy *and* The Public Interest. *In the following essay, which first appeared as "Shooting Up" in the* New Republic *on June 13, 1988, Nadelmann makes his claim that the legalization of drugs would eliminate the criminal activity associated with drug use.*

Hamburgers and ketchup. Movies and popcorn. Drugs and crime.

Drugs and crime are so thoroughly intertwined in the public mind that to most people a large crime problem seems an inevitable consequence of widespread drug use. But the historical link between the two is more a product of drug laws than of drugs. There are four clear connections between drugs and crime, and three of them would be much diminished if drugs were legalized. This fact doesn't by itself make the case for legalization persuasive, of course, but it deserves careful attention in the emerging debate over whether the prohibition of drugs is worth the trouble.

The first connection between drugs and crime—and the only one that would remain strong after legalization—is the commission of violent and other crimes by people under the influence of illicit drugs. It is this connection that most infects the popular imagination. Obviously some drugs do "cause" people to commit crimes by reducing normal inhibitions, lessening the sense of responsibility, and unleashing aggressive and other antisocial tendencies. Cocaine, particularly in the form of "crack," has earned such a reputation in recent years, just as heroin did in the 1960s and 1970s and marijuana did in the years before that.

Crack's reputation may or may not be more deserved than those 4 of marijuana and heroin. Reliable evidence isn't yet available. But no illicit drug is as widely associated with violent behavior as alcohol. According to Justice Department statistics, 54 percent of all jail inmates convicted of violent crimes in 1983 reported having used alcohol just prior to committing the offense. The impact of drug legalization on this drug-crime connection is hard to predict. Much would depend on overall rates of drug abuse and changes in the nature of consumption, both imponderables. It's worth noting, though, that any shift in consumption from alcohol to marijuana would almost certainly reduce violent behavior.

This connection between drugs and antisocial behavior—which 5 is inherent and may or may not be substantial—is often confused with a second link between the two that is definitely substantial and not inherent: many illicit drug users commit crimes such as robbery, burglary, prostitution, and numbers-running to earn enough money to buy drugs. Unlike the millions of alcoholics who support their habits for modest amounts, many cocaine and heroin addicts spend hundreds, maybe even thousands, of dollars a week. If these drugs were significantly cheaper—if either they were legalized or drug laws were not enforced—the number of crimes committed by drug addicts to pay for their habits would drop dramatically. Even if the drugs were taxed heavily to discourage consumption, prices probably would be much lower than they are today.

The third drug-crime link—also a byproduct of drug laws—is 6 the violent, intimidating, and corrupting behavior of the drug traffickers. Illegal markets tend to breed violence, not just because they attract criminally minded people but also because there are no legal institutions for resolving disputes. During Prohibition violent struggles between bootlegging gangs and hijackings of booze-laden trucks were frequent and notorious. Today's equivalents are the booby traps that surround marijuana fields; the pirates of the Caribbean, who rip off drug-laden vessels en route to the United States; and the machine-gun battles and executions of the more sordid drug mafias—all of which occasionally kill innocent people. Most authorities agree that the dramatic increase in urban murder rates over the past few years is almost entirely due to the rise in drug-dealer killings, mostly of one another.

Perhaps the most unfortunate victims of drug prohibition laws   7
have been the residents of America's ghettos. These laws have proved largely futile in deterring ghetto-dwellers from becoming drug abusers, but they do account for much of what ghetto residents identify as the drug problem. Aggressive, guntoting drug dealers often upset law-abiding residents far more than do addicts nodding out in doorways. Meanwhile other residents perceive the drug dealers as heroes and successful role models. They're symbols of success to children who see no other options. At the same time the increasingly harsh criminal penalties imposed on adult drug dealers have led drug traffickers to recruit juveniles. Where once children started dealing drugs only after they had been using them for a few years, today the sequence is often reversed. Many children start using drugs only after working for older drug dealers for a while.

The conspicuous failure of law enforcement agencies to deal   8
with the disruptive effect of drug traffickers has demoralized inner-city neighborhoods and police departments alike. Intensive crackdowns in urban neighborhoods, like intensive anti-cockroach efforts in urban dwellings, do little more than chase the menace a short distance away to infect new areas. By contrast, legalization of drugs, like legalization of alcohol in the early 1930s, would drive the drug-dealing business off the streets and out of apartment buildings and into government-regulated, tax-paying stores. It also would force many of the gun-toting dealers out of the business and convert others into legitimate businessmen. Some, of course, would turn to other types of criminal activities, just as some of the bootleggers did after Prohibition's repeal. Gone, though, would be the unparalleled financial gains that tempt people from all sectors of society into the drug-dealing business.

Gone, too, would be the money that draws police into the world   9
of crime. Today police corruption appears to be more pervasive than at any time since Prohibition. In Miami dozens of law enforcement officials have been charged with accepting bribes, ripping off drug dealers, and even dealing drugs themselves. In small towns and rural communities in Georgia, where drug

smugglers from the Caribbean and Latin America pass through, dozens of sheriffs have been implicated in corruption. In one New York police precinct, drug-related corruption has generated the city's most far-reaching police scandal since the late 1960s. Nationwide, over 100 cases of drug-related corruption are now prosecuted each year. Every one of the federal law enforcement agencies with significant drug enforcement responsibilities has seen an agent implicated.

It isn't hard to explain the growth of this corruption. The financial temptations are enormous relative to other opportunities, legitimate or illegitimate. Little effort is required. Many police officers are demoralized by the scope of drug traffic, the indifference of many citizens, a frequent lack of appreciation for their efforts, and the seeming futility of it all; even with the regular jailing of drug dealers, there always seem to be more to fill their shoes. Some police also recognize that their real function is not so much to protect victims from predators as to regulate an illicit market that can't be suppressed but that much of society prefers to keep underground. In every respect, the analogy to Prohibition is apt. Repealing drug prohibition laws would dramatically reduce police corruption. By contrast, the measures currently being proposed to deal with the growing problem, including more frequent and aggressive internal inspection, offer little promise and cost money.

The final link between drugs and crime is the tautological connection: producing, selling, buying, and consuming drugs is a crime in and of itself that occurs billions of times each year nationwide. Last year alone, about 30 million Americans violated a drug law, and about 750,000 were arrested, mostly for mere possession, not dealing. In New York City almost half of the felony indictments were on drug charges, and in Washington, D.C., the figure was more than half. Close to 40 percent of inmates in federal prisons are there on drug-dealing charges, and that population is expected to more than double within 15 years.

Clearly, if drugs were legalized, this drug-crime connection—which annually accounts for around $10 billion in criminal justice costs—would be severed. (Selling drugs to children would, of course, continue to be prosecuted.) And the benefits would run deeper than that. We would no longer be labeling as criminals the

tens of millions of people who use drugs illicitly, subjecting them
to the risk of arrest, and inviting them to associate with drug dealers (who may be criminals in many more senses of the word). The
attendant cynicism toward the law in general would diminish,
along with the sense of hostility and suspicion that otherwise
law-abiding citizens feel toward police. It was costs such as these
that strongly influenced many of Prohibition's more conservative
opponents. As John D. Rockefeller wrote in explaining why he
was withdrawing his support of Prohibition:

> That a vast array of lawbreakers has been recruited and
> financed on a colossal scale; that many of our best citizens,
> piqued at what they regarded as an infringement of their pri-
> vate rights, have openly and unabashedly disregarded the
> 18th Amendment; that as an inevitable result respect for all
> law has been greatly lessened; that crime has increased to an
> unprecedented degree—I have slowly and reluctantly come
> to believe.

Questions for Study and Discussion

1. What are the four connections Nadelmann makes between
   drugs and crime? According to Nadelmann, what changes
   would occur if drugs were legalized? Would anything remain unaffected? How does he explain this?
2. Nadelmann insists that the connection between drugs and
   crime is not inevitable. What kinds of evidence does he offer to support this argument? Which kinds of evidence did
   you find the most convincing? (Glossary: *Evidence*) The
   least convincing? Explain.
3. Nadelmann identifies several groups of people associated
   with the criminal aspects of drug use. What role does each
   group presently play? According to Nadelmann, how would
   that role change if drug use were made legal?
4. What is the analogy Nadelmann draws in paragraph 10?
   (Glossary: *Analogy*) Is it effective? Why or why not?
5. What is the "tautological connection" between drugs and
   crime that Nadelmann describes in paragraph 11? Is this
   connection clearly stated?

6. What exactly is Nadelmann's purpose in writing this essay? (Glossary: *Purpose*) Does he expect his readers to endorse the legalization of drugs or does he want something else? How do you know?

Vocabulary

Refer to your dictionary to define the following words as they are used in this selection. Then use each word in a sentence of your own.

inevitable (1)	deterring (7)
illicit (2)	conspicuous (8)
inhibitions (3)	implicated (9)
imponderables (4)	demoralized (10)
inherent (5)	predators (10)
bootlegging (6)	tautological (11)
sordid (6)	cynicism (12)
futile (7)	

Suggested Writing Assignments

1. In a brief essay, respond to Nadelmann's assertion that "any shift in consumption from alcohol to marijuana would almost certainly reduce violent behavior." What reasons do you have for agreeing or disagreeing? What is the relationship between alcohol and violent behavior? Marijuana and violent behavior?

2. Write an essay in which you establish the cause and effect relationship that exists in one of the following pairs.

   winter and depression
   poverty and crime
   wealth and power
   health and happiness
   old age and wisdom
   good looks and popularity
   drugs and sex

18

ARGUMENT

Argumentation is the attempt to persuade a reader to accept your point of view, to make a decision, or to pursue a particular course of action. Because the writer of an argument is often interested in explaining a subject, as well as in advocating a particular view, argumentation frequently adopts other rhetorical strategies. Nevertheless, it is the attempt to convince, not to explain, that is most important in an argumentative essay.

There are two basic types of argumentation: logical and persuasive. In *logical argumentation* the writer appeals to the reader's rational or intellectual faculties to convince him or her of the truth of a particular statement or belief. In *persuasive argumentation,* on the other hand, the writer appeals to the reader's emotions and opinions to move the reader to action. These two types of argumentation are seldom found in their pure forms, and the degree to which one or the other is emphasized in written work depends on the writer's subject, specific purpose, and intended audience. Although you may occasionally need or want to appeal to your readers' emotions, most often in your college work you will need to rely only on the fundamental techniques of logical argumentation.

There are two types of reasoning common to essays of argumentation: induction and deduction. *Inductive reasoning,* the more common type, moves from a set of specific examples to a general statement. In doing so, the writer makes what is known as an *inductive leap* from the evidence to the generalization. For example, after examining enrollment statistics, we can conclude that students do not like to take courses offered early in the morning or late in the afternoon. *Deductive reasoning,* on the other hand, moves from a general statement to a specific conclusion. It works on the model of the *syllogism,* a simple three-part argument that consists of a major premise, a minor premise, and a conclusion, as in the following example:

a. All women are mortal. (major premise)
b. Judy is a woman. (minor premise)
c. Judy is mortal. (conclusion)

A well-constructed argument avoids *logical fallacies,* flaws in the reasoning that will render the argument invalid. Following are some of the most common logical fallacies:

1. *Oversimplification.* The tendency to provide simple solutions to complex problems. "The reason we have high unemployment today is the war in the Middle East."

2. *Hasty generalization.* A generalization that is based on too little evidence or on evidence that is not representative. "The movie was very popular. It should get an Academy Award."

3. *Post hoc, ergo propter hoc* ("After this, therefore because of this"). Confusing chance or coincidence with causation. Because one event comes after another one, it does not necessarily mean that the first event caused the second. "Ever since I went to the hockey game, I've had a cold." The assumption here is that going to the hockey game had something to do with the speaker's cold when, in fact, there might be one or more different causes for the cold.

4. *Begging the question.* Assuming in a premise that which needs to be proven. "Conservation is the only means of solving the energy problem over the long haul; therefore, we should seek out methods to conserve energy."

5. *False analogy.* Making a misleading analogy between logically unconnected ideas. "Of course he'll make a fine coach. He was an all-star basketball player."

6. *Either/or thinking.* The tendency to see an issue as having only two sides. "There are good judges and there are bad judges."

7. *Non sequitur* ("It does not follow"). An inference or conclusion that does not follow from established premises or evidence. "She is a sincere speaker; she must know what she is talking about."

As you write your argumentative essays, you should keep the following advice in mind. Somewhere near the beginning of your essay, you should identify the issue to be discussed, explain why you think it is important, and point out what interest you and your readers share in the issue. Then, in the body of your essay, you should organize the various points of your argument. You may move from your least important point to your most important point, from the most familiar to the least familiar, from the easiest to accept or comprehend to the most difficult. For each point in your argument, you should provide sufficient appropriate supporting evidence—facts and statistics, illustrative examples and narratives, quotations from authorities. In addition, you should acknowledge the strongest opposing arguments and explain why you believe your position is more valid.

Be sure that you neither overstate nor understate your position. It is always wise to let the evidence convince your reader. Overstatement not only annoys readers but, more importantly, raises serious doubts about your own confidence in the power of your facts and reasoning. At the same time, no writer persuades by excessively understating or qualifying information with words and phrases such as *perhaps, maybe, I think, sometimes, most often, nearly always,* or *in my opinion.* The result sounds not rational and sensible but indecisive and fuzzy.

HATE, RAPE, AND RAP

Tipper Gore

Tipper Gore, the wife of Vice President Al Gore, was born in Washington, D.C., in 1948 and grew up in Arlington, Virginia. She graduated from Boston University with a degree in psychology in 1970 and pursued graduate studies in psychology at George Peabody College in Nashville, Tennessee. In 1983, Gore helped establish the Parents' Music Resource Center (P.M.R.C.) a group which addresses issues of obscenity and pornography in modern rock lyrics. In "Hate, Rape, and Rap," which first appeared in the Washington Post *in January 1990, Gore contends that the lyrics in some modern rap music inspire feelings of hatred among its listeners.*

Words like "bitch" and "nigger" are dangerous. Racial and sexual epithets, whether screamed across a street or camouflaged by the rhythms of a song, turn people into objects less than human—easier to degrade, easier to violate, easier to destroy. These words and epithets are becoming an accepted part of our lexicon. What's disturbing is that they are being endorsed by some of the very people they diminish, and our children are being sold a social dictionary that says racism, sexism, and antisemitism are okay.

As someone who strongly supports the First Amendment, I respect the freedom of every individual to label another as he likes. But speaking out against racism isn't endorsing censorship. No one should silently tolerate racism or sexism or antisemitism, or condone those who turn discrimination into a multimillion-dollar business justified because it's "real."

A few weeks ago television viewers saw a confrontation of depressing proportions on the Oprah Winfrey show. It was one I witnessed firsthand; I was there in the middle of it. Viewers heard some black American women say they didn't mind being called "bitches" and they weren't offended by the popular rap music artist Ice-T when he sang about "Evil E" who "f---ed the bitch with a flashlight/pulled it out, left the batteries in/so he could get a charge when he begins." There is more, and worse.

Ice-T, who was also on the show, said the song came from the heart and reflected his experiences. He said he doesn't mind other groups using the word "nigger" in their lyrics. That's how he described himself, he said. Some in the audience questioned why we couldn't see the humor in such a song.

Will our kids get the joke? Do we want them describing themselves or each other as "niggers?" Do we want our daughters to think of themselves as "bitches" to be abused? Do we want our sons to measure success in gold guns hanging from thick neck chains? The women in the audience may understand the slang; Ice-T can try to justify it. But can our children?

One woman in the audience challenged Ice-T. She told him his song about the flashlight was about as funny as a song about lynching black men.

The difference is that sexism and violence against women are accepted as almost an institutionalized part of our entertainment. Racism is not—or at least, it hasn't been until recently. The fact is, neither racism, sexism nor antisemitism should be accepted.

Yet they are, and in some instances that acceptance has reached startling proportions. The racism expressed in the song "One In A Million" by Guns N' Roses, sparked nationwide discussion and disgust. But, an earlier album, that featured a rape victim in the artwork and lyrics violently degrading to women, created barely a whisper of protest. More than 9 million copies were sold, and it was played across the radio band. This is only one example where hundreds exist.

Rabbi Abraham Cooper of the Simon Wiesenthal Center, who also appeared on the Oprah Show, voiced his concerns about the antisemitic statements made by Professor Griff, a non-singing member of the rap group, Public Enemy; statements that gain added weight from the group's celebrity. "Jews are wicked," Professor Griff said in an interview with The Washington Times. ". . . [Responsible for] a majority of wickedness that goes on across the globe."

The Simon Wiesenthal Center placed a full-page ad in Daily Variety calling for self-restraint from the music industry, a move that prompted hundreds of calls to the center. Yet Rabbi Cooper's concerns barely elicited a response from Oprah Winfrey's audience.

Alvin Poussaint, a Harvard psychiatrist who is black, believes 11 that the widespread acceptance of such degrading and denigrating images may reflect low self-esteem among black men in today's society. There are few positive black male role models for young children, and such messages from existing role models are damaging. Ice-T defends his reality: "I grew up in the streets—I'm no Bryant Gumbel." He accuses his critics of fearing that reality, and says the fear comes from an ignorance of the triumph of the street ethic.

A valid point, perhaps. But it is not the messenger that is so 12 frightening, it is the perpetuation—almost glorification—of the cruel and violent reality of his "streets."

A young black mother in the front row rose to defend Ice-T. Her 13 son, she said, was an A student who listened to Ice-T. In her opinion, as long as Ice-T made a profit, it didn't matter what he sang.

Cultural economics were a poor excuse for the South's continu- 14 ation of slavery. Ice-T's financial success cannot excuse the vileness of his message. What does it mean when performers such as Ice-T, Axl Rose of Guns N' Roses and others can enrich themselves with racist and misogynist diatribes and defend it because it sells? Hitler's antisemitism sold in Nazi Germany. That didn't make it right.

In America, a woman is raped once every six minutes. A ma- 15 jority of children surveyed by a Rhode Island Rape Crisis Center thought rape was acceptable. In New York City, rape arrests of 13-year-old boys have increased 200 percent in the past two years. Children 18 and younger now are responsible for 70 percent of the hate crime committed in the United States. No one is saying this happens solely because of rap or rock music, but certainly kids are influenced by the glorification of violence.

Children must be taught to hate. They are not born with ideas 16 of bigotry—they learn from what they see in the world around them. If their reality consists of a street ethic that promotes and glorifies violence against women or discrimination against minorities—not only in everyday life, but in their entertainment—then ideas of bigotry and violence will flourish.

We must raise our voices in protest and put pressure on those 17 who not only reflect this hatred but also package, polish, promote

and market it; those who would make words like "nigger" acceptable. Let's place a higher value on our children than on our profits and embark on a remedial civil rights course for children who
are being taught to hate and a remedial nonviolence course for
children who are being taught to destroy. Let's send the message
loud and clear through our homes, our streets and our schools, as
well as our art and our culture.

Questions for Study and Discussion

1. What is Gore's thesis? Where is it best stated? (Glossary:
   Thesis)
2. In paragraph 1 Gore says that words like "bitch" and "nigger" are dangerous. Does she say why? How do you respond
   to her charge?
3. Does Gore use inductive or deductive reasoning to argue
   her point? You may find it helpful to outline the essay so as
   to more easily see the logic of her development.
4. Gore makes the claim that performers such as Ice-T and
   Guns 'n' Roses are like Hitler. In what ways does she say
   they are similar? Is she convincing? Why or why not? Does
   she include the ways in which they are dissimilar? Explain.
5. What solutions does Gore offer as a means of minimizing
   children's exposure to objectionable music? In your opinion, is she advocating a form of censorship? Explain.
6. In paragraph 16 Gore says, "Children must be taught to
   hate." What does she mean? How does her statement relate
   to her thesis?
7. What is the relationship among the words "hate," "rape,"
   and "rap" in Gore's essay? How well do these words serve as
   a title for this essay? (Glossary: *Title*) Explain.

Vocabulary

Refer to your dictionary to define the following words as they
are used in this selection. Then use each word in a sentence of
your own.

epithets (1)   misogynist (14)
lexicon (1)   diatribes (14)
antisemitism (7)   remedial (17)

Suggested Writing Assignments

1. Based on what you have just read, write an essay in which you argue either for or against the labelling of music albums. Discuss the extent to which you believe such labelling would or would not constitute censorship.

2. Gore says "Children must be taught to hate," and she insists that they can learn hatred by listening to some modern rap music. Do you think Gore has made a good case for the harmful effects of rock music or has she oversimplified the issue? In an essay, address this question while discussing your own opinion as to why hatred, bigotry, and prejudice still exist in America.

As They Say, Drugs Kill

Laura Rowley

*Laura Rowley was born in Oak Lawn, Illinois, in
1965 and graduated from the University of Illinois
at Champaign-Urbana in 1987 with a degree in
journalism. While in college, Rowley was the city
editor for the* Daily Illini. *After graduation she
worked at the* United Nations Chronicle *in New
York City. Rowley works as a free-lance writer and
hopes some day to travel and work in Africa under
the auspice of either the United Nations or the
Peace Corps. In the following essay, which first
appeared in* Newsweek on Campus *in 1987, Rowley argues against substance abuse by recounting a
particularly poignant personal experience. As you
read her piece, notice how she attempts to persuade
without preaching.*

The fastest way to end a party is to have someone die in the   1
middle of it.

At a party last fall I watched a 22-year-old die of cardiac arrest   2
after he had used drugs. It was a painful, undignified way to
die. And I would like to think that anyone who shared the experience would feel his or her ambivalence about substance abuse
dissolving.

This victim won't be singled out like Len Bias as a bitter exam-   3
ple for "troubled youth." He was just another ordinary guy cele-
brating with friends at a private house party, the kind where they
roll in the keg first thing in the morning and get stupefied while
watching the football games on cable all afternoon. The living
room was littered with beer cans from last night's party—along
with dirty socks and the stuffing from the secondhand couch.

And there were drugs, as at so many other college parties. The   4
drug of choice this evening was psilocybin, hallucinogenic mushrooms. If you're cool you call them "'shrooms."

This wasn't a crowd huddled in the corner of a darkened room   5
with a single red bulb, shooting needles in their arms. People
played darts, made jokes, passed around a joint and listened to
the Grateful Dead on the stereo.

Suddenly, a thin, tall, brown-haired young man began to gasp.   6
His eyes rolled back in his head, and he hit the floor face first
with a crash. Someone laughed, not appreciating the violence
of his fall, thinking the afternoon's festivities had finally caught
up with another guest. The laugh lasted only a second, as the
brown-haired guest began to convulse and choke. The sound of
the stereo and laughter evaporated. Bystanders shouted frantic
suggestions:

"It's an epileptic fit, put something in his mouth!"   7

Roll him over on his stomach!"   8

"Call an ambulance; God, somebody breathe into his mouth."   9

A girl kneeling next to him began to sob his name, and he   10
seemed to moan.

"Wait, he's semicoherent." Four people grabbed for the tele-   11
phone, to find no dial tone, and ran to use a neighbor's. One
slammed the dead phone against the wall in frustration—and
miraculously produced a dial tone.

But the body was now motionless on the kitchen floor. "He has   12
a pulse, he has a pulse."

"But he's not breathing!"   13

"Well, get away—give him some f———ing air!" The three or   14
four guests gathered around his body unbuttoned his shirt.

"Wait—is he OK? Should I call the damn ambulance?"   15

A chorus of frightened voices shouted, "Yes, yes!"   16

"Come on, come on, breathe again. Breathe!"   17

Over muffled sobs came a sudden grating, desperate breath   18
that passed through bloody lips and echoed through the kitchen
and living room.

"He's had this reaction before—when he did acid at a concert   19
last spring. But he recovered in 15 seconds . . . ," one friend
confided.

The rest of the guests looked uncomfortably at the floor or   20
paced purposelessly around the room. One or two whispered,
"Oh, my God," over and over, like a prayer. A friend stood next to
me, eyes fixed on the kitchen floor. He mumbled, just audibly,
"I've seen this before. My dad died of a heart attack. He had the

same look. . . ." I touched his shoulder and leaned against a wall, repeating reassurances to myself. People don't die at parties. People don't die at parties.

Eventually, no more horrible, gnashing sounds tore their way 21 from the victim's lungs. I pushed my hands deep in my jeans pockets wondering how much it costs to pump a stomach and how someone could be so careless if he had had this reaction with another drug. What would he tell his parents about the hospital bill?

Two uniformed paramedics finally arrived, lifted him onto a 22 stretcher and quickly rolled him out. His face was grayish blue, his mouth hung open, rimmed with blood, and his eyes were rolled back with a yellowish color on the rims.

The paramedics could be seen moving rhythmically forward 23 and back through the small windows of the ambulance, whose lights threw a red wash over the stunned watchers on the porch. The paramedics' hands were massaging his chest when someone said, "Did you tell them he took psilocybin? Did you tell them."

"No, I . . ." 24

"My God, so tell them—do you want him to die?" Two people 25 ran to tell the paramedics the student had eaten mushrooms five minutes before the attack.

It seemed irreverent to talk as the ambulance pulled away. My 26 friend, who still saw his father's image, muttered, "That guy's dead." I put my arms around him half to comfort him, half to stop him from saying things I couldn't believe.

The next day, when I called someone who lived in the house, I 27 found that my friend was right.

My hands began to shake and my eyes filled with tears for 28 someone I didn't know. Weeks later the pain has dulled, but I still can't unravel the knot of emotion that has moved from my stomach to my head. When I told one friend what happened, she shook her head and spoke of the stupidity of filling your body with chemical substances. People who would do drugs after seeing that didn't value their lives too highly, she said.

But others refused to read any universal lessons from the inci- 29 dent. Many of those I spoke to about the event considered him the victim of a freak accident, randomly struck down by drugs as a pedestrian might be hit by a speeding taxi. They speculated that

the student must have had special physical problems; what
happened to him could not happen to them.
Couldn't it? Now when I hear people discussing drugs I'm   30
haunted by the image of him lying on the floor, his body straining
to rid itself of substances he chose to take. Painful, undignified,
unnecessary—like a wartime casualty. But in war, at least, lessons
are supposed to be learned, so that old mistakes are not repeated.
If this death cannot make people think and change, that will be
an even greater tragedy.

Questions for Study and Discussion

1. What is Rowley's purpose in this essay? What does she
   want us to believe? What does she want us to do? (Glossary: *Purpose*)
2. Rowley uses an extended narrative example to develop her
   argument. How does she use dialogue, diction choices, and
   appropriate details to enhance the drama of her story?
3. What does Rowley gain by sharing this powerful experience
   with her readers? How did Rowley's friends react when she
   told them her story?
4. Why do you think Rowley chose not to name the young man
   who died? In what ways is this young man different from
   Len Bias, the talented basketball player who died of a drug
   overdose after signing a contract with the Boston Celtics?
5. What in Rowley's tone—her attitude toward her subject and
   audience—particularly contributes to the persuasiveness of
   the essay? Cite examples from the selection that support
   your conclusion. (Glossary: *Tone*)
6. How did Rowley's opening paragraph affect you? What
   would have been lost had she combined the first two paragraphs? (Glossary: *Beginnings and Endings*)
7. For what audience do you suppose Rowley wrote this essay? In your opinion, would most readers be convinced by
   what Rowley says about drugs? Are you convinced? Why, or
   why not? (Glossary: *Audience*)

Vocabulary

Refer to your dictionary to define the following words as they are used in this selection. Then use each word in a sentence of your own.

ambivalence (2)	gnashing (21)
stupefied (3)	irreverent (26)
convulse (6)	unravel (28)
semicoherent (11)	speculated (29)
audibly (20)	tragedy (30)

Suggested Writing Assignments

1. Write a persuasive essay in which you support or refute the following proposition:

   Television advertising is in large part responsible for Americans' belief that over-the-counter drugs are cure-alls.

   Does such advertising in fact promote drug dependence and/or abuse?

2. Write an essay in which you argue against either drinking or smoking. What would drinkers and smokers claim are the benefits of their habits? What are the key arguments against these types of substance abuse? Use examples from your personal experience or from your reading to document your essay.

3. What is the most effective way to bring about social change and to influence societal attitudes? Concentrating on the sorts of changes you have witnessed over the last ten years, write an essay in which you describe how best to influence public opinion.

IN PRAISE OF THE F WORD

Mary Sherry

Mary Sherry was born in Bay City, Michigan, and received her B.A. degree from Rosary College in River Forest, Illinois. She is the owner of her own research and publishing company which specializes in information for economic and development organizations while at the same time pursuing an M.B.A. degree. A teacher in adult literacy programs, she has written essays on educational problems for various newspapers including the Wall Street Journal, *and* Newsday. *In the following essay reprinted from the May 6, 1991, issue of* Newsweek *Sherry takes a provocative stance, that the threat of flunking is a "positive teaching tool." She believes students would all be better off if they had a "healthy fear of failure."*

Tens of thousands of 18-year-olds will graduate this year and 1
be handed meaningless diplomas. These diplomas won't look any different from those awarded their luckier classmates. Their validity will be questioned only when their employers discover that these graduates are semiliterate.

Eventually a fortunate few will find their way into educational- 2
repair shops—adult-literacy programs, such as the one where I teach basic grammar and writing. There, high-school graduates and high-school dropouts pursuing graduate-equivalency certificates will learn the skills they should have learned in school. They will also discover they have been cheated by our educational system.

As I teach, I learn a lot about our schools. Early in each session 3
I ask my students to write about an unpleasant experience they had in school. No writers' block here! "I wish someone would have had made me stop doing drugs and made me study." "I liked to party and no one seemed to care." "I was a good kid and didn't

cause any trouble, so they just passed me along even though I didn't read well and couldn't write." And so on.

I am your basic do-gooder, and prior to teaching this class I blamed the poor academic skills our kids have today on drugs, divorce and other impediments to concentration necessary for doing well in school. But, as I rediscover each time I walk into the classroom, before a teacher can expect students to concentrate, he has to get their attention, no matter what distractions may be at hand. There are many ways to do this, and they have much to do with teaching style. However, if style alone won't do it, there is another way to show who holds the winning hand in the classroom. That is to reveal the trump card of failure.

I will never forget a teacher who played that card to get the attention of one of my children. Our youngest, a world-class charmer, did little to develop his intellectual talents but always got by. Until Mrs. Stifter.

Our son was a high-school senior when he had her for English. "He sits in the back of the room talking to his friends," she told me. "Why don't you move him to the front row?" I urged, believing the embarrassment would get him to settle down. Mrs. Stifter looked at me steely-eyed over her glasses. "I don't move seniors," she said. "I flunk them." I was flustered. Our son's academic life flashed before my eyes. No teacher had ever threatened him with that before. I regained my composure and managed to say that I thought she was right. By the time I got home I was feeling pretty good about this. It was a radical approach for these times, but, well, why not? "She's going to flunk you," I told my son. I did not discuss it any further. Suddenly English became a priority in his life. He finished out the semester with an A.

I know one example doesn't make a case, but at night I see a parade of students who are angry and resentful for having been passed along until they could no longer even pretend to keep up. Of average intelligence or better, they eventually quit school, concluding they were too dumb to finish. "I should have been held back," is a comment I hear frequently. Even sadder are those students who are high-school graduates who say to me after a few weeks of class, "I don't know how I ever got a high-school diploma."

Passing students who have not mastered the work cheats them and the employers who expect graduates to have basic skills. We excuse this dishonest behavior by saying kids can't learn if they come from terrible environments. No one seems to stop to think that—no matter what environments they come from—most kids don't put school first on their list unless they perceive something is at stake. They'd rather be sailing.

Many students I see at night could give expert testimony on unemployment, chemical dependency, abusive relationships. In spite of these difficulties, they have decided to make education a priority. They are motivated by the desire for a better job or the need to hang on to the one they've got. They have a healthy fear of failure.

People of all ages can rise above their problems, but they need to have a reason to do so. Young people generally don't have the maturity to value education in the same way my adult students value it. But fear of failure, whether economic or academic, can motivate both.

Flunking as a regular policy has just as much merit today as it did two generations ago. We must review the threat of flunking and see it as it really is—a positive teaching tool. It is an expression of confidence by both teachers and parents that the students have the ability to learn the material presented to them. However, making it work again would take a dedicated, caring conspiracy between teachers and parents. It would mean facing the tough reality that passing kids who haven't learned the material—while it might save them grief for the short term—dooms them to long-term illiteracy. It would mean that teachers would have to follow through on their threats, and parents would have to stand behind them, knowing their children's best interests are indeed at stake. This means no more doing Scott's assignments for him because he might fail. No more passing Jodi because she's such a nice kid.

This is a policy that worked in the past and can work today. A wise teacher, with the support of his parents, gave our son the opportunity to succeed—or fail. It's time we return this choice to all students.

Questions for Study and Discussion

1. What is the "F" word discussed in the essay? Does referring to it as the "F" word increase the effectiveness of the essay? Why?

2. Who is Sherry's audience? (Glossary: *Audience*) Is it receptive to the "F" word? Explain your answer.

3. What is Sherry's thesis? (Glossary: *Thesis*) What evidence does she use to support it? (Glossary: *Evidence*)

4. What does Sherry accomplish in paragraph 3?

5. In what way is Sherry qualified to comment on the potential benefits of flunking students? Do you think her induction is accurate? (Glossary: *Induction*)

6. Why does Sherry think flunking is a valuable tool for educators and for students?

Vocabulary

Refer to your dictionary to define the following words as they are used in this selection. Then use each word in a sentence of your own.

validity (1)   trump (4)
semiliterate (1)   testimony (9)
impediments (4)

Suggested Writing Assignments

1. Think of something that involves short-term pain or sacrifice, but can lead to a brighter future. For example, filling a cavity involves pain now, but it saves one from far more pain down the road. Studying and writing papers when you'd rather be having fun or even sleeping may seem painful, but a college degree leads to better jobs. Even if the benefits are obvious, imagine a skeptical audience and write an argument in favor of the short-term sacrifice over the long-term consequences of avoiding it.

2. Write an essay in which you argue against Sherry's thesis. In what ways is flunking bad for students? Are there techniques more positive than a "fear of failure" to use to motivate students?

LESS IS MORE:
A CALL FOR SHORTER WORK HOURS

Barbara Brandt

Barbara Brandt has written extensively on how our society places too high a value on work and productivity and not enough on quality of life in her book Whole Life Economics: Revaluing Daily Life *(1993). The following excerpt argues that shorter working hours would actually benefit our society economically, but that shorter work hours would be difficult to implement. Note how she argues her point to an audience that she knows will be skeptical.*

America is suffering from overwork. Too many of us are too busy, trying to squeeze more into each day while having less to show for it. Although our growing time crunch is often portrayed as a personal dilemma, it is in fact a major social problem that has reached crisis proportions over the past 20 years.

The simple fact is that Americans today—both women and men—are spending too much time at work, to the detriment of their homes, their families, their personal lives, and their communities. The American Dream promised that our individual hard work paired with the advances of modern technology would bring about the good life for all. Glorious visions of the leisure society were touted throughout the '50s and '60s. But now most people are working more than ever before, while still struggling to meet their economic commitments. Ironically, the many advances in technology, such as computers and fax machines, rather than reducing our workload, seem to have speeded up our lives at work. At the same time, technology has equipped us with "conveniences" like microwave ovens and frozen dinners that merely enable us to adopt a similar frantic pace in our home lives so we can cope with more hours at paid work.

A recent spate of articles in the mainstream media has focused on the new problems of overwork and lack of time. Unfortunately, overwork is often portrayed as a special problem of yuppies and professionals on the fast track. In reality, the unequal distribution of work and time in America today reflects the decline in both standard of living and quality of life for most Americans. Families whose members never see each other, women who work a double shift (first on the job, then at home), workers who need more flexible work schedules, and unemployed and underemployed people who need more work are all casualties of the crisis of overwork.

Americans often assume that overwork is an inevitable fact of life—like death and taxes. Yet a closer look at other times and other nations offers some startling surprises.

Anthropologists have observed that in pre-industrial (particularly hunting and gathering) societies, people generally spend 3 to 4 hours a day, 15 to 20 hours a week, doing the work necessary to maintain life. The rest of the time is spent in socializing, partying, playing, storytelling, and artistic or religious activities. The ancient Romans celebrated 175 public festivals a year in which everyone participated, and people in the Middle Ages had at least 115.

In our era, almost every other industrialized nation (except Japan) has fewer annual working hours and longer vacations than the United States. This includes all of Western Europe, where many nations enjoy thriving economies and standards of living equal to or higher than ours. Jeremy Brecher and Tim Costello, writing in *Z Magazine* (Oct. 1990), note that "European unions during the 1980s made a powerful and largely successful push to cut working hours. In 1987 German metalworkers struck and won a 37.5-hour week; many are now winning a 35-hour week. In 1990, hundreds of thousands of British workers have won a 37-hour week."

In an article about work-time in the *Boston Globe*, Suzanne Gordon notes that workers in other industrialized countries "enjoy—as a statutory right—longer vacations [than in the U.S.] from the moment they enter the work force. In Canada, workers are legally entitled to two weeks off their first year on the job. . . . After two or three years of employment, most get three weeks of vacation. After 10 years, it's up to four, and by 20 years, Canadian workers are off for five weeks. In Germany, statutes guarantee 18 days minimum for everyone, but most workers get five or six weeks. The same is true in Scandinavian countries, and in France."

In contrast to the extreme American emphasis on productivity 8 and commitment, which results in many workers, especially in professional-level jobs, not taking the vacations coming to them, Gordon notes that "In countries that are America's most successful competitors in the global marketplace, all working people, whether lawyers or teachers, CEOs or janitors, take the vacations to which they are entitled by law. 'No one in West Germany,' a West German embassy's officer explains, 'no matter how high up they are, would ever say they couldn't afford to take a vacation. Everyone takes their vacation.'"

And in Japan, where dedication to the job is legendary, Gordon 9 notes that the Japanese themselves are beginning to consider their national workaholism a serious social problem leading to stress-related illnesses and even death. As a result, the Japanese government recently established a commission whose goal is to promote shorter working hours and more leisure time.

Most other industrialized nations also have better family-leave 10 policies than the United States, and in a number of other countries workers benefit from innovative time-scheduling opportunities such as sabbaticals.

While the idea of a shorter workweek and longer vacations 11 sounds appealing to most people, any movement to enact shorter work-time as a public policy will encounter surprising pockets of resistance, not just from business leaders but even from some workers. Perhaps the most formidable barrier to more free time for Americans is the widespread mind-set that the 40-hour workweek, 8 hours a day, 5 days a week, 50 weeks a year, is a natural rhythm of the universe. This view is reinforced by the media's complete silence regarding the shorter work-time and more favorable vacation and family-leave policies of other countries. This lack of information, and our leaders' reluctance to suggest that the United States can learn from any other nation (except workaholic Japan) is one reason why more Americans don't identify overwork as a major problem or clamor for fewer hours and more vacation. Monika Bauerlein, a journalist originally from Germany now living in Minneapolis, exclaims, "I can't believe that people here aren't rioting in the streets over having only two weeks of vacation a year."

A second obstacle to launching a powerful shorter work-time movement is America's deeply ingrained work ethic, or its modern incarnation, the workaholic syndrome. The work ethic fosters the widely held belief that people's work is their most important activity and that people who do not work long and hard are lazy, unproductive, and worthless. 12

For many Americans today, paid work is not just a way to make money but is a crucial source of their self-worth. Many of us identify ourselves almost entirely by the kind of work we do. Work still has a powerful psychological and spiritual hold over our lives—and talk of shorter work-time may seem somehow morally suspicious. 13

Because we are so deeply a work-oriented society, leisure-time activities—such as play, relaxation, engaging in cultural and artistic pursuits, or just quiet contemplation and "doing nothing"— are not looked on as essential and worthwhile components of life. Of course, for the majority of working women who must work a second shift at home, much of the time spent outside of paid work is not leisure anyway. Also much of our non-work time is spent not just in personal renewal, but in building and maintaining essential social ties—with family, friends, and the larger community. 14

Today, as mothers and fathers spend more and more time on the job, we are beginning to recognize the deleterious effects— especially on our young people—of the breakdown of social ties and community in American life. But unfortunately, our nation reacts to these problems by calling for more paid professionals— more police, more psychiatrists, more experts—without recognizing the possibility that shorter work hours and more free time could enable us to do much of the necessary rebuilding and healing, with much more gratifying and longer-lasting results. 15

Of course, the stiffest opposition to cutting work hours comes not from citizens but from business. Employers are reluctant to alter the 8-hour day, 40-hour workweek, 50 weeks a year because it seems easier and more profitable for employers to hire fewer employees for longer hours rather than more employees—each of whom would also require health insurance and other benefits— with flexible schedules and work arrangements. 16

Harvard University economist Juliet B. Schor, who has been 17 studying issues of work and leisure in America, reminds us that we cannot ignore the larger relationship between unemployment and overwork: While many of us work too much, others are unable to find paid work at all. Schor points out that "workers who work longer hours lose more income when they lose their jobs. The threat of job loss is an important determinant of management's power on the shop floor." A system that offers only two options—long work hours or unemployment—serves as both a carrot and a stick. Those lucky enough to get full-time jobs are bribed into docile compliance with the boss, while the spectre of unemployment always looms as the ultimate punishment for the unruly.

Some observers suggest that keeping people divided into "the 18 employed" and "the unemployed" creates feelings of resentment and inferiority/superiority between the two groups, thus focusing their discontent and blame on each other rather than on the corporations and political figures who actually dictate our nation's economic policies.

Our role as consumers contributes to keeping the average work 19 week from falling. In an economic system in which addictive buying is the basis for corporate profits, working a full 40 hours or more each week for 50 weeks a year gives us just enough time to stumble home and dazedly—almost automatically—shop; but not enough time to think about deeper issues or to work effectively for social change. From the point of view of corporations and policymakers, shorter worktime may be bad for the economy, because people with enhanced free time may begin to find other things to do with it besides mindlessly buying products. It takes more free time to grow vegetables, cook meals from scratch, sew clothes, or repair broken items than it does to just buy these things at the mall.

Any serious proposal to give employed Americans a break by 20 cutting into the eight-hour work day is certain to be met with anguished cries about international competitiveness. The United States seems gripped by the fear that our nation has lost its economic dominance, and pundits, policymakers, and business leaders tell us that no sacrifice is too great if it puts America on top again.

As arguments like this are put forward (and we can expect them 21 to increase in the years to come), we need to remember two things. First, even if America maintained its dominance (whatever that means) and the economy were booming again, this would be no guarantee that the gains—be they in wages, in employment opportunities, or in leisure—would be distributed equitably between upper management and everyone else. Second, the entire issue of competitiveness is suspect when it pits poorly treated workers in one country against poorly treated workers in another; and when the vast majority of economic power, anyway, is in the control of enormous multinational corporations that have no loyalty to the people of any land.

Questions for Study and Discussion

1. According to Brandt, why has technology contributed to the problem of overwork in the United States instead of improved it?
2. What are some of the reasons that it will be difficult to enact a shorter workweek in the United States?
3. What does Brandt mean by the term "workaholic syndrome"? (paragraph 12) How is it related to America's work ethic?
4. What is Brandt's thesis? (Glossary: *Thesis*) Is it stated or implied?
5. What does Brandt accomplish in paragraphs 5–9? Why is the information relevant to her argument?
6. Analyze the structure of Brandt's essay, paragraph by paragraph. How does she organize her essay in order to best argue her opinion? (Glossary: *Organization*)

Vocabulary

Refer to your dictionary to define the following words as they are used in this selection. Then use each word in a sentence of your own.

detriment (2)	statutory (7)
spate (3)	workaholism (9)

clamor (11)   docile (17)
deleterious (15)   pundits (20)
determinant (17)

Suggested Writing Assignments

1. How long a workweek and how many weeks of vacation do you think represents the best compromise between productivity and adequate leisure time? Write an essay in which you argue for your "ideal" workweek. Imagine that your audience will be the management of a large corporation that currently maintains long workweeks and short vacations.

2. Write an argument paper in favor of fewer years of education in America, either in secondary school or college. How would students and the rest of society benefit? In what ways would it be better than maintaining the number of years that young people now devote to an education? Use Brandt's essay as a model, and be sure to acknowledge and effectively counter expected objections to each point you raise.

ABORTION IS TOO COMPLEX TO FEEL ALL ONE WAY ABOUT

Anna Quindlen

Columnist Anna Quindlen was born in 1952, and after graduating from Barnard College, she began her newspaper career at the New York Post. *Later she moved to the* New York Times *where she wrote the column "About New York," then was made deputy metropolitan editor at the age of thirty-one. Quindlen has contributed to the "Hers" column and for several years wrote the column "Life in the Thirties," in which she reflected on marriage, motherhood, secret desires and self-doubt, drawing on her own family for inspiration. The best of these columns were selected for her books* Living Out Loud *(1988) and* Object Lessons *(1991). In the following essay, which first ran in the* Times *as a "Life in the Thirties" column, Quindlen shares her struggle to come to some definite position on the issue of abortion.*

It was always the look on their faces that told me first. I was the freshman dormitory counselor and they were the freshmen at a women's college where everyone was smart. One of them could come into my room, a golden girl, a valedictorian, an 800 verbal score on the SATs, and her eyes would be empty, seeing only a busted future, the devastation of her life as she knew it. She had failed biology, messed up the math; she was pregnant.

That was when I became pro-choice.

It was the look in his eyes that I will always remember, too. They were as black as the bottom of a well, and in them for a few minutes I thought I saw myself the way I had always wished to be—clear, simple, elemental, at peace. My child looked at me and I looked back at him in the delivery room, and I realized that out of a sea of infinite possibilities it had come down to this: a specific person born on the hottest day of the year, conceived on a Christmas Eve, made by his father and me miraculously from scratch.

Once I believed that there was a little blob of formless protoplasm in there and a gynecologist went after it with a surgical instrument, and that was that. Then I got pregnant myself—eagerly, intentionally, by the right man, at the right time—and I began to doubt. My abdomen still flat, my stomach roiling with morning sickness, I felt not that I had protoplasm inside but instead a complete human being in miniature to whom I could talk, sing, make promises. Neither of these views was accurate; instead, I think, the reality is something in the middle. And there is where I find myself now, in the middle, hating the idea of abortions, hating the idea of having them outlawed.

For I know it is the right thing in some times and places. I remember sitting in a shabby clinic far uptown with one of those freshman, only three months after the Supreme Court had made what we were doing possible, and watching with wonder as the lovely first love she had had with a nice boy unraveled over the space of an hour as they waited for her to be called, degenerated into sniping and silences. I remember a year or two later seeing them pass on campus and not even acknowledge one another because their conjoining had caused them so much pain, and I shuddered to think of them married, with a small psyche in their unready and unwilling hands.

I've met 14-year-olds who were pregnant and said they could not have abortions because of their religion, and I see in their eyes the shadows of 22-year-olds I've talked to who lost their kids to foster care because they hit them or used drugs or simply had no money for food and shelter. I read not long ago about a teenager who said she meant to have an abortion but she spent the money on clothes instead; now she has a baby who turns out to be a lot more trouble than a toy. The people who hand out those execrable little pictures of dismembered fetuses at abortion clinics seem to forget the extraordinary pain children may endure after they are born when they are unwanted, even hated or simply tolerated.

I believe that in a contest between the living and the almost living, the latter must, if necessary, give way to the will of the former. That is what the fetus is to me, the almost living. Yet these questions began to plague me—and, I've discovered, a good many other women—after I became pregnant. But they became even more acute after I had my second child, mainly because he is so different from his brother. On two random nights 18 months apart the same two people managed to conceive, and on one occasion the tumult within turned itself into a curly-haired brunet with merry black eyes who walked and talked late and loved the whole world, and on another it became a blond with hazel Asian eyes and a pug nose who tried to conquer the world almost as soon as he entered it.

If we were to have an abortion next time for some reason or another, which infinite possibility becomes, not a reality, but a nullity? The girl with the blue eyes? The improbable redhead? The natural athlete? The thinker? My husband, ever at the heart of the matter, put it another way. Knowing that he is finding two children somewhat more overwhelming than he expected, I asked if he would want me to have an abortion if I accidentally became pregnant again right away. "And waste a perfectly good human being?" he said.   8

Coming to this quandary has been difficult for me. In fact, I believe the issue of abortion is difficult for all thoughtful people. I don't know anyone who has had an abortion who has not been haunted by it. If there is one thing I find intolerable about most of the so-called right-to-lifers, it is that they try to portray abortion rights as something that feminists thought up on a slow Saturday over a light lunch. That is nonsense. I also know that some people who support abortion rights are most comfortable with a monolithic position because it seems the strongest front against the smug and sometimes violent opposition.   9

But I don't feel all one way about abortion anymore, and I don't think it serves a just cause to pretend that many of us do. For years I believed that a woman's right to choose was absolute, but now I wonder. Do I, with a stable home and marriage and sufficient stamina and money, have the right to choose abortion because a pregnancy is inconvenient right now? Legally I do have that right; legally I want always to have that right. It is the morality of exercising it under those circumstances that makes me wonder.   10

Technology has foiled us. The second trimester has become a time of resurrection; a fetus at six months can be one woman's   11 late abortion, another's premature, viable child. Photographers now have film of embryos the size of a grape, oddly human, flexing their fingers, sucking their thumbs. Women have amniocentesis to find out whether they are carrying a child with birth defects that they may choose to abort. Before the procedure, they must have a sonogram, one of those fuzzy black-and-white photos like a love song heard through static on the radio, which shows someone is in there.

I have taped on my VCR a public-television program in which 12 somehow, inexplicably, a film is shown of a fetus in utero scratching its face, seemingly putting up a tiny hand to shield itself from the camera's eye. It would make a potent weapon in the arsenal of the antiabortionists. I grow sentimental about it as it floats in the salt water, part fish, part human being. It is almost living, but not quite. It has almost turned my heart around, but not quite turned my head.

Questions for Study and Discussion

1. Exactly what is the "ambiguity" of the abortion issue as far as Quindlen is concerned?

2. What kind of language does Quindlen use to describe the different participants in the abortion debate? (Glossary: *Diction*) Citing examples of her diction from the essay, discuss Quindlen's attitudes toward the members of the different groups she names. Who are the "thoughtful" people Quindlen describes? Does she count herself among them? How do you know?

3. Although Quindlen faces the "quandary" of the abortion issue, she has in fact taken a position. What is it? Does she offer any reasons for taking this position? Explain.

4. Cite examples of Quindlen's use of rational and emotional appeals. What is characteristic of each kind of appeal? Which did you find more convincing? In what ways are her appeals appropriate or inappropriate to her subject? Explain.

5. Quindlen wrote this essay for a liberal, educated, mostly middle-class audience. (Glossary: *Audience*) What risks did

she take in writing such an article for this audience? Why do you suppose she was willing to take such risks? What does she want her readers to do?

Vocabulary

Refer to your dictionary to define the following words as they are used in this selection. Then use each word in a sentence of your own.

valedictorian (1)	tumult (7)
elemental (3)	nullity (8)
protoplasm (4)	quandary (9)
unraveled (5)	monolithic (9)
sniping (5)	stamina (10)
conjoining (5)	amniocentesis (11)
execrable (6)	

Suggested Writing Assignments

1. The above column generated many letters to the editor. In a brief essay, write a letter of your own in which you express your reaction to Quindlen's essay. What kinds of appeals will you use to support your position? Can you make a good argument for your position using only rational or only emotional appeals?

2. Participants on both sides of the abortion debate have objected to the labels the other side uses to describe themselves. They say the press has an obligation not to use terms a group designates for itself, especially if that term makes assumptions about the thinking or attitude of the other side. What is your reaction to the terms "Pro-Life" and "Pro-Choice"? What do these terms imply about the group so labelling itself, and what do they imply about the opposition? Can you think of other terms to describe the two major positions on legalized abortion that are less loaded? Write an essay in which you argue for or against the use of the labels "Pro-Life" and "Pro-Choice."

EXPOSING MEDIA MYTHS:
TV DOESN'T AFFECT YOU AS MUCH
AS YOU THINK

Joanmarie Kalter

Joanmarie Kalter was born in Mineola, New York, in 1951. After graduating from Cornell University, she worked as a book editor for Belmont-Tower for two years. She began her free-lance writing career in 1976, and has written many pieces about the television and entertainment industries. In the following selection, note how she uses her evidence to chip away at some "false truths" about television news.

Once upon a time, there was a new invention—television. It became so popular, so quickly, that more American homes now have a TV set (98 percent) than an indoor toilet (97 percent). Around this new invention, then, an industry rapidly grew, and around this industry, a whole mythology. It has become a virtual truism, often heard and often repeated, that TV—and TV news, in particular—has an unparalleled influence on our lives.

Over the past 20 years, however, communications scholars have been quietly examining such truisms and have discovered, sometimes to their surprise, that many are not so true at all. *TV Guide* asked more than a dozen leading researchers for their findings and found an eye-opening collection of mythbusters. Indeed, they suggest that an entire body of political strategy and debate has been built upon false premises. . . .

Myth No. 1: Two-thirds of the American people receive most of their news from TV. This little canard is at the heart of our story. It can be traced to the now-famous Roper polls, in which Americans are queried: "I'd like to ask you where you usually get most of your news about what's going on in the world today. . . ." In 1959, when the poll was first conducted, 51 percent answered "television," with a steady increase ever since. The latest results

421

show that 66 percent say they get most of their news from TV; only about a third credit newspapers.

Trouble is, that innocent poll question is downright impossible to answer. Just consider: it asks you to sort through the issues in your mind, pinpoint what and where you learned about each, tag it, and come up with a final score. Not too many of us can do it, especially since we get our news from a variety of sources. Even pollster Burns Roper concedes, "Memories do get fuzzy."

Scholars have found, however, that when they ask a less general, more specific question—Did you read a newspaper yesterday? Did you watch a TV news show yesterday?—the results are quite different. Dr. John Robinson, professor of sociology at the University of Maryland, found that on a typical day 67 percent read a newspaper, while 52 percent see a local or national TV newscast. Dr. Robert Stevenson, professor of journalism at the University of North Carolina, analyzed detailed diaries of TV use, and further found that only 18 percent watch network news on an average day, and only 13 percent pay full attention to it. Says Robinson, "TV is part of our overall mix, but in no way is it our number one source of news."

Yet it's a myth with disturbing consequences. Indeed, it is so widespread, says Dr. Mark Levy, associate professor of journalism at the University of Maryland, that it shapes—or misshapes—our political process. In the words of Michael Deaver, White House deputy chief of staff during President Reagan's first term, "The majority of the people get their news from television, so . . . we construct events and craft photos that are designed for 30 seconds to a minute so that it can fit into that 'bite' on the evening news." And thus the myth, says Levy, "distorts the very dialogue of democracy, which cannot be responsibly conducted in 30-second bites."

Myth No. 2: TV news sets the public agenda. It was first said succinctly in 1963, and has long been accepted: while the mass media may not tell us what to think, they definitely tell us what to think about. And on some issues, the impact of TV is indisputable: the Ethiopian famine, the Challenger explosion. Yet for the more routine story, new research has challenged that myth, suggesting TV's influence may be surprisingly more limited.

For one thing, TV news most often reacts to newspapers in framing issues of public concern. Dr. David Weaver, professor of journalism at Indiana University, found that newspapers led TV through the 1976 campaign. Given the brevity of broadcasts, of course, that's understandable. "TV has no page 36," explains Dr. Maxwell McCombs, professor of communications at the University of Texas. "So TV journalists have to wait until an issue has already achieved substantial public interest." TV, then, does not so much set the public agenda as spotlight it.

Even among those issues spotlighted, viewers do make inde- 9 pendent judgments. It seems the old "hypodermic" notions no longer hold, says Dr. Doris Graber, political science professor at the University of Illinois. "We're not sponges for this stuff, and while TV may provide the raw material, people do select."

Indeed, even TV entertainment is less influential than once 10 was thought. According to Robinson, studies found no difference in racial attitudes among those who saw *Roots* and those who didn't. Ditto "The Day After" on nuclear war, and *Amerika* on the Soviets. As for news, Graber notes that the public took a long time to share the media's concern about Watergate, and even now are lagging the media on Iran-Contragate. And finally, there are many issues on which the press must belatedly catch up with the public. Which brings us to . . .

Myth No. 3: TV news changed public opinion about the war in 11 Vietnam. Contrary to this most common of beliefs, research shows just the opposite. Lawrence Lichty, professor of radio/television/ film at Northwestern University, analyzed network war coverage and found that it did not become relatively critical until 1967. By then, however, a majority of Americans already thought U.S. involvement in Vietnam was a mistake. And they thought so not because of TV coverage, but because of the number of young Americans dying.

Yet this fable about the "living-room war" is so accepted it has 12 become "fact": that gory TV pictures of bloody battles undermined public support for the war; that, in a 1968 TV-news special, Walter Cronkite mistakenly presented the Tet offensive as a defeat for the U.S.; and that, because President Johnson so believed in the power of TV, he concluded then that his war effort was lost.

In fact, Lichty found few "gory" pictures. "TV presented a dis- 13 tant view," he says, with less than five percent of TV's war reports showing heavy combat. Nor, as we now know, was a rapt audience watching at home in their living rooms. As for Cronkite's report on the Tet offensive, the CBS anchor said on the evening news, "First and simplest, the Vietcong suffered a military defeat." And, in his now-famous TV special, Cronkite concluded, "we are mired in a stalemate," and should "negotiate." By that time, Lichty says, "public opinion had been on a downward trend for a year and a half. A majority of Americans agreed." And so Johnson's concern, it seems, was not that Cronkite would influence public opinion, but rather that he reflected it.

Indeed, Prof. John Mueller of the University of Rochester has compared the curve of public opinion on the war in Vietnam, covered by TV, with that of the war in Korea, hardly covered. He found the two curves strikingly similar: in both cases, public support dropped as the number of American deaths rose.

Disturbingly, the misconception about TV's influence in Vietnam has had broad consequences, for it has framed an important debate ever since. Can a democratic society, with a free flow of dramatic TV footage, retain the public will to fight a war? Many argue no. And this has been the rationale more recently for censoring the Western press in the Falklands and Grenada. Yet it is, says Lichty, a policy based on a myth.

Myth No. 4: TV today is the most effective medium in communicating news. Most of us think of TV fare as simple, direct, easy to understand—with the combination of words and pictures making it all the more powerful. But recent research shows that TV news, as distinct from entertainment, is often very confusing. In study after study, Robinson and Levy have found that viewers understand only about a third of network news stories.

Why is TV news so tough to understand? Dr. Dan Drew, professor of journalism at Indiana University, suggests that the verbal and visual often conflict. Unlike TV entertainment, in which the two are composed together, TV-news footage is gathered first, and the story it illustrates often diverges. We may see fighting across the Green Line in Beirut—for a story about peace talks. We may see "file footage" of Anglican envoy Terry Waite walking down the street—for a story on his disappearance. As viewers try to make sense of the visual, they lose the gist of the verbal. "The myth," says Levy, "is that since we are a visual medium, we must always have pictures. . . . But that's a disaster, a recipe for poor communication."

Journalists also are much more familiar with the world of public affairs, says Levy, and rely on its technical jargon: from "leading economic indicators" to "the Druse militia." Their stories, say researchers, are overillustrated, with most pictures on the screen for less than 20 seconds. They assume, mistakenly, that viewers pay complete attention, and so they often do not repeat the main theme. Yet while understanding TV news takes concentration, watching TV is full of distractions. In one study, researchers mounted cameras on top of sets and recorded the amount of time viewers also read, talked, walked in and out of the room. They concluded that viewers actually watch only 55 percent of what's on.

The audience does recall the extraordinary, such as a man on the moon, and better comprehends human-interest stories. But since most news is not covered night after night, tomorrow's broadcast tends to wash away today's. "People don't remember much from TV news," says Graber. "It's like the ocean washing over traces that have been very faintly formed." 19

Today's TV news is carefully watched by politicians, who keep a sharp eye on how they're covered. But while it may provide theater for a handful, this research increasingly shows it's lost on the American public. And sadly, then, hard-working TV journalists may be missing an opportunity to inform. 20

Yet TV remains a medium with great potential. And studies show that it does extend the awareness of the poor and ill-educated, who cannot afford additional sources. What's more, research suggests that the clarity of TV news can be improved— without compromising journalistic standards. "We have been glitzed by the glamour of TV, all these gee-whiz gimmicks," says Robinson. "And we have lost sight of one of the oldest and most durable findings of communications research. . . . The most important element is the writer, who sits at a typewriter and tries to tell the story in a simple and organized way. That's the crucial link." 21

Research also shows that viewers want a broadcast they can understand. The success of "60 Minutes" proves there's an audience still hungry for sophisticated factual information. "When someone does this for news, they'll grab the ratings," says Levy. "Nobody loses!" Ironically, no corporation would launch an ad campaign without extensive testing on how best to reach its audience. But many broadcast journalists, working under intense pressure, remain unaware of the problems. "There's a lot we have 22 to learn about how people comprehend," says William Rubens, NBC research vice-president. "But no, it hasn't been the thrust of our research." According to Robinson and Levy, this requires the attention of those in charge, a collective corporate will. With the networks under a financial squeeze, their news audiences having recently declined some 15 percent, "This may be the time for them to rethink their broadcasts," says Levy.

And if they do, they may just live . . . happily ever after. 23

Questions for Study and Discussion

1. Kalter uses the term "myth" to describe assumptions about TV news. Look up the definition of myth in your dictionary. How does the use of this term help Kalter influence her audience? (Glossary: *Audience*)

2. How can general survey questions lead to inaccurate data? How have the Roper polls contributed to the myths about television news?

3. According to Kalter, why is it a myth that TV news changed public opinion about the Vietnam War? What are the broad consequences of this myth?

4. Kalter begins by discussing television—and her title implies that the article is about television in general—but the focus of her article is television news. (Glossary: *Focus*) In what ways does narrowing her focus help her argue her point?

5. How does Kalter organize her argument in paragraphs 16–20? (Glossary: *Argumentation*) What does each paragraph accomplish? (Glossary: *Paragraph*)

6. In what ways does TV remain a "medium with great potential"? How can TV news be changed to make it more effective? Why hasn't it been changed in the past?

Vocabulary

Refer to your dictionary to define the following words as they are used in this selection. Then use each word in a sentence of your own.

truism (1)   rapt (13)
canard (3)   rationale (15)
succinctly (7)   gist (17)
brevity (8)   glitzed (21)

Suggested Writing Assignments

1. How much has television—and television news in particular—affected you? Write an argument paper in which you either agree with Kalter's argument or disagree based on your personal experiences.

2. How would you change television news in order to make it more effective for you? Write a letter to the head of a network news show in which you argue for your proposed changes in the format of the show.

DEATH AND JUSTICE: HOW CAPITAL PUNISHMENT AFFIRMS LIFE

Edward I. Koch

Democrat Edward I. Koch was mayor of New York City from 1978 to 1990. A New Yorker by birth, Koch quickly established himself as a no-holds-barred, nothing-left-unsaid, tough-guy spokesman for the people he served. He led his city through a period of economic and social change characterized by labor strikes, a rise in violent street crime, and unemployment. Koch has written the following books: Mayor *(1984),* Politics *(1985),* All the Best Letters from a Feisty Mayor *(1990), and* Citizen Koch: An Autobiography *(1992). In the following article, which first appeared in the* New Republic *in April 1985, Koch argues in favor of the death penalty. Using a technique in keeping with his personality, Koch sets up his opponents' arguments like so many cans on a fence and then attempts to shoot them full of holes. As you read his essay, notice how he uses facts, statistics, quotations, and numerous examples to develop his paragraphs.*

Last December a man named Robert Lee Willie, who had been convicted of raping and murdering an 18-year-old woman, was executed in the Louisiana state prison. In a statement issued several minutes before his death, Mr. Willie said: "Killing people is wrong. . . . It makes no difference whether it's citizens, countries, or governments. Killing is wrong." Two weeks later in South Carolina, an admitted killer named Joseph Carl Shaw was put to death for murdering two teenagers. In an appeal to the governor for clemency, Mr. Shaw wrote: "Killing is wrong when I did it. Killing is wrong when you do it. I hope you have the courage and moral strength to stop the killing."

It is a curiosity of modern life that we find ourselves being lectured on morality by cold-blooded killers. Mr. Willie previously had been convicted of aggravated rape, aggravated kidnapping, and the murders of a Louisiana deputy and a man from Missouri. Mr. Shaw committed another murder a week before the two for which he was executed, and admitted mutilating the body of the 14-year-old girl he killed. I can't help wondering what prompted these murderers to speak out against killing as they entered the deathhouse door. Did their newfound reverence for life stem from the realization that they were about to lose their own?

Life is indeed precious, and I believe the death penalty helps to affirm this fact. Had the death penalty been a real possibility in the minds of these murderers, they might well have stayed their hand. They might have shown moral awareness before their victims died, and not after. Consider the tragic death of Rosa Velez, who happened to be home when a man named Luis Vera burglarized her apartment in Brooklyn. "Yeah, I shot her," Vera admitted. "She knew me, and I knew I wouldn't go to the chair." 3

During my twenty-two years in public service, I have heard the pros and cons of capital punishment expressed with special intensity. As a district leader, councilman, congressman, and mayor, I have represented constituencies generally thought of as liberal. Because I support the death penalty for heinous crimes of murder, I have sometimes been the subject of emotional and outraged attacks by voters who find my position reprehensible or worse. I have listened to their ideas. I have weighed their objections carefully. I still support the death penalty. The reasons I maintain my position can be best understood by examining the arguments most frequently heard in opposition. 4

1. The death penalty is "barbaric." Sometimes opponents of capital punishment horrify with tales of lingering death on the gallows, of faulty electric chairs, or of agony in the gas chamber. Partly in response to such protests, several states such as North Carolina and Texas switched to execution by lethal injection. The condemned person is put to death painlessly, without ropes, voltage, bullets, or gas. Did this answer the objections of death penalty opponents? Of course not. On June 22, 1984, the *New York Times* published an editorial that sarcastically attacked the new "hygienic" method of death by injection, and stated that "execution can never be made humane through science." So it's not the method that really troubles opponents. It's the death itself they consider barbaric. 5

Admittedly, capital punishment is not a pleasant topic. How-   6
ever, one does not have to like the death penalty in order to support it any more than one must like radical surgery, radiation, or
chemotherapy in order to find necessary these attempts at curing
cancer. Ultimately we may learn how to cure cancer with a simple
pill. Unfortunately, that day has not yet arrived. Today we are
faced with the choice of letting the cancer spread or trying to cure
it with the methods available, methods that one day will almost
certainly be considered barbaric. But to give up and do nothing
would be far more barbaric and would certainly delay the discovery of an eventual cure. The analogy between cancer and murder is imperfect, because murder is not the "disease" we are trying
to cure. The disease is injustice. We may not like the death penalty, but it must be available to punish crimes of cold-blooded
murder, cases in which any other form of punishment would be
inadequate and, therefore, unjust. If we create a society in which
injustice is not tolerated, incidents of murder—the most flagrant
form of injustice—will diminish.

2. No other major democracy uses the death penalty. No other ma-   7
jor democracy—in fact, few other countries of any description—
are plagued by a murder rate such as that in the United States.
Fewer and fewer Americans can remember the days when unlocked doors were the norm and murder was a rare and terrible
offense. In America the murder rate climbed 122 percent between
1963 and 1980. During that same period, the murder rate in New
York City increased by almost 400 percent, and the statistics are
even worse in many other cities. A study at M.I.T. showed that
based on 1970 homicide rates a person who lived in a large American city ran a greater risk of being murdered than an American
soldier in World War II ran of being killed in combat. It is not surprising that the laws of each country differ according to differing
conditions and traditions. If other countries had our murder
problem, the cry for capital punishment would be just as loud as
it is here. And I daresay that any other major democracy where 75
percent of the people supported the death penalty would soon
enact it into law.

3. An innocent person might be executed by mistake. Consider   8
the work of Hugo Adam Bedau, one of the most implacable foes
of capital punishment in this country. According to Mr. Bedau,
it is "false sentimentality to argue that the death penalty should

be abolished because of the abstract possibility that an innocent person might be executed." He cites a study of the 7,000 executions in this country from 1893 to 1971, and concludes that the record fails to show that such cases occur. The main point, however, is this. If government functioned only when the possibility of error didn't exist, government wouldn't function at all. Human life deserves special protection, and one of the best ways to guarantee that protection is to assure that convicted murderers do not kill again. Only the death penalty can accomplish this end. In a recent case in New Jersey, a man named Richard Biegenwald was freed from prison after serving 18 years for murder; since his release he has been convicted of committing four murders. A prisoner named Lemuel Smith, who, while serving four life sentences for murder (plus two life sentences for kidnapping and robbery) in New York's Green Haven Prison, lured a woman corrections officer into the chaplain's office and strangled her. He then mutilated and dismembered her body. An additional life sentence for Smith is meaningless. Because New York has no death penalty statute, Smith has effectively been given a license to kill.

But the problem of multiple murder is not confined to the nation's penitentiaries. In 1981, 91 police officers were killed in the line of duty in this country. Seven percent of those arrested in the cases that have been solved had a previous arrest for murder. In New York City in 1976 and 1977, 85 persons arrested for homicide had a previous arrest for murder. Six of these individuals had two previous arrests for murder, and one had four previous murder arrests. During those two years the New York police were arresting for murder persons with a previous arrest for murder on the average of one every 8.5 days. This is not surprising when we learn that in 1975, for example, the median time served in Massachusetts for homicide was less than two and a half years. In 1976 a study sponsored by the Twentieth Century Fund found that the average time served in the United States for first-degree murder is ten years. The median time served may be considerably lower.

4. *Capital punishment cheapens the value of human life.* On the contrary, it can be easily demonstrated that the death penalty strengthens the value of human life. If the penalty for rape were lowered, clearly it would signal a lessened regard for the victims'

suffering, humiliation, and personal integrity. It would cheapen their horrible experience, and expose them to an increased danger of recurrence. When we lower the penalty for murder, it signals a lessened regard for the value of the victim's life. Some critics of capital punishment, such as columnist Jimmy Breslin, have suggested that a life sentence is actually a harsher penalty for murder than death. This is sophistic nonsense. A few killers may decide not to appeal a death sentence, but the overwhelming majority make every effort to stay alive. It is by exacting the highest penalty for the taking of human life that we affirm the highest value of human life.

5. *The death penalty is applied in a discriminatory manner.* This factor no longer seems to be the problem it once was. The appeals process for a condemned prisoner is lengthy and painstaking. Every effort is made to see that the verdict and sentence were fairly arrived at. However, assertions of discrimination are not an argument for ending the death penalty but for extending it. It is not justice to exclude everyone from the penalty of the law if a few are found to be so favored. Justice requires that the law be applied equally to all.

6. *Thou Shalt Not Kill.* The Bible is our greatest source of moral inspiration. Opponents of the death penalty frequently cite the sixth of the Ten Commandments in an attempt to prove that capital punishment is divinely proscribed. In the original Hebrew, however, the Sixth Commandment reads "Thou Shalt Not Commit Murder," and the Torah specifies capital punishment for a variety of offenses. The biblical viewpoint has been upheld by philosophers throughout history. The greatest thinkers of the 19th century—Kant, Locke, Hobbes, Rousseau, Montesquieu, and Mill—agreed that natural law properly authorizes the sovereign to take life in order to vindicate justice. Only Jeremy Bentham was ambivalent. Washington, Jefferson, and Franklin endorsed it. Abraham Lincoln authorized executions for deserters in wartime. Alexis de Tocqueville, who expressed profound respect for American institutions, believed that the death penalty was indispensable to the support of social order. The United States Constitution, widely admired as one of the seminal achievements in the history of humanity, condemns cruel and inhuman punishment, but does not condemn capital punishment.

7. The death penalty is state-sanctioned murder. This is the defense with which Messrs. Willie and Shaw hoped to soften the resolve of those who sentenced them to death. By saying in effect, "You're no better than I am," the murderer seeks to bring his accusers down to his own level. It is also a popular argument among opponents of capital punishment, but a transparently false one. Simply put, the state has rights that the private individual does not. In a democracy, those rights are given to the state by the electorate. The execution of a lawfully condemned killer is no more an act of murder than is legal imprisonment an act of kidnapping. If an individual forces a neighbor to pay him money under threat of punishment, it's called extortion. If the state does it, it's called taxation. Rights and responsibilities surrendered by the individual are what give the state its power to govern. This contract is the foundation of civilization itself.   13

Everyone wants his or her rights, and will defend them jealously. Not everyone, however, wants responsibilities, especially the painful responsibilities that come with law enforcement. Twenty-one years ago a woman named Kitty Genovese was assaulted and murdered on a street in New York. Dozens of neighbors heard her cries for help but did nothing to assist her. They didn't even call the police. In such a climate the criminal understandably grows bolder. In the presence of moral cowardice, he lectures us on our supposed failings and tries to equate his crimes with our quest for justice.   14

The death of anyone—even a convicted killer—diminishes us all. But we are diminished even more by a justice system that fails to function. It is an illusion to let ourselves believe that doing away with capital punishment removes the murderer's deed from our conscience. The rights of society are paramount. When we protect guilty lives, we give up innocent lives in exchange. When opponents of capital punishment say to the state, "I will not let you kill in my name," they are also saying to murderers: "You can kill in your *own* name as long as I have an excuse for not getting involved."   15

It is hard to imagine anything worse than being murdered while neighbors do nothing. But something worse exists. When those same neighbors shrink back from justly punishing the murderer, the victim dies twice.   16

Questions for Study and Discussion

1. In your own words, what is Koch's thesis, and where does he present it?

2. Is Koch's argument in favor of capital punishment based more on his desire for punishment or on his belief that it functions as a deterrent? Cite references from the text to support your answer.

3. How do paragraphs 1–3 function in the context of Koch's essay? Could Koch have made his argument just as effectively without them? Explain.

4. What kinds of evidence does Koch use to support his arguments for the death penalty? How does Koch organize his evidence within each paragraph? Which kinds of evidence did you find the most convincing? Why?

5. Koch begins paragraphs 5, 7, 8, 10, 11, 12 and 13 with his opponent's argument against capital punishment. How well does this strategy work? Did you find Koch's refutation of each of these arguments convincing? Explain why or why not.

6. Identify the analogy that Koch uses in paragraph 6. (Glossary: *Analogy*) Explain how the analogy works in the context of Koch's argument?

7. Explain the meaning of Koch's title. In what ways can the death penalty actually affirm that which it so blatantly snuffs out?

Vocabulary

Refer to your dictionary to define the following words as they are used in this selection. Then use each word in a sentence of your own.

clemency (1)	median (9)
constituencies (4)	sophistic (10)
heinous (4)	proscribed (12)
reprehensible (4)	ambivalent (12)
lethal (5)	seminal (12)
implacable (8)	extortion (13)

Suggested Writing Assignments

1. Koch supports the death penalty for what he calls "heinous crimes of murder." What do you suppose Koch means by "heinous crimes of murder"? If a society can decide in favor of the death penalty, how does it then decide which crimes will be so punished? Write an essay in which you present your thinking on this issue.

2. In a letter to the editor, argue against Koch's proposal. What materials in Koch's essay can you turn to your own use? What kinds of appeals will you make to your audience? Can it be argued that the death penalty is nothing more than legalized murder?

THE DEATH PENALTY IS A STEP BACK

Coretta Scott King

Coretta Scott King was the spouse of civil rights leader Martin Luther King, Jr., who was assassinated in 1968. Born in Heiberger, Alabama, on April 27, 1927, she graduated from Antioch College with a degree in music and education. She met her future husband while pursuing an advanced degree in music at the New England Conservatory of Music in Boston. In keeping with the philosophy of nonviolence that they both promoted during the civil rights struggle, she continues to oppose the execution of violent criminals. She argues that our legal system is dangerously imperfect—far too imperfect to have the authority to legally put someone to death.

When Steven Judy was executed in Indiana [in 1981], America took another step backwards towards legitimizing murder as a way of dealing with evil in our society.

Although Judy was convicted of four of the most horrible and brutal murders imaginable, and his case is probably the worst in recent memory for opponents of the death penalty, we still have to face the real issue squarely: Can we expect a decent society if the state is allowed to kill its own people?

In recent years, an increase of violence in America, both individual and political, has prompted a backlash of public opinion on capital punishment. But however much we abhor violence, legally sanctioned executions are no deterrent and are, in fact, immoral and unconstitutional.

Although I have suffered the loss of two family members by assassination, I remain firmly and unequivocally opposed to the death penalty for those convicted of capital offenses.

An evil deed is not redeemed by an evil deed of retaliation. ₅
Justice is never advanced in the taking of a human life.

Morality is never upheld by legalized murder. Morality apart, ₆
there are a number of practical reasons which form a powerful
argument against capital punishment.

First, capital punishment makes irrevocable any possible mis- ₇
carriage of justice. Time and again we have witnessed the specter
of mistakenly convicted people being put to death in the name of
American criminal justice. To those who say that, after all, this
doesn't occur too often, I can only reply that if it happens just
once, that is too often. And it has occurred many times.

Second, the death penalty reflects an unwarranted assumption ₈
that the wrongdoer is beyond rehabilitation. Perhaps some individuals cannot be rehabilitated; but who shall make that determination? Is any amount of academic training sufficient to en-
title one person to judge another incapable of rehabilitation?

Third, the death penalty is inequitable. Approximately half of ₉
the 711 persons now on death row are black. From 1930 through
1968, 53.5% of those executed were black Americans, all too
many of whom were represented by court-appointed attorneys
and convicted after hasty trials.

The argument that this may be an accurate reflection of guilt, ₁₀
and homicide trends, instead of a racist application of laws lacks
credibility in light of a recent Florida survey which showed that
persons convicted of killing whites were four times more likely to
receive a death sentence than those convicted of killing blacks.

Proponents of capital punishment often cite a "deterrent effect" ₁₁
as the main benefit of the death penalty. Not only is there no hard
evidence that murdering murderers will deter other potential killers, but even the "logic" of this argument defies comprehension.

Numerous studies show that the majority of homicides com- ₁₂
mitted in this country are the acts of the victim's relatives, friends
and acquaintances in the "heat of passion."

What this strongly suggests is that rational consideration of ₁₃
future consequences is seldom a part of the killer's attitude at the
time he commits a crime.

The only way to break the chain of violent reaction is to prac- ₁₄
tice nonviolence as individuals and collectively through our laws
and institutions.

Questions for Study and Discussion

1. What is King's thesis, and where does she present it? (Glossary: *Thesis*)
2. What are King's three main arguments against the death penalty? What evidence does she present to support each argument? (Glossary: *Evidence*).
3. Why has the death penalty gained more support from the public in recent years? Why is King a good spokesperson for opponents of the death penalty?
4. Why does King believe that capital punishment does not deter crime, as many proponents of capital punishment proclaim?
5. How does King propose to combat violence in our society?
6. If you are a proponent of the death penalty, do you find King's argument persuasive? (Glossary: *Audience*) Why, or why not?

Vocabulary

Refer to your dictionary to define the following words as they are used in this selection. Then use each word in a sentence of your own.

legitimizing (1)   irrevocable (7)
capital punishment (3)   miscarriage (7)
abhor (3)   specter (7)
sanctioned (3)   inequitable (9)
unequivocally (4)   deterrent (11)

Suggested Writing Assignments

1. Do you support or oppose the death penalty? Why? Have King's arguments influenced your opinion? Write an essay in which you argue for your position on this important issue.
2. King says that the increase in support for the death penalty has been caused by the increase in violent crime in our society. Write an essay in which you argue that solutions to this increase in violent crime need to be made in society rather than with our system of justice and punishment.

GLOSSARY OF USEFUL TERMS

Abstract   See *Concrete/Abstract.*

Allusion   An allusion is a passing reference to a familiar person, place, or thing often drawn from history, the Bible, mythology, or literature. An allusion is an economical way for a writer to capture the essence of an idea, atmosphere, emotion, or historical era, as in "The scandal was his Watergate" or "He saw himself as a modern Job" or "The campaign ended not with a bang but a whimper." An allusion should be familiar to the reader; if it is not, it will add nothing to the meaning.

Analogy   Analogy is a special form of comparison in which the writer explains something unfamiliar by comparing it to something familiar: "A transmission line is simply a pipeline for electricity. In the case of a water pipeline, more water will flow through the pipe as water pressure increases. The same is true of electricity in a transmission line."

Anecdote   An anecdote is a short narrative about an amusing or interesting event. Writers often use anecdotes to begin essays as well as to illustrate certain points.

Argumentation   Argumentation is one of the four basic types of prose. (Narration, description, and exposition are the other three.) To argue is to attempt to persuade a reader to agree with a point of view, to make a given decision, or to pursue a particular course of action. There are two basic types of argumentation: logical and persuasive. See the introduction to Chapter 18 (pp. 392–94) for a detailed discussion of argumentation.

Attitude   A writer's attitude reflects his or her opinion of a subject. The writer can think very positively or very negatively about a subject, or somewhere in between. See also *Tone.*

Audience   An audience is the intended readership for a piece of writing. For example, the readers of a national weekly news magazine come from all walks of life and have diverse interests, opinions, and educational backgrounds. In contrast, the readership for an organic chemistry journal is made up of people whose interests and education are quite similar. The essays in *Models for Writers* are intended for general readers, intelligent people who may lack specific information about the subject being discussed.

Beginnings and Endings   A beginning is that sentence, group of sentences, or section that introduces an essay. Good beginnings usually identify the thesis or controlling idea, attempt to interest readers, and establish a tone.

An ending is that sentence or group of sentences that brings an essay to a close. Good endings are purposeful and well planned. They can be a summary, a concluding example, an anecdote, or a quotation. Endings satisfy readers when they are the natural outgrowths of the essays themselves and give the readers a sense of finality or completion. Good essays do not simply stop; they conclude. See the introduction to Chapter 4 (pp. 69–73) for a detailed discussion of *Beginnings and Endings*.

Cause and Effect   Cause and effect analysis is a type of exposition that explains the reasons for an occurrence or the consequences of an action. See the introduction to Chapter 17 (pp. 372–73) for a detailed discussion of cause and effect. See also *Exposition*.

Classification   See *Division and Classification*.

Cliché   A cliché is an expression that has become ineffective through overuse. Expressions such as *quick as a flash, jump for joy,* and *slow as molasses* are clichés. Writers normally avoid such trite expressions and seek instead to express themselves in fresh and forceful language. See also *Diction*.

Coherence   Coherence is a quality of good writing that results when all sentences, paragraphs, and longer divisions of an essay are naturally connected. Coherent writing is achieved through (1) a logical sequence of ideas (arranged in chronological order, spatial order, order of importance, or some other appropriate order), (2) the purposeful repetition of key words and ideas, (3) a pace suitable for your topic and your reader, and (4) the use of transitional words and expressions. Coherence should not be confused with unity. (See *Unity*.) See also *Transitions*.

Colloquial Expressions   A colloquial expression is characteristic of or appropriate to spoken language or to writing that seeks its effect. Colloquial expressions are informal, as *chem, gym, come up with, be at loose ends, won't,* and *photo* illustrate. See also *Diction*. Thus, colloquial expressions are acceptable in formal writing only if they are used purposefully.

Comparison and Contrast   Comparison and contrast is a type of exposition in which the writer points out the similarities and differences between two or more subjects in the same class or category. The function of any comparison and contrast is to clarify—to reach some conclusion about the items being compared and contrasted. See the introduction to Chapter 16 (pp. 342–45) for a detailed discussion of comparison and contrast. See also *Exposition*.

Conclusions   See *Beginnings and Endings*.

Concrete/Abstract   A concrete word names a specific object, person, place, or action that can be directly perceived by the senses: *car, bread, building, book, John F. Kennedy, Chicago,* or *hiking*. An abstract word, in contrast, refers to general qualities, conditions, ideas, actions, or relationships that cannot be directly perceived by the senses: *bravery, dedication, excellence, anxiety, stress, thinking,* or *hatred*. See also the introduction to Chapter 8 (pp. 161–66).

Connotation/Denotation   Both connotation and denotation refer to the meanings of words. Denotation is the dictionary meaning of a word, the literal meaning. Connotation, on the other hand, is the implied or suggested meaning of a word. For example, the denotation of *lamb* is "a young sheep." The connotations of *lamb* are numerous: *gentle, docile, weak, peaceful, blessed, sacrificial, blood, spring, frisky, pure, innocent,* and so on. See also the introduction to Chapter 8 (pp. 161–66).

Controlling Idea   See *Thesis*.

Coordination   Coordination is the joining of grammatical constructions of the same rank (e.g., words, phrases, clauses) to indicate that they are of equal importance. For example, *They ate hotdogs,* and *we ate hamburgers*. See the introduction to Chapter 7 (pp. 136–40). See also *Subordination*.

Deduction   Deduction is the process of reasoning from stated premises to a conclusion that follows necessarily. This form of reasoning moves from the general to the specific. See the introduction to Chapter 18 (pp. 392–94) for a discussion of deductive reasoning and its relation to argumentation. See also *Syllogism*.

Definition   Definition is one of the types of exposition. Definition is a statement of the meaning of a word. A definition may be either brief or extended, part of an essay or an entire essay itself. See the introduction to Chapter 14 (pp. 297–98) for a detailed discussion of definition. See also *Exposition*.

Denotation   See *Connotation/Denotation*.

Description   Description is one of the four basic types of prose. (Narration, exposition, and argumentation are the other three.) Description tells how a person, place, or thing is perceived by the five senses. See the introduction to Chapter 12 (pp. 250–51) for a detailed discussion of description.

Dialogue   Conversation of two or more people as represented in writing. Dialogue is what people say directly to one another.

Diction   Diction refers to a writer's choice and use of words. Good diction is precise and appropriate—the words mean exactly what the writer intends, and the words are well suited to the writer's subject, intended audience, and purpose in writing. The word-conscious writer knows that there are differences among *aged, old,* and *elderly; blue, navy,* and *azure;* and *disturbed, angry,* and *irritated.* Furthermore, this writer knows in which situation to use each word. See the introduction to Chapter 8 (pp. 161–66) for a detailed discussion of diction. See also *Cliché, Colloquial Expressions, Connotation/Denotation, Jargon, Slang.*

Division and Classification.   Division and classification is one of the types of exposition. When dividing and classifying, the writer first establishes categories and then arranges or sorts people, places, or things into these categories according to their different characteristics, thus making them more manageable for the writer and more understandable and meaningful for the reader. See the introduction to Chapter 15 (pp. 318–19) for a detailed discussion of division and classification. See also *Exposition.*

Dominant Impression   A dominant impression is the single mood, atmosphere, or quality a writer emphasizes in a piece of descriptive writing. The dominant impression is created through the careful selection of details and is, of course, influenced by the writer's subject, audience, and purpose. See also the introduction to Chapter 12 (pp. 250–51).

Emphasis   Emphasis is the placement of important ideas and words within sentences and longer units of writing so that they have the greatest impact. In general, what comes at the end has the most impact, and at the beginning nearly as much; what comes in the middle gets the least emphasis.

Endings   See *Beginnings and Endings.*

Evaluation   An evaluation of a piece of writing is an assessment of its effectiveness or merit. In evaluating a piece of writing, one should ask the following questions: What is the writer's purpose? Is it a worthwhile purpose? Does the writer achieve the purpose? Is the writer's information sufficient and accurate? What are the strengths of the essay? What are its weaknesses? Depending on the type of writing and the purpose, more specific questions can also be asked. For example, with an argument one could ask: Does the writer follow the principles of logical thinking? Is the writer's evidence sufficient and convincing?

Evidence   Evidence is the information on which a judgment or argument is based or by which proof or probability is established. Evidence usually takes the form of statistics, facts, names, examples or illustrations, and opinions of authorities.

Example   An example illustrates a larger idea or represents something of which it is a part. An example is a basic means of developing or clarifying an idea. Furthermore, examples enable writers to show and not simply to tell readers what they mean. See also the introduction to Chapter 10 (pp. 205–6).

Exposition   Exposition is one of the four basic types of prose. (Narration, description, and argumentation are the other three.) The purpose of exposition is to clarify, explain, and inform. The methods of exposition presented in *Models for Writers* are process analysis, definition, illustration, classification, comparison and contrast, and cause and effect. For a detailed discussion of these methods of exposition, see the appropriate chapter introductions.

Fallacy   See *Logical Fallacies.*

Figures of Speech   Figures of speech are brief, imaginative comparisons that highlight the similarities between things that are basically dissimilar. They make writing vivid, interesting, and memorable. The most common figures of speech are:

> *Simile:* An explicit comparison introduced by *like* or *as.* "The fighter's hands were like stone."
> *Metaphor:* An implied comparison that makes one thing the equivalent of another. "All the world's a stage."

Personification: A special kind of simile or metaphor in which human traits are assigned to an inanimate object. "The engine coughed and then stopped."

See the introduction to Chapter 9 (pp. 186–87) for a detailed discussion of figurative language.

Focus   Focus is the limitation that a writer gives his or her subject. The writer's task is to select a manageable topic given the constraints of time, space, and purpose. For example, within the general subject of sports, a writer could focus on government support of amateur athletes or narrow the focus further to government support of Olympic athletes.

General   See *Specific/General.*

Idiom   An idiom is a word or phrase that is used habitually with special meaning. The meaning of an idiom is not always readily apparent to nonnative speakers of that language. For example, *catch cold, hold a job, make up your mind,* and *give them a hand* are all idioms in English.

Illustration   Illustration is the use of examples to explain, elucidate, or corroborate. Writers rely heavily on illustration to make their ideas both clear and concrete. See the introduction to Chapter 10 (pp. 205–6) for a detailed discussion of illustration.

Induction   Induction is the process of reasoning to a conclusion about all members of a class through an examination of only a few members of the class. This form of reasoning moves from the particular to the general. See the introduction to Chapter 18 (pp. 392–94) for a discussion of inductive reasoning and its relation to argumentation.

Inductive Leap   An inductive leap is the point at which a writer of an argument, having presented sufficient evidence, moves to a generalization or conclusion. See also *Induction.*

Introductions   See *Beginnings and Endings.*

Irony   The use of words to suggest something different from their literal meaning. For example, when Jonathan Swift proposes in *A Modest Proposal* that Ireland's problems could be solved if the people of Ireland fattened their babies and sold them to the English landlords for food, he meant that almost any other solution would be preferable. A writer can use irony to establish a special relationship with the reader and to add

an extra dimension or twist to the meaning. See also the introduction to Chapter 8 (pp. 161–66).

Jargon Jargon, or technical language, is the special vocabulary of a trade, profession, or group. Doctors, construction
workers, lawyers, and teachers, for example, all have a specialized vocabulary that they use "on the job." See also *Diction.*

Logical Fallacies A logical fallacy is an error in reasoning
that renders an argument invalid. See the introduction to
Chapter 18 (pp. 392–94) for a discussion of the more common
logical fallacies.

Metaphor See *Figures of Speech.*

Narration One of the four basic types of prose. (Description,
exposition, and argumentation are the other three.) To narrate
is to tell a story, to tell what happened. While narration is most
often used in fiction, it is also important in expository writing,
either by itself or in conjunction with other types of prose. See
the introduction to Chapter 11 (pp. 225–26) for a detailed discussion of narration.

Opinion An opinion is a belief or conclusion, which may or
may not be substantiated by positive knowledge or proof. (If
not substantiated, an opinion is a prejudice.) Even when based
on evidence and sound reasoning, an opinion is personal and
can be changed, and is therefore less persuasive than facts and
arguments.

Organization Organization is the pattern of order that the
writer imposes on his or her material. Some often used patterns of organization include time order, space order, and order
of importance. See the introduction to Chapter 3 (pp. 52–53)
for a more detailed discussion of organization.

Paradox A paradox is a seemingly contradictory statement
that is nonetheless true. For example, "We little know what we
have until we lose it" is a paradoxical statement.

Paragraph The paragraph, the single most important unit of
thought in an essay, is a series of closely related sentences.
These sentences adequately develop the central or controlling
idea of the paragraph. This central or controlling idea, usually
stated in a topic sentence, is necessarily related to the purpose
of the whole composition. A well-written paragraph has several
distinguishing characteristics: a clearly stated or implied topic

sentence, adequate development, unity, coherence, and an appropriate organizational strategy. See the introduction to Chapter 5 (pp. 97–100) for a detailed discussion of paragraphs.

Parallelism   Parallel structure is the repetition of word order or grammatical form either within a single sentence or in several sentences that develop the same central idea. As a rhetorical device, parallelism can aid coherence and add emphasis. Franklin Roosevelt's statement, "I see one third of the nation ill-housed, ill-clad, and ill-nourished," illustrates effective parallelism.

Personification   See *Figures of Speech*.

Point of View   Point of view refers to the grammatical person in an essay. For example, first-person point of view uses the pronoun *I* and is commonly found in autobiography and the personal essay; third-person point of view uses the pronouns *he, she,* or *it* and is commonly found in objective writing. See the introduction to Chapter 11 (pp. 225–26) for a discussion of point of view in narration.

Process Analysis   Process analysis is a type of exposition. Process analysis answers the question *how* and explains how something works or gives step-by-step directions for doing something. See the introduction to Chapter 13 (pp. 275–76) for a detailed discussion of process analysis. See also *Exposition*.

Purpose   Purpose is what the writer wants to accomplish in a particular piece of writing. Purposeful writing seeks to *relate* (narration), to *describe* (description), to *explain* (process analysis, definition, classification, comparison and contrast, and cause and effect), or to *convince* (argumentation).

Rhetorical Question   A rhetorical question is asked for its rhetorical effect but requires no answer from the reader. "When will nuclear proliferation end?" is such a question. Writers use rhetorical questions to introduce topics they plan to discuss or to emphasize important points. See the general introduction (pp. 1–16) and the introduction to Chapter 4 (pp. 69–73).

Sentence   A sentence is a grammatical unit that expresses a complete thought. It consists of at least a subject (a noun) and a predicate (a verb). See the introduction to Chapter 7 (pp. 136–40) for a discussion of effective sentences.

Simile   See *Figures of Speech*.

Slang   Slang is the unconventional, very informal language of particular subgroups in our culture. Slang, such as *bummed, coke, split, rap, dude,* and *stoned,* is acceptable in formal writing only if it is used selectively for specific purposes.

Specific/General   General words name groups or classes of objects, qualities, or actions. Specific words, on the other hand, name individual objects, qualities, or actions within a class or group. To some extent the terms *general* and *specific* are relative. For example, *clothing* is a class of things. *Shirt,* however, is more specific than *clothing* but more general than *T-shirt.* See also *Diction.*

Strategy   A strategy is a means by which a writer achieves his or her purpose. Strategy includes the many rhetorical decisions that the writer makes about organization, paragraph structure, sentence structure, and diction. In terms of the whole essay, strategy refers to the principal rhetorical mode that a writer uses. If, for example, a writer wishes to show how to make chocolate chip cookies, the most effective strategy would be process analysis. If it is the writer's purpose to show why sales of American cars have declined in recent years, the most effective strategy would be cause and effect analysis.

Style   Style is the individual manner in which a writer expresses his or her ideas. Style is created by the author's particular choice of words, construction of sentences, and arrangement of ideas.

Subordination   Subordination is the use of grammatical constructions to make one part in a sentence dependent on rather than equal to another. For example, the italicized clause in the following sentence is subordinate: They all cheered *when I finished the race.* See the introduction to Chapter 7 (pp. 136–40). See also *Coordination.*

Supporting Evidence   See *Evidence.*

Syllogism   A syllogism is an argument that utilizes deductive reasoning and consists of a major premise, a minor premise, and a conclusion. For example,

> All trees that lose leaves are deciduous. (major premise)
> Maple trees lose their leaves. (minor premise)
> Therefore, maple trees are deciduous. (conclusion)

See also *Deduction.*

Symbol   A symbol is a person, place, or thing that represents something beyond itself. For example, the eagle is a symbol of the United States, and the maple leaf, a symbol of Canada.

Syntax   Syntax refers to the way in which words are arranged to form phrases, clauses, and sentences, as well as to the grammatical relationship among the words themselves.

Technical Language   See *Jargon.*

Thesis   A thesis is the main idea of an essay, also known as the controlling idea. A thesis may sometimes be implied rather than stated directly in a thesis statement. See the introduction to Chapter 1 (pp. 19–20) for a detailed discussion of thesis.

Title   A title is a word or phrase set off at the beginning of an essay to identify the subject, to state the main idea of the essay, or to attract the reader's attention. A title may be explicit or suggestive. A subtitle, when used, explains or restricts the meaning of the main title.

Tone   Tone is the manner in which a writer relates to an audience, the "tone of voice" used to address readers. Tone may be friendly, serious, distant, angry, cheerful, bitter, cynical, enthusiastic, morbid, resentful, warm, playful, and so forth. A particular tone results from a writer's diction, sentence structure, purpose, and attitude toward the subject. See the introduction to Chapter 8 (pp. 161–66) for several examples that display different tones.

Topic Sentence   The topic sentence states the central idea of a paragraph and thus limits the content of the paragraph. Although the topic sentence normally appears at the beginning of the paragraph, it may appear at any other point, particularly if the writer is trying to create a special effect. Not all paragraphs contain topic sentences. See also *Paragraph.*

Transitions   Transitions are words or phrases that link sentences, paragraphs, and larger units of a composition in order to achieve coherence. These devices include parallelism, pronoun references, conjunctions, and the repetition of key ideas, as well as the many conventional transitional expressions such as *moreover, on the other hand, in addition, in contrast,* and *therefore.* See the introduction to Chapter 6 (pp. 117–19) for a detailed discussion of transitions. See also *Coherence.*

Unity   Unity is that quality of oneness in an essay that results when all the words, sentences, and paragraphs contribute to the thesis. The elements of a unified essay do not distract the reader. Instead, they all harmoniously support a single idea or purpose. See the introduction to Chapter 2 (pp. 35–36) for a detailed discussion of unity.

Verb   Verbs can be classified as either strong verbs (*scream, pierce, gush, ravage,* and *amble*) or weak verbs (*be, has, get,* and *do*). Writers often prefer to use strong verbs in order to make writing more specific or more descriptive.

Voice   Verbs can be classified as being in either the active or the passive voice. In the active voice the doer of the action is the subject. In the passive voice the receiver of the action is the grammatical subject:

Active: Glenda questioned all of the children.
Passive: All the children were questioned by Glenda.

Acknowledgments (continued from copyright page)

Page 54. "Reach Out and Write Someone" by Lynn Wenzel. From "My Turn," *Newsweek on Campus*, January 9, 1984. Reprinted with the permission of the author.

Page 58. "Made to Order Babies" by Geoffrey Cowley. From *Newsweek* special issue, Winter/Spring 1990. Copyright © 1990 Newsweek, Inc. Reprinted with the permission of *Newsweek*.

Page 65. "The Corner Store" by Eudora Welty. From *The Eye of the Story: Selected Essays and Reviews*. Originally titled "The Little Store." Copyright © 1975 by Eudora Welty. Reprinted with the permission of Random House, Inc.

Page 74. "Advertisements for Oneself" by Lance Morrow. From *Fishing in the Tiber*. Copyright © 1988 by Lance Morrow. Reprinted with the permission of Henry Holt and Company, Inc.

Page 79. "Of My Friend Hector and My Achilles Heel" by Michael T. Kaufman. From *The New York Times*, November 1, 1992. Copyright © 1992 by The New York Times Company. Reprinted with the permission of *The New York Times*.

Page 84. "Even You Can Get It" by Bruce Lambert. From *The New York Times*, March 11, 1989. Copyright © 1989 by The New York Times Company. Reprinted with the permission of *The New York Times*.

Page 91. "How to Take a Job Interview" by Kirby W. Stanat. From *Job Hunting Secrets and Tactics* by Kirby W. Stanat with Patrick Reardon. Copyright © 1977 by Kirby Stanat and Patrick Reardon. Reprinted with the permission of Westwind Press, a division of Raintree Publishers Limited.

Page 101. "Simplicity" by William Zinsser. From *On Writing Well*, Fifth Edition (New York: Harper, 1994). Copyright © 1976, 1980, 1985, 1988, 1990, 1994 by William Zinsser. Reprinted with the permission of the author and Carol Brissie.

Page 108. "Bilingualism's Goal" by Barbara Mujica. From *The New York Times*, February 26, 1984. Copyright © 1984 by The New York Times Company. Reprinted with the permission of *The New York Times*.

Page 112. "I Just Wanna Be Average" by Mike Rose. From *Lives on the Boundary*. Copyright © 1989 by Mike Rose. Reprinted with the permission of The Free Press, a division of Macmillan, Inc.

Page 120. "Why I Want to Have a Family" by Lisa Brown. From "My Turn," *Newsweek*, October 1984. Reprinted with the permission of the author.

Page 125. "How I Got Smart" by Steve Brody. From *The New York Times*, September 21, 1986. Originally titled "Love, With Knowledge Aforethought." Copyright © 1986 by The New York Times Company. Reprinted with the permission of *The New York Times*.

Page 131. "Facing Violence" by Michael T. Kaufman. From *The New York Times*, May 13, 1984. Copyright © 1984 by The New York Times Company. Reprinted with the permission of *The New York Times*.

Page 145. "Playing to Win" by Margaret A. Whitney. From *The New York Times*, July 3, 1988. Copyright © 1988 by The New York Times Company. Reprinted with the permission of *The New York Times*.

Page 150. "A Brother's Murder" by Brent Staples. From *The New York Times Magazine*, 1987. Copyright © 1987 by The New York Times Company. Reprinted with the permission of *The New York Times*.

Page 155. "Salvation" by Langston Hughes. From *The Big Sea*. Copyright © 1940 by Langston Hughes, renewed © 1969 by Arna Bontemps and George Houston Bass. Reprinted with the permission of Hill & Wang, a division of Farrar, Straus & Giroux, Inc.

Page 167. "On Being 17, Bright, and Unable to Read" by David Raymond. From *The New York Times*, April 25, 1976. Copyright © 1976 by The New York Times Company. Reprinted with the permission of *The New York Times*.

Page 172. "The Flight of the Eagles" by N. Scott Momaday. From *House Made of Dawn*. Copyright © 1968 by N. Scott Momaday. Reprinted with the permission of HarperCollins Publishers, Inc.

Page 175. *"La Vida Loca* (The Crazy Life): Two Generations of Gang Members" by Luis J. Rodriguez. From *Los Angeles Times*, June 21, 1992, Section M. Reprinted with the permission of the author.

Page 181. "The Fourth of July" by Audre Lorde. From *Zami*. Copyright © 1982 by Audre Lorde. Reprinted with the permission of The Crossing Press, Freedom, CA.

Page 188. "The Barrio" by Robert Ramirez. Reprinted with the permission of the author.

Page 194. "The Death of Benny Paret" by Norman Mailer. Reprinted with the permission of Wylie, Aitken & Stone, Inc.

Page 197. "The Thirsty Animal" by Brian Manning. From *The New York Times*, October 13, 1985. Copyright © 1985 by The New York Times Company. Reprinted with the permission of *The New York Times*.

Page 207. "A Crime of Compassion" by Barbara Huttmann. From *Newsweek*, 1983. Reprinted with the permission of the author.

Page 212. "Winter Birds" by Gale Lawrence. From *The Beginning Naturalist*. Copyright © 1979 by Gale Lawrence. Reprinted with the permission of The New England Press, Inc., Shelburne, VT.

Page 217. "On Dumpster Diving" by Lars Eighner. From *Travels with Lizbeth*. Copyright © 1991, 1993 by Lars Eighner. This essay first appeared in *The Threepenny Review*, Fall 1991. Reprinted with the permission of St. Martin's Press.

Page 221. "Controlling the Electronic Home" by Ellen Cobb Wade. From *Newsweek*, 1984. Reprinted with the permission of the author.

Page 227. "Shame" by Dick Gregory. From *Nigger: An Autobiography*. Copyright © 1964 by Dick Gregory Enterprises, Inc. Reprinted with the permission of Dutton, an imprint of New American Library, a division of Penguin Books USA, Inc.

Page 232. "38 Who Saw Murder Didn't Call Police" by Martin Gansberg. From *The New York Times*, March 17, 1964. Copyright © 1964 by The New York Times Company. Reprinted with the permission of *The New York Times*.

Page 237. "The Dare" by Roger Hoffman. From "About Men," *The New York Times Magazine*, January 1, 1986. Originally titled "There's Always the Dare." Copyright © 1986 by The New York Times Company, Inc. Reprinted with the permission of *The New York Times*.

Page 242. "Momma, the Dentist, and Me" by Maya Angelou. *From I Know Why the Caged Bird Sings*. Copyright © 1969 by Maya Angelou. Reprinted with the permission of Random House, Inc.

Page 252. "The Sounds of the City" by James Tuite. From *The New York Times*, August 6, 1966. Copyright © 1966 by The New York Times Company, Inc. Reprinted with the permission of *The New York Times*.

Page 256. "Unforgettable Miss Bessie" by Carl T. Rowan. From *Reader's Digest*, March 1985. Copyright © 1985 by The Reader's Digest Association, Inc. Reprinted with the permission of *Reader's Digest*.

Page 262. "Grocer's Daughter" by Marianne Wiggins. From *Herself in Love and Other Stories*. Originally appeared in *Parade*, June 18, 1989. Copyright © 1989 by Marianne Wiggins. Reprinted with the permission of Martin Secker & Warburg, Ltd.

Page 268. "Borders" by Barry Lopez. From *Crossing Open Ground* (New York: Scribner's 1988). Originally appeared in *Country Journal.* Copyright © 1988 by Barry Lopez. Reprinted with the permission of Sterling Lord Literistic.

Page 277. "How to Build a Fire in a Fireplace" by Bernard Gladstone. From *The New York Times Complete Manual of Home Repair.* Copyright © 1972 by The New York Times Company. Reprinted with the permission of the publishers.

Page 280. "How to Put Off Doing a Job" by Andy Rooney. From *Word for Word.* Copyright © 1986 by Essay Productions, Inc. Reprinted with the permission of The Putnam Publishing Group.

Page 283. "How to Organize Your Thoughts for Better Communication" by Sherry Sweetnam. From *Personnel,* March 1986. Copyright © 1986 American Management Association. Reprinted with the permission of the publishers.

Page 290. "The Spider and the Wasp" by Alexander Petrunkevitch. From *Scientific American,* August 1952. Copyright 1952 and renewed © 1980 by Scientific American, Inc. Reprinted with the permission of *Scientific American.*

Page 299. "A Jerk" by Sidney J. Harris. From "Strictly Personal." Copyright © North American Syndicate, Inc. Reprinted with the permission of King Features, a division of Hearst Corporation.

Page 302. "Inflation" by Marilu Hurt McCarty. From *Dollars and Sense: An Introduction to Economics,* Second Edition. Copyright © 1979, 1976 by Scott, Foresman and Company. Reprinted with the permission of HarperCollins College Publishers.

Page 307. "The Underclass" by Herbert J. Gans. From *The Washington Post,* September 10, 1990. Originally titled "So Much for the 'Underclass'." Copyright © 1990 by The Washington Post Writers Group. Reprinted with the permission of *The Washington Post.*

Page 311. "They've Gotta Keep It: People Who Save Everything" by Lynda W. Warren and Jonnae C. Ostrom. From *San Francisco Chronicle,* May 1, 1988. Originally titled "Pack Rats: World Class Savers." Copyright © 1988 by Sussex Publishers. Reprinted with the permission of *Psychology Today.*

Page 320. "The Ways of Meeting Oppression" by Martin Luther King, Jr. From *Stride Toward Freedom* (New York: Harper & Row, 1958). Copyright © 1958 by Martin Luther King, Jr., renewed 1986 by Coretta Scott King, Dexter King, Martin Luther King, III, Yolanda King, and Bernice King. Reprinted with the permission of Joan Daves Agency.

Page 325. "Friends, Good Friends—and Such Good Friends" by Judith Viorst. From *Redbook,* 1977. Copyright © 1977 by Judith Viorst. Reprinted with the permission of Lescher & Lescher, Ltd.

Page 332. "What You Do Is What You Are" by Nickie McWhirter. From *San Jose Mercury News,* March 8, 1982. Reprinted with the permission of the *Detroit Free Press.*

Page 336. "The Ten Most Memorable Bores" by Margot Mifflin. From *Cosmopolitan,* April, 1990. Reprinted with the permission of the author.

Page 346. "That Lean and Hungry Look" by Suzanne Britt. From "My Turn," *Newsweek On Campus,* 1978. Reprinted with the permission of the author.

Page 351. "Grant and Lee: A Study in Contrasts" by Bruce Catton. From *The American Story,* edited by Earl Schenk Miers. Copyright © United States Capitol Historical Society. Reprinted with the permission of the United States Capitol Historical Society, Washington, DC.

Page 357. "My Son, My Teacher" by Barney Cohen. From *Parenting,* June/July 1990. Copyright © 1990 by *Parenting* magazine, a publication of The Time Inc. Magazine Company. Reprinted with the permission of *Parenting* magazine.

Page 362. "A Case of 'Severe Bias' " by Patricia Raybon. From *Newsweek,* October 1989. Reprinted with the permission of the author.

Page 367. "A Battle of Cultures" by K. Connie Kang. From *Asian Week,* May 25, 1990. Reprinted with the permission of the author.

Page 374. "Never Get Sick in July" by Marilyn Machlowitz. From *Esquire,* July 1978. Reprinted with the permission of the author.

Page 378. "The Bounty of the Sea" by Jacques Cousteau. Reprinted with the permission of The Cousteau Society, Inc.

Page 381. "Halfway to Dick and Jane" by Jack Agueros. From *The Immigrant Experience,* edited by Thomas C. Wheeler. Copyright © 1971 by Doubleday, a division of Bantam Doubleday Dell Publishing Group, Inc. Reprinted with the permission of the publishers.

Page 386. "Legalize Drugs" by Ethan A. Nadelmann. From *The New Republic,* June 13, 1988. Copyright © 1988 by The New Republic, Inc. Reprinted with the permission of *The New Republic.*

Page 395. "Hate, Rape, and Rap" by Tipper Gore. From *The Washington Post,* January 8, 1990. Copyright © 1990 by *The Washington Post.* Reprinted with the permission of *The Washington Post.*

Page 400. "As They Say, Drugs Kill" by Laura Rowley. From *Newsweek On Campus,* February 1987. Reprinted with the permission of the author.

Page 405. "In Praise of the F Word" by Mary Sherry. From *Newsweek,* May 6, 1991. Reprinted with the permission of the author.

Page 409. "Less Is More: A Call for Shorter Work Hours" by Barbara Brandt. From *Utne Reader,* July/August 1991. Reprinted with the permission of the author.

Page 416. "Abortion Is Too Complex to Feel All One Way About" by Anna Quindlen. From "Hers," *The New York Times Magazine,* March 6, 1986. Copyright © 1986 by The New York Times Company, Inc. Reprinted with the permission of *The New York Times.*

Page 421. "Exposing Media Myths: TV Doesn't Affect You as Much as You Think" by Joanmarie Kalter. From *TV Guide,* May 30, 1987. Copyright © 1987 by News America Publications, Inc. Reprinted with the permission of *TV Guide.*

Page 428. "Death and Justice: How Capital Punishment Affirms Life" by Edward I. Koch. From *The New Republic,* April 15, 1985. Copyright © 1985 by New Republic, Inc. Reprinted with the permission of *The New Republic.*

Page 436. "The Death Penalty Is a Step Back" by Coretta Scott King. Copyright © 1981 by Coretta Scott King. Reprinted with the permission of the Joan Daves Agency.

INDEX

Instructor's Manual to Accompany

FIFTH EDITION

MODELS
for Writers

Short Essays for
Composition

Alfred Rosa
Paul Eschholz

Prepared by Mark Wanner

Instructor's Manual
to Accompany

MODELS FOR WRITERS

SHORT ESSAYS FOR COMPOSITION
Fifth Edition

Editors

Alfred Rosa
Paul Eschholz

Prepared by
Mark Wanner

ST. MARTIN'S PRESS   NEW YORK

Manufactured in the United States of America.
98765
fedcba

For information, write:
St. Martin's Press, Inc.
175 Fifth Avenue
New York, NY 10010

ISBN: 0-312-10121-X

Preface

The purpose of this *Instructor's Manual* is to help you use *Models for Writers* with the greatest effectiveness. We therefore provide for each selection in the book a fairly detailed analysis of the essay as a whole. In these sections of the manual, labeled *Essay Analysis and Discussion*, we try to share with you our experiences in teaching the essays—what to stress, what to explain, what to ask about, what to expect generally from discussions. In addition, a typical analysis might do one or more of the following:

- explore one or more content issues
- point out stylistic features
- suggest classroom activities that reinforce rhetorical strategies
- suggest one or more other essays in the text that might be usefully taught in conjunction with the present one
- explain where students are likely to have difficulty understanding either content or rhetorical techniques

In addition, we provide in the section called *Questions for Study and Discussion* suggested responses to the questions following each selection. Our intent is to save you time, not to dictate answers. On occasions you may disagree with our interpretation or emphasis, but we trust that the suggested responses here will be useful at least as starting points. There are no substitutes for your own experience with each essay or for common sense about what will challenge and engage your students.

The essays in *Models for Writers* are grouped into eighteen chapters, each devoted to a separate rhetorical topic. The first seven chapters focus on specific elements of essays: thesis, unity, organization, beginnings and endings, paragraphs, transitions, and effective sentences. The next two chapters concern some uses and effects of language: diction and tone, and figurative language. The final nine chapters explore types of essays: illustration, narration, description, process analysis, definition, division and classification, comparison and contrast, cause and effect, and argument.

The arrangement of the chapters suggests a logical teaching sequence, from the elements of an essay through the language of an essay to the types of essays. An alternative teaching strategy is to structure your course according to the types of essays, teaching other chapters as necessary or having students use them for reference. Finally, because each chapter is self-contained, you can design your own teaching sequence, omitting or emphasizing particular chapters according to the special needs of your class.

To help you use the book effectively, we would like to call your attention to the following special features:

General Introduction. An enlarged introduction provides guidelines for reading and writing short essays and includes three sample student papers with annotations that highlight the elements of an essay that are emphasized in the text proper. The sample papers and the analyses that accompany them provide the opportunity to show and discuss with your class how three students went about completing typical writing assignments. Moreover, the sample papers give students a good idea of the length and quality of writing they should be striving to produce. We suggest, therefore, that you assign this introduction early in the course and that you spend as much time as possible discussing the student papers and their salient features.

Chapter Introductions. Before reading the essays in a particular chapter, students should read the chapter introduction. There they will find an explanation of the rhetorical principle under consideration and a discussion of how it can be used. The information in the introductions will also help students to answer the questions and do the writing assignments that accompany each selection.

Questions for Study and Discussion. The study questions for each selection focus on its content, its author's purpose and the rhetorical principle used to achieve that purpose. Some of the questions require brief answers, and others are intended to stimulate class discussion. Since students' knowledge of rhetorical techniques and patterns will increase as the course proceeds, we have included for each essay one or more questions about rhetorical elements other than the one highlighted in the particular essay.

Vocabulary. We have tried to emphasize each author's choice of words and have included an exercise on vocabulary building for almost every essay. The vocabulary words in these exercises are defined in this manual and can be used for a vocabulary test for each essay or chapter.

Suggested Writing Assignments. Two writing assignments accompany each essay in the textbook. They offer students the opportunity to apply the rhetorical principle at hand. Often these assignments are related to the content of the essays as well; but most can be assigned independently if you prefer not to assign all the readings.

Glossary of Useful Terms. This glossary is located at the end of the book and provides students with concise definitions of terms useful for discussing the readings and their own writing. Wherever we have felt that information in the glossary might assist students in answering a study question, we have placed a cross-reference to the appropriate entry next to the question.

Thematic Table of Contents. If a particular essay evokes strong student response, this alternative table of contents makes it easier for you to choose thematically related pieces in other sections of *Models for Writers*. Nearly all the readings are entered under at least one subject heading, and many appear under two or three. Admittedly, some of these classifications may seem a bit arbitrary, but we believe that none are misfits. And, beyond calling attention to the content of individual essays, this listing allows you to point out different rhetorical approaches to common themes.

Finally, we are very much interested in hearing from anyone who has constructive ideas about the content or use of either *Models for Writers* or this manual. We can be reached at the Department of English, 315 Old Mill, University of Vermont, Burlington, Vermont 05405.

Alfred Rosa
Paul Eschholz
Mark Wanner

Contents

PART I   THE ELEMENTS OF THE ESSAY

CHAPTER 1   THESIS

THE MOST IMPORTANT DAY (p. 21)
Helen Keller

Essay Analysis and Discussion

The first paragraph of this essay, though short, is vital to establishing focus and direction for the paragraphs that follow. The first sentence states the thesis, but without the two sentences following it, the essay would lose the unity Keller has achieved. To get students to see the connection between the thesis statement and the opening paragraph as a whole, and their relation to the rest of the essay, have them consider what each of the first three sentences accomplish in regard to the other paragraphs. It may help to look at the stage of Keller's narration (as they are outlined in study question 6) to see if there is a correlation between those stages and the three sentences in the opening paragraph. The students' analysis should reveal that though the thesis statement focuses on a particular day, the essay can include discussion of other days and other events and remain unified because of the context established by the entire first paragraph.

Questions for Study and Discussion

1. Keller's thesis is the first sentence of the essay.
2. Keller's purpose is to *tell* why the day that Anne Sullivan came to her was the most important day in her life.
3. For several weeks before Anne Sullivan arrived, Keller was angry and bitter. When that passed she fell into a "deep languor." She compared the feeling to being a ship in a fog of darkness groping its way to shore.
4. Every new name gave birth to a new thought. Words would "make the world blossom for me."
5. Keller understood the connection between words and the things they describe one day, after many such days, when her teacher placed one of Keller's hands under running water while she spelled the word water in the other. "Suddenly I felt a misty consciousness as of something forgotten, a thrill of returning thought; and somehow the mystery of language was revealed to me."
6. On the first day, she meets Anne Sullivan and they embrace. On the next day, Anne gives her a doll and spells the word *doll* on her hand until Keller is able to imitate the spelling. Several weeks later, Anne again tries to make the connection between objects and words (e.g., mug and water and dolls) and is finally able to accomplish this at the well-house with the word *water* and the actual water.

1

Vocabulary

dumb (2) lacking the faculty of speech; mute
preyed (2) exerted an injurious effect
languor (2) sluggishness
passionate (2) expressing or revealing strong emotion
plummet (3) a weight tied to a line that is used to measure the depth of the sea
tussle (6) struggle or scuffle
vainly (8) unsuccessfully

GIVE US JOBS, NOT ADMIRATION (p. 25)
Eric Bigler

Essay Analysis and Discussion

Bigler waits until the second sentence of his essay to state his thesis that the handicapped are passed over in job interviews, even when they are qualified. A second part of his thesis, that more needs to be done to employ the handicapped, is put forth in the examples Bigler gives in the rest of the essay. Bigler strengthens his argument in the way he organizes his essay. In the first two paragraphs he sets the scene: a future job interview that he expects will end without a commitment from the company. Then he offers his thesis that the handicapped often don't get jobs they are qualified to fill. At this point, the reader may or may not be convinced. However, beginning with paragraph three, Bigler enumerates the different methods that government and the private sector use to deal with the handicapped. By the time he ends his essay, back in the interview, we have enough information to share his doubt. Students can try this technique with similar experiences of their own; being denied a job because they are too young, or because they are female, or because they belong to some minority group. Ask them to set the scene for the reader, develop the "facts," and then bring the reader full circle to the opening scene. Have students note that Bigler's tone is never self-pitying; he relies on the facts to make his case.

Questions for Study and Discussion

1. Bigler thinks these programs do not necessarily spend their money wisely. They might be more successful, Bigler said, "If they concentrated on the perceptions of employers as well as the skills of applicants."
2. Bigler's thesis is that the disabled are not hired for jobs they are qualified to fill, and that little is being done about it. The first part of the thesis is stated most clearly in paragraph two. The second part is stated indirectly in the examples he gives of government and private programs which he claims are not working.
3. Bigler gives a few reasons for the disabled not being hired (paragraph 7).

2

However, his thesis does not depend on reasons but on two more general assumptions. One, on some level he knows that we know why they aren't hired. He knows that the public at large shares prejudices and fears about the handicapped. Two, if the handicapped are being treated unfairly, those fears are irrelevant.

4. Bigler anticipates a job interview in both the beginning and end of his essay. The beginning is effective because it presents the scene to the reader immediately, before the reader has any information. Then, after he uses several good examples, Bigler presents the same scene to a now convinced reader who can shake his head saying, "Now I see what you mean."

5. Bigler refers to such events as National Employ the Handicapped Week as cosmetic because they adorn the issue, and help people feel they are doing something; they do not effect significant change.

6. The average person—who is also the average employer, legislator, voter, anyone who harbors prejudice or misinformation—is the audience Bigler addresses because these are the people who can effect change.

Vocabulary

worrisome (2) causing distress or worry
seminars (5) conferences
enhance (6) to make greater in value or desirability
forthright (7) direct; straightforward
proclamations (8) public declarations
self-esteem (9) esteem for oneself; pride

ANXIETY: CHALLENGE BY ANOTHER NAME (p. 30)
James Lincoln Collier

Essay Analysis and Discussion

Collier arranges his essay chronologically, beginning with his youth and coming into the present, to demonstrate his thesis that we can learn to overcome the stultifying effects of anxiety. At each era of his life, he pauses to use examples from philosophy, psychology, and other peoples' lives to illustrate and strengthen his argument. The examples he uses are everyday enough that the reader can sympathize with and relate to the author's point of view. At three different points, Collier also punctuates the essay with his "rules," the conclusions he has drawn about anxiety and its relationship to learning. Ask students to think about some of the "rules" they have learned for themselves. Then ask them to describe, using examples, how these rules might have universal application. Remind them to use examples of situations that are easily identified by the other students in the class. They might try writing about lessons they learned over time, as well as ones they learned quickly, after one hapless episode. How would the arrangement of material differ in that case?

Questions for Study and Discussion

1. Collier states his thesis in paragraph 20: "The new, the different, is almost by definition scary. But each time you try something, you learn, and as the learning piles up, the world opens to you." Students will explain their own experience with Collier's thesis.
2. Collier explains extinction in paragraph 14.
3. "Do what makes you anxious; don't do what makes you depressed." The corollaries to his rule are: "You'll never eliminate anxiety by avoiding the things that caused it," and "You can't learn if you don't try." Collier means that the second and third rules are true once we accept the truth of his basic rule.
4. Collier means to demonstrate,. based on his own experience that we can overcome anxiety and in so doing can live a richer, fuller life.
5. Collier uses "personification" to depict anxiety as a traveling companion.
6. These paragraphs contrast with the first paragraph in Collier's essay to show that over time he has learned to overcome the kind of anxiety that kept him "safe" at home when he was a young adult.

Vocabulary

daunted (2) lessened the courage of
proposition (3) something proposed for consideration
anxiety (5) abnormal apprehension and fear
depression (5) an emotional disorder marked by sadness, inactivity, difficulty in concentration
butterflies (5) a fluttery sensation accompanying nervousness
crack (6) attempt; try
venture (10) an understanding involving chance or risk
corollary (15) a natural consequence, result, or conclusion

CHAPTER 2   UNITY

THE MEANINGS OF A WORD (p. 37)
Gloria Naylor

Essay Analysis and Discussion

In her essay Naylor uses illustration to argue that there are two different definitions of the word "nigger," depending on who is using it and to what purpose. In so doing, Naylor makes the larger point that all of language is similarly subject to interpretation and change depending on the "context." Readers will notice that Naylor concentrates most of her essay on illustrating the lesser known meaning of the word "nigger" as it is used in African American culture. This imbalance is based on Naylor's assumption that most of her readers will be familiar with the racist connotation of the word as it is used in the white culture. Students can choose a word that has both a familiar and a lesser known meaning to discuss in an essay. Then using Naylor's essay as a guide they can illustrate the ways in which the understanding of that word changes from culture to culture or from speaker to speaker.

Questions for Study and Discussion

1. While Naylor has the greatest respect for the written word, she considers the spoken word more powerful for coming at the instant of a thought and being expressed in the full dynamic interplay of all the senses. "Context" is the result of that interplay, enriched by a consensus of meaning which in turn orders reality.

2. Naylor best defines "nigger" in its role as a racial slur in paragraph 14: "a word that whites used to signify worthlessness or degradation." "Nigger" as used by African Americans is best expressed in the same paragraph: "Gathering there together, they transformed *nigger* to signify the varied and complex human beings they knew themselves to be."

3. Naylor means simply that the word "nigger" was used in her family in a context of love, admiration, and affection that allowed it to dwell there comfortably and unnoticed. In her third-grade class, she heard it expressed in a hostile context, for an altogether different purpose—as an insult. In other words, it was not the same word she had heard all her life and so she was hearing it for the first time.

4. Naylor includes details of her family's history, its structure, the neighborhood in which they all lived, the activities they enjoyed, the ways they earned their livings, and the substance of their conversations as a means of establishing the context in which their use of the word "nigger" arose. The little she offers in the way of a definition of the word "nigger" as used by the white community is disquieting to any reader who notices the omission and so is jolted to an awareness of not needing to be told what the word means.

5. Naylor could hardly have been faulted had she used an angry tone to describe the different meanings of the word "nigger." However, she has chosen to use a level, objective tone—as if she were standing back casting a cold, educated glance at the phenomenon which has hurt so many of her people. In paragraph 3, when she recounts the moment she first heard the word "nigger" as a slur, Naylor describes the event rather matter-of-factly: "I remember the first time I heard the word *nigger*. . . . Had he called me a nymphomaniac or a necrophiliac, I couldn't have been more puzzled." Throughout her essay she analyzes the meaning of the word "nigger" as an anthropologist might under the white light of science. It is not until her final sentence that Naylor reveals the sadness and fatigue that we can assume came after who knows how long an effort to assimilate her initial feelings of confusion, shock, anger, and betrayal.

6. Naylor's final sentence is effective for reminding the reader once again that "in America" the primary use of the word "nigger" will be as a racial slur and is one that most readers do not have to sit on their mothers' laps to have explained.

Vocabulary

transcendent (1) exceeding usual limits; passing beyond material existence
consensus (2) collective opinion
innocuous (2) harmless; inoffensive
nymphomaniac (3) a female with excessive sexual desire
necrophiliac (3) one who is sexually attracted to the dead
mecca (4) a place sought as a goal by many people, usually religious
clamor (5) vigorous, noisy protest or demand
anecdotes (5) brief stories of interesting, usually biographical, incidents
inflections (5) the changes in form that words undergo to make case, gender, number, tense, person, mood or voice; changes in the tone or mood in speech that signal a word's connotations and the emotions it is being used to express
unkempt (10) disheveled; not combed
trifling (10) of little value or importance
internalization (14) the incorporation of an attitude into one's thinking
impotent (14) helpless; lacking in power or strength

WHY "MODEL MINORITY" DOESN'T FIT (p. 42)
Deane Yen-Mei Wong

Essay Analysis and Discussion

Using personal experience to bring immediacy to a general argument can be an effective technique to grab the reader's attention. It is often difficult to mesh the two elements into a unified essay, however. Wong's essay is effective and unified because she uses her personal experience to draw the reader in, then establishes it as a springboard to address the larger issues involved. Paragraph 4 leads the reader smoothly from one point of view to the other. She adds paragraph 13 to put her general argument back in the context of her original story, yielding a more unified essay. How do your students react to Wong's assertion that there are no good stereotypes?

Questions for Study and Discussion

1. Wong begins with a personal anecdote to grab the reader's attention and to provide a motivation for her essay. By starting with a specific experience that backs up the general argument presented later, she makes the reader ready to accept her point of view. The paragraphs help unify her essay by

allowing her to reference her personal experience again in paragraph 13. By doing this, she brings the essay together as she reveals the consequences of the problems in the Asian American community.

2. Wong's thesis is that it is wrong to stereotype the Asian American community. She states it in paragraph 5. The advantages of stating it so late in the essay are explored above.

3. Wong's audience is society as a whole, since she states that people both in and out of the Asian American community perpetuate the model minority stereotype.

4. The model minority stereotype is harmful because it encourages people to ignore the increasing problems in the Asian American community. She illustrates her argument by identifying the problems that are present, such as poverty and violence.

5. Wong implies that increased interaction between distinct Asian American ethnic groups may lead to more crime. Answers will differ for the second part of the question.

6. See question 1.

Vocabulary

render (2) give
septuagenarian (2) person in his or her seventies
extort (2) obtain through threats
valedictorians (7) high school academic leaders
espouses (7) advocates; supports
mantra (8) chant; prayer

DON'T LET STEREOTYPES WARP YOUR JUDGMENTS (p. 46)
Robert L. Heilbroner

Essay Analysis and Discussion

Heilbroner's essay is an excellent example of how to make use of support—objective, gathered information—to convey an idea. When you discuss this essay, point out the references to persons and events outside of the author's immediate realm of experience. For example, in the first few paragraphs, as he describes the nature and scope of stereotyping, Heilbroner relies on the authority of questionnaires, university studies, and the findings of criminologists and optometrists rather than just his own observations. In later paragraphs, he incorporates quotes from persons noted for their observations on human behavior (William James, Walter Lippmann, S. I. Hayakawa, F. Scott Fitzgerald) to amplify his statements about stereotypes and prejudice. As you look at these references with students, discuss how Heilbroner makes sure they are consistent with his central point and, therefore, lend credibility and support.

Heilbroner's essay can show students how to incorporate various types of supporting information into a clearly focused and tightly connected essay.

Questions for Study and Discussion

1. Heilbroner feels that stereotypes do an injustice to others and also impoverish those who think in terms of stereotypes.
2. Paragraph 6 is an example of our tendency to prejudge people. Paragraph 8 shows how stereotypes affect adults. Paragraph 15 shows how difficult it is to get rid of stereotypes. In each case the paragraph is directly related to the preceding paragraph. All three paragraphs illustrate Heilbroner's thesis about stereotypes.
3. Heilbroner uses a number of transitional devices: relative pronouns, repeated key words and ideas, conjunctions, transitional expressions. By indicating the relationships between paragraphs, these devices enhance the unity of the essay.
4. We stereotype for many reasons beginning with childhood when we learn to tell the good guys from the bad guys on television. Later, as adults we ingrain stereotypes through the jokes we listen to and repeat: we pick up other stereotypes in ads, books, and movies. Finally, "we tend to stereotype because it helps us make sense out of a highly confusing world." Stereotyping is dangerous, according to Heilbroner, because it becomes a "substitute for observation." Even when we do observe, "stereotypes get in the way of our judgment." In addition to the harm stereotypes do to others, "they impoverish ourselves," robbing us of the opportunity to see the world in our own, unique way. We can shed stereotypes on three fronts, according to Heilbroner. One, we can become aware of them in our thinking, the thinking of others, and in the world around us. Two, we can become suspicious of all rules that we allow the exception to "prove." Three, "we can learn to be chary of generalizations about people."
5. Heilbroner uses the word *picture* as a near-synonym for a stereotype because a stereotype really is a mental image. His repetition of the world culminates in his gallery metaphor in the final paragraph.

Vocabulary

irrational (7) illogical; contrary to reason
perpetuated (8) continued without interruption
infinite (10) having no boundaries or limits
preconceptions (11) opinions formed in advance of actual knowledge
vindicated (11) cleared, as from suspicion
impoverish (12) deprive of natural richness or strength
chastening (18) refining or purifying
edifice (18) building
chary (19) cautious

CHAPTER 3   ORGANIZATION

REACH OUT AND WRITE SOMEONE (p. 54)
Lynn Wenzel

Essay Analysis and Discussion

Wenzel offers the reasons we should cultivate and cherish the art of letter writing. She begins with historical reasons and finishes with the implications for our own lives, which she deems the most important. She argues that good writing demands all the components of good thinking. In presenting her case, Wenzel contrasts old-fashioned values with the ease and convenience. of the modern world. She reminds her reader that modern technology exacts a toll, in this case, a literal monetary one as well as the loss of the art of personal correspondence. Students can discuss whether they agree with Wenzel. Then ask them to write letters to each other, specifically about topics they have recently discussed over the phone with friends or family. Have them read the letters aloud in class and discuss how, if at all, the quality and content of a letter differ from those of a phone call

Questions for Study and Discussion

1. Wenzel states her thesis in paragraph 2.
2. Other forms of creative writing such as fiction and poetry are alive and well in our culture. It is the art of letter writing that is in danger of becoming extinct.
3. "Much of our knowledge of events and the people who lived them is based on such commonplace communication," Wenzel says in her essay. Without them we would be left with dates and names but would be bereft of the causes and effects. Letters have also contributed enormously to our knowledge of women's lives and thus have given us much of the women's history which is taking its place alongside "weighty tomes about men's contributions to the changing world."
4. Letter writing requires thinking in a way that a phone call does not, because the words can never be taken back. It demands "thought, logic, organization, and sincerity," qualities that Wenzel believes we must not lose, but must cultivate and "bring to luster."
5. Wenzel uses chronological and logical order in developing her essay. Students will find examples from the early days of our history in the beginning of the essay, examples of recent history in the middle, and the shortcomings of the telephone at the end. Wenzel considers all of her reasons important; however, she labels "thinking" at the end of the essay as the most important reason of all.
6. Wenzel uses a common device in rhetoric. She begins and ends with the same thought. When we first read of the breaking up of the phone com-

pany and the resulting dependency on letter writing, we may feel panicky. By the end of the essay, we are convinced that we need to worry more about losing the gentle art of letter writing.

Vocabulary

exorbitant (1) exceeding what is usual or proper
fomenting (6) stirring up; instigating
tomes (8) books, especially large or weighty ones
accouterments (10) personal clothing, accessories, etc.
seal (10) a device having a raised design that can be stamped on clay or wax

MADE TO ORDER BABIES (p. 58)
Geoffrey Cowley

Essay Analysis and Discussion

Cowley dispenses a lot of information and raises a lot of issues on the way to his concluding argument in paragraph 18, so it was imperative that he organize his essay well. Note how he begins his essay with the clear-cut benefits of genetic screening, thus establishing its usefulness to society. In paragraphs 5 and 6, he raises the possibility of abuse of the new technology, then expands upon some of the morally questionable practices it might encourage, such as cosmetic screening. He makes his scenarios more disturbing as he goes along until paragraph 17, where, after raising the specter of eugenics, he brings the reader back to the current benefits of the technology. This organization of the information makes the reader very receptive to Cowley's argument in paragraph 18, which is, of course, Cowley's objective. This subject should yield good classroom discussions. How do your students view the future potential of genetic screening? Would they want to know if their fetus would be prone to obesity or other cosmetic imperfections?

Questions for Study and Discussion

1. Paragraphs 1–3 deal with the benefits of genetic screening for a specific severe genetic disease, Tay-Sachs. Paragraphs 4–6 introduce the possibilities involved with using the technology for other purposes. Paragraphs 7–9 summarize the present situation, then introduce specific possibilities for abusing the technology. Paragraphs 10–12 introduce the human desire to control the genetic makeup of children, if possible, and paragraphs 13–15 support that possibility with statistics. Finally, paragraphs 16–18 summarize the issues and argue Cowley's point that society must deal with this issue. Cowley uses logical organization in his essay. The final question is a matter of opinion, but if the student argues that it isn't effective, make sure that the opinion is backed up well.

2. Answers will differ, but Cowley's title refers to the dangers of genetic screening he refers to in his essay, so he invokes the thought of "made to order babies" to disturb the reader right from he beginning.
3. Cowley simply wants to encourage his audience to consider the implications of the technology of genetic screening. His essay establishes the validity of the technology at first, but it then progresses to more and more disturbing potential uses of the technology, emphasizing the dangers involved in not taking time out to think about the moral implications presented.
4. Cowley quotes medical experts when he discusses potential problems of genetic screening that are not currently issues. He does this to underline that he is talking about real technology, not science fiction, and to reveal the mindset of the people who doctors work with. He can then state that the potential for problems with this technology is very real without having the reader doubt him.
5. The main benefit is that severe genetic diseases can be screened and eliminated. The primary danger is that parents will go beyond severe problems and want to select for certain physical characteristics.
6. Cowley establishes that many doctors and parents would, given access to the technology, use genetic screening to screen for cosmetic or gender-related characteristics.
7. Cowley's tone is cautionary. He is scientific in tone for much of the essay, but talks about "bizarre, scifi scenarios." His message to beware the potential consequences is conveyed very well.

Vocabulary

abet (3) aid, assist
analogous (6) similar to; equivalent
prenatal (6) before birth
adamant (8) insistent; resolute
impetus (10) motivation; force
ethicist (13) specialist who studies ethical questions
stigmatized (16) cast out; ostracized
eugenics (17) controlling genetic makeup of children
rife (18) full; common

THE CORNER STORE (p. 65)
Eudora Welty

Essay Analysis and Discussion

Welty makes good use of detail and organization as she moves through the corner store of her childhood. In a few words, she manages to fill our minds as full as Mr. Sessions fills his shelves. Note how Welty uses sensory description to paint a picture that is real, without overusing detail. Also, students can analyze the way Welty acquaints us with Mr. Sessions without having him speak. Then students can discuss the author's use of hard detail as contrasted with her poetic impressions. The exercise will help them understand how difficult it is to say enough without saying too much.

Questions for Study and Discussion

1. Students will find examples of chronological and spatial organization throughout the essay. Welty organizes the essay chronologically through the sequence of events from the time she enters the store until she leaves. Her body movement around the store and the movement of her eyes as she looks over the shelves and the counters are examples of spatial organization.

2. Welty creates an impression of the old-fashioned plenty associated with a nineteenth-century country store by describing shelves, counters, and barrels stocked with the numberless goodies and smells available in such places.

3. The countless items on the shelves might seem confusing, according to Welty, even though they are arranged in an orderly fashion. The confusion arises from the shopper's own memories and desires which cannot distinguish between what is needed and what is not.

4. Mr. Sessions is warm and friendly, a man who invites a child's hand to reach for a choice of penny candies, who knows what the child's favorite drink is, who weighs small children on his scale before they leave the store, and who will "remember what you weighed the last time."

5. Welty puts certain phrases in parentheses to set them apart. This information characterizes the era in even more detail than the rest of the essay. A personal quality, which identifies the things that were especially dear to the writer, would be lost if these asides to the reader were left out.

6. Students should give reasons that demonstrate their understanding of endings.

Vocabulary

frame (1) having a wood frame
tangible (2) perceptible, especially by the sense of touch
brine (2) water saturated with salt
motes (3) small particles
signet (3) a small intaglio seal
agates (4) children's' marbles of agate or material resembling agate
concoction (8) a mixture prepared by combining diverse ingredients
scales (9) a weighing machine

CHAPTER 4   BEGINNINGS AND ENDINGS

ADVERTISEMENTS FOR ONESELF (p. 74)
Lance Morrow

Essay Analysis and Discussion

Personal ads make many people uncomfortable, so Morrow adds levity to the subject right from the beginning of his essay. "Haiku of self-celebration" is at once an elegant and humorous way to describe the ads, and the reader knows that the article will be playful rather than serious. Even his Jane Austen "personal" at the end is meant to add humor and offset the "forlorn vibrations" that many get from personal ads. Discuss how your students view personal ads. Do they read them? If so, do they find them amusing or sad? Do they agree with Morrow that writing a personal ad is good training in self-assertion? Discuss where else such training might be useful.

Questions for Study and Discussion

1. As stated above, Morrow injects a playful tone into the first paragraph. He uses short sentences and euphemisms such as "chum the waters and bait the hook" to set the tone. The final part of the question is a matter of personal opinion.
2. Personals have become more popular and accepted in society over the past few years.
3. Morrow's purpose is, on the surface, to show his audience what personal ads can be like, but his larger purpose is to entertain and amuse his audience.
4. Composing a personal ad is usually a brazen act of self-promotion. The idea obviously makes Morrow uncomfortable, as he focuses on it in two places in his essay. Writing an ad can be good practice in self-promotion, or a somewhat pitiful cry for companionship, depending on how it's viewed.
5. This is a matter of opinion, but it is apparent that Morrow is intrigued and amused by the subject of personal ads. He also seems to view it as something that other people do, not himself.
6. Morrow's Jane Austen quote is a tongue-in-cheek reference to the personals writing "style." It adds humor to the essay, as well as a sort of faux respectability.

Vocabulary

haiku (1) short, strict form of Japanese poetry
cerebral (1) brainy; intelligent
sultry (1) sexy; steamy
euphemisms (2) slightly skewed synonyms

gnosis (3) intuitive knowledge of spiritual matters
callipygian (4) having shapely buttocks
suffused (5) saturated; permeated
self-effacement (6) deprecation; modesty
hyperbolic (6) exaggerated
incorrigibly (6) hopelessly; unstoppably
cotillions (10) formal balls

OF MY FRIEND HECTOR AND MY ACHILLES HEEL (p. 79)
Michael T. Kaufman

Essay Analysis and Discussion

Kaufman's first paragraph is unusual and grabs the reader's attention. Two short sentences admitting prejudice contrast sharply with the finger pointing, subtle or not, that forms the backbone of most essays about prejudice. Kaufman's story is not dramatic or even noteworthy until the end, but he hooks the reader into bearing with him to find out the nature of his so-called "prejudice and stupidity." Have your students write a short personal essay that uses a concise, attention-grabbing first paragraph. Have them discuss the essays and identify the type of essay for which it might be most effective and why. Kaufman's ending stays with the reader for two reasons. First, it is a situation that everyone can empathize with, since getting back in touch with an old, wrongfully neglected friend is something that most of us should do—but haven't. Second, it is an open-ended conclusion. The reader hopes that perhaps Kaufman will reunite with Hector somehow. Have your students discuss their reaction to the ending. How effective would the essay have been with a resolution at the end?

Questions for Study and Discussion

1. Achilles was a Greek hero who had a weak spot on his heel, a fatal flaw that eventually killed him. Kaufman is referring to his own flaw, which is prejudice.

2. Such an admission is unusual in a first-person essay, so it grabs the reader's attention and encourages the reader to finish the essay to find out what provoked such a statement. It also leads the reader to pay close attention to Kaufman's writing in hopes of discovering the roots of his stated stupidity. The second part of the question is personal experience.

3. The essay is organized chronologically.

4. Kaufman's purpose is to demonstrate how easy it is to form prejudices and segregate oneself from other people based on assumptions. His organization helps him express his purpose by allowing him to trace when, why, and how his prejudice was formed.

14

5. Kaufman ignored Hector because he assumed him to be a physical laborer with whom he would have difficulty holding a conversation. It tells him that "tracking," as he calls it, may not be unusual, and it may be damaging to people from the entire range of socioeconomic "tracks."
6. Kaufman's ending is effective because it describes a painful situation that most people can identify with. By keeping the ending open-ended, he emphasizes the ongoing nature of his—and presumably many others'—problem.

Vocabulary

intellectually (6) concerning the ability to learn or the mind
perfunctory (9) short; without elaboration
contemporaries (10) people of the same age
acclaimed (13) praised; celebrated
concocted (14) made; manufactured

EVEN YOU CAN GET IT (p. 84)
Bruce Lambert

Essay Analysis and Discussion

Lambert startles his reader to attention with his opening line and again when he closes his essay. In between he chronicles the emotional journey from the moment a young woman learns she has AIDS until the present. While the reader is raptly involved in the story of Alison Gertz, it would be easy to miss how skillfully Lambert moves from one phase of the woman's feelings to another. Ask students to study Lambert's essay with attention to the way in which he pulls the reader from one step to another on this painful odyssey. Then ask them to chronicle a personal voyage of their own, mindful of the fact that time is not the only thing that divides the eras of our lives—feelings, a change in social status, financial security or the lack of it, relationships, and other things mark the steps we take.

Questions for Study and Discussion

1. Lambert's beginning is intended to startle readers with a truth they either were unaware of or chose to ignore. The opening is effective for catching readers' attention, thus compelling them to stick around to hear the facts.
2. Alison got AIDS from a one-night sexual encounter. Hopefully , students today are aware that a well-to-do, heterosexual, white female who does not do drugs is still at risk for contracting AIDS. It is not the disease of the poor, of homosexual men, and of I.V. drug users only.

3. Gertz believes that AIDS is a gift because it has focused her attention on the tragedy of the disease and in so doing has offered her a purpose in life: the education she is able to offer others about the disease.

4. Gertz especially wants to reach "these kids who think they are immortal." Her message is simple—one casual sexual encounter can result in a case of AIDS. In response to their assurance that such things can't happen to them Gertz offers herself as tragic proof that they are wrong—AIDS can happen to anyone.

5. Lambert recognizes AIDS for what it is: a killer that must be dealt with immediately. In quoting Gertz's appeal for early and widespread education about AIDS, and by his choice of this subject for a story, Lambert demonstrates his own sense of urgency concerning the disease.

6. Lambert opens his essay with an attention-grabbing sentence and then in the first four paragraphs concentrates on Alison Gertz's present feelings about having AIDS. Beginning with the fifth paragraph, Lambert divides the essay into clear sections recalling Alison's feelings from the time she learned she had AIDS until the present. Each paragraph is a step in that painful journey, and the running titles point out events or short quotations that are emblematic of the emotional stage described in each section.

Vocabulary

promiscuous (2) engaging in sexual intercourse indiscriminately or with many persons

affluent (5) wealthy; rich

rampant (11) spreading unchecked; widespread

embark (18) to begin a journey

ebullience (21) an overflow of enthusiasm; high spirits

fervor (21) great warmth of emotion; ardor; zeal

optimistic (22) of or characterized by optimism; hopeful

opportunistic (24) adapting one's actions, thoughts or utterances to take advantage of circumstances for personal gain

ostracized (32) banished, barred, shut out

bolster (44) support so as to keep from falling

HOW TO TAKE A JOB INTERVIEW (p. 91)
Kirby W. Stanat

Essay Analysis and Discussion

The ending of the essay makes use of a kind of evidence writers often use to provide effective support for personal opinions—the experiment. Students sometimes hesitate to draw conclusions in their essays fearing they lack the necessary objective information to back them up. The experiment is one way of putting those opinions to a test, while also providing a way to develop the body of an essay. When you approach Stanat's essay, have students look at the conclusion he reaches in paragraph 28. In the paragraph following it, he uses objective data to support that conclusion. Ask your students if that data is as effective as the experiment he goes on to describe in paragraphs 30 through 36. Though the information in paragraph 29 serves the same purpose as the experiment, most students will probably agree the closing paragraphs finally convince readers that Stanat's opinion is correct. The specific case study gives authenticity to the generic description in paragraph 29 by presenting a more concrete and visual connection for the reader.

Questions for Study and Discussion

1. Stanat's beginning and ending work together to provide an orderly progression of ideas. He opens the essay by establishing a key point about his topic—the recruiter is coming from corporate headquarters—and uses the first three paragraphs to drive that point home. Paragraphs 4 through 11 illustrate how *not* to approach an interview, given the opening lesson; and after a nice transition in paragraph 12, Stanat explains in detail how a recruiter operates (paragraphs 13 through 29). The last seven paragraphs present a fitting climax by once again providing a sample experience to illustrate his preceding lesson and, at the same time, reemphasize the point made at the beginning.

2. Stanat's purpose is to provide information about the interview process to help college students succeed in campus job interviews. His thesis is that in order to succeed in an interview, one has to know what the recruiter is looking for as well as where he or she is "coming from."

3. The sequence of steps in the process is: (1) recruiter examines résumé or data sheet, (2) recruiter goes to lobby and calls for interviewee, (3) recruiter looks to see who moves, (4) recruiter waits for interviewee to approach, (5) recruiter scrutinizes interviewee's physical actions as well as dress and appearance, (6) recruiter introduces self and leads way to interviewing room, (7) recruiter opens door and gestures interviewee into room, (8) recruiter gives close-up inspection, (9) recruiter smells interviewee, (10) recruiter checks interviewee's backside, (11) recruiter asks interviewee to sit down (Stanat believes that at this point the decision on the interviewee is 75 to 80 percent made), and (12) recruiter talks to interviewee.

4. Body movement alerts the recruiter to the applicant's attitude. If you come across like a brisk, young professional hopping out of your seat, he will assume that will be your attitude on the job. If you slouch now, you'll probably slouch through the workday.

5. Most recruiters have made up their minds before the actual interview begins. The essay is useful for advising young job applicants that recruiters need to be impressed with the whole person, not just a résumé and a grade point average.

17

6. The structural and technical devices Stanat uses to establish this informal tone include: (a) the pronoun *you*, (b) contractions, (c) imperative mood, (d) informal diction, (e) active voice, and (f) loose (as opposed to periodic) sentences. Stanat's use of slang and colloquial expressions reinforces the informality. To make his tone more formal, Stanat could have used: (a) third-person pronouns, (b) passive constructions, (c) periodic sentences, (d) no contractions, and (e) no slang or colloquial expressions

Vocabulary

cubicle (3) any small compartment or room
deteriorates (10) decreases in quantity, character, or value
résumé (13) a summary of experience submitted with a job application
adamant (35) firm in purpose or opinion; unyielding

CHAPTER 5 PARAGRAPHS

SIMPLICITY (p. 101)
William Zinsser

Essay Analysis and Discussion

Freshmen are often surprised by Zinsser's suggestion to simplify, simplify. Many have come through high school writing courses believing that more is better and that the thesaurus is the basic tool for selecting vocabulary. To reinforce the notion of revising for simplicity's sake, have your students look over Zinsser's sample revision from manuscript. Then, using examples from past student papers (or some other suitable source), present students with paragraphs needing simplifying. As students trim words or alter vocabulary or rearrange sentences, be sure they keep in mind the elements for an effective paragraph—controlling idea, unity, development, and coherence. When they've finished, analyze the deletions and changes and see if they can identify common types of clutter.

Questions for Study and Discussion

1. As Zinsser states in paragraph 1, clutter is a writing disease, the symptoms of which include "unnecessary words, circular constructions, pompous frills and meaningless jargon."
2. Students may have several theories. One possibility is that some educated and high-ranking people confuse erudition with long words and obscured meanings.
3. "Clear thinking becomes clear writing: one can't exist without the other. It's impossible for a muddy thinker to write good English."
4. The writer must ask himself constantly: What am I trying to say? Have I said it? Is it clear to someone encountering the subject for the first time?

These questions are important to Zinsser because good writing doesn't come naturally or easily. And the clear thinking that precedes it "is a conscious act that writers must force upon themselves."

5. The first paragraph introduces the essay by defining "clutter" and establishing what Zinsser hopes to eliminate by writing his essay. It provides a necessary context for his thesis about simplicity. The final paragraph is a reminder that good writing does not come naturally but is the result of hard work. It is effective because it reemphasizes the importance of revision to successful writing.

6. Paragraphs 4 and 5 illustrate the points Zinsser makes in his first three paragraphs. He provides examples of cluttered writing by highly educated people to demonstrate the need for simplicity, and then presents simplified versions to underscore what he advocates.

7. Zinsser uses the questions in paragraph 2 to get readers to identify with the problem of clutter. By using the questions, he blames the writer rather than the reader for the reader's failure to understand. This helps establish his main point that writing should be simplified for the reader's sake.

Vocabulary

pompous (1) characterized by an exaggerated show of dignity or self-importance
decipher (2) to read or interpret something ambiguous, obscure, or illegible
adulterants (3) extraneous or improper ingredients that make something impure or inferior
mollify (4) to allay anger; placate
enviable (6) desirable
tenacious (9) persistent
bearded (11) confronted boldly

BILINGUALISM'S GOAL (p. 108)
Barbara Mujica

Essay Analysis and Discussion

Have your students read Mujica's first five paragraphs again in class. Her thesis comprises paragraph 5, emphasized by her use of a single-sentence paragraph. Note how she prepares her readers for it. She uses her first two paragraphs to provide the framework for her argument, establishing her views of the role of the school system versus her role as an Hispanic parent. She presents the argument she seeks to overcome in paragraph 3, then a concise rebuttal in paragraph 4. In essence, the whole essay is right here, concise and convincing, and the body of the essay serves only to bolster the point she has already made. Discuss the role of schools versus the role of parents with your students. Do they agree with Mujica's assertion that ethnic heritage is strictly a family matter? How effectively can schools teach children from a strictly Spanish household?

Questions for Study and Discussion

1. Mujica argues that the teaching of ethnicity and heritage should be done in the home and the teaching of tools to use in society, specifically the English language, should be taught in the schools.
2. Mujica begins her essay with this sentence to establish a context for her argument. Her point of view as a Spanish speaker carries much more weight than if she were from an Anglo household commenting on a situation that she didn't have to deal with.
3. Mujica uses a one-sentence paragraph to emphasize the main argument of her essay.
4. The topic sentence is the first sentence. All the subsequent sentences relate directly to the topic. The paragraph serves to allow exceptions to Mujica's general argument. It helps establish Mujica as a reasonable person who knows that exceptions will exist to her basic argument.
5. Bilingual education is of particular importance to Hispanics because they are the fastest-growing minority in the United States, and they lag behind non-Hispanics economically.
6. Bilingualism's goal is to teach English to non-English-speaking students so that they are prepared to excel in American society. It can best be achieved by leaving the teaching of ethnic heritage to the parents and concentrating on providing the students with the language skills they need.

Vocabulary

instilling (1) inspiring; providing
inculcate (2) teach
advocate (3) support; propose
curricula (6) (plural of curriculum) courses of study
notoriously (8) well-known for negative reasons
menial (9) unrewarding; simple; drudgery

"I JUST WANNA BE AVERAGE" (p. 112)
Mike Rose

Essay Analysis and Discussion

Students will likely find Rose's tribute to Jack MacFarland entertaining, but some may find it wordy or drawn out. Yet when they study the essay, they will find that each anecdote, each personal reference, and each seemingly casual statement directly relates to the topic Rose wants to present in a particular paragraph. Rose proves that you don't have to be overly concise or conservative in your writing to write an effective essay, but you do have to have a purpose and to stick to it in each paragraph. Rose makes MacFarland and his own situation real to the reader while maintaining a flow in his essay that would be impossible to maintain with sloppy paragraphs. Have your students closely examine a paragraph of their choice and explain how each sentence relates to the paragraph's topic. If they write an essay about a teacher, emphasize the importance of using examples and anecdotes to liven up their essay—as long as they directly contribute to the paragraph containing them.

Questions for Study and Discussion

1. The title gives the reader a sense of just how much Rose's standards were raised by MacFarland. By the end of the essay Rose obviously goes well beyond the average in a number of areas—he has exceeded his academic dreams.
2. MacFarland is a slob with wrinkled pants, a sorry tie, and stained teeth. Obviously, his abilities as a teacher have nothing to do with the way he looks.
3. Jack MacFarland looked awful, but he was a very good teacher. MacFarland's lectures were well crafted and intellectually stimulating, and his course covered a lot of ground. He was able to handle the difficult students and earn everyone's respect. MacFarland inspired Rose to work hard and do well. Good grades from MacFarland were things of value. MacFarland encouraged Rose into working to get into college. And succeeded in helping him go.
4. The transition between paragraphs 2 and 3 both has to do with language—Rose's somewhat idyllic view in paragraph 2 and the real world of Mercy High in paragraph 3. The transition between paragraphs 3 and 4 brings the reader to what MacFarland did for Rose in particular. Rose shows what MacFarland did in class and how he interacted with others before he begins an in-depth account of his own relationship with MacFarland.
5. Rose introduces the reader to real people, kids like everyone knows in high school. It makes the essay more entertaining, and it gives the reader a way to see what MacFarland had to contend with. By making them real people, Rose shows the interaction MacFarland had with a variety of students, and the respect he earned from all.
6. Rose has difficulty getting into college because his grades are awful. He makes it by doing well in MacFarland's class and having him pull strings at his alma mater.

Vocabulary

beatnik (1) hippie; counterculture person
curriculum (1) course of study

21

paradox (2) incongruity; puzzle
existentialism (2) philosophy focusing on human responsibility
rejoin (3) respond; counterattack
indomitable (3) dauntless; irrepressible
linguistic (3) relating to language
incipient (3) developing; budding
ministrations (4) attention; care
extrinsic (5) from outside
spectroscopic (5) concerning a spectroscope, an optical instrument
gangly (6) tall; lanky

CHAPTER 6   TRANSITIONS

WHY I WANT TO HAVE A FAMILY (p. 120)
Lisa Brown

Essay Analysis and Discussion

Since students may find it intimidating to argue against Brown's thesis in class, try playing devil's advocate when considering this essay. Develop a series of points opposed to Brown's, paying particular attention to her reasons for wanting to raise a family, and present your own set of contrasting situations. See what kind of reactions this generates. You may stimulate a discussion similar to one that has occurred more than once in the students' dorms and apartments, but one they are initially reluctant to broach in a classroom situation. Such a discussion could reveal aspects of the underlying motive in Brown's approach to her audience.

Questions for Study and Discussion

1. Brown argues for what she calls a "package deal"—the personal fulfillment of relationships and family life in conjunction with the individual awareness that a college education can produce. Her attitude began to change when her sister and a friend had babies, and she noticed the positive influence that raising children can have on parents.

2. Brown argues against those women whose obsessiveness in pursuing a career insulates them from the people around them and prevents them from seeing the inherent value of relationships and family life.

3. In paragraph 6, Brown discusses the "abstract happiness" associated with raising children and explains what children offer parents: (1) teaching them patience and sensitivity; (2) serving as clues to their own pasts; and (3) reminding them to ensure a quality future. The culmination of her reasoning appears in paragraph 7, when she states: "I want to be unselfish. But I've spent most of my life working in the opposite direction. . . ."

4. In the first sentence of paragraph 2, the transitional *though* sets up a contrast with the point made in paragraph 1; similarly, the "good news-bad news" transition at the beginning of paragraph 3 sets up a contrast with paragraph 2. Paragraph 4 begins with a transitional concession (*granted*) that provides a contrast between "now" and "then"; the final sentence in paragraph 4 is a summary (*in short*) that offers a transition into the writer's second reason that motherhood came to be seen as an obstacle. The fourth sentence in paragraph 6 uses *though* to point out a transition in the way Brown herself began to think about motherhood. In paragraph 8 the first sentence answers a question posed at the end of paragraph 7, providing a transition into Brown's concluding arguments. The first word in paragraph 9 (*today*) sets up a transitional contrast to the final sentence in paragraph 8.
5. Children require patience and sensitivity if we care to see the world as they see it and want them to see our needs as well. Seeing the world through their eyes reminds us of how the world once looked to us, which in turn strengthens our sensitivity. It is a circle that points to the future. We give them the memories and quality of compassion that they will someday pass on to their children.
6. Though this essay is aimed at a female audience, especially those who have ruled out a family in their future plans (as evidenced by the questions at the end of paragraph 3), its arguments can be applied to males too. Brown's ideas about the roles of women, egocentrism, education, and what children can teach us transcend any limitations of gender.

Vocabulary

relegating (2) sending or consigning to an obscure place, position, or condition
autonomy (2) the condition or quality of being self-governing
insular (3) detached and isolated in outlook and experience
bravado (3) defiant or swaggering behavior
precepts (5) rules or principles that impose a particular standard of action or conduct
contingent (5) dependent upon
doting (6) showing excessive love or fondness
tandem (10) one behind the other

HOW I GOT SMART (p. 125)
Steve Brody

Essay Analysis and Discussion

Brody uses the first three paragraphs of his essay to set up his point that sometimes a love of education is not born, it is made. The rest is a narrative presented chronologically to take us from his distaste for book learning to his "thirst" for it. This is a "one-joke" essay: The excerpts from the encyclopedia not only are used to support his thesis, they also form the bulk of the dialogue with the girl Brody wants to impress. His lengthy discourses are punctuated with her short responses which moves the narrative along smoothly. Brody makes good use of transitions to keep his story easy to read. However, just as frequently, he gets the reader from paragraph to paragraph by moving them in time and space. Students can study Brody's essay to observe his movement from one paragraph or one sentence to another with and without the use of transitional words.

Questions for Study and Discussion

1. He had already "savored the heady wine of knowledge" and could not alter his course.
2. Brody's humor is affected by the stilted encyclopedia-style prose he tries to pass off as casual conversation.
3. In each case, the following paragraph begins with a transitional expression, such as "and," "so," "occasionally," etc. In paragraph 35 Brody uses "but," "and," and "where."
4. Coleridge was an English poet, 1772–1834. *The Rime of the Ancient Mariner* is probably his best known work. It describes in "exotic and supernatural themes" the plight of a mariner, alone at sea with an albatross around his neck. Agamemnon, leader of the Greek forces in the Trojan War, was murdered by his wife Clytemnestra and her lover. Alexander Pope, 1688–1744, was an English poet.
5. Brody's denial of any innate erudition at the beginning of his essay and his enthusiasm for learning at the end emphasize that the revelation of learning can happen to anyone and has little to do with higher intelligence. Also, by referring to Volume P, Brody reveals that he stuck to his resolve to read the encyclopedia.
6. Brody's substitution of encyclopedia entries for conversation is funny and contributes to the tone of the essay. His selections are also humorous for being outside the usual context of interest for most teenage boys and girls. They are dry and humorless, yet become funny when Debbie is kind and tolerant enough to take them as serious conversation. By including so many of them, Brody has several opportunities to elaborate on his joke.

Vocabulary

misconception (1) incorrect interpretation
prodigies (1) highly talented children
devotee (2) a zealous follower, supporter, or enthusiast
bearish (3) apt to sell securities or commodities in expectation of a price decline
dabbled (3) worked without serious effort

surge (9) to move in waves
erudition (9) learning; scholarship
snout (16) a long, projecting muzzle
sidled (20) moved sideways or side foremost
forbidding (24) disagreeable; repellent
subsist (26) receive the means of maintaining life
amorous (32) being in love
expatiated (32) talked or wrote at length
adenoids (32) an enlarged mass of tissue near the opening of the nose into the
    throat
voracious (35) excessively eager
disgorging (39) discharging forcefully or confusedly
savored (43) tasted with pleasure

FACING VIOLENCE (p. 131)
Michael T. Kaufman

Essay Analysis and Discussion

As with many aspects of good writing, the skillful use of transitions is sometimes barely noticeable to the reader. In Kaufman's essay, not only does he
move almost effortlessly from one idea to another, he also uses transition to
move us over the course of several years. To examine the way Kaufman achieves
the easy flow of his essay, students can outline the text, identifying the key idea
in each paragraph. Then they can identify the different time periods Kaufman
refers to and discuss how he uses transition to move his readers backwards and
forwards in time while still maintaining the overall unity of his essay. In their
discussion, students should refer to the role played in Kaufman's essay by the
three types of transitions referred to at the beginning of this chapter. This exercise should help students understand that a good piece of writing does not
merely string ideas one after the other—it establishes a relationship among
them and transitions play a key role in making that relationship clear to readers.

Questions for Study and Discussion

1. Kaufman states his thesis, "the greatest moral pitfall is not that we witness
   too much bang bang, but that for the most part, we perceive it vicariously,"
   in paragraph 2, and paraphrases it in paragraph 9.
2. Kaufman's uncle said that unless children played with toy guns, they were
   bound to "play" with them as adults. If the statement is to be taken as
   intended as literally true then it is puzzling, since many children who play
   with toy guns trade them for the real thing when they grow up. The uncle's

declaration makes a little more sense, although it is still shaky, if he intended to convey the idea that children possess some kind of innate tendency to violence that must be satisfied in childhood if it is not to be played out in adulthood.

3. Kaufman uses both emotional appeals and thoughtful examples to make his point that Americans perceive death from too safe a vantage point. In paragraph 5, for example, he lists some of the television shots of violence that occurred during the fighting in Beirut. As they failed to move him emotionally, so they fail to move the reader, but are simply examples of the kind of vicarious witnessing of American television audiences. However, at the end of this paragraph when he tells about his mother's death, we are grieved and shocked by his sudden and intimate confession. He masterfully uses examples, both thoughtful and emotional, to recapitulate the two different kinds of experience of death—the kind that is two-dimensional and the kind that involves participation.

4. The expression "visual clichés" refers to the expected, hackneyed shots of battle-torn areas of the world that we see on television all the time. They fail to be horrible because they are two-dimensional and don't seem real to us. We are not there. We cannot even imagine ourselves there.

5. Readers will be shocked and saddened by Kaufman's account of the way in which he left his mother to die. We agree that it is a terrible thing to do to a parent. It is an effective and emotional example of Kaufman's thesis, because he knows that it is the solution more and more Americans are choosing for their elderly relatives. By including it he is forcing readers to face an act that they are capable of and to participate in the guilt and horror that are the consequences of turning away from death.

6. All seven of these sentences sets the paragraph that follows it in time and place, each of which was the occasion or the setting for Kaufman's evolving realization of the way in which Americans shun death.

7. Jack Troake met death head on, without lying to himself or anyone else. Yet he was judged, and in his mind, judged wrongly by those who stood at too great a distance to know what they were talking about. Such a man could probably be counted on to be fair and pragmatic in judging others.

Vocabulary

alleged (1) stated as a fact without proof
impaired (2) damaged; lessened
vicariously (2) realized or experienced by one person through the sympathetic sharing in the experience of another
flabbergasted (4) astounded
sensitized (6) to make or become sensitive or hypersensitive
antidote (8) a remedy to counteract the effects of poison

CHAPTER 7   EFFECTIVE SENTENCES

AN EYE-WITNESS ACCOUNT OF THE SAN FRANCISCO EARTHQUAKE (p. 141)
Jack London

Essay Analysis and Discussion

The introductory section to this chapter briefly explains the difference between active and passive sentences. Though students may understand this difference when it is presented to them in sample form, many will still find it difficult to recognize the distinction when writing or reading an essay. Therefore. it may be useful to devote some class time to looking at examples of each in London's essay, and discussing the role that active and passive voice play. To prepare, identify a number of sentences to use as examples. Then, have your students decide if a sentence is active or passive, and why. You can also have them consider how each sentence might read if it were constructed in the other manner, and what effect such a change would have on the paragraph from which it is taken. Students should begin to see that London's selection of active and passive sentences is not simply a matter of chance, but serves a function vital to the vividness of his description.

Questions for Study and Discussion

1. London pits the forces of nature against the forces of man and nature wins. The earthquake and the fire easily snuff out the matchstick world of man. However, even in defeat man emerges a noble foe.
2. The rising heat of the intense fire created a chimneylike column. The fire was fanned by fresh air at the base of the column.
3. London tells us in paragraph 4 that he gives his account from a vantage point in the bay.
4. These short sentences are used for dramatic emphasis.
5. By using the passive voice London avoids the tiresome repetition of "the earthquake" as the subject in each sentence.
6. The parallelism in sentences 1 and 2 of paragraph 1 emphasizes the contrast between the earthquake and the fire. In sentences 7 and 8 of paragraph 1, London emphasizes by parallelism the extent of the desolation. In paragraph 2, the parallel triad "reddening the sun, darkening the day, and filling the land with smoke" serves to highlight the awesome proportions of the fire. In paragraph 6, the four sentences beginning with "An enumeration of" emphasize the totality of the destruction.

Vocabulary

conflagration (1) a large and destructive fire
nabobs (1) men of wealth and prominence
lurid (2) glowing or glaring through a haze
contrivances (3) mechanical devices or clever plans
vestiges (6) all visible traces of evidence

PLAYING TO WIN (p. 145)
Margaret A. Whitney

Essay Analysis and Discussion

The strength of Whitney's essay lies in many areas: her easy, glib, style; her punchy sentences; and her smooth transitions from one aspect of her story to another. But what sets it apart is her integration of her daughter's point of view into the body of the essay. By not using quotation marks to set off her daughter's words, Whitney allows them to come through almost as if they were being spoken by Whitney herself. The mother and daughter speak in one voice. It is not so surprising then when Whitney finally integrates her daughter's attitudes with her own. Students can learn from this essay to present a point of view while simultaneously allowing for the opposite point of view in a nonthreatening, friendly way. Students can practice this technique in an essay of their own, perhaps in a dialogue with a younger sibling, a parent or a roommate of opposing likes and attitudes.

Questions for Study and Discussion

1. Whitney was surprised that her daughter became interested in sports since she had shown little interest in sports before entering high school. Whitney explains that Ann was not very good at sports, and didn't seem to try hard. Whitney also explains that her daughter did not fit the "jock" stereotype. Social attitudes working against Ann were that pretty women did not need or like to play sports. The author shares these attitudes.
2. The vast majority of ads depict beautiful women as anything but athletic. We see just the woman's face or a beautiful form draped with jewelry or fine clothes, and always at rest. Even Virginia Slims ads, which purport to admire the liberated woman, still glorify the slim, beautiful, inert female.
3. The author was treated as the "typical girl" when she was younger. She was not expected to do anything athletic. Whitney's daughter has shown her that competition and team spirit are beneficial to a young adult and produce a more well-rounded person, better able to meet life's challenges.
4. Whitney is "resigned" to the fact that attitudes about what is "feminine" have changed. Her tone remains consistent throughout the essay and is evident in her choice of words such as: *marginally interested, simply sit and*

enjoy, athletic indifference, sports is a natural activity for females, and *advocacy of women.*

5. Paragraph 3 contains both short, dramatic sentences and longer ones. Whitney does this to make the essay more readable. The shorter sentences serve as mini-transitions from one idea to another, mimicking the author's thought process.

Vocabulary

marginally (1) minimally; slightly
titter (1) to laugh at in a half-suppressed way, suggestive of foolishness, nervousness, etc.
bode (2) to be an omen of; presage
bedraggled (3) soiled and wet; unkempt
scathing (6) searing; blasting; withering; usually figurative as in scathing remarks
wane (6) to gradually decrease in power, importance, prosperity, intensity, etc.
admonish (7) to warn; caution against specific faults
paroxysm (9) a sudden attack or intensification of symptoms (as in a disease) usually recurring periodically
unctuous (10) characterized by a smug, smooth suave manner; extremely suave, to the point of phoniness
machinations (12) plots; schemes
wrought (13) formed, fashioned, made

A BROTHER'S MURDER (p. 150)
Brent Staples

Essay Analysis and Discussion

Staples achieves power in his essay through his blows-to-the-head description of his brother's terrifying hurtle to death. However, by including the details of his own safe, rewarding life, Staples establishes the "might-have-been" that adds even greater tragedy to the story of his brother's short, piteous life. Thus by the time we read his final sentence, it is more than a confession of a gentle if tardy reaching into empty space. It has assumed the weight of despair great enough to throw us across the room out of reach of Blake's shimmering tragedy. Students can practice the power of sentences in a similar way. But they will have to remember that a sentence such as Staples's last one and others in his essay do not gain their power simply by being shocking. They gain it by the weight of all that has come before.

Questions for Study and Discussion

1. The opening of this essay is an effective one precisely because it is jarring, the first of many times we will feel that sensation throughout Staples's

essay. He wants us to feel, as he did, the suddenness, the unreality that comes with such a phone call even if it is (as it was for him) entirely expected.

2.   Staples was introduced to mortality during the 1960s when he first beheld the bodies of the young who had been wrecked "after sudden explosions of violence." It seemed odd to Staples to find death among the young instead of among the "old and failing."

3.   The Vietnam veterans and the sergeant helped characterize the circumstances under which young blacks kill one another—circumstances in which a desire to be "real men" makes them vulnerable to insult. Taken to extreme that desire defines manhood in the cruelest terms possible: the willingness to kill or be killed.

4.   Students will find plenty of examples of Staples's use of poetic language to add emotionalism and drama to his essay. Especially in phrases such as "beautiful young men," "Wesley, whom I loved very much," and "His eyes shining like black diamonds, he smiled and danced just beyond my grasp," Staples conveys not only the depth of his affection for his brother and friends, but he also inspires in readers a vision of these men as valuable and beautiful to the people who loved them. By so doing Staples saves them from the anonymity inflicted by death in the streets.

5.   The longer sentences set readers up, lulling them or hypnotizing them with a series of facts and images. The short stark sentences come without warning to shock us awake to the grim realities of the inner city. They are the sudden jab that follows an easy dance in the ring.

6.   Staples "got out," got educated, and never went back. His brother, on the other hand, stayed behind and got lost in the teeming despair of his environment. Yet it is not only what Staples says but what he does not say that reveals his point of view over his brother's fate. At no time does he compare his brother's character to his own. Such an omission suggests strongly that Staples believed life and circumstances rather than a flawed character conspired to kill his brother.

7.   The line is intended to convey Staples's feeling of despair and hopelessness as his brother moves beyond his reach to death. Staples conveys in his tone and his choice of details that he has confused and sad feelings about his brother's death. On the one hand, he wishes he had done more to save him. On the other, he knows his brother was "enamored" of the terrifying life he led. In the end, there is no one to blame unless one can give a name and a face to the terror and despair of life in the inner city.

Vocabulary

escalated (1): increased in extent, volume, number, intensity or scope
affluent (3): wealthy; well-to-do; privileged
machismo (3): a strong or exaggerated pride in one's masculinity
incursions (3): sudden, usually temporary invasions; raids

ensconced (4): settled snugly or securely
umbilical (4): the cord that joins the unborn child with its mother
forays (5): raids, especially in search of plunder; pillages
hustler (6): one who works energetically
swagger (6): to walk with a conceited swing or strut

SALVATION (p. 155)
Langston Hughes

Essay Analysis and Discussion

In addition to Hughes's use of different sentence lengths and patterns in this essay, he varies the manner of his material, particularly for the scene at the church. To add a sense of the revival meeting's liveliness, he includes bits of conversation that enhance the essay's main idea. In paragraph 3 he presents the preacher's words: in paragraph 6, Westley's whispered mutterings; and in paragraphs 8 through 10, an exchange between the minister and Langston's aunt. To illustrate the effects of these passages, read the essay aloud to your students and ask them to pay attention to what the dialogue contributes. Your discussion should focus, especially, on the dialogue's relation to the first and last paragraphs, and on how the inclusion of conversation helps convey Hughes's central idea. Students should also note that he includes only enough dialogue to serve his purpose.

Questions for Study and Discussion

1. According to Hughes, salvation is being "saved from sin" when Jesus and the Holy Ghost come into your life. Young Langston "wanted to see Jesus." However, his salvation was more important to his aunt who cared about his soul and didn't want to be embarrassed in front of the congregation by his being the only one left who had not been saved.
2. Hughes expects to be saved because his aunt and the other townspeople had built up the expectation during the weeks of preparation for the revival meeting. In paragraph 3 we see the various appeals made by the preacher, and the preacher's appeals are reinforced by the prayers and songs of the congregation.
3. The boy cried out because he lied to the congregation about seeing Jesus, because he regretted not seeing Jesus, and because he now doubted that Jesus existed at all. The irony of the tale is that Langston's "salvation from sin" was based on a lie.
4. If these two sentences had been combined, the dramatic effect of the reversal of thought and statement would have been lost.
5. Hughes uses coordinating conjunctions throughout his essay. When he wants to link closely related actions and not give any one of them empha-

sis, he does so in a long sentence. When he wants to link closely related ideas but give emphasis to each idea, he uses short sentences that begin with coordinating conjunctions.

6. The subordinating conjunctions in paragraph 15 are: *for, for, because, because, because, that, that, since.* In this last paragraph Hughes reflects on the experience, and, therefore, makes explicit connections.

7. Some of the words Hughes uses to remind us that we are at a revival meeting are *sin, mourners' bench, preached, sermon, hell, prayed, Jesus, congregation,* and *wall.* In addition, Hughes uses traditional religious figures of speech such as "to bring the young lambs to the fold," "when you were saved you saw a light," "lower lights are burning," and "all the new young lambs were blessed in the name of God."

Vocabulary

dire (3) dreadful or terrible
gnarled (4) deformed; twisted
vain (11) without due respect or piety
punctuated (14) interrupted periodically
ecstatic (14) enraptured

PART II   THE LANGUAGE OF THE ESSAY

CHAPTER 8   DICTION AND TONE

ON BEING 17, BRIGHT, AND UNABLE TO READ (p. 167)
David Raymond

Essay Analysis and Discussion

This essay contains some good examples for demonstrating the use of abstract and concrete diction. For instance, in paragraphs 5, 11, and 13, Raymond makes abstract statements and then interprets their meanings by providing concrete supporting information. Before your students look at these paragraphs, ask them how they would define the following three terms: *dumb, change, problem.* Unless they use examples, their definitions will likely be general and abstract— intangible rather than concrete ideas. This is how Raymond uses the three words:

> I just felt *dumb.* And *dumb* was how the kids treated me.
> Life began to *change* for me then, because I began to feel better about myself.
> Homework is a real *problem.*

In each case, Raymond goes on to show what he means in very concrete terms. Have students look over this concrete supporting information and discuss what distinguishes it from the statements above. Let them consider the elements of sensory perception and the identification of facts as they are described in the introductory section to this chapter. Once the distinction between concrete and abstract is clear, have them do a short writing exercise in which they develop a concrete representation for an abstract idea.

Questions for Study and Discussion

1. Dyslexia is a learning disorder in which the brain cannot interpret spatial relationships or has trouble distinguishing the difference between audio and visual information. The definition is not included, because the essay is not about dyslexia. Raymond is writing about the effect on a child of being labeled as different or stupid.
2. Raymond's purpose for telling his story is related in paragraph 16.
3. Raymond's story warns us that negative early-childhood experiences can have a devastating effect on a child's self-esteem, academic performance, and achievement, and that this effect can define us as adults.
4. Other examples include "but from where I sit," "unless you've been there," "I wish I were dead," "I guess I couldn't read," "I didn't talk as good as other kids," and "It was awful." These colloquialisms are the authentic expressions of a seventeen-year-old youth, and they add to the realism and credibility of the essay.
5. In each instance, the word suggested as a substitute is inferior either because it is imprecise or because it lacks the rich connotative value of Raymond's diction.
6. Raymond's tone is intimate and sincere and, though informal, serious enough to establish his central point. The colloquial expression suggests that his reflections are honest.

Vocabulary

dyslexia (2) a disturbance of the ability to read

psychiatrists (6) persons whose profession is the study, diagnosis, treatment, or prevention of mental illness

THE FLIGHT OF THE EAGLES (p. 172)
N. Scott Momaday

Essay Analysis and Discussion

Momaday admittedly describes a spectacular event in his essay, but he does it justice with his compelling language. He avoids elaborate or pretentious phrases. Instead, his skillfully chosen mixture of adverbs, adjectives, and verbs paints a complete picture of the flight in a very brief and accessible essay. Emphasize Momaday's choice of verbs—the eagles don't just fly, they cavort, spin, spiral, swerve, sail, feint, and scream. Note also how he concentrates on one bird at a time in order to give each his full attention. The female's grandeur and control contrasts with the male's quickness "sliding down in a blur of motion to the strike." The rattlesnake connects the two birds—otherwise, they are individuals. See how well your students can follow Momaday's example in the suggested writing assignments.

Questions for Study and Discussion

1. The female is large, controlled, and elegant. The male is smaller and quicker.
2. The rattlesnake connects the two birds. The reader follows it from the female to the male.
3. Verbs such as *feinting, screaming, cavorting, fanned, writhing, swerved,* and *sailed* add to the description.
4. In describing the female, Momaday is very specific with his diction. He refers to her broad wings and her pivots and wheels. The rattlesnake is specifically identified, as is its long body. The female's crop and hackles gleam like copper. The male is just more than half as large as the female. By using concrete and specific diction, Momaday paints a very defined picture in his essay.
5. Momaday uses several similes. The snake is like a bit of silver thread, the female's crop and hackles gleam like copper, the male cracks the snake like a whip and swings upward in a long pendulum arc, then the female recedes like a mote into the haze. Momaday also personifies the eagles by saying they feint and scream with delight.

Vocabulary

cavorting frolicking; playing
feinting dodging; bluffing
spectral ghostly
carrion meat of a dead animal
mote speck

LA VIDA LOCA (THE CRAZY LIFE): TWO GENERATIONS OF
GANG MEMBERS (p. 175)
Luis Rodriguez

Essay Analysis and Discussion

Rodriguez uses vivid imagery to communicate the despair associated with gang life and his pain at seeing his son follow the same destructive path. The first paragraph is a good example—Rodriguez shows the dreariness of winter in an urban neighborhood by juxtaposing the streets filled with "dark scum" and "the whiskers of old men" hanging from the buildings. Paragraph 6 is particularly poignant: "As Ramiro speeds off, I see my body enter the mouth of darkness, my breath cut the frigid flesh of night—my voice crack open the night sky." The choice of words is poetic and striking, and it effectively readies the reader for the tone of anger and despair found in the rest of the essay. It would be hyperbolic in a different context, but here it is very effective in conveying Rodriguez's passionate involvement in his topic. Have your students find other examples of unusual word choices and images. Has the essay helped them understand the motivations of gang members?

Questions for Study and Discussion

1. Words such as *scum, decay, whiskers of old men, bone-chilling,* and *fever* add to the description by painting a vivid image. The reader has a better sense of the hostile conditions Rodriguez faces both inside and outside of his apartment.
2. Rodriguez brought Ramiro to Chicago to escape the California gangs that he had joined when he was Ramiro's age.
3. Gangs offer their members a way to get both power and respect within a group. Rodriguez had been made to feel powerless in school and society, so he was very susceptible to gangs.
4. The tone is indicated in the first sentence of the passage—tired. Tired of the dying, tiring his mother, tired of his pain. His escape from the streets is not a grand release, but a drawn-out battle against his pain and hopelessness. His use of phrases such as "post-traumatic syndrome," "fallen through the cracks," and wanting his "self-consuming hate to wither in the sunlight" gives the reader a sense of how deep his hopelessness was—and how difficult it must have been to climb out of it.
5. It often means "kill me." Gang murders involve members killing the people most like themselves—in killing someone like themselves, they are, in a way, committing suicide.
6. Rodriguez says that collective action by schools, parents, and the law is needed. He is vague about exactly what should be done, and he doesn't say it will be easy. The ending is optimistic because Ramiro is off the streets, but it is a tenuous optimism. The battle for Ramiro's future is not yet won.

Vocabulary

admixture (1) mixture; substance created by mixing
dissipating (3) disappearing; dissolving
kindred (10) similar; related
absolution (12) redemption; forgiveness
impotence (22) being powerless; inability to change a situation *disenfranchised* (24) displaced; outside of society
innate (35) natural; instinctive

THE FOURTH OF JULY (p. 181)
Audre Lorde

Essay Analysis and Discussion

Lorde's essay is a carefully crafted slow boil, her restraint at the beginning serving to emphasize the blazing anger at the end. She progresses from documenting the ingenuous pleasure of traveling as a young girl to the fury of confronting racism, and her tone follows suit. Yet even in the first four paragraphs, where she doesn't mention race, she foreshadows things to come with her disappointment at not seeing the Liberty Bell and the "violently yellow" cakes. See how many other details your students can find that foreshadow the rage at the end of the essay. The reader senses that she passively accepts her parents' method of shielding her from racism—it is a "new and crushing reality" for them, but it is private. It is not until she and the reader confront racism head-on in the essay that the tone becomes angry. Have your students reread the last paragraph, including the stinging "that summer I left childhood was white." Have them discuss it in the context of current racial issues. How have things changed since Lorde wrote her essay and how have they stayed the same?

Questions for Study and Discussion

1. Lorde describes the food to emphasize the celebrational nature of her family's trip. She also implies that the food—and her family—is very American and proper, at least when discussed outside of the context of her family's color. Finally, her description of the food in paragraph 4 provides a natural lead-in to the next paragraph where we get our first glimpse of racism in the essay.
2. Lorde found the bright sunlight and glare painful for her eyes as a child. As an adult, she dislikes it because it celebrates ideals about the United States that don't exist for her and her family.
3. The Fourth of July represents American ideals of liberty and equality, ideals that don't extend to Black citizens in Lorde's essay. The second part of the question is a matter of opinion, but most students should find that the irony of the title contributes to the effectiveness of the essay.
4. Lorde describes racism as crushing, but private for her parents. She describes her physical agony on the Fourth of July as a child, implying that it is now a mental agony for her regarding the travesty of the holiday for Black people. Lorde's repetition of white in the one-sentence final paragraph brings home the disgust and physical sickness she felt at confronting racism head-on for the first time.
5. Lorde writes an angry essay, but it is a restrained anger until the very end. The choice of words listed above shows the progression of her understanding and anger toward racism as it unfolds in the essay. Early on, she uses subtle and indirect methods to discuss racism, but in the last three paragraphs, detailing how she is confronting it for the first time, she is very direct and very angry.

6. Lorde's parents are probably people who don't like to make waves. Though they are dismayed by racism, their personalities lead them to avoid confronting it and living in a way that they try to be comfortable without conflict. Lorde is obviously a confrontational person, so she reacts in an aggressive, confrontational manner to the injustice she faces.

Vocabulary

ensconced (3) settled; firmly placed
measly (6) pathetic; unsatisfactory
injunction (7) order; command
corolla (10) circular arrangement; petals in a flower
travesty (10) ridiculous or farcical representation
pinafored (16) dressed in a pinafore (a sleeveless dress or apron)
emphatic (18) heated; strong

CHAPTER 9   FIGURATIVE LANGUAGE

THE BARRIO (p. 188)
Robert Ramirez

Essay Analysis and Discussion

Ramirez points out the sights of the barrio from a moving train that emerges in the "deep sleep" of night in the opening paragraph, and reappears to the "yawns and stretchings" of a new dawn in the closing paragraph. Students can discuss this use of figurative language in the asking of two questions: why does Ramirez use a train to establish a context for his description of the barrio?; and why does he take us into the barrio only through the still hours of the night? What does he intend as the symbolism of the train and the street lamp? What do they add to his portrayal of the barrio?

Questions for Study and Discussion

1. Barrio is a Spanish word which refers to a chiefly Spanish-speaking neighborhood (typically in a city) in the United States.
2. The Spanish phrases, spoken as if the reader understands them, lend an aura of authenticity and color to Ramirez's essay. These words allow us to "hear" the people of the barrio. The other words connote warmth, community, intimacy, and friendliness. They are meant to emphasize the positive feelings of life in the barrio that are known only to its inhabitants.
3. "[T]his pulsing light . . . beats slower, like a weary heartbeat" (paragraph 1). "[F]rom the angry seeds of rejection grow the flowers of closeness between outcasts, not the thorns of bitterness" (paragraph 4). "[T]he warmth of the tortilla factory is a wool *serape*" (paragraph 5). "Their houses, aged and

bent, oozing children, are fissures in the horn of plenty" (paragraph 17). These metaphors are particularly apt since they compare things common to the barrio with other things which are relevant to it. The wool serape is as common as the factory. The horn of plenty, broken and empty, is also a metaphor for the people of the barrio.

4. Ramirez intends his comparison of the fences in the barrio with the walls of the Anglo community to symbolize the easy access among the people of his culture as compared with the isolation and separation of the Anglo world.

5. The shopkeeper extends credit to those unable to pay. The young men perform rituals of manhood for the approval or disapproval of the old men who only watch. Families, extended, large, inclusive of neighbors, maintain the sense of belonging, order, and tradition that keeps the people of the barrio here. Even the poor of the barrio serve as a visual reminder of the attitudes and isolation of the Anglo community outside its borders.

6. Had Ramirez begun his description of the barrio with the negative aspects of life there he would have risked having reader's misunderstand the intent of his essay. Ramirez wants us to understand that life in the barrio is integral, satisfying, and necessary. He saves the sadder aspects of life there until the end, so that we do not confuse his desire for our understanding with a desire for pity.

Vocabulary

paradoxical (2) seemingly contradictory
eludes (2) escapes or evades
permeated (3) pervaded
stoical (4) suffering silently and without complaint
pariahs (4) outcasts
complacently (9) with satisfaction or acceptance, especially self-satisfaction
Chicano (11) an American of Mexican descent
countenances (12) human faces, especially as an indication of mood or character
fissures (17) narrow openings or cracks
elusive (19) evasive; out of reach
adverse (19) unfavorable

THE DEATH OF BENNY PARET (p. 194)
Norman Mailer

Essay Analysis and Discussion

Mailer brings the action of the boxing ring alive in this essay through his use of concrete and vivid similes. Descriptions of scenes of action often depend on figurative devices to convey the energy contained in them; to rely only on literal depictions can result in a flat rendering of what was an extremely charged situation. You may wish to have students practice using figurative language by modeling a writing exercise on Mailer's essay. First, have students describe in a paragraph or two an action scene from a sporting event or recreational activity they have witnessed. For the initial draft they should concentrate on getting the details down so that the scene is developed completely. Then, ask them to go back over what they've written and look for places where they might enliven their descriptions with a simile or metaphor or the use of personification. Remind students they are trying to recreate the sensations they experienced by using figurative language that will evoke the same sensations in the reader. When they've finished, ask for volunteers to read their descriptions aloud and find out if class members respond to the figurative devices as the writers hoped they would.

Questions for Study and Discussion

1. Paret was "a proud club fighter," while Griffith was a killer "back on a hoodlum's street." Paret was the champion.
2. Griffith's actions changed boxing from a sport between men to a battle between animals fought to the death.
3. Mailer uses the following similes: "like a cat ready to rip the life out of a huge boxed rat" (paragraph 2); "like a piston rod which had broken through the crankcase" (paragraph 2); "like a baseball bat demolishing a pumpkin" (paragraph 2); "as if some spasm had passed its way through him" (paragraph 2); "as if he were saying, 'I didn't know I was going to die just yet'" (paragraph 3); "like a large ship which turns on end and slides second by second into its grave" (paragraph 3); and "like a heavy ax in the distance chopping into a wet log" (paragraph 3). These similes help convey the physical and mental sensations of sitting in the arena watching the fight in a way that a literal depiction cannot.
4. Students' answers will vary. The question places the focus for the paragraph on Paret and asks the reader, in an emphatic way, to consider the effects of the fight on him.
5. Although Mailer doesn't state directly who is to blame for Paret's death, his emphasis on the audience's reactions to it in the final paragraph suggests that the spectators' and his own thirst for the spectacle helps create the opportunity for such a tragedy to occur.
6. Mailer personifies death in the final paragraph by giving qualities of animation to an abstract concept. In the fourth sentence he states that death "reached out to us," and in the sentence following, that it "hovered" in the air. In sentence 6 he says that Paret's death "came to breathe about him." By using personification, Mailer is better able to evoke the scene in the ring as the life passed out of Benny Paret.

Vocabulary

wilt (2) to become less active or energetic; weaken
spasm (2) a sudden, involuntary contraction of a muscle or a group of muscles
psychic (3) pertaining to extrasensory and nonphysical mental processes
hover (3) to remain floating or suspended in the air over a particular place

THE THIRSTY ANIMAL (p. 197)
Brian Manning

Essay Analysis and Discussion

One of the elements that makes Manning's piece effective is the lack of bitterness and recrimination in his tone, and he uses a metaphor to help him accomplish this. He allows the reader to see his longing for the positive associations he had with alcohol. The negatives—the hangovers and lost days—are ever-present and reveal the magnitude of his problem, but they are not presented with self-pity or newly found disgust. Only through his use of the thirsty animal metaphor does he demonstrate his knowledge of the insidiousness of alcoholism. He does not introduce the thirsty animal until paragraph 11, when the reader is familiar with its nature and how hard it is for Manning to refuse to let it drink. It is therefore very effective, giving substance to an urge that most readers can only try to comprehend. Discuss how Manning characterizes the thirsty animal with your students. Have them come up with metaphors for various aspects of their own personalities.

Questions for Study and Discussion

1. Manning drank in college to try to define a self-image that he could feel comfortable with and, to a lesser degree, to emulate his literary heroes. It took him a long time to deal with his alcoholism because he did not want to believe he was an alcoholic and he did not want to lose the camaraderie he felt with his drinking buddies.
2. Paragraphs 1–8 are organized chronologically, and they summarize the progression of his alcoholism and recovery. By beginning his essay in this way, he gives the reader an overview of the severity of his problem and the difficulties he faces in trying to stay sober.
3. Manning's purpose is to provide an intimate portrait of his own struggles with alcohol. He does not argue against drinking, but explores what it did to him in particular. The positive things include the camaraderie and sense of belonging that drinking gave him, and the sensory pleasures associated with its consumption. The negative things include hangovers, wasted money, and days lost to drinking.

4. Manning describes his urge to drink as a thirsty animal that is always begging for a drink. He uses the metaphor to give shape to his urge, which many of his readers may not understand in the abstract.
5. Manning, as a child, was aware at some level that there was something to beware in the wine cellar. Manning, as an adult, was not wary of the dangers there.
6. Personal opinion may differ, but caging the thirsty animal is a very understandable and compelling image.

Vocabulary

wafting (1) drifting gently
raucously (1) loudly
accouterments (7) things that accompany an event or activity
vintage (9) for port, a particularly good year
sustenance (11) nourishment; food

PART III   TYPES OF ESSAYS

CHAPTER 10   ILLUSTRATION

A CRIME OF COMPASSION (p. 207)
Barbara Huttmann

Essay Analysis and Discussion

At the heart of Huttmann's dramatic and often shocking essay is the story of her young patient. In the beginning of her essay we meet him, a strong, confident, healthy young man. Then Huttmann proceeds in a chronological order to describe the rapid deterioration that ends in his death. Other things are happening as well: the falling apart of his family and the nurse's own evolution from a rule-abiding health worker to mercy "killer." Yet as dramatic as Huttmann's tale is, it remains a model of "show-don't tell." For Huttmann never asks us to weep—she moves us to tears with the details of the events she witnessed and the emotions she experienced. Even those who condemn her actions would be hard pressed to remain unmoved by the horrors that the young family went through. Ask students to reread Huttmann's essay carefully to see how she sustains the dramatic atmosphere of her story. Which kinds of evidence were convincing and which were not? In the end, is she successful in convincing readers of the justness of her actions?

Questions for Study and Discussion

1. Huttmann did not have the legal right to end her patient's life. By that definition, she is a murderer. However, her defenders no doubt will point out that the definition of murder as premeditated and malicious killing of a human being does not fit the circumstances of Huttmann's deed. She killed out of love, not hate, and the decision to do so was painful given her attitude that life is something which must be sustained and nurtured. As Huttmann wondered at the right of doctors to sustain life beyond reasonable bounds, she no doubt questioned their right, and hers, to end it. That is why she argues so strenuously for a patient's right to make this terrible decision.

2. Huttmann's essay is as much a tale of her own struggle as it is the story of her patient's decline and death. She begins in paragraph 7 by telling us how often Mac had to be resuscitated and the terrible and grisly agony he went through. By paragraph 8, she is praying he will die but she has not yet thought of helping him to do it. In paragraph 9 she asks for a "no-code order," which only a doctor can issue. In other words, it is not illegal for doctors to allow a patient to die, only for a nurse. When her request was refused she contemplated the implications of failing to press the button. By paragraph 10, when Mac had undergone fifty-two codes, she began appealing to a higher court, a spiritual judge to question the necessity of her actions. She began to be haunted by the question that modern technology has made inevitable—"do we have the right to play God," not in taking life, but in sustaining it beyond all hope? Finally she makes us witness her panic and fear as she makes the decision not to press the button. Her story is compelling and terrifying and she spares us little of the terror she experienced in making her final decision.

3. As Huttmann explains in paragraph 18, a doctor may legally issue a no-code order. The hypocrisy for her is that the charge of murder is based not on intent but on which uniform a person wears.

4. In paragraph 7 Huttmann describes the work a team of nurses had to do over Mac's body: "The nurses stayed to wipe the saliva that drooled from his mouth, irrigate the big craters of bedsores that covered his hips, suction the lung fluids that threatened to drown him, clean the feces that burned his skin like lye, pour the liquid food down the tube attached to his stomach, put pillows between his knees to ease the bone-on-bone pain, turn him every hour to keep the bedsores from getting worse, and change his gown and linen every two hours to keep him from being soaked in perspiration." Such graphic descriptions are necessary to force the reader to see what Huttmann saw and, however feebly, to feel what Mac felt. She knows it is easy to make philosophical decisions about life and death from a distance. She wants to rub the readers' noses in the truth.

5. As her essay moves forward, Huttmann intensifies the story by going into lengthier detail about shorter periods of time. No doubt this is meant to

parallel as much as possible the way in which Mac's pain escalated, not only in intensity but in the horror of its detail.

6. Quite simply Huttmann means to say that as long as medical science and its practitioners have the means to keep patients alive and believe that they must do so, and as long as the decision not to resuscitate rests with the doctors, patients cannot legally choose to die.

Vocabulary

resuscitate (3) to revive from a condition resembling death
irrigate (7) to flush with liquid
lucid (10) clear-minded; alert
imperative (11) power to restrain, control, or direct
waxen (15) resembling wax (as in color or consistency)
pallor (15) paleness

WINTER BIRDS (p. 212)
Gale Lawrence

Essay Analysis and Discussion

Lawrence is writing for an audience that is just beginning to learn about nature, and she uses illustration very skilfully to both interest her readers in her subject and instruct them about it. The different species of birds are described more according to personality than according to appearance. Chickadees are "one-at-a-timers," blue jays are "gobblers," evening grosbeaks are "feeder bums." Such characterizations are much more intriguing than simple physical descriptions that would soon be made superfluous by the field guide she recommends. As she moves beyond the feeder, she continues to expand upon her subject in interesting ways. For instance, a ruffed grouse taking off is very frightening— more than a simple "sudden rush of wings" would convey—and she indicates this in an amusing and readily understood way. Have your students find the places where Lawrence uses illustration to catch her reader's interest. What experiences have they had observing nature?

Questions for Study and Discussion

1. Winter is a good time to begin to study nature because it is a less daunting task to begin when there are few animals and fewer plants available to study. Feeding birds is a good first step for anyone who wants to learn more about nature.
2. By discussing the birds' personalities and character, Lawrence makes the prospect of observing them much more appealing. Leaden descriptions and how-to instructions would do little to encourage the interest in nature that Lawrence wishes to convey.

43

3. One feeder would contain sunflower seeds, one mixed seeds, and the other suet. The sunflower seeds would attract chickadees, blue jays, and evening grosbeaks; the mixed seeds would bring juncos, redpolls, sparrows, and pine siskins; and the suet would appeal to woodpeckers. Buying a field guide is a good way to identify birds that have similar appearances.

4. Lawrence's audience is people who do not know much about nature but would like to learn. Students should find her style suitable to her audience.

5. Ruffed grouse, owls, gulls, crows, and pigeons are also present during the winter months. To observe them one has to leave the house and look for them in the surrounding trees. Such an exploration provides a good way for Lawrence to bridge the gap between passive observation from inside a house to active exploration outside.

6. Lawrence's larger purpose is to get her audience interested in the natural world in general—watching winter birds is merely a good way to start. Her last sentence indicates that birds are only a starting point that will lead to other observations and—she hopes—a wider appreciation of nature.

Vocabulary

diapause (1) period of cold-weather inactivity
cram (6) stuff; pack forcefully
hoarding (6) saving large amounts; stashing
gluttonous (7) voracious, greedy eater
nocturnal (15) active at night

DUMPSTER DIVING (p. 217)
Lars Eighner

Essay Analysis and Discussion

It is hard for anyone who has never faced homelessness to imagine life on the streets. Eighner, who became homeless after working and having a home for ten years, understands this. His essay about one aspect of homeless life, Dumpster diving—what he likes to call scavenging—incorporates concrete examples of the dangers and rewards of Dumpster diving. The image of pristine, still-frozen ice cream in a Dumpster is a powerful one, and one Eighner uses to explain the odd appeal of Dumpster diving. Discuss the final five paragraphs with your students, and how Eighner's essay may have changed the way they look at the material things that clutter everyone's life.

Questions for Study and Discussion

1. The word scavenging is frank, implying that it involves living off of the leavings of others. Students' impressions of Eighner will differ.

2. The examples that Eighner uses—the running shoes, calculator, ice cream—initiate the reader into the possibilities of Dumpster diving. Few people know that such things can be found in Dumpsters, and it makes the odd appeal of it that Eighner discusses more understandable.

3. Eighner repeats the phrase "perfectly good" to describe the items he finds in Dumpsters. This repetition emphasizes the waste that Eighner sees in our consumer society.

4. Eating from Dumpsters separates the so-called professionals from the rest of those who do it.

5. Eighner has learned to take what he can use and let the rest go and that material objects are transient.

6. Scavenging is harmful physically because of the dysentery. It is beneficial because of what it has taught Eighner, as discussed in the previous question.

7. The concrete elements are the actual physical goods found in the Dumpsters—the shoes and peanut butter and so on. The abstract elements are the lessons learned about transience and the true value of objects. Had Eighner used only the concrete elements his essay would have been nothing more than a description of the contents of a typical Dumpster. On the other hand, the essay would lack a basis in fact with only the abstract elements. By using both concrete and abstract elements, Eighner allows the reader to see how he derives his philosophy.

Vocabulary

refuse (3) garbage
niche (3) specialized role or place
dilettanti (9) dabblers; amateurs
qualms (10) misgivings; apprehensions
transience (14) lack of permanence
sated (16) satisfied
rat-race (16) wearisome rush

CONTROLLING THE ELECTRONIC HOME (p. 221)
Ellen Cobb Wade

Essay Analysis and Discussion

In an era when technology is seen as a driving force behind many improvements in our lives, Wade's argument that many technological "advances" have become too complicated is likely to be greeted with at least a little skepticism. By using familiar examples, however, she makes her point very clear. Almost everyone has faced remote controls or phone systems that are sure to baffle a new user, and she documents both annoyances in the first paragraph. Throughout her essay, Wade strengthens her argument by using anecdotes about familiar experiences, such as reprogramming a clock radio or trying to choose a telephone. By doing so, she forces the reader to concede that technology can be annoying at times, and, perhaps, to think about what might be done about it. Your students will probably have some good anecdotes about struggling with "new and improved" gadgets. Do they agree that there should be some standardization established?

Questions for Study and Discussion

1. Wade's thesis is that technology has run amok and left the consumer with more headaches from the lack of standards of operations than benefits from the new technological features. She does not state it clearly until paragraph 7.
2. Wade's story about her parent's unanswered call conjures the helplessness that many readers have felt when confronted by the array of buttons on a new remote control. By using this familiar example, she makes it easy for the reader to identify with her argument.
3. The difference between 1960s appliances and 1980s appliances is that the old technology was standardized and user-friendly, while the new technology is neither.
4. The "market mechanism" (competition) has failed to weed out all but the few very best new products. The third part of the question is a matter of personal opinion, but the answer should be well defended.
5. Wade reinforces her opinion of the new appliances by using adjectives such as "baffling," "distressing," and "formidable" to describe them. Also, they "confront" her, and she "fumbles" while trying to manipulate them. By using such diction, she shows very clearly the effect the machines have on her and, presumably, on many of her readers.
6. Personal opinion will differ. On one hand it undermines her argument because, although the confusion in the technology marketplace confuses her, she continues to patronize it. On the other hand, it is an amusing and open-ended way to end the piece, indicating that she will not give up.

Vocabulary

hostile (2) relating to an enemy; openly opposed
trilling (2) type of ringing sound
proliferated (3) grown quickly in number
transmogrified (3) to change or alter greatly
inherently (5) basically; essentially
cornucopia (7) variety; plenty
haphazardly (7) carelessly; without direction

CHAPTER 11   NARRATION

SHAME (p. 227)
Dick Gregory

Essay Analysis and Discussion

The heart of this essay is the incident Gregory relates about being shamed in front of Helene Tucker. Gregory chooses a chronological organization, but the chronology does not begin until the fourth paragraph because Gregory needs to establish a context for the incident in paragraphs 1 through 3. To give your students an indication of how vital such a context is to this essay, have them reexamine the first three paragraphs and consider what they contribute to Gregory's narration of the schoolroom incident in paragraphs 4 through 27, and what effect the removal of these three paragraphs would have on the essay. If you wish to narrow the focus of the discussion even further, ask them how the following sentences from those initial paragraphs interact with elements from Gregory's anecdote:

> "It was a lady's handkerchief, but I didn't want Helene to see me wipe my nose on my hand." (paragraph 1)
> "Everybody's got a Helene Tucker, a symbol of everything you want." (paragraph 2)
> "And she had a Daddy, and he had a good job." (paragraph 2)
> "When I played the drums in high school it was for Helene and when I broke track records in college it was for Helene and when I started standing behind microphones and heard applause I wished Helene could hear it, too." (paragraph 3)

After you've discussed the relationship between the opening paragraphs and the episode at school, have students analyze how those three paragraphs connect with Gregory's conclusion. The intent of your discussion should be to clarify what it means to establish a clear context for a narration.

Questions for Study and Discussion

1. For Gregory, *shame* means "disgrace," in this case disgrace in an environment where he least expected to find it. Gregory was ashamed of his poverty and for not having a father; however, that day in school was the day "I learned to be ashamed of myself."
2. In the first three paragraphs of the essay, Gregory introduces Helene Tucker and tells of his infatuation with her. This information provides the motivation for his later behavior.
3. Because Gregory lived the experience he is telling, it is most natural for him to narrate it in the first person. The third-person point of view would give the narrative an objective, perhaps even a sociological, bent.

4. The teacher thought Gregory was stupid, he said, but didn't stop to consider that he had trouble in school because he wasn't getting enough to eat at home. She also thought he was a troublemaker, again not taking time to consider that he was looking for attention he didn't get at home. Nevertheless, until the day of his shaming, he thought she liked him. "She always picked me to wash the blackboard on Friday, after school . . . it made me feel important." Ultimately she showed contempt for "you and your kind," and publicly humiliated him when she announced his secret to the class: "We know you don't have a daddy."

5. This is not a story about racism. In fact, there's nothing to indicate that his teacher wasn't black. The lack of money is the basis of Gregory's shame, just as it would be the having of money that erased it. Helene Tucker, the little girl who was light-complexioned, clean, and well-dressed, became the symbol of what he wasn't. "It wasn't until I was twenty-nine years old and married and making money that I finally got her out of my system."

6. Examples of Gregory's use of descriptive details abound in the essay. (By locating examples, students will become aware of how such details help to create vivid and interesting prose.)

7. Gregory's repeated use of the word *shame* in paragraph 28 emphasizes the importance of the incident in his life and the burden that shame carries with it. It is appropriate that Gregory narrate his early childhood experience in simple language. A more sophisticated vocabulary would soften the drama and realism of the narrative.

Vocabulary

nappy (2) shaggy or fuzzy
mackinaw (28) a short double-breasted coat of heavy woolen material

38 WHO SAW MURDER DIDN'T CALL POLICE (p. 232)
Martin Gansberg

Essay Analysis and Discussion

Gansberg uses a third-person point of view in this essay since he was not involved in the events described. But third person is appropriate because it lets the facts speak for themselves. When you discuss this essay, mention that at no point does Gansberg editorialize about what happened to Kitty Genovese. Yet, it is clear after reading the essay how he feels about the incident. Ask them how Gansberg manages to display his attitude about the lack of response to Kitty's attack, even though he uses third person and interjects no opinions of his own. Have students look closely at his selection of details and ordering of events, and at his choices of diction. His use of dialogue is another important element in the narrative. After they've examined these aspects, the students should see that though the facts seem to speak for themselves, deliberate choices about which facts to present help the essay achieve its purpose.

Questions for Study and Discussion

1. Gansberg's purpose is to show how apathy and fear have gripped the lives of New Yorkers, making them indifferent to the suffering of others. His use of narration has the advantage of illustrating the stark results of such apathy and fear, but the disadvantage of relying on readers to draw their own conclusions about the incident, conclusions which might not reflect what Gansberg hoped to achieve.

2. Gansberg's narrative of Kitty Genovese's murder begins with paragraph 7. As with Dick Gregory's essay "Shame," the introductory paragraphs establish an appropriate context in which to consider the events of the narrated incident. Without that context, the neighbors' reactions to Genovese's attack would not have as much emotional appeal.

3. Some neighbors claimed they "thought it was a lover's quarrel." Other excuses included being too afraid, too tired, and unwilling to get involved. The events dramatize a sense of separateness so acute that we can ignore a neighbor's cries for help one minute and fall asleep the next.

4. Gansberg uses a tone of controlled anger and subdued amazement. Though he describes events objectively in third person, his arrangement of details and use of diction and dialogue hint at a more aggressive attitude toward his subject.

5. Quotes from eleven people in the essay lend authenticity to Gansberg's narrative and illustrate, through the words of those involved, exactly how appalling the situation is.

6. Students may have various opinions. One reason might be that anyone who reads Gansberg's essay and has information about either the murders (recognizing the case by the address), but has not come forward with it, will be motivated to do so.

7. Gansberg might appear didactic if he were to analyze the meaning of his narrative at the end. Though he is forced to rely on readers to formulate an appropriate meaning for his essay, that is better than if he were to appear "preachy" and create hostility between himself and his audience. Students may or may not agree.

Vocabulary

stalk (1) to pursue
recitation (4) the act of repeating or uttering aloud memorized materials
assailant (5) a person who attacks or assaults another
staid (6) prudently reserved and colorless in style, manner, or behavior
shrouded (9) concealed; hidden
sheepishly (21) in an embarrassed manner, as though conscious of a fault
apprehensive (28) anxious or fearful

THE DARE (p. 237)
Roger Hoffman

Essay Analysis and Discussion

Hoffman begins his story with a description of the terrible, frightening thing he does to win the dare. Then he explains that he would never do it again as an adult. He allows the present, the lesson to be learned from all this, to interrupt his narrative only one other time—just after he accepts the dare. The author wants us to know two things: what the moment was like for a young boy and how it fit into his picture of himself as a man. Ask students to compare episodes of their lives that were significant when they happened and then took on even more significance in retrospect. How would they write such a story?

Questions for Study and Discussion

1. Hoffman took the dare because he wanted to be accepted by the rest of the 12-year-old boys in his class. He implies in paragraph 4 that by taking the dare at 12, he doesn't have to prove anything to himself or anyone else at 38.
2. Paragraph 4 explains the author's purpose in telling us his story.
3. Hoffman organizes his narration chronologically. He covers the first years of his schooling in the first five paragraphs. In the last seven he covers one day. A narration needs to spend less time setting the scene or the context of the story than it does on the story itself.
4. Hoffman uses several very effective figures of speech to convey his feelings of dread. And in the final sentences he tells us he has wet his pants.
5. "a circle on another planet" (7) metaphor
   "Their silhouette resembled a round-shouldered tombstone." (8) metaphor
   "The train sounded like a cow going short of breath." (9) simile
   "The monkey clawing my back was Teacher's Pet." (3) metaphor

   Hoffman uses the different figures of speech to sharpen his images and to present the world the way it seemed to a frightened boy.
6. Using the third person, whether from the perspective of O.T. or Dwayne or omnisciently, would "fictionalize" the narrative. It would also distance readers from the central action: We could not lie under the train with Hoffman or experience his terror firsthand. In addition, using third person would limit Hoffman's ability to reflect as an adult on his childhood experience. However, a third-person narrator *would* be able to give readers greater insight into the responses and motives of O.T. and Dwayne.

Vocabulary

shards (1) broken pieces; fragments
baited (1) nagged, teased, tempted

50

cronies (2) close friends, especially of long standing
escalated (2) increased in intensity
guerrilla (2) one who engages in irregular warfare
evaporating (3) disappearing quickly
implicit (4) understood though not directly stated
ambiguous (4) capable of being understood in more than one way
convulsive (11) violently disturbing

MOMMA, THE DENTIST, AND ME (p. 242)
Maya Angelou

Essay Analysis and Discussion

The editors of this text placed their own title on this selection from Angelou's *I Know Why the Caged Bird Sings*. Their title is appropriate for the content of the essay, but, given the complexity of Angelou's narration, other suitable options may also exist. This essay can, therefore, serve as a catalyst for discussion of how to choose an effective title. Ask your students to reread the essay with an eye toward providing it with a new title. Then, have them write suggested titles on slips of paper and turn them in so you can compile an anonymous listing on the board. Once you've completed it, ask the students to vote on which they like best, and when they've indicated their preferences, discuss why some titles were chosen over others. You will want to consider originality, ability to stimulate interest, and appropriateness to the content of the essay, as well as other factors the students may see as significant.

Questions for Study and Discussion

1. Angelou's purpose is to show the kind of pain that bigotry and injustice inflict, and to show that such cruelty often fosters the desire for retribution in its victims.
2. The content of the two interchanges between Momma and the dentist is similar in that, in both cases, Momma exacts revenge on the dentist for his refusal to treat the young girl. But the way she achieves that revenge is different. In Maya's version, Momma "obliterates" the dentist with her angry words, rendering him weak and submissive under her power and authority. In Momma's version, although she speaks of the dentist and his nurse with contempt, the scene she describes is more subdued and less vengeful, but ultimately, more productive in getting Maya's toothache treated The style of the two versions is very different. To use Angelou's words, the first displays an "eloquent command of English," both in the way Momma speaks and in Maya's description of events, while in the second, Momma uses her usual vernacular to recall the scene.

51

3. Angelou's chronological presentation helps her establish a clear and purposeful context for the scene at the dentist's office. In the narration leading up to the visit, she builds a sense of tension and frustration as she describes the pain of her toothache and her anxiety about approaching a white dentist. The chronological pattern also helps to juxtapose the two versions of what occurred between Momma and the dentist. The first-person point of view is crucial to the central idea of the essay because it shows Maya's desire for retribution firsthand, and that desire creates the fantasized version of the confrontation between Momma and the dentist. Her version becomes more poignant since readers come to feel what she is like and what motivates her, before they reach that scene. This makes the final statement more potent.

4. Angelou's essay contains the following similes: "as if a white breeze blew off whitefolks and cushioned everything in their neighborhood" (paragraph 6); "the way people hunt for shells" (paragraph 18); "like little claps of thunder" (paragraph 29); "like filling in a pie crust" (paragraph 46); "like a piece of lint" (paragraph 48); "thick as thieves" (paragraph 48); and "like he was sitting on a pin" (paragraph 48). Each simile works in its paragraph, and together they provide a more vivid description of events.

5. Angelou's version of the episode describes what, for her, is a more just resolution of the situation: a Dodge-City-style triumph over bigotry. The dentist is not only confronted, he is driven from town frightened and disgraced. To the child, it must have been a pale consolation that the dentist had to pay a few more dollars on his debt to the grandmother.

6. Angelou first uses exaggerated descriptions to indicate the magnitude of her pain: "I prayed earnestly that I'd be allowed to sit under the house and have the building collapse on my left jaw" (paragraph 1); "seriously considering the idea of jumping in the well" (paragraph 2); "I was certain that I'd be dead" (paragraph 2); "the pain was more serious than that which anyone had ever suffered" (paragraph 4). She then presents some startling metaphors to show her intimate connection to that pain: "I had frozen to the pain" (paragraph 4); "the pain was my world, an aura that haloed me for three feet around" (paragraph 5). These references are important because they establish the extent to which she suffers physically; yet, the physical pain subsides when Maya confronts the psychic pain of bigotry and injustice described in paragraphs 6 through 9, culminating in the dentist's refusal to treat her.

Vocabulary

bailiwick (1) specific area of interest, skill, or authority

calaboose (7) jail

mite (22) a very small creature

vernacular (34) the nonstandard everyday speech of a country or region

varlet (39) rascal; knave

concoct (42) to prepare by mixing ingredients
snippety (49) impertinent
retributive (50) characterized by the giving or demanding of repayment, especially punishment.

CHAPTER 12 DESCRIPTION

THE SOUNDS OF THE CITY (p. 252)
James Tuite

Essay Analysis and Discussion

Tuite's images appeal to the reader's sense of hearing, which is a common source for descriptive details. To round out your students' consideration of sensory images, ask them to do some writing in which they appeal to the senses of smell, taste, and touch as well. They should spend 10 to 12 minutes on each of the three, trying to evoke corresponding images by choosing appropriate descriptive details. For example, to convey an image through smell a student might describe a carnival or festival at which ethnic foods send off an array of distinctive aromas. Since these three senses are appealed to infrequently, when a successful image directed to one of them does appear, it is all the more effective. Read some of the students' selections aloud and see if they bear this out.

Questions for Study and Discussion

1. Tuite's purpose is to show that New York is a city of sounds and that these sounds are part of the life of the city. He points out that New Yorkers don't hear these sounds because they are constantly around them.
2. Tuite has organized his essay chronologically. He starts in the nighttime, moves through the daylight hours, and ends with nightfall. This organization is effective because it gives readers an overview of the city's sounds on a typical day.
3. Among the sounds Tuite includes are: "tinseled honky-tonk," "firm beat of rock 'n' roll," "frenzied outbursts of the discotheque," "shrill language," "bottle shatters," "whine of a police siren," "guttural halt," "snarling, arrogant bickering of automobile horns," "Taxicabs blaring," "Trash cans rattle," "satisfied groan of gears," "rat-a-tat-tat," and "whistles . . . chirp." With each of the adjectives and verbs that he uses, Tuite gets at the essence of the sound and so enlivens his description.
4. Visitors are more sensitive to city sounds because they do not hear them all the time, whereas for "cliff dwellers," they are "constant and eternally urban." City people who do not stop to listen are asphalt-kin to those who do not stop to smell the roses. Noises are the life of the city and people ought to stop to listen, "to think about them, to be appalled or enchanted."

53

5. Among the metaphors and similes Tuite uses are: "The cliff dwellers of Manhattan," "Somewhere in the canyons below," "The growl of a predatory monster," "Metallic jaws . . . gulp and masticate . . . then digest," "as jarring as the glare of a sun," and "like birds calling for their mates." Each of these figures of speech gives a naturalistic picture of the city.
6. The dominant impression that Tuite creates is one of ceaseless, discordant sound.

Vocabulary

muted (1) muffled; softened
inaudible (2) incapable of being heard
restive (2) restless, uneasy
raucous (4) rough-sounding or harsh
tentative (5) not definite or positive
precocious (8) prematurely developed
taunts (8) challenges
vibrant (9) resonant or resounding
perpetuate (10) to continue without interruption

UNFORGETTABLE MISS BESSIE (p. 256)
Carl T. Rowan

Essay Analysis and Discussion

Rowan's essay offers students the opportunity to analyze the effective use of the dash. Many students have problems recognizing the proper place for this helpful form of punctuation and either use it too much or not at all. Rowan uses it in seven of his paragraphs, and for various purposes. Look over these instances with your students and have them identify which of the two most common reasons for using a dash each case falls under (see extract below). When you've finished with Rowan's examples, have the students develop sentences of their own, using dashes in each of the ways described.

1. Use dashes to highlight parenthetical material, informal explanations, and afterthoughts that warrant emphasis.
2. Use dashes to signal a dramatic reversal of thought or tone.*

---

* From Alfred Rosa and Paul Eschholz, *The Writer's Brief Handbook* (New York: Macmillan, 1994).

Questions for Study and Discussion

1. In the first paragraph, Rowan describes Miss Bessie as about 5 feet tall and 110 pounds. In paragraph 4 he notes that she had large brown eyes and, in paragraph 12, that she was "frail-looking." Though these characteristics do not seem to fit the image of the tough and towering figure from Rowan's school days, by the end of the essay they seem less inconsistent with the warm-hearted and compassionate teacher he looks back on as an adult.

2. A firm, committed, wise and caring individual emerges from Rowan's description of Miss Bessie. Some of the words used to convey this are: *towering, tough* (paragraph 1); *informed, dedicated, blessing, asset* (paragraph 8); *essence of pride and privacy* (paragraph 9); *bearing of dignity* (paragraph 10); *softness and compassion* (paragraph 22); *love and motivation, wisdom and influence* (paragraph 25); and *wise, educated, warm-hearted* (paragraph 28)

3. The details of Miss Bessie's background appear in paragraphs 9 and 10. Rowan delays presenting this information so that he can first describe what Miss Bessie was like and why he is writing about her. This provides a stimulating opening and establishes a context for the biographical details, since it helps to know what role Miss Bessie will play in the essay before being given information about her background.

4. Rowan's use of dialogue presents a more vivid picture of Miss Bessie's personality. Rather than rely on only a subjective, third-person description of her, Rowan allows the dialogue to provide a few more realistic glimpses into her character.

5. Students' opinions may vary as to whether Miss Bessie's drinking influences their view of her. Rowan's feeling of a "new sense of equality" suggests that his discovery that she drank made Miss Bessie more lifelike, dispelling some of the larger-than-life images from his grade school perception of her, while not diminishing her significance to his life.

6. Miss Bessie gave her students a sense of pride and self-worth by encouraging their talent and curiosity. In opening to them the world of literature, writing, self-expression, and a solid notion of this country's time in history, Miss Bessie taught young black children to stretch beyond the limits a segregated world had set for them.

Vocabulary

civics (1) the branch of political science that deals with civic affairs

barrios (16) chiefly Spanish-speaking communities or neighborhoods within U.S. cities

conscience (18) the faculty of recognizing the distinction between right and wrong, coupled with a sense that one should act accordingly

cajoling (20) coaxing gently and persistently

osmotic (20) characterized by a gradual, often unconscious process of assimilation or absorption

measure (25) an evaluation or basis of comparison

GROCER'S DAUGHTER (p. 262)
Marianne Wiggins

Essay Analysis and Discussion

Wiggins' personal description of her father flows like most memories—disjointed and sometimes rambling. In fact, the essay often seems disorganized and not well crafted. It is held together by a consistent focus, however, established in the very first sentence: "I am shameless in the way I love my father." That opening propels the reader through an intimate description of a man who was probably seen as unsuccessful by his peers and who must have been, at times, difficult to live with. Yet Wiggins shows so many facets of her father that by the end of the essay, the reader knows him and the reasons behind Wiggins' difficult love for him far better than he or she would from a stiffer, more formal written presentation. Have your students emulate Wiggins' technique in their personal essays, concentrating less on form than on creating a complete portrait of their chosen subject.

Questions for Study and Discussion

1. The first sentence emphasizes that, despite all the faults and struggles Wiggins describes later on, John Wiggins was a good father and a man who earned his daughter's respect and love.
2. The list indicates that he was a simple, honest, and hard-working man, who probably had more success in keeping his customers happy than in running a profitable business.
3. The writing emulates memory, in that it describes her father in a series of fragments that add up to a very complete picture. It should be effective for most students, but some may be put off by the lack of readily seen organization.
4. The Wiggins family moved so often because John Wiggins' small grocery stores kept getting squeezed out by the larger suburban supermarkets.
5. He taught his daughter important values, including perserverance and honesty. He obviously loved her and both educated and entertained her. And it is obvious that his legacy lives on in her.
6. Wiggins explores the impact he had on her both in life and after death, so what is important to her is how he lived, not how he died. Perhaps, too, the event of his death is a painful memory that she prefers to leave out of her description. It is obvious that he died suddenly, but students will need to use some creative research to answer the rest of the question.

Vocabulary

pathology (2) referring to disease
concocted (15) developed; made
germinated (15) sprouted; emerged from a seed

charisma (18) personal charm; appeal
portenting (21) disturbing
novitiate (22) beginner; novice
piecemeal (24) in pieces; broken into bits

BORDERS (p. 268)
Barry Lopez

Essay Analysis and Discussion

If you ask your students for a one-sentence description of Lopez's essay, they will probably respond with a sentence something like "It is an essay about a trip he took to the international border between Alaska and the Yukon Territories." That this is a correct response indicates how difficult it is to adequately summarize the essay. Lopez starts with a day trip to the border and uses it as a springboard for a series of vivid descriptions of the harsh conditions in the northern territories and the wildlife that manages to survive in these conditions. He also uses it to ponder the meaning of borders—natural, physical, and spiritual. Study each paragraph with your students and discuss what it accomplishes. For example, paragraph 4 combines trip observations with wildlife description. Paragraphs 5 and 6 introduce Lopez's philosophical interest in borders in the abstract, beyond the one he actually travels to see. Paragraphs 7, 8, and 9 interweave events that occur on the trip with further thoughts about the nature of borders, but by paragraph 11, Lopez is back to his trip and descriptions of the natural world. All three elements of his essay encourage the reader to think—about borders, about the vast wilderness in the Northwest Territories, and about the fun of taking a day off for a small adventure.

Questions for Study and Discussion

1. Students should discuss Lopez's philosophical discussions about the meanings of borders, including the natural, political, and spiritual kinds. His day trip serves as a catalyst to discuss the random nature of political borders, the borders of theoretical society structures, the different meanings that different borders have, and so on.
2. Lopez frequently mentions the ice and its encroachment upon the boat. He also uses such descriptions as "logs weathered gray-white," "tundra," the "lack of habitation," the "white, frozen ocean," and the "low chance of survival for the swans."
3. The Eskimos claim a right of prior use in a Wildlife Refuge because of the house.
4. The men are euphoric because of the romance of reaching the border and because of the beauty of the day, contrasted with the days of hard work they have endured.

5. Lopez indicates the problems that can arise from assigning an arbitrary international border. As the old saying goes, you can see no political borders from the air. The paragraph ties in with his musings about borders, and reinforces his implied disdain for political ones.

6. Lopez encounters two young swans. That they are imminently doomed brings home what a fine line exists between survival and death in the arctic, even for an animal that is merely caught in the wrong place a week or two late.

7. After the expanse of the Arctic, it is clear that the petty border issues of his hometown will take a while to get used to.

Vocabulary

austerity (1) spare; plainness
lee (3) sheltered from wind
bioregionalism (6) using natural borders instead of political ones
decentralize (6) scatter; move away from a central point
askew (7) tilted
fortuitous (9) fortunate; lucky
arbitrary (12) without plan; haphazard
whimsical (14) lighthearted
engendered (14) caused; generated
conscientiousness (16) care; attention to detail

CHAPTER 13   PROCESS ANALYSIS

HOW TO BUILD A FIRE IN A FIREPLACE (p. 277)
Bernard Gladstone

Essay Analysis and Discussion

Gladstone's brief essay is an excellent example of a directional process analysis. Although the essay contains only four short paragraphs, readers learn an accepted method for building a fire, why this method is effective, and reasons for avoiding other fire-building methods. Note how Gladstone presents the entire process in the first paragraph, then summarizes it again in the fourth. The rest of the essay is used to present common mistakes and the problems they can create. Challenge your students to write an understandable directional process analysis that emulates Gladstone's concise but thorough presentation.

Questions for Study and Discussion

1. Gladstone's essay is a directional analysis, appropriate for his purpose of teaching how to perform a specific task.

2. The steps for building a fire in a fireplace are:
   1. Crumple newspaper and spread it on the hearth.
   2. Spread a generous amount of kindling over the newspaper.
   3. Place a large log near the back of the fireplace, across the back of the andirons.
   4. Place another log an inch in front of the first log.
   5. Put more kindling over the two logs.
   6. Place a final log on top in a pyramid shape, leaving air spaces for the flames.
3. Paragraphs 2, 3, and 4 present common mistakes and their consequences. In addition to preventing a repetition of the mistakes, they help to underscore the relative effectiveness of the method presented.
4. The use of "first" and the repeated use of "is then" makes the sequence readily identifiable.
5. Too big a fire can create more smoke and draft than the chimney can handle, increasing the likelihood of smoke and/or sparks coming out into the room.

Vocabulary

hearth (1) the base of the fireplace
andirons (1) a two-piece metal stand used to raise logs off the hearth
kindling (1) small pieces of wood helpful in lighting fires

HOW TO PUT OFF DOING A JOB (p. 280)
Andy Rooney

Essay Analysis and Discussion

The humor in Rooney's essay is obvious, particularly in an age filled with books and TV shows about how to do just about anything. Yet the essay is a very effective process analysis on procrastination. Note how he organizes the essay. He begins his list of procrastination techniques with one of his "most dependable putter-offers," in paragraph 3, then, after presenting a few others, he presents his most effective, but most dangerous, "last resort" in paragraph 9. He thus imposes a structure to the essay that implies that he is not just being silly. His humor also has an edge to it—in paragraph 6, near the middle of the essay, he describes how to use the very "how-to" books he parodies as tools for procrastination. Your students are sure to have more techniques for procrastination, if they will admit to them. Also, choose another topic to parody—such as how not to get ahead in business or how not to dress for success—and have your students write a short, humorous process analysis based on Rooney's model.

Questions for Study and Discussion

1. The irony is that Rooney is writing a "how-to" article about how to *not* do jobs that need to be done.
2. February seems like the longest month because it is a difficult time of year to put off doing jobs. The implication for the rest of the article is that Rooney uses the techniques described in the article a lot each February.
3. Going to the store gets Rooney out of the house, away from his job, and can lead him to something else entirely.
4. Philosophizing is Rooney's last resort for putting off a job. Rooney implies that it can lead to not just putting off the job, but a reevaluation of one's life in general.
5. Rooney's tone is casual and helpful. His humor is mainly derived from the irony in the article. His tone doesn't differ much from that found in many legitimate "how-to" articles

Vocabulary

adhesive (3) glue
accomplish (6) achieve
how-to (6) a category of article or book meant to teach how to perform one or more tasks
interim (8) interval; break
philosophize (9) think about life
mold (9) form; pattern

HOW TO ORGANIZE YOUR THOUGHTS FOR BETTER COMMUNICATION (p. 283)
Sherry Sweetnam

Essay Analysis and Discussion

An interesting thing to note in Sweetnam's article is that she doesn't frontload her main point, which is that frontloading is the most effective way for people in business to write. Instead, she uses a question to hook interested readers and an example to demonstrate the need for the techniques presented later in the article. Based on her later analysis, it is likely Sweetnam thinks that she is writing to a skeptical audience. Discuss what else can be figured out about Sweetnam's intended audience from the way she presents the article and addresses her readers. Also have your students note the use of concrete examples in each paragraph that describe how to use frontloading. Why are they important in her article?

Questions for Study and Discussion

1. Sweetnam's first paragraph is effective if her readers want to analyze the way they communicate and organize their thoughts. It also gives them a starting point for this analysis, and a sense of what the article will discuss.

2. Frontloading is the technique of placing the most important thought or point of a written communication very early in the piece. It avoids wasting time and helps capture the reader's interest.

3. People do not use frontloading because they don't want to appear bold or aggressive, because they were taught to organize their writing differently, because they don't know what's important to their audience, or because they have not organized their thoughts well enough. Frontloading should be avoided when there is the possibility that your reader will not be receptive to your ideas.

4. Sweetnam's subheads serve to focus the reader's attention on the main divisions of her article. Of special note are the three categories that she delineates under the heading "How to Frontload Writing." In general, Sweetnam's advice in the subheads moves from the easiest to "trickiest" tasks to accomplish.

5. The middle of the page is "no-man's land" because it does not need to catch the reader's attention like the first section does, and it does not stay in the reader's mind like the conclusion does.

6. Sweetnam uses concrete examples, lists, short paragraphs, and repetition to help hold the reader's attention and communicate the information.

7. Sweetnam's intended audience is people in business. Because she does not frontload her discussion of frontloading, it is likely that Sweetnam thinks her audience is either skeptical of her advice or reluctant to follow it.

Vocabulary

personnel (2) employees; staff
credibility (4) believability; integrity
clarify (4) make clear
sheerly (4) exclusively; only
chronologically (4) arranged by time
captive (5) unable to escape; bound
inadvertently (14) accidentally; unintentionally
nonmanipulative (18) without manipulation or trickery

THE SPIDER AND THE WASP (p. 290)
Alexander Petrunkevitch

Essay Analysis and Discussion

As a scientist, Petrunkevitch writes to teach an audience that is more or less unfamiliar with his information. To do this, he relies on many forms of writing. Although "The Spider and the Wasp" is a process analysis, it also has effective description, has anecdotes and other forms of illustration, and uses definitions to further the reader's understanding of what happens between the spider and the wasp. Ask your students to identify these and other writing techniques that

Petrunkevitch uses in the essay. How does each contribute to the essay as a whole? Also note Petrunkevitch's diction, particularly the use of such words as *ghastly enterprise* (paragraph 12) and *pawing* (paragraph 15). These words indicate that Petrunkevitch is writing for a lay audience that can better identify with familiar terms than scientific. How else does he make his article accessible to nonscientists and make the battle between spider and wasp interesting?

Questions for Study and Discussion

1. The Pepsis wasp displays what looks like intelligence by discriminating between species of tarantula and by carefully avoiding the spider's defense and/or attack responses. The spider relies on instinct in that it responds in a passive way to what is in fact a grave threat—in effect, it lets the wasp win by only following instinctual reactions to the wasp's interference.
2. Petrukevitch organizes his essay using logical order. In order for the reader to appreciate the interaction between the wasp and the spider, each combatant must be clearly described. Then the process analysis of the wasp's lethal attack on the spider can begin, and the questions it raises can be explored. For an outline, Petrunkevitch's opening paragraph introduces the reader to the situation he wishes to present. In the next several paragraphs he carefully describes tarantulas, including their mating habits and response to external stimuli, and the Pepsis wasp. Once the reader is familiar with the two, he writes a process analysis about the interaction between the wasp and tarantula. He concludes by pondering the reasons why the tarantula lets it all happen.
3. The three tactile responses are pressure against the body wall, stroking of the body hair, and air movement against the trichobothria. Understanding the spider's response to these stimuli is crucial to understanding possible reasons the wasp can get away with harassing the spider before paralyzing it.
4. The process analysis is about the actual paralyzing of the spider. Petrunkevitch finishes his discussion of the spider's tactile responses with a transitional sentence that introduces the Pepsis wasp. His discussion of the Pepsis wasp includes a summary of the whole egg-laying process and brings the reader back to the tarantula with the topic sentence of paragraph 10. He can then move into his process analysis.
5. It is possible that the wasp applies pressure in such a way that the tarantula reacts passively to that rather than to the wasp's antennae. Or it could be that the wasp somehow avoids stimulating the escape instinct in the spider, so that the spider, doing what is most efficient for survival, dooms itself.
6. The spider is able to survive as a species because its reproductive prowess is so much greater.

Vocabulary

progeny (1) offspring; child
tactile (7) sense of touch
Gargantuan (9) big; huge
chitinous (9) composed of chitin, which forms the hard outer skeleton of insects and spiders
molestation (11) abuse; interference
qualitatively (14) relating to quality or kind
olfactory (14) sense of smell
initiative (16) drive; motivation

CHAPTER 14   DEFINITION

A JERK (p. 299)
Sydney J. Harris

Essay Analysis and Discussion

Harris's essay, though short, contains a good number of delightfully expressed ideas. The entire piece can serve as a case study in "choosing the right words to get the job done." His unique use of words and images combined with his ease and naturalness of expression makes Harris's subject matter more interesting and entertaining than it might otherwise be. To illustrate, have your students consider the following fragments from the essay:

   I *fluffed* her off with some *inane* answer (paragraph 2)

   It is a *marvelously apt* word (paragraph 3)

   it is, rather, a kind of *subtle but persuasive aroma emanating from the inner part of the personality* (paragraph 4)

   he is totally incapable of *looking into the mirror of his soul and shuddering at what he sees there* (paragraph 5)

   most of us—unlike the jerk—are *perfectly and horribly aware of it when we make asses of ourselves* (paragraph 6)

Noting, especially, the italicized portions, discuss why these fragments are so effective in conveying Harris's ideas. In their responses, students should recognize the role that originality of expression plays in arousing the appropriate connotations and mental imagery for an essay. In this respect, Harris's manipulation of language is "marvelously apt," and demonstrates the need for students, also, to make the language they use in their writing uniquely their own.

Questions for Study and Discussion

1. The term *jerk* is a widely used slang term, and people use it without really knowing what it means. The question from Harris's son Michael prompts him to define the term. According to Harris, "a jerk . . . is a man (or woman) who is utterly unable to see himself as he appears to others." (paragraph 6)
2. According to Harris, boobs and simps are lovable, and jerks never are; fools and dopes lack intelligence, and a jerk may not.
3. Harris sees no relationship between the two.
4. The example of the college president shows that being a jerk has little to do with intelligence.
5. The episode points out our tendency to use words whose meaning we cannot easily define. We "intuit" the meaning of words such as *jerk*. The anecdote works because it gets the reader thinking about not only the meaning of the word jerk (how would I define it for one of my children?), but other similarly slippery words in our vocabulary.

Vocabulary

inane (2) empty; lacking sense or substance
apt (3) appropriate
coined (3) invented
emanating (4) coming from
amenities (5) courtesies, pleasantries, or civilities
tactless (6) offensively blunt; undiplomatic

INFLATION (p. 302)
Marilu Hurt McCarty

Essay Analysis and Discussion

Inflation is a familiar word to most people, and its impact is readily understood at supermarket checkout lines. Yet the reasons it exists and gets better and worse are mysterious to almost everybody, including, as McCarty admits, economists. Her definition of inflation is very efficient and easy to read because of its structure and diction. It is particularly effective because it starts at the beginning of economic development to give the reader a sense of the basic economics of our society. From there she can explain how economic progress and expansion lead to the imbalances in the supplies of goods and money that in turn lead to inflation or deflation. McCarty also avoids using economic jargon to make her essay accessible to lay readers. Discuss the techniques McCarty uses to put her readers at ease with a difficult topic.

Questions for Study and Discussion

1. A number of interpretations are possible, but her intent is probably to put the reader at ease by implying the fallibility of the experts in the field she is discussing. It is effective at putting the reader at ease while preparing them to learn about a complex topic.
2. It is best to establish what inflation is before discussing the reasons behind it to ensure that all of her readers know how she defines inflation.
3. McCarty avoids jargon to make her essay easy to understand for a general audience.
4. Inflation should be of concern because of the impact it has on people with fixed incomes or salaries that are on a set scale. Inflation also tends to discourage prudent saving practices and long-term lending.
5. A recession or depression usually follows a period of inflation because of overproduction and stockpiling of inventories during expansion. When investment and production fall off, a recession follows.

Vocabulary

haphazardly (2) carelessly
self-sufficiency (4) ability to survive without outside help
barter (5) trade
obsolete (11) outdated; no longer in use
frivolous (12) foolhardy; impractical
virtuous (13) good; ethical
rampant (15) excessive; widespread

THE UNDERCLASS (p. 307)
Herbert J. Gans

Essay Analysis and Discussion

Sexism and racism depend, in part, on the ability to lump people into large groups and not view them as individuals. Gans argues that the term underclass performs the same thing along socioeconomic lines, providing a label that makes it easy to group poor people together, then condemn or dismiss them. To make his point clear, Gans begins his essay with easily understood references. Both the proverb and the examples Gans uses to label it "patent nonsense," are familiar to the reader. It is not until the end of paragraph 2 that Gans introduces the term "underclass," then he immediately defines its traditional and current meanings. He is then able to use the rest of the essay to support his assertion that "underclass" is an insidious pejorative that may be a harbinger of worse things to come. Can your class come up with any other terms that are nonoffensive on the surface, but support or create negative stereotypes or associations? What can be done to discourage the use of such words in the media and conversation?

Questions for Study and Discussion

1. America has always tended to look down upon its poor as undeserving of assistance and deserving of insults. Some of the terms used for the poor include bums, hoboes, vagrants, and paupers.

2. According to Myrdal, the underclass are the unemployed and unemployables created by the modern economy. It has come to mean all those who are socioeconomically disadvantaged for whatever reason.

3. Underclass sounds technical and proper, not outwardly pejorative or biased.

4. This question is a matter of personal opinion. Gans uses an academic writing style that some students may not like, but such phrases as "growing horde of beggars" and "threatening" convey the knee-jerk reaction to the term "underclass" that Gans wishes to demonstrate, and the phrase "respectable substitute word with which to condemn them" is both refined and very cutting in its expression.

5. The underclass may be the symptom of a dark American future because the economy may start displacing workers through no fault of their own. In this situation, the original meaning of underclass—describing people who have been displaced by the modern economy—may be used more appropriately, but in America we will use it not only to describe but also to condemn.

6. Gans writes with a very academic style, so his tone is subdued, but it is scathing and angry nonetheless. Such sentences as the third sentence in paragraph 4 and the first sentence in paragraph 7 show the reader what Gans really thinks about those who work against the "underclass," as they like to call them, in our society.

Vocabulary

paupers (2) poor people
condemn (3) declare to be evil or wrong
pejorative (4) insult
biases (4) prejudices
rationale (6) justification

THEY'VE GOTTA KEEP IT: PEOPLE WHO SAVE EVERYTHING (p. 311)
Lynda W. Warren and Jonnae C. Ostrom

Essay Analysis and Discussion

One of the difficulties faced by scientists is selecting an appropriate way to communicate their findings to the rest of the world. Warren and Ostrom obviously aim for a broad audience in their piece, from the catchy title to the relative informality and accessibility of their prose. Even their name for the phenomenon they define in the article—"pack rat" behavior—is easily understood and free of intimidating scientific terminology. Have your students identify other techniques the authors use to make it easy for a broad audience to understand their research and findings. Discuss the deeper questions that the authors suggest need further study. What other studies can be done on this topic? Finally, what do your students think about the final paragraph? Do they feel that it is an appropriate way to end the article. Why or why not?

Questions for Study and Discussion

1. A pack rat is someone who saves compulsively, with little or no reason for doing so. A collector saves particular things and usually has an order to what they save—pack rats save many things that have no immediate value to them or anyone else, and they usually have no order to what they save.

2. The authors became interested in pack rat behavior through personal experience with relatives and clients. Little work has been done in this area before.

3. The quotes make it easier to understand the thought patterns of the pack rats and their family members, and they make the article as a whole more accessible.

4. Miserliness, orderliness, stubbornness are all anal-retentive characteristics. Many pack rats also resemble compulsive personalities through their avoidance of decisions, and some display a depressive side.

5. Warren and Ostrom write for a general lay audience. The purpose of the article is to inform their audience about pack rat behavior and to encourage further inquiry into the phenomenon.

6. The authors' attitude toward pack rats is the same as they would display toward a client with any other psychological disorder. They view pack rats as subjects to be studied so that their disorder can be better understood.

7. The second to last paragraph provides a good base for further inquiry into the problem, and it raises issues to consider for everyone who either is or knows a pack rat. The last paragraph reinforces the informality of the piece, but it seems odd and out of place in a scientific article. Whether or not it is an effective end to the article is a matter of personal opinion, but have your students defend their answers.

Vocabulary

winnow (1) weed out; reduce
haphazardly (3) with organization; randomly
hoarding (5) excessive saving
miserliness (8) excessively thrifty
buttressed (11) supported
compulsive (12) obsessive

inordinate (12) exceeding reasonable limits
akin (13) similar; like
irks (20) irritates; annoys
impotent (22) powerless
deprivation (25) lacking; deprived of something

CHAPTER 15   DIVISION AND CLASSIFICATION

THE WAYS OF MEETING OPPRESSION (p. 320)
Martin Luther King, Jr.

Essay Analysis and Discussion

In addition to being an excellent example of division and classification, King's essay is a model of how to achieve unity between paragraphs. To illustrate this, have students identify the topic sentence in each of King's paragraphs and make a list of those statements. They should come up with the following:

1. One way is acquiescence: The oppressed resign themselves to their doom.
2. There is such a thing as the freedom of exhaustion.
3. So acquiescence—while often the easier way—is not the moral way.
4. A second way that oppressed people sometimes deal with oppression is to resort to physical violence and corroding hatred.
5. Violence as a way of achieving racial justice is both impractical and immoral.
6. Violence is not the way.
7. The third way open to oppressed people in this quest for freedom is the way of nonviolent resistance.
8. It seems to me that this is the method that must guide the actions of the Negro in the present crisis in race relations
9. Nonviolent resistance makes it possible for the Negro to remain in the South and struggle for his rights.
10. By nonviolent resistance, the Negro can also enlist all men of good will in his struggle for equality.

This list demonstrates how tightly King's ideas are connected as he moves from paragraph to paragraph. The supporting information that surrounds these topic sentences explains and strengthens the main idea of each paragraph, but it is the close connection between those main ideas that gives the essay its unity and makes King's logical argument and the presentation of the ways to meet oppression so easy to follow and understand.

Questions for Study and Discussion

1. For King, one who acquiesces "increases the oppressor's arrogance and contempt." One who resorts to violence uses a means that "never brings permanent peace."

2. Slaves become accustomed to being slaves. They will bear the ills slavery offers rather than risk other, unknown ills.

3. The freedom of exhaustion refers to a kind of "giving up" that engulfs the slave to the extent that he doesn't even "mind" his slavery anymore, and if he doesn't mind, then he is "free" to do nothing about it.

4. King's purpose in classifying the types of resistance is to make clear that there are essentially three ways to deal with oppression, and that for him only one of these options, nonviolent resistance, is viable.

5. The principle of division that King uses is the way oppressed people react to the oppression.

6. The order that King uses runs from the option that is easiest and least effective for the oppressed to the option that is most difficult and most effective.

7. King shows that he does not favor acquiescence by using the following words and phrases: *resign* (paragraph 1), *doom* (paragraph 1), *prefer to remain oppressed* (paragraph 1), *slaves* (paragraph 1), *fleshpots of Egypt* (paragraph 1), *worn down* (paragraph 2), *give up* (paragraph 2), *negative freedom* (paragraph 2), *cooperate* (paragraph 3), *evil* (paragraph 3), *coward* (paragraph 3), *inferiority* (paragraph 3), *sell* (paragraph 3). King shows that he does not favor violent resistance by using the following words and phrases: *resort* (paragraph 4), *corroding hatred* (paragraph 4), *momentary* (paragraph 4), *temporary* (paragraph 4), *impractical* (paragraph 5), *immoral* (paragraph 5), *humiliate* (paragraph 5), *annihilate* (paragraph 5), *thrives* (paragraph 5), *bitterness* (paragraph 5), *brutality* (paragraph 5), *clutter* (paragraph 5), *wreckage* (paragraph 5), *succumb* (paragraph 6), *temptation* (paragraph 6), *desolate night of bitterness* (paragraph 6), *endless reign of meaningless chaos* (paragraph 6). King shows that he favors nonviolent resistance by using the following words and phrases: *quest* (paragraph 7), *truths* (paragraph 7), *guide* (paragraph 8), *rise to the noble height* (paragraph 8), *loving* (paragraph 8), *passionately* (paragraph 8), *unrelentingly* (paragraph 8), *full stature as a citizen* (paragraph 8), *great opportunity* (paragraph 9), *lasting contribution* (paragraph 9), *sublime example of courage* (paragraph 9).

Vocabulary

acquiescence (1) passive assent or agreement
tacitly (1) quietly, without open expression
corroding (4) consuming
annihilate (5) destroy utterly

desolate (6) barren; miserable
synthesis (7) the combining of separate elements to form a new, coherent whole
sublime (9) inspiring or impressive

FRIENDS, GOOD FRIENDS—AND SUCH GOOD FRIENDS (p. 325)
Judith Viorst

Essay Analysis and Discussion

An analysis of the division and classification section of this essay will reveal two important features: its consistency in structure and its variety in development. For the most part, Viorst uses a three-step approach in her categories of friends: first, she defines the type of friend being discussed; second, she offers examples of the type; and third, she provides further clarification to reinforce her definition. The consistency of this pattern makes it easier to follow along as she goes down her list of numerous kinds of friends. She achieves variety in the ways she presents the further clarification in step three. She makes use of examples from women friends, dialogue from women friends, her own additional analysis, examples from her own experience, and various combinations of these to clarify the main points of her categories. Discuss this method of organization and development with your students and, when you've finished, see if they can offer additional supporting evidence for any of Viorst's categories, based on their own experiences. Then have them decide where that evidence would fit within the three-step structure of her essay.

Questions for Study and Discussion

1. Viorst has come to see that friendships are "conducted at many levels of intensity, serve many different functions, meet different needs and range from "…soul sisters to…the most casual playmates."
2. Viorst's purpose in this essay is to make her readers understand the many different kinds of relationships that fall into the general class of friendship. Classification is clearly an appropriate strategy.
3. Viorst's categories are: (1) convenience friends; (2) special-interest friends; (3) historical friends; (4) crossroads friends; (5) cross-generational friends; (6) part-of-a-couple friends; (7) men who are friends; and (8) medium friends, pretty good friends, very good friends.
4. Viorst states in paragraph 3 the principles of division that she uses in this essay.
5. Viorst numbers each category, labels each category ("convenience friends," "special-interest friends," etc.), and provides at least one memorable example of each type of friendship.
6. Her categories, with the exception of "men who are friends," would probably stay the same. Her examples, of course, would be men and would reflect the interests they share.

Vocabulary

ardor (2) passion
nonchalant (3) appearing casual, unconcerned, indifferent
sibling (16) brother or sister
forge (18) make or fashion
dormant (19) inactive
perspective (20) point of view

WHAT YOU DO IS WHAT YOU ARE (p. 332)
Nickie McWhirter

Essay Analysis and Discussion

Start your discussion of McWhirter's article by asking your students about their classmates. What words do they use to describe them? Then ask them to describe their parents, friends' parents, and other adults they know. It is likely that they will use adjectives to describe their peers, but they will follow McWhirter's pattern of identifying adults at least partially by their professions. Do they think that the pressure of being identified with one's job will influence their career choices? Do they agree with McWhirter's assertion that "We're supposed to be a classless society, but we are not"? McWhirter's essay should lead to lively discussion because of its informal style and open-ended structure. She presents the problem of how we tend to classify others, using offbeat but entertaining examples (e.g., "Loyal Order of Hibernating Hibiscus"), and then gives no answers about how to solve the problem. Discuss how McWhirter's final three paragraphs serve her purpose in the essay.

Questions for Study and Discussion

1. McWhirter's thesis is that Americans judge and define people in terms of the work they do, and that it is a peculiar phenomenon. The central part of her thesis is stated outright in the first sentence, the secondary part in the first sentence of paragraph 2.
2. Make sure the student understands McWhirter's meaning. Lists can include "just" an assistant manager at McDonald's, "just" a supermarket bagger, "just" a ski bum, and so on.
3. We should teach children how the system works so that, if they crave respect and/or privilege, they will go into a suitable profession. The second part of the question can be argued either way—teaching children about the system perpetuates it, which McWhirter does not want, but it can be argued that she views it as a necessary evil to educate children about how the system works, for their sakes.
4. McWhirter's tone is slightly cynical. This can be seen in her use of such phrases and clauses as "swell" (paragraph 5), "diddly dot" (paragraph 6), and "That apparently doesn't count" (paragraph 2).

5. Income is a factor, but not the only one. Prestige, difficulty of the job, the perspective of one's peers, and other factors all play roles.
6. Unemployed people are assigned to limbo.

Vocabulary

validate (1) accept
limbo (1) a place of neglect or oblivion
prestige (3) standing in the eyes of other people
dynastic (4) having to do with a dynasty; family lineage
deference (6) respect; esteem
fawn (7) court favor by flattery

THE TEN MOST MEMORABLE BORES (p. 336)
Margot Mifflin

Essay Analysis and Discussion

Classifying boring people was, it would seem, an amusing exercise for Mifflin, and she relies on humor to get her point across. She also falls into a trap, because at times she resembles some of the bores she describes. See how many instances of this your students can find in the article. Still, Mifflin has structured her essay well. She begins by providing three concise definitions of a bore, from her own perspective as well as from two other sources. She introduces the humorous element right away with a Henny Youngman quote in the first paragraph, so the reader is prepared for a lighthearted read and not a series of psychological profiles. Also, it is clear that she carefully organizes her presentation of "bore classes." Leading off with the gasbag and the vain bores is effective, because nearly everyone has had to suffer through conversations with such people. The less common bores such as the chemically altered bores and the techno-bores are tucked into the middle of the article, where the reader will presumably keep going even if he or she is unfamiliar with these types. Boring relatives make an effective close, because they are universal. Discuss other classifications that can be made about people. Can your students come up with a more positive type of person to classify?

Questions for Study and Discussion

1. The quotes provide a couple of definitions of bores in general, and they indicate that the article will be humorous.
2. One trait that all bores share is that they are not aware that they are boring. They are also thick-skinned and do not notice their effect on other people.
3. Mifflin uses humorous anecdotes and specific examples to keep her essay lively. She also presents situations that will be familiar to most of her readers to involve her audience and convince them that her classifications are valid.

72

4. The use of "you" makes the essay more familiar and immediate. It puts the reader in the situation of having to deal with the bore, so it makes Mifflin's descriptions more poignant.

5. Mifflin's article is not intended to be taken very seriously, so her use of such phrases as "You, sucker, are gonna get educated," "for God's sake, go to the movies," "see little floppy disks spinning in their eyes," and "(snort, giggle) 'Gosh, don't be so literal!'" reinforces her humorous style. Some students may think that she got a little too informal with her writing.

6. Mifflin ends with boring relatives because it is a universal hazard, and because it is a situation in which everyone is boring. The self-aware reader is likely to go back and find the kind of bore he or she turns into at family gatherings.

Vocabulary

lapel (1) part of a coat or blazer
pathological (3) altered or caused by disease
paralytics (5) people who are paralyzed
copacetic (7) very satisfactory
pontificating (7) expressing opinions in a pompous manner
manifest (7) become evident
diatribe (8) forceful speech
hyperbolic (11) overstated; exaggerated
cadence (15) rhythm
incant (18) recite
ennui (19) boredom

CHAPTER 16   COMPARISON AND CONTRAST

THAT LEAN AND HUNGRY LOOK (p. 346)
Suzanne Britt

Essay Analysis and Discussion

Britt's skillful use of first-person point of view can be a focus for discussion of this essay. She establishes it right at the beginning when she reveals her thesis: "Thin people need watching. *I've* been watching them for most of *my* adult life, and *I* don't like what *I* see." By emphasizing the first person, Britt implies a personal identification with fat people as she contrasts the attributes of those both thin and fat. That implication is carried through the first three paragraphs and then, in paragraph 4, becomes explicit: "Some people say . . . that all of *us* chubbies are neurotic, sick, sad people." For the rest of the essay her remarks about fat people, though presented in third person, are more convincing and appear more good-humored because she has connected herself with that group.

This connection also allows her to act as "fat spokesperson" in her analysis of thin people. Discuss these elements with your students and ask them to note how the first and third person are integrated throughout the essay. Have them consider how the essay would be affected if the first-person references were removed, or if *all* the references to fat people were presented from a first-person standpoint. The students should find that the integration of first and third person is crucial to the essay's tone and, hence, its success.

Questions for Study and Discussion

1. Britt uses a point-by-point pattern of organization. She discusses numerous traits of thin and fat people, explaining how the two differ as she mentions each trait. The points of her comparison and contrast fall roughly into the following categories:

THIN PEOPLE		FAT PEOPLE
A. Aren't funny, always "adoring," bustle briskly	vs.	Goof off, sluggish, inert, easy-going
B. Surly, hard, mean	vs.	Gooey and soft, much nicer
C. Logical, face truth, get to the heart of the matter	vs.	Know mystery of life—there is no truth, life is illogical
D. Oppressive, are downers: expound, prognose, probe, prick	vs.	Whoop it up, are convivial: gab, giggle, guffaw

2. Thin people are a sharp, nervous, predatory breed as contrasted with fat people who are softer, warmer, and in general more trustworthy. Thin people are not close to being as attractive and likeable as the fat people she describes.

3. Thin people are more apt to insist that other people do things their way even to the point of being oppressive. We can be sure Britt herself is a "fat" person, because she uses the pronoun *we* in a couple of places when she is referring to fat people. Also, her tone and diction indicate not only affection for, but a sense of comaraderie with, fat people.

4. Britt's purpose is to expose the personality traits of two human "types." Though she presents her discussion under the labels "thin" and "fat," the character traits she mentions deal with approaches to life that have little to do with physical appearance. Yet, she relies on the stereotypes surrounding "fat" and "thin" to help readers visualize the different characteristics she discusses. Britt's essay is mostly humorous, but there is an underlying seriousness to her point about the "severity" with which some people run their lives.

5. There are four examples in this essay of sentences with three words or less:
   1. *Caesar was right.* (paragraph 1). This sentence, which alludes to Shakespeare's famous line, pulls us right into the essay. It is an effective opening sentence.
   2. *I disagree.* (paragraph 4). This sentence works as a short, emphatic rebuttal to the sentence that precedes it.
   3. *They know better.* (paragraph 5). This sentence clarifies the meaning of the sentence before it, and the two work together to refute thin people's belief in logic, which the rest of paragraph 5 develops.
   4. *Phrases like that.* (paragraph 7). After listing the phrases that thin people "spout," Britt seems to wink at the reader, as if to say, "You know what I mean."

6. Though clichés are overused and tired expressions, they evoke predictable mental associations. Britt relies on these associations to help draw out the personalities of the two "types" she describes. Twelve examples of clichés in her essay are:
   1. aren't enough hours in the day
   2. problems to tackle
   3. to the heart of the matter
   4. face the truth
   5. the key thing
   6. get a grip on yourself
   7. fit as a fiddle
   8. ducks in a row
   9. neat as a pin
   10. cry in your beer
   11. put your name in the pot
   12. let you off the hook

7. Britt uses alliteration in the last two paragraphs to sum up the difference between thin and fat people. For thin people, she uses an alliterative "p"—short and raspy, to fit her descriptions of them; for fat people, an alliterative "g," which has a lazier quality to it. As with Britt's use of clichés, the alliteration relies on connotative associations that are attached to certain aspects of language, beyond the meaning of words.

Vocabulary

menacing (1) troublesome or annoying
adoing (2) bustling; fussing
metabolism (3) the complex of physical and chemical processes involved in the maintenance of life
inert (3) moving or acting very slowly
chortling (4) uttering or expressing a snorting, joyful chuckle
nebulous (5) indistinct; vague

rutabagas (10) variety of turnips having a large, yellowish root
prognose (11) variant form of "prognosticate," meaning to predict or foretell
convivial (12) fond of feasting, drinking, and good company; sociable
gallant (12) high-spirited and courageous

GRANT AND LEE: A STUDY IN CONTRASTS (p. 351)
Bruce Catton

Essay Analysis and Discussion

Catton begins his essay describing Lee and Grant as two men with differences that not only encompass their own personalities, but that embody the ideals that divided the North and the South during the Civil War. Beginning with paragraph 4, Catton uses a subject-by-subject organization of his material to elaborate on the personality of each man. Then, in paragraphs 10 through 12, he summarizes those differences using a point-by-point organization. Catton describes the similarities between the two men in the final four paragraphs, again in a point-by-point organization. By spending the better part of the essay describing the features that separated the two leaders, Catton heightens our expectations as to what the two men can possibly have in common. By using subject-by-subject to contrast them, he keeps them separate for twelve paragraphs. Then, using point-by-point to compare them, he draws them together within paragraphs and sentences as they were drawn together with the same purpose at the end of the war. Students can discuss to what extent the impact of the essay might have been lessened had Catton presented the generals' similarities first or if he had presented the entire essay in subject-by-subject or point-by-point contrast and comparison. Students can also plot the essay to see with what precision and equality Catton organizes his discussion of the two generals.

Questions for Study and Discussion

1. As Catton sees it, the most striking difference between Grant and Lee was that Lee's first loyalty was to aristocratic society and the region in which it existed, whereas Grant would fight for society at large. Lee resisted change, while Grant defended national development.

2. The similarities that Catton sees between Grant and Lee include:
   a. Both men were marvelous fighters.
   b. Both men possessed utter tenacity and fidelity.
   c. Both men possessed an indomitable quality
   d. Both generals had daring and resourcefulness.

   Catton feels that their most important similarity was "the ability, at the end, to turn quickly from war to peace." (16) Catton felt this similarity to be most important because it allowed the postwar unification of the country.

3. Catton first contrasts the diametrically opposed backgrounds of the two generals, demonstrating how social philosophy and regional mores determined the conflicting attitudes of the North and South. The later comparison, then, moves from conflict to union: we see that both men had "tenacity and fidelity," an indomitable fighting will, the ability to outthink the enemy, and the great soldier's ability to turn from war to peace. Because the similarity between these two men provides a natural conclusion to the essay, it is appropriate that similarities be discussed after differences. To end with contrasts would leave the conflict unresolved.

4. The subjects of the paragraphs in the body of this essay are as follows:

INTRODUCTION
    paragraph 3: Grant and Lee

DIFFERENCES
    paragraph 4: Lee
    paragraph 5: Lee
    paragraph 6: Lee
    paragraph 7: Grant
    paragraph 8: Grant
    paragraph 9: Grant

MOST STRIKING DIFFERENCE
    paragraph 10: Lee
    paragraph 11: Grant

SIMILARITIES
    paragraph 12: Grant and Lee
    paragraph 13: Grant and Lee
    paragraph 14: Grant and Lee
    paragraph 15: Grant and Lee

MOST STRIKING SIMILARITY
    paragraph 16: Grant and Lee

5. The profound "inequality in the social structure" (a landed leisure class supported by slaves) resembles the social structure of feudalism; also, a "class of men" with a "strong sense of obligation to the community" and its protection resembles knights.

6. Catton's identification of Grant as "the modern man emerging" is convincingly supported by his presentation of Grant as the mobile man, one of the adventurous entrepreneurial types whose wealth was due not to aristocratic, hereditary landownership, but to personal initiative and vigor.

7. Paragraphs 2, 3, 8, 14, and 15: pronoun references; paragraphs 9, 10, and 13: conjunctions; paragraphs 4 and 11: transitional phrases; paragraphs 5, 6, 7, and 12: name repetition; paragraph 16: convention of order. These transitional devices make Catton's essay coherent and easy to read.

Vocabulary

poignant (2) incisive; to the point
chivalry (5) medieval institution of knighthood
sanctified (6) consecrated
sinewy (7) lean and muscular
obeisance (7) deference or homage
tidewater (8) low coastal land drained by tidal streams
tenacity (11) holding or tending to hold firmly; persistence; stubbornness
aspiration (13) strong desire, longing, ambition

MY SON, MY TEACHER (p. 357)
Barney Cohen

Essay Analysis and Discussion

In just a few short paragraphs, Cohen uses several different comparisons in order to make his central point that our children are our teachers as much as we are theirs. In his opening paragraph he recounts the analogy of the small boy and the calf, which he will later compare to his tennis lessons with his son. He also compares his tennis game to that of an old friend to illustrate the moment at which he became aware of the central truth he expresses in his essay. After explaining the way in which the tennis game revealed the steady, unseen growth of his own and his son's tennis skills, Cohen restates the original analogy confident that its relevance to the point of his essay will now be clear to readers. Cohen reveals the purpose of his essay in his conclusion when he compares what he has learned to an even larger truth, one that is relevant for all parents. Although Cohen has used comparisons on several occasions, he achieves economy of expression and detail by relying on a single analogy (the boy and the calf to the tennis games) to make his point. Students can learn from Cohen the way in which writers can move from the specific to the general in a small space, without a lot of detail, by also relying on the use of analogy to make their point. Have them apply this technique in an essay of their own in which they attempt to find, in the specific truth of something they have learned in their own lives, a larger truth that is widely applicable.

Questions for Study and Discussion

1. The story of the small boy and the calf establishes the point of Cohen's essay. It is particularly apt for his essay since it suggests that as the calf strengthened the boy, so do children affect changes in their parents' lives—slowly, subtly, and for the better.
2. Cohen failed to recognize his son's progress because he failed to recognize his own until he was able to compare it with that of someone who had remained at a steady level of skill.

3. Cohen thinks it is "the ultimate insult to compete against someone at anything less than your best." Some students will argue that in some instances, especially with a very young child, it may profit that child to experience winning, but that it might still be wise to let them know that the game is being thrown to them.

4. Cohen wants to make the point that while parents think they are teaching and nurturing their children, children are also "sharpening you, polishing you, making you better tennis players, better parents—and better people."

5. Words such as *kids, bunch, guy, old man, dude,* and *surrender,* suggest that the author is a mellow, down-to-earth sort of person. Such an image suggests a parent who probably has an easy camaraderie with his son.

Vocabulary

mythological (1) pertaining to or arising from a myth; a usually legendary narration that presents part of the beliefs of a people or explains a practice or natural phenomenon

epistemological (4) philosophical; knowing the nature, methods, and limits of human knowledge

martinet (5) a rigid disciplinarian

recruited (9) secured the services of

proficient (13) adept; expert in an art, skill, or branch of learning

throw (14) to lose intentionally

demolition (16) smashing; destruction

suffice (16) be sufficient; satisfy a need

resolve (17) determination; fixity of purpose

notch (18) V-shaped hollow in an edge or surface

surrender (18) capitulate; to yield to the power of another; to give up

A CASE OF "SEVERE BIAS" (p. 362)
Patricia Raybon

Essay Analysis and Discussion

Prejudice is often strengthened by stereotypes, by members of a certain group being lumped together. When the negative stereotypes of a small segment of a group are transferred to the whole group, as often happens, the whole group suffers the consequences. Raybon argues that the American media does exactly this to African Americans by slanting its coverage of blacks strongly towards images of poverty, crime, drug addiction, and other problems. As a result, the millions of African Americans who are responsible citizens become unfairly saddled with negative associations. To make her point, she begins her essay by listing what she is not—her life, she asserts, is not dysfunctional, unlike the lives so often depicted in media stories about African Americans. What is accepted as the norm for African Americans contrasts sharply with reality, which Raybon argues leads to problems for all of American society. Discuss the disadvantages of being associated with a negative stereotype with your students. How would they feel if they saw a group they identify with portrayed in a bad light much of the time?

Questions for Study and Discussion

1. Raybon establishes the contrast between the stereotype of African Americans and the life she and her friends actually lead. She uses examples used by the media to depict African Americans.
2. By saying who she is not, Raybon is directly arguing against what she perceives is the image that the media constructs about African Americans. She perceives that readers will wonder: "If she is not this, not that, and does not do that, how can she still be an African American?" It underscores the absurdity, and the harm, of the media's depictions.
3. Both paragraphs 1 and 6 say what she and African Americans are not. She repeats this style to reinforce her debunking of media myths.
4. Her thesis is that the news media presents an image of African Americans that is misleading and damaging. She presents it in paragraph 3. The final part of the question is personal opinion, but it should be defended.
5. Raybon uses the comparison and contrast technique to work toward overcoming the stereotypes that have been presented by the media, because she perceives that there is a large contrast between the media image and reality. She wants more balanced coverage of African Americans in the media, and she would like her readers to work toward achieving this.
6. Raybon's tone is angry and frustrated. It can be readily seen in the way she describes the media's actions, such as the use of the word "insidious," and in the way she concludes her essay by saying that "it's time to let the truth be known."

Vocabulary

tenement (1) crowded housing unit, usually run-down or cramped
dysfunctional (3) unable to function in society
insidious (3) underhanded; harmful
myopic (7) with poor vision
besetting (8) plaguing; provoking
scenario (9) script; imagined scene
aberrant (9) irregular; unconventional
pervasive (10) widespread; extensive
subtleness (16) indirectness; implication
enterprise (16) undertaking; project

A BATTLE OF CULTURES (p. 367)
K. Connie Kang

Essay Analysis and Discussion

Kang's comparison-and-contrast piece is based on conflict. The presence of the conflict implies that differences exist between African Americans and Koreans right in the first sentence. Kang then contrasts the two cultures to explain the root causes of the conflict. Kang organizes her essay very effectively. Paragraphs 1–5 are used to establish the surface problems. Note how Kang makes paragraph 6 a very effective one-sentence transition into the cultural contrasts that underlie the problem. She can then explore what these differences are and how they contribute to the misunderstanding, such as the Koreans' cultural bias against smiling, in paragraphs 7–14. Paragraphs 15–20 suggest simple solutions to the problem, and comment on the role of everyone in an ethnically diverse democracy. Have your students write a comparison and contrast essay based on conflict. Direct them to follow Kang's organization by beginning with the surface conflict, then making a transition to the contrasts that contribute to the conflict.

Questions for Study and Discussion

1. The battle of cultures noted in the title stems from the differences between the Korean and African American cultures.
2. After a long period of tension between the two groups, the African Americans are boycotting the Korean grocers because a woman was attacked by a grocery employee.
3. Cultural misunderstanding and a lack of cultural insight is causing the problem, according to Kang. She contrasts the two cultures to argue her thesis.
4. Most Asian immigrants are ill-equipped to run businesses in the United States because they lack cultural and social knowledge of their new country. They are indebted to African Americans because of the civil rights work done by them, which means that Koreans face less discrimination today.
5. Kang is writing from the point of view of a Korean American, so she understands many of the elements of Korean culture that make it difficult for them to assimilate into American neighborhoods. She also understands the American point of view toward new Korean immigrants.
6. One element that makes it difficult for Koreans to adapt is that the "Confuican ethos lacks the value of social conscience." Koreans tend to focus on themselves and their own success. They are not tolerant of other cultures and they don't reach out to people from other cultures, which has helped to exacerbate the situation in New York.

Vocabulary

volatile (1) dangerous; explosive
boycotting (1) protesting by not buying from
bilingual (3) able to speak two languages
intervene (3) step in; come between
brusque (4) rude; curt
sporadic (4) occasional; infrequent
gregarious (9) friendly; comfortable in groups
inclination (10) tendency
ethos (16) guiding beliefs of a person, group, or institution

CHAPTER 17   CAUSE AND EFFECT

NEVER GET SICK IN JULY (p. 374)
Marilyn Machlowitz

Essay Analysis and Discussion

Machlowitz relies on a number of quotes from sources in the medical profession to support her claim that medical care is adversely affected by the influx of new interns in July. These quoted passages are important to the strength of Machlowitz's thesis, but the way she introduces them contributes to the essay's success as well. To demonstrate this, have your students examine the paragraphs that contain quoted material (3, 4, 7, and 9) and consider how Machlowitz has prepared for the quotation in each case. They should determine, in particular, how much and what kind of information she presents, and what it adds to the quoted passages. Once you've discussed these elements, ask your students to do a follow-up exercise in which they must provide introductory phrases, similar to Machlowitz's, for a series of quotes. (You may want to assign another essay in the text from which they can choose quotations.) The explanatory information they use should fit the context of the supporting quotations. The point is to familiarize students with the format for introducing quotes and the role it can play in the success of an essay.

Questions for Study and Discussion

1. The opening anecdote is an effective beginning because the author states her thesis from the horse's mouth—in this case, a member of the medical community.
2. According to Machlowitz, the immediate causes are: (1) every July 1 the house staffs at hospitals across the country turn over, and (2) there is a great influx of new inexperienced interns.

3. Machlowitz attributes intern inadequacy to inexperience and long hours. She substantiates this cause-and-effect relationship by using examples and citing authorities as the bulk of her essay.
4. Interns order tests so that they are covered "in case a resident or attending physician decides to give them the third degree."
5. Ways to minimize patient risk during the month of July include: "rely upon a physician in group practice whose partners can provide substitute coverage"; "select a physician who has hospital privileges at the best teaching institution in town"; and don't enter the hospital for elective surgery in July.
6. Boxt confirms Machlowitz's feeling that if you have a choice you should not enter the hospital in July.

Vocabulary

meticulous (4) extremely careful about details
diagnoses (6) conclusions about the nature of a disease
unwarranted (6) having no justification
compromised (7) exposed or made liable to danger
affiliated (8) associated with
prestigious (8) having a high reputation
vigilant (9) on the alert; watchful

THE BOUNTY OF THE SEA (p. 378)
Jacques Cousteau

Essay Analysis and Discussion

The cause and effect of Cousteau's grim essay can be summed up in one phrase: "If the oceans die, we will too." But in his desire to present the enormity and immediacy of the problem facing us, Cousteau creates strong images to get his point across. After using paragraph 1 to quickly document the sickening of the oceans and the indifference of many people to the problem, Cousteau uses each paragraph to paint an increasingly horrible picture. Paragraph 2 contains an "insupportable stench"; paragraphs 3 and 4 contain the "greenhouse effect" and the "famine, fighting, chaos, and disease" it would create; paragraph 5 depicts an ocean "scummed over with a thick film of decayed matter"; and the essay is concluded with humans "bewildered, starving, struggling to survive" and finally "[man] gasping out his life on some barren hill." Discuss why Cousteau describes these scenes in such detail, and how it might relate to his purpose in writing the essay (see question 5). Have your students write a cause-and-effect essay using vivid imagery to describe the effect, making sure that the imagery supports their purpose for writing the essay.

Questions for Study and Discussion

1. Cousteau's thesis is that the death of the oceans will be the death of the human race.
2. Cousteau's standing in the oceanographic field means that his personal observations carry a lot of weight. Thus, it is sufficient for him to say that he himself has seen oil, trawling, and toxic effluents destroy pieces of the ocean.
3. The human race will eventually die from anoxia after enduring terrible suffering. All that will remain will be bacteria and insects.
4. The greenhouse effect is a warming of the earth caused by the buildup of carbon dioxide in the atmosphere. It will melt the polar icecaps and create massive flooding of all lands near the oceans.
5. Cousteau uses such words as *insupportable stench, catastrophic, chaos, wretched,* and *barren* to strengthen the impact of his essay. He is writing to what he feels is an apathetic audience with an attitude that "they're only fish," so he needs to write as forcefully as he can to grab the reader's attention and provoke his or her concern.
6. The cause of the death of the oceans may well be through human generated pollution. The effect of the death of the oceans will be the death of the human race.

Vocabulary

teemed (1) swarmed
effluents (1) runoffs; emissions
fundamental (1) basic; necessary
buffer (3) something that cushions or balances
radiates (3) moves outward
famine (4) large-scale starvation

HALFWAY TO DICK AND JANE (p. 381)
Jack Agueros

Essay Analysis and Discussion

Agueros's contrast of his prewar, "Dick and Jane-like" childhood with the tumultuous postwar world of his adolescence is a striking one. Notice how the writing style and, indeed, the whole tone of the essay changes between the two descriptions. The idyllic childhood is depicted with warmth and a childlike innocence. The repetitive use of the word *always* in paragraph 2 and *clean* in paragraph 3 give the section a childish tone, the obvious hyperbole reinforcing the youthful writing style. Agueros makes the technique obvious with the sentence "There was always music, there seemed to be no rain, and snow did not become slush," but it is effective nonetheless. After the move and the disillusionment, the writing becomes staccato as the tone becomes angry. "Mambo.

Spics, Spooks, and Wops. . . . Dick and Jane were dead, man. Education collapsed." By mixing in the rhythm and slang of adolescent conversation, he conveys his anger and confusion much more clearly than he could with simple description. Have your students write two short descriptive passages, one about a pleasant memory and one about an unpleasant one, and have them change their writing style for each to help them get their point across.

Questions for Study and Discussion

1. Agueros implies that minority groups in the United.States cannot live the idyllic, protected lives that Dick and Jane lead in the children's books. By identifying his life with Dick and Jane's, he makes a readily understood comparison between the change in his life—after he got halfway to a Dick and Jane life-style—compared with the life-styles of the "Dicks" and "Janes" beyond Cooney's Hill.

2. Agueros's early childhood was very happy and idyllic. He describes it in detail to establish that his life was very much like Dick and Jane's.

3. He uses exaggeration in this part of the essay to establish a tone of childish hyperbole. In his memory, everything *was* just about ideal.

4. The end of the war led to massive immigration, unemployment, and a rise in prejudices and ethnic tensions.

5. The ethnically diverse nature of his school and his neighborhoods led to prejudice, a lack of security, and an educational system that obviously could not meet the ever changing needs of its students.

6. Puerto Ricans risk fights in the Italian and black neighborhoods and police harassment in the white neighborhoods.

7. The rise in prejudice caused by the influx of immigrants leads to the death of the American dream for Agueros and his friends.

Vocabulary

compensation (2) payment
declaim (2) speak rhetorically or pompously
immaculate (3) very clean
consolidate (6) merge; bring together
pathologically (7) relating to disease

LEGALIZE DRUGS (p. 386)
Ethan A. Nadelmann

Essay Analysis and Discussion

The strength of Nadelmann's essay rests on his ability to convince his readers that legalizing drugs will have the effects he states. Because he relies to a great degree on general, unsupported statements to establish the cause of drug-related crimes and the effects of drug legalization, he puts himself in a vulnerable position. You may wish to have students examine Nadelmann's statements to see if they find them convincing or if they would insist on more documented kinds of evidence. Further discussion can assess the reasons Nadelmann may have had for avoiding the use of more numbers and expert testimony. Is there anything about his subject matter or audience that made such an opinion-oriented approach more suitable than a more fact-filled one? Students need to decide in what ways Nadelmann's approach is or is not effective for his purpose.

Questions for Study and Discussion

1. Nadelmann makes connections between drugs and acts of violence committed by people on drugs because of the drugs' effect on their judgment; the commission of crimes to support the drug habit; the intimidating behavior of drug traffickers; and the "crime" of drugs itself. If drugs were legal, crimes of burglary, prostitution, and others committed to obtain money would be "unnecessary," as would be the "violent, intimidating, and corrupting behavior of drug traffickers." Thirdly, dealing, producing, and using drugs would no longer be a crime and millions of users and sellers would no longer be criminals. Only acts of violence committed by people on drugs would not decrease if drugs were made legal simply because, by their nature, they are inevitable and therefore not preventable.

2. Although Nadelmann uses statistics and cites authorities on the subject of drug related crimes, he relies most heavily on simple statements of fact with which his audience is apt to be familiar. For example: "cocaine and heroin addicts spend hundreds, maybe even thousands of dollars a week"; "(Drug dealers) are symbols of success to children who see no other options"; and "Intensive crackdowns in urban neighborhoods . . . do little more than chase the menace a short distance away to infect new areas." These statements, because they are commonly understood, are persuasive. Some students may find Nadelmann's omission of expert testimony a weakness in his essay. Others may point out that making drugs legal may not reduce crime since those who profit from the drug trade will simply move into another area of criminal activity.

3. Those who commit violent crimes while under the influence of drugs would not change if drugs were to become legal. However, those who commit nonviolent crimes would no longer have to do so to obtain drugs and that segment of the criminal population would be reduced. Drug traffickers, obviously, would be out of business and police officers who have been corrupted by the financial temptations of the drug trade would no longer be drawn into the world of crime. Finally, drug users would remain drug users but would no longer be criminals if drugs were made legal.

4. In paragraph 10 Nadelmann draws an analogy between the prohibition of drugs and of alcohol. He points out that both alcohol and drugs reap great profits to sellers whether they are legal or illegal. Both are widely used and

desired and both breed crime and violence when they are made illegal. The analogy seems apt in its negative aspects as well. Just as violent crime will not disappear with the legalization of drugs, so too will the abusers of alcohol continue to be batterers and killers.

5. Nadelmann's fourth connection says simply that when drug use ceases to be a crime, users and producers cease to be criminals.

6. Public opinion has prompted many of the laws governing the use of drugs and alcohol. A new awareness of the dangers of mixing drinking and driving has resulted in harsher drunk driving laws throughout the country. No doubt then, Nadelmann seeks to urge his readers to action on behalf of his point of view concerning the legalization of drugs.

Vocabulary

inevitable (1) incapable of being avoided or evaded; bound to happen
illicit (2) not permitted; unlawful
inhibitions (3) inner checks or restraints on free activity, expression, or functioning
imponderables (4) things or issues incapable of being weighed or evaluated with exactness
inherent (5) intrinsic; an essential part of
bootlegging (6) making, transporting, or selling (as liquor) illegally
sordid (6) marked by baseness or grossness; vile
futile (7) useless; vain
deterring (7) inhibiting; turning aside; discouraging
conspicuous (8) attracting attention; prominent
implicated (9) involved
demoralized (10) weakened in discipline or spirit
predators (10) those who prey upon or exploit others
tautological (11) a needless repetition of an idea, statement, or word
cynicism (12) a predisposition to attribute all actions to selfish or otherwise base motives

CHAPTER 18 ARGUMENT

HATE, RAPE, AND RAP (p. 395)
Tipper Gore

Essay Analysis and Discussion

Tipper Gore has earned a reputation among her critics as advocating the censoring of rock lyrics; a charge she vehemently denies. In this essay, Gore seems to be arguing her thesis in anticipation of this bias; readers may even find her tone somewhat defensive. Students should read this essay with attention to a couple of points they can use to good advantage in their own writing; notice to what extent and with what means she dispatches her opposition. Is her tone overly defensive? Would her essay have been more or less effective had she ignored the unspoken criticism of her detractors? Secondly, readers will want to determine to what extent her evidence reveals her political profile. Does she seem conservative in her point of view or liberal? In what ways is her position on rock lyrics consistent or inconsistent with her social attitudes? Students can write an essay of their own in which they argue for or against something that is inconsistent with their social or political views. What additional kinds of evidence must a writer consider in undertaking such a task?

Questions for Study and Discussion

1. Gore's thesis is stated in the second sentence of the first paragraph.
2. "Words like 'bitch' and 'nigger' are dangerous" because they dehumanize people thus making them easier to diminish. Unfortunately, these words are becoming accepted, even among the people they dehumanize, to the point that children learn that "racism, sexism, and antisemitism are okay."
3. Gore uses inductive reasoning to argue her thesis, moving from the general to the particular.
4. Gore claims that Ice-T and Guns N' Roses, like Hitler, promote degradation and violence toward minorities in their lyrics, and reap large financial benefits in the process. The reference to Hitler is a compelling and shocking reminder, if such a reminder is needed, that economic success is not a justification for murder and hatred. Gore does not include ways in which Hitler and the rock groups are dissimilar because this would not serve the purpose of her essay.
5. Gore believes we should educate our children as to the dangers of "sexism," "racism," and "misogyny." But more than that she wants us to raise our voices publicly against anything that promotes dehumanizing attitudes. Some will argue that her desire to speak out and put pressure on the music industry to clean up its act is a form of censorship. Others will argue that since she is not arguing for the banning of objectionable lyrics, she is not advocating censorship.
6. As Gore states later in paragraph 16, "[children] are not born with ideas of bigotry—they learn from what they see in the world around them." And this is precisely the point she wants to make in her essay and why she is so vehemently opposed to rap music, which "glorifies violence against women or discrimination against minorities." Instead, Gore calls for "a remedial civil rights course for children who are being taught to hate and a remedial nonviolence course for children who are being taught to destroy" (17).
7. These three words form a perfect title for Gore's essay because they capture the essence of what she has to say. For Gore, it is the objectionable *rap* lyrics which teach unsuspecting children to *hate* and these children in turn come to think that *rape* is acceptable behavior.

Vocabulary

epithets (1) disparaging or abusive words or phrases

lexicon (1) the vocabulary used in a language or by an individual speaker or group of speakers

antisemitism (7) hostility toward or discrimination against Jews as a religious group

misogynist (14) one who hates women

diatribes (14) bitter and abusive speech or compositions

remedial (17) designed to correct a faulty study habit or cover material that should have been mastered already

AS THEY SAY, DRUGS KILL (p. 400)
Laura Rowley

Essay Analysis and Discussion

Rowley arranges her argument into four sections: an opening statement, in which she presents the subject of her essay; the narrative, which gives an eyewitness account of the young man's death; her reaction to his death; and the conclusions she draws from the experience. The first three sections argue persuasively; by telling us her feelings and by forcing us to witness the man's agonizing and sudden death, Rowley makes an emotional case for not using drugs. In her conclusion, she is more logical, almost saying that it is unreasonable to witness or hear about an incident such as this and remain unconvinced. Students can go through the different sections to see what emotions Rowley inspires and what effect those feelings have on the reader. She says in her essay that friends remained unconvinced and thought it could not happen to them. What has Rowley done to ensure that her written narrative will be more convincing than her spoken one?

Questions for Study and Discussion

1. Rowley wants us to consider that death by drugs can happen to anyone; she wants us to think about this fact and if we are users, she wants us to stop.

2. Rowley uses very emotional, graphically disturbing language in her dialogue, her diction, and her choice of details. For example, "His face was grayish blue, his mouth hung open, rimmed with blood, and his eyes were rolled back with a yellowish color on the rims."

3. Rowley is able to shock the reader and force our attention to the issue with her eyewitness account of the death. Her friend seemed to sympathize with Rowley that bearing witness to such a death would be convincing enough to prevent anyone's using drugs again.

4. Rowley may have chosen not to violate the man's privacy. However, his anonymity also gives an "everyman" quality to the story and underlines her proposition that what happened to him could happen to anyone. The young man's ordinariness distinguishes him from celebrity victims such as Len Bias.

5. Rowley shares openly her sense of helplessness and sorrow for the man who died and her concern for others who might die the same way. "It seemed irreverent to talk as the ambulance pulled away." "My hands began to shake and my eyes filled with tears for someone I didn't know." "If this death cannot make people think and change, that will be an even greater tragedy."

6. Rowley's opening paragraph is apparently glib, which makes it shocking and grabs the reader's attention. The impact would have been diluted if the reader could have continued reading into the next sentence.

7. Rowley wants to reach drug users, of course. However, she wants everyone to think about the issue, so that a general complacency may be destroyed. Some students will feel that, as with many such events, the impact eventually dissolves and people resume their old habits. Whether someone is convinced may depend on how they feel about drug use to begin with.

Vocabulary

ambivalence (2) simultaneous attraction toward and repulsion by a person, object, or action
stupefied (3) made dull, torpid, or numb by or as if by drugs
convulse (6) to agitate violently
semicoherent (11) semi-logically consistent
audibly (20) capable of being heard
gnashing (21) grinding together
irreverent (26) showing lack of reverence
unravel (28) solve, especially a mystery
speculated (29) reasoned; thought; deliberated
tragedy (30) a disastrous event

IN PRAISE OF THE F WORD (p. 405)
Mary Sherry

Essay Analysis and Discussion

Anything that involves short-term sacrifice to achieve long-term benefits is hard to sell in our society, and Mary Sherry knows it. But she also knows that her perspective as a adult literacy teacher carries weight when it comes to addressing those who would argue that failing is too traumatic for kids. In particular, note how she organizes paragraphs 2–4. She begins by saying what she does, then progresses to what she has learned about her school, what difficulties students and teachers there face, and only at the end of paragraph 4 does she bring up the word "failure." By the time she gets to that word, she has established her experience and credibility. She has also implied that the schools have, in some cases, failed their students by not being willing to fail them. Also note how paragraphs 10–12 comprise what is essentially a three-paragraph conclusion. Much of the text in the three paragraphs would be repetitive and unnecessary if Sherry felt she was addressing sympathetic readers, but it is clear that she feels that it is important to drive her point home. Discuss these and other techniques Sherry uses to persuade her presumably reluctant audience.

Questions for Study and Discussion

1. The "F" word can mean either failure or flunking. By calling it the "F" word, Sherry implies that it has now become a taboo concept to flunk kids.
2. Sherry's audience is presumably educators and parents. It does not appear to be receptive to the "F" word. Students should note the gradual introduction of the concept of failure, the long conclusion, and the personal examples.
3. Sherry's thesis is that flunking kids—or even the possibility of flunking them—can motivate many of them in the short term and prevent many long-term problems. She uses her experience as both an adult literacy program teacher and as a parent as evidence.
4. Sherry establishes her adult literacy students' dissatisfaction with the laissez-faire attitude of their schools.
5. Sherry has seen the results of passing marginally literate and illiterate students—severe problems after graduation and a need to go back to school. The second part is a matter of personal opinion.
6. Flunking gets the attention of the students in the classroom, it can be used as a long-term motivator, and it prevents the integration of incapable high school graduates into society.

Vocabulary

validity (1) justifiability; correctness
semiliterate (1) barely able to read and write
impediments (4) obstacles
trump (4) powerful; especially valuable
testimony (9) statement; description

LESS IS MORE: A CALL FOR SHORTER WORK HOURS (p. 409)
Barbara Brandt

Essay Analysis and Discussion

Brandt, like Mary Sherry in "In Praise of the F Word," faces the task of arguing her point to a skeptical audience. But, unlike Sherry, she does not rely on personal perspective and credibility—the reader, in fact, never finds out in the article what Brandt does or what her area of expertise might be. Instead, following her blunt, attention-getting opening, she uses a more academic approach, invoking statistics, examples, and expert testimony to argue her point of view. She also writes with an aggressive tone. Having stated the fact that "America is suffering from overwork" in the first section and backing it up in paragraphs 4–10, she addresses the impediments to achieving shorter working hours with the assumption that she has already proven her point to the reader. All of the problems identified in paragraphs 11–21 are problems only if you agree with Brandt's argument. Discuss Brandt's technique versus Sherry's technique. Which do your students find most effective? If your students disagree with Brandt, challenge them to suggest ways that Brandt may have made her argument more effective.

Questions for Study and Discussion

1. Technology has speeded up the pace not only in the workplace but at home as well, making it possible to live one's entire life at a frenetic pace and to cram more hours in at work.

2. Many workers in the United States believe that the current workweek is some sort of natural rhythm. There is also a strong work ethic here, and jobs form the basis of many people's sense of self-worth, so to cut work time would be traumatic to many workers. Business leaders would also fight a cut, because the current system is very profitable for them, and it allows them to hire fewer workers. Also, the potential impact of shorter hours on consumer spending would create resistance.

3. The workaholic syndrome is the tendency of many to work too much, to the exclusion of almost everything else in their lives. They tend to be admired in American culture because of its traditional work ethic and workaholism is a kind of modern incarnation of that work ethic.

4. Brandt's thesis is that Americans work too much and that they need to have shorter working hours. It is stated in her title and the first sentence of the essay.

5. Brandt is showing that cultures and countries that are competitive with us actually work shorter hours. She is trying to show that long workweeks and short vacations are not necessary for productivity, and, with the exception of Japan, are peculiar to the United States. She includes the information to show skeptics that the American workweek structure is not necessary to maintain a healthy economy.

6. The structure of Brandt's essay is as follows:

Paragraphs 1–3	general statements postulating that overwork is hurting American culture
Paragraphs 4–10	citing examples from other cultures that shorter workweeks and more vacation time have historical and current precedent in productive societies in order to prove that overwork is not an inevitable fact of life

Paragraphs 11-14	discussing the possibility that many American workers will resist shorter workweeks because of lack of information, work ethic, lack of recognition of the value of leisure time, and identification with their jobs
Paragraph 15	specific discussion of the country's reaction to the deleterious effects of overwork, and how it demonstrates a lack of understanding of the problem
Paragraphs 16–21	overview of the likely reactions of the business community to the call for a shorter workweek and more vacation time, and the reasons behind them

Brandt perceives that her readers need to be convinced of the validity of the shorter workweek, so she begins her essay by arguing that Americans are suffering from overwork and that other countries do not work as many hours per week and as many weeks per year as we do. Thus, she has established the problem, overwork, and a valid solution. She then explores the potential objections, and why Americans feel the way they do. By putting the objections section last, she has the reader thinking that these are things that need to be overcome in order to achieve the goal, instead of thinking that these are things that are facts of life and will never change.

Vocabulary

detriment (2) damage; injury
spate (3) flurry; sudden outburst
statutory (7) relating to law
workaholism (9) overworking to great degree
clamor (11) make noise
deleterious (15) harmful
determinant (17) crucial factor
docile (17) tame; easy to control
pundits (20) experts

ABORTION IS TOO COMPLEX TO FEEL ALL ONE WAY ABOUT (p. 416)
Anna Quindlen

Essay Analysis and Discussion

Quindlen seems to take a side in the debate but that position is less central to her essay than her discussion of the debate itself and the ways in which it has lost credibility or direction by virtue of being too entrenched at its poles, or as she puts it by becoming too "ambiguous." Quindlen carefully and sensitively analyzes both sides in the abortion issue. Her tone is sorrowful out of deference to the women and babies she argues for. Ask students to take on a hot topic of their own, for example the use of drugs, and with humor or poignancy, put themselves into the debate, but with the eye of a referee rather than the eye of a contestant. What do they gain in insight into the elements of debate by taking this approach?

Questions for Study and Discussion

1. Quindlen states the quandary in paragraph 4, "hating the idea of abortions, hating the idea of having them outlawed." Although she never states it directly, the problem for Quindlen is that no matter which way the issue goes, somebody loses, either the mother or the unborn child.

2. Quindlen does not refer directly to pro-choice people, other than herself, except on one occasion, when she contrasts them with antiabortion people: "some people who support abortion rights are most comfortable with a monolithic position" (paragraph 9) Throughout her essay, Quindlen refers to antiabortion people in negative terms: "those people who hand out those execrable little pictures of dismembered fetuses" (paragraph 6); "the so-called right-to-lifers" (paragraph 9); and "the smug and sometimes violent opposition." Although Quindlen is in a quandary over the abortion issue, she has little use for the antiabortion position. Instead she counts herself among the "thoughtful," those for whom the issue is not cut-and-dried. "In fact, I believe the issue of abortion is difficult for all thoughtful people . . . I don't feel all one way about abortion anymore."

3. Quindlen is pro-choice for a variety of reasons: "it is the right thing in some times and places" (paragraph 5); "the extraordinary pain children may endure after they are born when they are unwanted, even hated or simply tolerated" (paragraph 6); and "in a contest between the living and the almost living, the latter must, if necessary, give way to the will of the former." (paragraph 7)

4. In paragraph 11 Quindlen cites the technological advances that have made the pros and cons of abortion less clear. However, most of her examples are of the emotional kind, for example: "I remember sitting in a shabby clinic far uptown with one of those freshman . . . and watching with wonder as the lovely first love she had had with a nice boy unraveled over the space of an hour as they waited for her to be called" (paragraph 5); and "If we were to have an abortion next time . . . which infinite possibility becomes, not a reality, but a nullity?" (paragraph 8) All of Quindlen's appeals, like most of her writing, bear the stamp of her humanity, her concern for the feelings of others. In that sense, even when she is using rational appeals, she appeals to feelings, rather than to logic. In fact it could be said without stretching the point too far, that because her appeals so accurately measure and reflect the feelings of most of her readers they become the most logical appeals she could make.

5. Quindlen risks the wrath of an audience that is likely to be pro-choice for the most part and which expects her to maintain the staunch feminist position she has in the past. However, having faced the quandary herself she is betting that many of her "liberal" readers have also been confused by the issue, but are reluctant to say so for fear of not being politically correct. Since Quindlen has already proved her loyalty to women's issues, she can safely voice her doubts.

Vocabulary

valedictorian (1) the student of the graduating class who, having achieved one of the best academic records, is asked to deliver the farewell address at commencement

elemental (3) rudimentary; exhibiting the simplest principles

protoplasm (4) the complex colloidal, largely protein, living substance of plant and animal cells

unraveled (5) undone, as in threads unweaving; separated

sniping (5) snapping; curt fighting

conjoining (5) joining together

execrable (6) detestable

tumult (7) disturbance; turbulent movement

nullity (8) something invalid; void; an absence of something

quandary (9) a state of perplexity or doubt

monolithic (9) something held to be single, massive, whole; exhibiting solid uniformity

stamina (10) vigor; endurance

amniocentesis (11) the surgical insertion of a hollow needle through the wall of the abdomen and uterus of a pregnant woman especially to obtain amniotic fluid for the determination of sex or chromosomal abnormality of the fetus

EXPOSING MEDIA MYTHS: TV DOESN'T AFFECT YOU AS MUCH AS YOU THINK (p. 421)
Joanmarie Kalter

Essay Analysis and Discussion

Facing the task of arguing against accepted truths, Kalter organizes her essay well. She brings up each so-called myth, states the actual situation as she sees it, then backs up her statements with statistics and expert opinions. Also note how she chooses her words. Researchers do not find data, they find "an eye-opening collection of mythbusters." An accepted truth becomes a "little canard" or "fable." Kalter does not overdo it, but her choice of words helps build the reader's confidence in the new research and erode confidence in the old accepted truths. This essay should promote a good discussion in your class. Although Kalter addresses only TV news, there is a strong suggestion that many other accepted truths about other forms of programming may in fact be false. Have your students write about how they think TV has affected them and their friends. Do they believe that the current concern over the strong sexual and violent content of some shows is merited?

Questions for Study and Discussion

1. The word myth has come to be associated with old stories that rely more on imagination than fact. Kalter uses it to imply that certain assumptions about TV news rely more on imagination than fact.
2. General survey questions can yield skewed results because they can be confusing and/or very difficult to answer correctly. The Roper polls indicated that people received most of their news from television, thus increasing the perceived importance of TV news, but when more specific questions were asked, the responses indicated that fewer people watch TV news each day than read a newspaper.
3. Kalter says that public opinion helped shape TV coverage of the Vietnam War, not vice versa. The tone of the coverage of the war followed public opinion trends. The perceived ability of TV media to shape public opinion about conflicts has been used as a rationale for censoring coverage of recent battles.
4. Kalter is able to focus on a particular body of research about TV news, the impact of which has probably been studied more intensively than that of other television programs. By limiting her argument to the news, she is able to make a clearly organized argument, and she does not need to make any potentially questionable extrapolations of the data she presents.
5. Kalter introduces the myth that TV news is easily understood and explains that studies have shown it is not in paragraph 16. She then uses the next four paragraphs to detail why it is not always an effective medium. Thus the reader is not only convinced about the veracity of what she is saying, he or she also understands the reasons behind it. Paragraph 17 states why the visual medium is not always clear. Paragraph 18 explains how the content and structure of news stories does not correlate with normal viewing habits. Paragraph 19 differentiates between the public's reaction to the extraordinary, which is remembered, and the ordinary, which is not. Paragraph 20 concludes that TV news is useful to a select few but lost on the general public.
6. TV reaches a larger audience than other medium and it can be improved. It can be changed by improving the writing and studying how people watch news and what they want to get from watching it. It has not changed because journalists and networks, under pressure to produce, have not sufficiently analyzed how best to present the news.

Vocabulary

truism (1) something held to be a true statement
canard (3) false story
succinctly (7) without wasting words
brevity (8) conciseness; being brief
rapt (13) entranced; playing close attention
rationale (15) reasoning; explanation
gist (17) essence; meaning
glitzed (21) jazzed up; made shiny or fancy

DEATH AND JUSTICE: HOW CAPITAL PUNISHMENT AFFIRMS LIFE (p. 428)
Edward I. Koch

Essay Analysis and Discussion

Koch brings the tough-talking no-nonsense style of rhetoric for which the liberal former New York mayor became famous or notorious depending on your point of view. The fact that Koch uses his brash style to argue for a position most liberals shun makes his essay even more powerful. The strength of Koch's essay lies on two points: his ability to state as unequivocal fact, that which he believes to be true, and his then proceeding to back up opinion with hard facts. To accomplish this, Koch uses paragraphs to their best advantage. Each one, though somewhat lengthy and detailed, stands as an essay in itself just as a good paragraph should. Koch begins each one with an argument from the opposing point of view. Then in a bold swipe he refutes that point and offers fact, not opinion, to put it down. Nearly every paragraph closes with a bold assertion so loud that the reader can almost hear Koch speaking.

Questions for Study and Discussion

1. Koch states his thesis in paragraph 3: "Life is indeed precious, and I believe the death penalty helps to affirm this fact."
2. Students will find references that confirm Koch's attention both to deterrence and to punishment. However, the weight of his argument comes down, not only on the side of deterrence, but on the side of "social order," a subtle understanding that society has the right and the obligation to prove its regard for human life by denying it to those who would take it from others. "If we create a society in which injustice is not tolerated, incidents of murder—the most flagrant form of injustice—will diminish." (paragraph 6) "Human life deserves special protection, and one of the best ways to guarantee that protection is to assure that convicted murderers do not kill again." (paragraph 8) "The greatest thinkers of the 19th century . . . agreed that

natural law properly authorizes the sovereign to take life in order to vindicate justice." (paragraph 12)

3. The first three paragraphs serve a useful purpose and perhaps Koch's argument would be less effective without them. They permit the reader to glimpse inside the heads of the killers themselves. Once these men have spoken, revealing on the one hand a fear of dying and on the other a disregard for a system that does not exact the highest price for their crimes, they become advocates for Koch's point of view.

4. Koch cites examples of actual murder cases, and he quotes murderers, experts on the subject of criminal justice, the arguments of the opposition, and statistics on homicides to support his argument for the death penalty. Koch begins most paragraphs by stating and then immediately refuting each of seven key arguments against the death penalty. He then offers evidence to support his point of view and finishes with a bold reassertion of his position. Certainly the statistics Koch cites are stunning enough, but the recounting of actual crimes is apt to grab the reader's attention even more dramatically.

5. Koch's bold, easy dismissal of the opposition in these paragraphs effectively leaves the opposition standing with its mouth open while Koch goes on to explain his position. His use of diverse and thorough evidence to support his position is convincing for showing that he has done his homework, is familiar with his subject, and is not relying on his own opinion to persuade his audience.

6. In paragraph 6, Koch likens the injustice of murder to cancer that must be "cured" through the use of capital punishment: "one does not have to like the death penalty in order to support it any more than one must like radical surgery, radiation, or chemotherapy in order to find necessary these attempts at curing cancer." Koch admits that "The analogy between cancer and murder is imperfect." Therefore the analogy cannot be pursued too far. His point is simply that, as with cancer, sometimes drastic, even unpleasant means must be pursued to effect a cure for murder—"the most flagrant form of injustice."

7. Koch himself says it in paragraph 10, "When we lower the penalty for murder, it signals a lessened regard for the value of the victim's life. . . . . It is by exacting the highest penalty for the taking of human life that we affirm the highest value of human life."

Vocabulary

clemency (1) a disposition to be merciful
constituencies (4) those entitled to vote for a representative to a district
heinous (4) hatefully or shockingly evil
reprehensible (4) deserving blame or censure; culpable
lethal (5) deadly; fatal
implacable (8) not capable of being appeased, pacified, mitigated or changed

median (9) a value in an ordered set of values below and above which there are an equal number of values

sophistic (10) arguing in correct form but embodying a subtle fallacy

proscribed (12) outlawed

ambivalent (12) simultaneous attraction toward and repulsion from a person, object, or action

seminal (12) formative; original

extortion (13) use of force or improper pressure to obtain something from someone

THE DEATH PENALTY IS A STEP BACK (p. 436)
Coretta Scott King

Essay Analysis and Discussion

You should probably make sure that all of your students know who Coretta Scott King is before you assign the essay. It might even be a good idea to discuss how students think her point of view might influence their impression of her argument before they actually read it. Then see if their predictions hold true. King's short piece <u>is</u> strengthened by her perspective. She lays out her arguments against capital punishment clearly and concisely, but the impact of what she says is greatly increased by the fact that she is the one arguing against executing her husband's murderer, among others. Her crisp, dispassionate writing clearly demonstrates the lack of vindictiveness that she argues for in the judicial system, yet the reader knows that she has been severely provoked. Indeed, all of her negative feeling is directed specifically toward capital punishment. It is an "evil deed," "legalized murder," and an act of "murdering murderers." This is a very controversial issue, so encourage a debate on the merits of capital punishment. How do proponents of capital punishment counter King's arguments?

Questions for Study and Discussion

1. King's thesis is that she is opposed to the death penalty. She states it in paragraph 4.
2. King argues first that the death penalty is final, so any miscarriage of justice is also final, and even one such case is unacceptable. She states "it has occurred many times" as evidence. Second, she argues that the death penalty assumes that the convicted person is beyond rehabilitation, and that this is a difficult thing to determine. Finally, she argues that it is applied unevenly between blacks and whites, and backs up this contention with statistical evidence.
3. The death penalty has gained support through public backlash against the increase in criminal violence. King has been a victim of such crimes and

still steadfastly opposes capital punishment, so she is a good spokesperson. No one can tell her that she does not know what it is like to lose a loved one to violent crime.
4. King says that most murders are committed in the heat of passion between people who know each other. Most murderers do not think of consequences when they commit their crimes, so the death penalty will not be a deterrent for them.
5. King argues that we should practice nonviolence as individuals and work to use nonviolence in our institutions.
6. This is a matter of personal opinion.

Vocabulary

legitimizing (1) making legitimate; validating
capital punishment (3) using execution as a punishment
abhor (3) hate; despise
sanctioned (3) officially approved
unequivocally (4) without question; definitely
irrevocable (7) irreversible
miscarriage (7) malfunction
specter (7) unpleasant image
inequitable (9) unequal; unfair
deterrent (11) obstacle; hindrance

St. Martin's